ROCKERS, JAZZBOS & VISIONARIES

Bill Milkowski

BILLBOARD BOOKS
An imprint of Watson-Guptill Publications
New York

To my daughter, Sophie, who turned three
on the day I finished this book

Senior Editor: Bob Nirkind
Associate Editor: Alison Hagge
Production Manager: Hector Campbell
Cover and interior design: Robin Lee Malik, Buddy Boy Design

First published in 1998 by Billboard Books
an imprint of Watson-Guptill Publications
a division of BPI Communications, Inc.
1515 Broadway, New York, NY 10036

Library of Congress Cataloging-in-Publication Data
Milkowski, Bill, 1954–
    Rockers, jazzbos & visionaries / Bill Milkowski.
      p. cm.
    ISBN 0-8230-7833-7
    1. Rock musicians—Interviews.   2. Jazz musicians—Interviews.
  I. Title.
  ML385.M425 1998
  781.66'092'2—dc21   98-19249
                                               CIP
                                               MN

Manufactured in the United States of America

First printing, 1998

1 2 3 4 5 6 7 8 9 / 06 05 04 03 02 01 99 98

CONTENTS

ACKNOWLEDGMENTS

BEING A COLLECTION of interviews that have previously appeared in various magazines around the world, this project was made possible by numerous editors and publishers. I'd like to give my thanks to the following people: Mike Joyce, Lee Mergner, and Glenn and Ira Sabin at *Jazz Times*; Art Lange, Charles Doherty, Frank Alkyer, John Ephland, and Jack and Kevin Maher at *Down Beat*; Gene Santoro, Wayne Garcia, and Larry Alan Kay at *Fi*; Noe Goldwasser, Joe Bosso, Dennis Page, and Stanley Harris at *Guitar World*; Laurie MacIntosh, Jackson Brian Griffith, and Mike Farrace at *Pulse!*; Bill Miller and Ronald Spagnardi at *Modern Drummer*; Jim Roberts at *Bass Player*; Blair Jackson and David Schwartz at *MIX*; Kiyoshi Koyama and Bunichi Murata at *Swing Journal*; Keiko Yuasa, Albert Elegino, and Koichi Sakaue at Rittor Music, Inc. (*Bass, Keyboard, Guitar, Drums, Sound & Recording* in Japan); Rossana Pasturenzi and Marco Nobili at *Guitar Club* (Italy); Richard Branciforte and Mark Schlau at *Good Times*. Thanks to Bob Nirkind of Billboard Books for the opportunity and to Bruce Gallanter of the Downtown Music Gallery for introducing me to Bob. And, of course, thanks to all the musicians who have allowed me to interview them over the past 20 years.

INTRODUCTION

I DIDN'T SET OUT TO BECOME A FREELANCE music writer. But certain events conspired to push me in that direction. Number one, I had been an avid music listener all my life. Number two, I studied journalism in high school and college. Number three, the position of pop music reviewer at *The Milwaukee Journal* was magically laid in my lap in the summer of 1976 when the previous scribe, my good pal Steve Wiest, was busted for raping an old girlfriend and carted away to the Fox Lake State Penitentiary (where he once played checkers with Ed Gein, the notorious Wisconsinite who inspired the ghoulish horror film *Texas Chainsaw Massacre*). With a sudden vacancy in the feature department, the newspaper offered me the position. In my humble Midwestern manner, I replied, "Sure."

So there I was—22 years old, working as an intern at a major metropolitan daily newspaper that bicentennial summer, suddenly finding myself reviewing concerts by everybody from Kiss and the Kinks to Dolly Parton and Tammy Wynette to Dave Brubeck and Ella Fitzgerald. A couple of thousand bylines later and I'm still churning out copy on a daily basis for a dozen or so music magazines around the world. And my parents are still waiting for me to get a real job with regular paychecks, health insurance, and a dental plan—the whole security package. Of course, they're still waiting for my juvenile fascination with New York to end so I can do the right, responsible thing and move back to Milwaukee. Sorry to disappoint you, folks. Or as they say in New York... fuhgeddaboudit!!!

After migrating to The Big Apple in 1980, I worked for two years as managing editor at *Good Times*, a bi-weekly entertainment publication based on Long Island, before striking out on the freelance trail. It was extremely slow going at first but I finally made some significant breakthroughs with two magazines, *Down Beat* and *Guitar World*, both of which began feeding me cover story assignments in 1983. The workload picked up from there as I added *Guitar Player, Music Sound Output,* and *International Musician* to my list of regular clients.

The magazine work, along with record company bios and liner notes, kept the rent paid for a few years. I was able to make a fiscal leap when I finally connected with a Japanese magazine publishing company, Rittor Music, which began reprinting several of my stateside stories and feeding me regular assignments on the side. My writing has since appeared in numerous publications, including *Billboard, MIX, Interview,* the *New York Daily News, Swing Journal* (Japan), and *Fachblatt* (Germany). I currently am a regular contributor to *Jazz Times, Modern Drummer, Jazziz, Bass Player, Pulse!, Audio,* and *Fi* magazines. I also write a monthly column on New York happenings for *Jazzthing* magazine in Germany and contribute regularly to *Guitar Club* magazine in Italy.

I feel like I've developed a keen ear over the past 20-plus years as a critic, coupled with an ever-expanding grasp of music history, theory, and vocabulary. And though I confess to becoming increasingly jaded about the rock scene—probably since the emergence of the Pixies, the Cranberries, Fiona Apple, and other whining, no-playing charlatans—my appreciation for jazz, blues, and the essence of improvisation has deepened tenfold. I began losing interest in rock as the players became younger than me. Oh well, I guess there's always The Rolling Stones.

My musical aesthetic may have been formed early by my older siblings. With my brother, Tom, being four years older than me and my sister, Sue, being six years older, I was naturally privy to the popular music of the day long before I came of age and could make my own choices about what was cool or hip. I was younger brother, so I just sat back and soaked it all up. I remember Sue being heavily into the Everly Brothers. She must've thought "Wake up Little Susie" was written for her. And, naturally, she dug Elvis Presley. In fact, the first record I ever purchased with my own money was a copy of Presley's post-GI soundtrack, *Blue Hawaii,* a present for Sue on the occasion of her 15th birthday. She and her teenage friends were also into all the latest dances, often corralling me as a partner to practice down in the basement. So I had firsthand knowledge of the Twist, the Fly, the Pony, the Mashed Potato, the Philly Dog, the Continental, the Hully Gully, the Bristol Stomp, and every other new step of the day. Sue eventually got into the surf music scene, via the Beach Boys and Jan & Dean. I vividly recall her insisting that the family go en masse to see *Beach Blanket Bingo* with Frankie Avalon and Annette Funicello at the drive-in theater (remember those?). It was a memorable event, not for the movie but for the sexual epiphany I experienced during the coming attractions for *Yesterday, Today and Tomorrow* with Sophia Loren and Marcello Mastroianni. It was somewhat reminiscent of that scene in the original Blues Brothers movie—John Belushi standing in the Baptist church, light pouring down on him from above, when suddenly he's hit with an epiphany: "The band! The band!!!" Only in my case it was more like, "The breasts! The breasts!!!"

I was right there alongside sister Sue, gawking at the old black and white TV in the living room, when The Beatles appeared on "The Ed Sullivan Show." I remember her crying. Naturally, she went for the cute Beatle, Paul. My brother Tom had much hipper taste in music. And because I slept in the same room (good God, was it the same bed?) with him for the first 12 years of my life, I had direct and immediate access to the sounds of Fats Domino, Jerry Lee Lewis, Chuck Berry, The Coasters, Sam the Sham & The Pharoahs, Del Shannon, Gary U. S. Bonds, and Duane Eddy. He later introduced me to *The Rolling Stones, Now!* and *12x5, Fresh Cream,* The Beatles' *White Album,* and *Da Capo* by Arthur Lee & Love.

I began to exert my own direction in music listening when Jimi Hendrix came out with *Are You Experienced?* Something about the title track and "The Wind Cries Mary" held me transfixed. And

Axis: Bold as Love put me over the top. Not having headphones at the time, I used to lie on my bed with the speakers from an el cheapo stereo system crushed up against my ears, cranking the volume to 10 and listening to "Little Miss Lover" over and over again, just to let that humongous low end seep directly into my brain as I convulsed on the bed. One day my mother barged into my bedroom, caught me in this compromising position, and let out with a scream. I got so into Hendrix at one point that I actually concocted book covers out of a Jimi photo spread that appeared in *Life* magazine. While everyone else at Samuel Morse Junior High had The Monkees bookcovers, I had this psychedelic gypsy cat with eye shirts, a Fu Manchu mustache, and a wild Afro do.

Ironically, Hendrix opened for The Monkees that year at The Milwaukee Auditorium. He was soon yanked from the tour for his overt sexuality and "dangerous" demeanor. Those 14-year-old girls screaming for Davy Jones, Mike Nesmith, Peter Tork, and Mickey Dolenz didn't know what the hell to make of "Foxy Lady" or "Purple Haze."

Around that same time, I benefited greatly from a social experiment that began in Milwaukee—so-called "forced busing" to desegregate the public schools. Overnight, our lily-white junior high school was "invaded" by these black kids from the inner city. Through a mutual love of basketball, I began hanging out with Mack Bennett, Larry Buck, Richard Williamson, and Michael Higgins. They in turn hipped me to James Brown at a time when he had come out with his anthemic "Say It Loud, I'm Black and I'm Proud." I was one of the few white kids in the audience that summer of 1968 (the year of the riots in Watts, Detroit, Milwaukee, elsewhere...) to see James Brown get up and do his thing. And it was a major epiphany in my ongoing musical education.

Frank Zappa provided an important bridge from rock and blues into something a bit headier instrumentally, particularly *Hot Rats* with "Peaches En Regalia" and *Weasles Ripped My Flesh* with "The Eric Dolphy Memorial Barbecue." Jazz didn't begin to filter into my vocabulary until the early-1970s, via two sources—local guitar great George Pritchett, a Joe Pass–inspired player who gigged regularly with a swinging trio at a downstairs lounge adjacent to a bowling alley in the hippie part of town, and late night DJ Ron Cuzner, who went on the air at midnight and played unfiltered, unadulterated jazz until sunrise, five nights a week. Cuzner was my guru, sort of like a Wolfman Jack figure who served as the muse for the Richard Dreyfuss character in *American Grafitti*. He not only introduced me, via the airwaves, to everybody from Wes Montgomery, Barney Kessel, and Larry Coryell to McCoy Tyner, Oscar Peterson, and Miles Davis, he also hipped me to Jaco Pastorius, Miroslav Vitous, and The Crusaders. In 1975, I was the editor of the campus newspaper, the *UWM Post*. And during those frantic production nights when we were putting the semi-weekly paper together, we would invariably stay up until sunrise with the radio tuned to Cuzner's ultra-hip show, "The Dark Side" on WFMR. That show gave me a deeper understanding of and appreciation for jazz, as well as a hunger to learn more about it.

I also got a serious schooling by hanging out at the Jazz Gallery, a hip nightclub opened by Cuzner and Chuck LaPaglia. It was there that I got to see the likes of McCoy Tyner, Betty Carter, Eddie Jefferson, Clifford Jordan, Dizzy Reece, the Thad Jones–Mel Lewis big band, Art Blakey & The Jazz Messengers, and countless other jazz heavyweights—up close and in person. It made a huge impression on me and helped formulate my aesthetic.

Moving to New York in 1980, of course, opened my head up to a myriad of musical worlds. Not only were there regular doses of Jackie McLean, Freddie Hubbard, and the Thad Jones–Mel Lewis big band at the Village Vanguard, but there was a very vital "weird music" scene going on Downtown with renegades like John Zorn, Elliott Sharp, Arto Lindsay, Christian Marclay, David Moss, Bill Laswell, and Fred Frith who were making strange and wonderful sounds at joints like Armageddon, Roulette, and Danceteria. I was open to it all, soaking up as much as I could—the "out" jazz thing with James "Blood" Ulmer, Arthur Blythe, and Leroy Jenkins; the punk-funk thing with James White & The Blacks, The Contortions, and Defunkt; the straightahead jazz scene headed by Art Blakey &

The Jazz Messengers. I saw Grandmaster Flash & The Furious Five perform "The Message" at the old Peppermint Lounge. I saw Devo at Carnegie Hall on Halloween night. I witnessed the first American performances by King Sunny Ade and the Bulgarian Women's Choir. I saw The Clash at Bond International Casino on Broadway—the night the audience nearly trashed the place. I caught Don Cherry and Sun Ra together at a summer solstice sunrise concert in Battery Park. I watched The Plasmatics' Wendy O. Williams smashing TV sets with a sledgehammer at the old Ritz. I dug Tiny Grimes at Sweet Basil on the night John Lennon was murdered. In fact, it was Tiny who broke the news to me ("Hey man, they done shot that Beatle!"). And I watched a slightly crazed Jaco Pastorius play "The Star Spangled Banner" on the Fourth of July—in the middle of the West 4th Street basketball court!

A few thousand interviews have flown by—at least three a week for the past 22 years. (For the record, my first published music piece was a Stanley Clarke interview appearing in a February '75 issue of Milwaukee's counterculture mag, *The Bugle American*.) Compiling a mere 30 interviews for this book was no easy task. But for the sake of variety, I split it up into three sections—rockers, jazzbos, and visionaries. The format here is strictly Q&A, although very few of the pieces originally appeared in that form. It was my hope to retain the language and cadence of the individuals as much as possible, which I feel results in some colorful and sometimes insightful storytelling. I have added new intros to all the pieces to update what these artists have been up to since the time of these interviews and also to provide some personal hindsight of my own.

I can't say that the life of a freelance writer is a lucrative one. On the contrary, it's a struggle. Sometimes the cash flow is poor, sometimes payment is late, sometimes magazines declare bankruptcy and screw you altogether. I've heard every delay tactic and excuse imaginable: "Sorry, our accounts payable person has... a) been on vacation b) been fired c) misplaced your invoice." Or how about, "The office where we keep all of our financial records burned down." I even got this one from a Japanese magazine I write for: "Honorable check in mail."

Sure, I could've stayed in Milwaukee and gotten a gig at the post office. But every day I witness something inspiring at the Village Vanguard or the Knitting Factory or Birdland or the Blue Note or any of countless clubs around town that continue to pump out live music on a continual basis, I thank God I'm still here. Recently, I've produced a couple of records (including Pat Martino's Blue Note debut, *All Sides Now*) and I have a book that is being made into a movie (my 1995 biography, *Jaco: The Extraordinary and Tragic Life of Jaco Pastorius, the World's Greatest Bass Player*, published by Miller Freeman Books). I hope to get into more of that, producing and screenwriting, in the future. But I'm still a freelancer at heart. I'm still churning out the copy. And I'm still excited about the music.

ROCKERS

BILLY GIBBONS

KEITH RICHARDS

CARLOS SANTANA

STEVIE RAY VAUGHAN

DR. JOHN

JOHNNY WINTER

BOOTSY COLLINS

ROBERT QUINE

JOE SATRIANI

DANNY GATTON

BILLY GIBBONS

THE OVERWHELMING SUCCESS of ZZ Top's *Eliminator* (Warner Bros., 1983) had everything to do with MTV. The music video network was in its infancy back then and those bearded baggy-suited entrepreneurs took full advantage of the new vehicle with hot and humorous videos featuring leggy babes in short, tight red dresses, cool guitars, and the band's trademark '34 Ford coupe. Videos for "Sharp Dressed Man," "TV Dinners," and "Legs" helped push *Eliminator* well over the three million mark. Clearly, the "Little Ol' Band from Texas" had gone beyond its initial cult following of two-fisted drinkers from their hometown of Houston.

This interview took place over the phone just after the *Eliminator* tour of 1983 had ended and a few days before Billy's 34th birthday. It appeared in a May 1984 issue of *Guitar World.* A few months after it hit the newsstands—in an act of fiscal desperation that I shall regret for the rest of my life—I flew down to Houston to sell Gibbons my prized 1928 National Steel triolian that I speak of in the following interview. Billy gave me a check for $600 for the shiny instrument. I learned some years later that the going price on that collector's item was in the neighborhood of $3,500. To quote Homer Simpson... "Doh!"

DECEMBER 20, 1983

It was just a little more than 14 years ago that Billy Gibbons joined forces with drummer Frank Beard and bassist Dusty Hill to create perhaps the most formidable blues-based rock group to ever come out of Texas—ZZ Top. The bearded boys are still thoroughly immersed in basic three-chord blues patterns, albeit a crunchier variety than the blues stylings of their Texas colleagues. But it's this stripped-down heavy metal approach to the blues that has won ZZ Top a huge international following. And with their slick videos of "Sharp Dressed Man" and "TV Dinners" seeing heavy rotation on MTV and winning favor with call-in voters on NBC's "Friday Night Videos," it seems that ZZ Top is destined for even greater success in the coming year. "Without a doubt, MTV has had an effect on our success," admits Gibbons. "Personally, I feel that the videos have been instrumental in popularizing the image of the group. For one thing, I can't drive that hot rod around anymore without being recognized. But beyond that, I think MTV is offering an added dimension that has certainly extended the popularity of modern music and has certainly stimulated record sales."

Unfortunately, 1983 wasn't entirely rosy for the Texas trio. At the outset of their *Eliminator* tour, which began in May of '83, tragedy struck. "The second night out we came up missing an entire semi-load of equipment. All the amps, guitars, basses, drums, accessories, including our lasers—all gone. Everything we had prepared for the tour had suddenly disappeared," explains Gibbons. Luckily, Dean Guitars of Houston came to their rescue, quickly supplying Gibbons and Hill with a matched set of instruments. "We were quite pleased with the instruments," says Billy, "but it was quite a challenge to show up three days later with an entirely new set of guitars to work out on. That'll really make you learn fast."

Tell me about your family. Was it a musical household?
Oh yes. Dad was an entertainer. In fact, he was in show business all of his life. He was a keyboard artist—organ, piano, and anything else that happened by. He was versed in just about every facet of show business you can imagine—silent movies, the circus, funerals, the movies of Hollywood during the '20s and '30s, arranged for Bob Hope, worked with Johnny Carson. I mean, the guy was really something. He did it all. He was quite a fascinating character. He was Houston's Society Orchestra leader for years. And it was under those influences that me and my sister grew up. So it was kind of impossible to say that we weren't hearing the floating notes from day one.

Was your father interested in having his kids learn music? Did he give you lessons at an early age?
Absolutely not. It was my parents' expressed desire that we would never take an interest in music. But after seeing Elvis Presley on television—you know the story, like so many others.

What were your other early guitar inspirations?
There was a guy who lived on the corner who had a '61 Les Paul. His brother played a Fender Jazzmaster. Bobby and Mickey. The two of them had a teen combo that was out of sight and it was just impossible to ignore it because, even though we lived down the block, you could hear it for miles. That was another great source of inspiration. That's really what turned me on to electric guitar was those guys.

How old were you when you first picked it up?
My first guitar, which was a Gibson Melody Maker, arrived Christmas Day when I turned 13. And it was really great because I opened the wrapping paper and was flipping out, then peaked around the corner and saw a little Fender Champ amp sitting next to it. So I knew it was time to burn.

Did you start taking lessons right away.

No, I locked myself in my room and learned "What'd I Say" by Ray Charles and "Found Love" by Jimmy Reed. We had those records lying around the house. My mom, believe it or not, would bring home these records. She really didn't know what they were all about, but both my sister and I would ask for records that we would hear on the R&B radio station, KYOK here in Houston, that featured most of the hits by Ray Charles, Jimmy Reed, B. B. King, and all of the great influential R&B and blues artists of the day. It seems like everybody was turning onto these sounds back then. That's how we heard them in Houston, over KYOK, and, of course, the great station out of Mexico, XZRF. Between those two sources of input we were able to plug right in.

Once you started playing and practicing, did your parents encourage you?

Well, they were, I think, amused by it. They would inform me from time to time that the china was rattling in the china cabinet. Other than that, they were somewhat amused when we started a band called The Saints. We had a great time. Our first party paid $5 a head. It was a beer party sponsored by Hoffa Hi Ronka, an unauthorized social club during the high school days. We were not only paid but the experience was memorable in as much as the party was raided halfway through the night...sent us scrambling over the back fence holding our guitars and amps, getting cut, and bruised...smiling all the way down. So we were stung. We were definitely hooked at that point. That was the summer of 1965 and it was the beginning of what led to more of the same thing.

And you went through a succession of bands?

Yes. We continued with the Saints and progressed, eventually changing the name to the Coachmen. That took us right into about 1967. By then we were well into the local Texas music scene, which was a very curious blend of white R&B and what was emerging as the psychedelic scene, which was fronted by the 13th Floor Elevators. They became such a local favorite that they were inspiring bands to try out new sounds and different kinds of musical stylings. The psychedelic offerings from the Lone Star State were nothing short of mind-frying. Because not only was it experimental instrumental, but it was based with such a heavy bottom end that you could really feel it and it was very easy to get into. So we formed the Moving Sidewalks and dove headfirst into as much psychedelia as we could. The lineup that captured the Sidewalks on vinyl was D. M. Mitchell on drums, Tommy Moore on keyboards, D. F. Summers on bass, and myself on guitar.

Before delving into psychedelia, had you played other more conventional styles of music that were popular around Texas?

Yeah, previous to going into the psychedelic scene the Sidewalks had been featured as Billy G & His Ten Blue Flames, a horn band. We had about eight pieces, but every night somebody would invariably sit in and we'd end up with a dozen or so. It was strictly white R&B with a little blues thrown in. It was really not too different from everybody else but we were trying to capture that heavy tone.... Freddie King was always popping up in town and he was a big inspiration for me and the group. Not only was it moving to hear those notes being bent just right, but it was so heavy. Everybody concentrated on a thick tone in those days, which is a Texas trademark. There were days where it was uncertain what exactly the music was doing, but there was a dedication just on a level of musicianship, which I guess is another trademark of what Texas musicians are. Very dedicated.

When you started getting serious about being a musician, did you also start dipping into the past and looking at guitar players from earlier periods?

By earlier days I'd have to limit it to B. B. King, Muddy Waters, Howlin' Wolf—all the easily accessible bluesmen on records. We would try and emulate those styles and it came out sounding like a modernized version of what they had been laying down. Then after the modernization it became psychedelic—lots of feedback.

I understand the Sidewalks opened for some celebrated players in those days.
Shortly after the Sidewalks had been on the scene, we joined up touring with Jimi Hendrix. That was a real eye-opener, to say the least, because we were all about 18. He'd come ripping in late at night in the hotel room and say, "Do you know this?" and slam down a lick that would last for ten minutes and I would shake my head and say, "No, could you maybe run through it once again?" And, of course, he knew all the tricks—five-way position on the toggle switch, bending the bar up so that it would go down farther and completely immobilize the strings. It was just great.

What year was that?
1968. We were opening for Soft Machine and Jimi Hendrix. We worked with them on and off for about six months. We started in Texas, then went on out West and wound up in California at the end of summer of '68. It was really an experience.... No pun intended.

Did you get to know Jimi's band well?
Oh yeah, we were running buddies. They were great players, man. I can't say enough about 'em. That was the definitive trio at the time. We were still working a four-piece as the Sidewalks but what they were able to do with the trio was just phenomenal. At that time there was a fellow who was representing Sunn amps and had brought a new development from the Sunn amp company. They started using Sunn equipment for the bass sound and we kept wondering what was making this great sound. Shortly thereafter, we also went with Sunn and we eventually all switched over to Marshall amps, which of course was a Hendrix trademark.

Any other interesting Hendrix anecdotes?
Yeah. Part of the Sidewalks' act was a fluorescent rainfall. There was a water-based fluorescent liquid that we used in a trough above the stage and it would rain purple raindrops at the end of the set. And Hendrix was intrigued by it. He really thought it was neat. One night after one of the shows he had attached a great big Bahamian sponge at the end of his guitar neck and he said, "I got something for the act." He had three washtubs with different colored fluorescent paint and he had this huge white backdrop installed and was doing painting with his Strat. He had tied one onto my guitar and said, "Come on, let's do it." Here it was three o'clock in the morning, the hall manager was trying to kick us out—eight Marshalls turned up to ten doing fluorescent paintings on a huge backdrop. It was wild! We never got to work it into the act but for one night it was great.

What events led up to forming ZZ Top?
That Sidewalks tour took us to the end of 1969, which is when we met up with manager Bill Ham. We had performed with the Sidewalks and jammed with John Mayall, who had come through Houston. Shortly thereafter, I peeled off and joined forces with Frank Beard, the drummer. He introduced me to Dusty Hill, the bass player. We met on February 10 of 1970, that's our official anniversary celebration day. We threw a jam session together—did a shuffle in C that lasted for two hours. We decided it was so much fun we just kept on cookin'. That lineup has remained intact to this day, which is not only phenomenal but it's still a lot of fun.

How has your phenomenal success affected the band's overall approach?
Well, this year has been a banner year for ZZ Top. It's remarkable that we're selling records in numbers far beyond our wildest dreams at this point in time. However, technically, things have changed

to allow ZZ Top not to change. That is, I don't think by listening to *Eliminator* you'll hear something so radically different from what you may have heard in the beginning. We're experimenting with new instruments now, but first and foremost is an intense interest in the music and the personal chemistry between us. That is the basis from which you can utilize new equipment. I think you'll find on the *Eliminator* record there's a little bit of synth popping through. Most of our synth work is geared for guitar-like tones or bass line passages or rhythm fills. It's dialed in for a ZZ Top guitar patch rather than something maybe a little more symphonic. The foundation of the band is still guitar, bass, and drums.

I understand that you're involved in designing guitars?
Yeah, I'm the holder of nine patents at the moment and a couple pending. Several of the designs are being distributed through the Hondo line and the Dean line here in Texas.

Is that something that grew out of your natural interest in guitars?
Well, I had a design background from art school. I went to the University of Texas. Of course, that fell by the wayside as soon as music started kicking in. In fact, it was during the time with the Sidewalks.... We had released a couple of records and started getting some notoriety.... That's when I really decided to make music a full-time endeavor. But not wanting to get away from my design background, I've kept my interest up.

You're also an avid collector and have several very rare guitars.
Indeed. My collection is strictly electric. The only acoustic instruments that you'll find here are a couple of Dobro-styled instruments, a National Steel duolian, and a triolian.

I picked up a National triolian at a farmer's auction in Lake Geneva, Wisconsin, for $10. I was bidding against an old lady who wanted to use it as a wall hanging. She dropped out of the bidding at $7. A mighty high price for a wall hanging, but a great price for a guitar.

And it sounds excellent.
Yeah, they are loud. They do have a piercing tone and they're fun to play. My National Steels date from about 1935. I've also got some Rickenbacker bakelite lapsteels from the early-1940s. What happened, what started this whole thing was Pearly Gates, the '59 Les Paul that I've had for years. When the humbucking sound was identified as the source for a rich, thick tone, I picked up a Flying V, which was a '58 model. An illustrious instrumentalist named Red Pharoah, who is here in Houston, sold me the Flying V for about $300. About a month later, I gave a car to a young lady who was auditioning for a part in a movie. She had no way to get to California. It was a 1939 Packard and I said, "Here, take the car, go to California and see if you can get the part." Well, she did indeed get the part so we named the car Pearly Gates because it had divine connections to get her the part in the movie. And she drove the thing for a few months and one afternoon a check arrived in the mail. She called me up and said, "I've sent you $450. I sold the car and I wanted you to have the money." I said, "Oh great, it came just in time because I just found a guitar." So I went over and bought it and she said, "We're going to name the guitar Pearly Gates because you're going to be playing divine music on it." It's the instrument pictured on the cover of the first ZZ Top album. That is Pearly Gates leaning up against the doorjamb of a '49 Chevrolet, sitting in a bed of polk salad.

So that's how that started. Well, the instrument had such a remarkable tone that I started looking for another one just like it. And these were back in the days when you could find a good vintage instrument for small change—$200–$300 was the price you'd pay for an instrument. And try as I might I was coming up against a brick wall in finding another instrument that sounded like Pearly. Meanwhile, the closet was filling up with guitar case after guitar case. And after realizing that there were over 100 guitars sitting there, I decided to branch out and not remain so one-pointed in trying to duplicate the sound of one instrument and started realizing the fascinating aspect of a wide variety of tone throughout all instruments. The differences may be subtle but I think most players will agree that there's a rightful place for just about any sound that can be created if it's put in the right context. It's been a battle to try and find a replacement for Pearly Gates but it's also been fun collecting instruments that have a wide variety of tone. And they all manage to not only be played, but a lot of them get used on records.

What are some other favorite guitars in your collection?
A gift that was rather unexpected was a Teisco Del Ray. A lot of people have now started collecting Japanese instruments and off-the-wall brand instruments like that because they're accessible price-wise and they provide a new outlet for outrageous sound. We had one part of the collection reserved for instruments that had been mutilated or shall we say customized beyond belief. Some of those instruments are really great. One is a Fender Stratocaster that had the body removed and was replaced by a replica that was carved out of an old Model T. That's really something. I don't know if Henry Ford or Leo Fender, either one, would approve. That's quite a rare piece. I have several Japanese instruments that would do better to appear in a cartoon series. And I have one guitar shaped like the state of Texas that is big enough to throw a party on.

Can you describe what is the Texas sound? A quality that seems to be pervasive in Texas music.
The Texas sound could be described as heavier than light and bluesier than anything else. Even the country and western players always refer to the bluesiness that is prevalent in Texas. And I think that's because Texas was a major blues center thanks to the recording scene in Dallas going back even to the '30s. And the popularity of the guitar seems to be foremost in the musicians' minds here in Texas because there's just nothing else to do here. There's endless days and endless nights and some of the best playing comes from just having nothing else to do but to pick up the ol' six-string and bang out a tune. And the flamboyancy of most Texans, which is now an established fact throughout the world, has created the flashiness that goes right along with the technical skills of most musicians. That kind of aim, that flamboyant style. Not only speed, but an understanding of the spirit of what you can do with a guitar—that you can bend a note and make somebody turn to the right in their chair or bend it another way and make 'em lean back and laugh. Those subtle nuances are exemplary of what you would find in the Texas player, I would say.

Are there any guitar players around Texas who are considered local legends but are unknown outside Texas?
Yes, there's a host of gunslingers. There's no more six-shooters in Texas, there's only six-strings. Red Pharoah is a player of note. He is a white guy that is pretty mean on the blues. You can hear him on Archie Bell & The Drells' albums. He is currently into gospel music with a Texas brand of bluesiness. Eric Johnson is a name that has come up in many articles. His playing is superb—lightning quick and residing in Austin. He's fronting a three-piece group and is currently traveling. He's quite a guy. He recorded an album a couple years ago with a band called the Electromagnets that is really fine. It's like Jeff Beck meets Jimi Hendrix on the Mexican border. It's really an extension of what you might expect from them...a very modern player. Van Wilks is an extremely talented player. He and Eric are old running buddies from Austin. Of course, the Vaughan brothers...their story need not be told. They're great. True artists, I might add. Joey Long is a bluesman from way back. His records number into the hundreds for the great Gulf Coast sound that was popular from the late-

1950s through the mid-1960s. He is still fronting a five-piece band. Great bluesman. Doug Sahm is still active on the Texas scene. Johnny Winter is still tearing it up. I just ran across him in London. He's still waving the Texas flag. He's still got those licks, first and foremost. And there's another fellow named David Johnson. He's like a second generation Eric. He's quite a stylist himself. He plays a little bit more fluid, open runs, jazz-like. And yet his speed is of that flamboyancy that certainly qualifies as a Texas player. Bugs Henderson is another great player around Dallas. He's been fronting a great blues band for about ten years himself. His claim to fame is ridiculous speed. He'd be doing runs down by the tuning keys and then fire up to the stratosphere in the blink of an eye and hit about every fret in between on the way up and back down again. He is a tremendous player. So is Denny Freeman out of Austin. He's been with the Cobras for quite a while and is really tearing it up. My bass player's brother, Rocky Hill, is also somebody to watch. But these are some great, great players and it's a real pleasure to be in that Texas guitar fraternity with them. It's really allowed us a freedom as players to express a spiritual side of music. Even though rock'n'roll is what I do and what most of these guys do, it's got that old Texas flavor.

KEITH RICHARDS

IN 1965 THERE WAS A RAGING DEBATE regarding the relative merits of The Beatles vs. The Rolling Stones that split fans into distinct camps. Girls tended to fall for The Beatles' cute looks and upbeat charms, while boys were more attracted to the harsher sound and nasty demeanor of The Stones. Moreover, "good" kids tended to prefer The Beatles while "bad" kids were won over by The Stones' more rebellious stance. Being basically a good kid who dug cool guitar riffs, I naturally gravitated toward The Stones and was immediately grabbed by *The Rolling Stones, Now!* (Abkco, 1965) and *12x5*, which featured their hard-edged covers of Buddy Holly's "Not Fade Away," Bobby Womack/Valentino's "It's All Over Now," Bo Diddley's "Mona," and Howlin' Wolf's hit "Little Red Rooster." And by the time their riff-laden originals like "(I Can't Get No) Satisfaction," "The Last Time," and "19th Nervous Breakdown" (from *Out of Our Heads*, Abkco, 1965) came along, I was hooked. But there was a price to pay. I distinctly remember, while waiting on lunch line in the school cafeteria, being punched in the stomach by some overzealous Beatles fan in the fourth grade for professing my allegiance to The Stones. In retrospect, I guess that was my first critical stance, and my first hostile reaction. But I stand by my original review—"I Wanna Hold Your Hand" and "She Loves You" are sissy tunes, "Get Off of My Cloud" is really tough.

Nearly 25 years, thousands of reviews, and a pile of hate mail later, I was face to face with Keith Richards—riffmeister extraordinaire behind The Stones' classic rock sound—interviewing him for an October '88 cover story in *Pulse!* magazine. He and lifelong writing partner Mick Jagger had endured many celebrated rifts throughout The Stones' odyssey and were currently enjoying a period of separation. Keith had just come out with *Talk Is Cheap,* his 1988 solo debut project. Mick had already debuted with *She's the Boss.* And while both were admirable offerings, neither one was charged with the magic created by the chemistry of the two of them writing together. It was the Lennon-McCartney story all over again.

The Rolling Stones, of course, have reunited for several mega-lucrative album/tour packages since the time of this interview—*Steel Wheels* ('89), *Flashpoint* ('91), *Voodoo Lounge* ('94), and *Bridges to Babylon* ('97). But at the time of this interview, Keith sounded somewhat dubious about the future of "the world's greatest rock'n'roll band."

AUGUST 25, 1988

Our designated appointment was for noon. But that relatively early call didn't stop the legendary Stone—looking as ravaged as all the jokes say he is—from dipping into a bottle of Jack Daniels. So we imbibed, sipping and chatting about Keith Richards' first solo project after being so intimately associated with long-time writing partner Mick Jagger. Like Gamble & Huff, Leiber & Stoller, and Lennon & McCartney, the names Jagger & Richards are indelibly tied and enshrined in rock'n'roll's Hall of Fame. So it was no small feat for Keith to sever that tie and strike out on his own for the first time since the Rolling Stones formed back in 1964. Several cups into our interview, Keith was feeling no pain and looking forward with great enthusiasm to the release of *Talk Is Cheap* and his first tour as leader of The X-Pensive Winos.

The new album is really strong. There's like five "Start Me Ups" on there.
Well, you know... I mean, it's like not surprising. I can only play one way. It's just a matter of coming up with something. It might have had something to do with the fact that I wasn't making a Stones album and I decided to write new stuff entirely. I didn't want to have any hangovers with old songs I had written for the Stones, which usually over the years I've done. I might hold onto a song for four or five years before we actually record it just 'cause it's not right yet. So I made a clean break with that material I had been working on before, and maybe that has something to do with it. I mean, if I'm gonna do a Keith Richards album, I didn't want any hangovers into the other guys. Which is why, apart from a Mick Taylor solo, there's no Stones or anything on this album. As much as I love to work with 'em, I just like to keep it separate.

Was it difficult for you to tackle this solo project without any of The Stones?
I said at the beginning, if I'm gonna make a record, who am I gonna play with? If I ain't gonna have Charlie Watts for the first time in 20-odd years, what am I gonna do? To me, that's a big thing. But with Steve Jordan, I had a basis for something to build on.

But you had played with other drummers before, like the New Barbarians tour you did in the '70s with the Meters' drummer Zigaboo Modeliste and bassist Stanley Clarke.
Oh yeah, I played with some great drummers like Zigaboo. But the idea of making my solo record and not playing with Charlie—it was hard for me. I didn't even want to ever make a solo record. To me, it was something you did if you had nothing else to do, until I got into it. And then I started to really enjoy it. It turned me on a lot and gave me a whole different perspective. I found out a lot

about other musicians, too, in the process. In The Rolling Stones you're in a bubble and the rest of the world sort of goes around it. But inside the bubble things don't really change that much. That's the inevitable thing and it's been that way for so long. It can almost ignore the rest of the world if it wants. And at various times people inside the bubble... When The Stones don't want anything to do with the rest of the world they can actually retreat. It's not necessarily a good thing but it's easy to stay inside the bubble and let everything happen around you. And you just—usually that means you do your bare minimum. You just sort of do with what you know exactly and never push a little bit more. And that's understandable. Anybody who's that successful and didn't expect to be but they were and they are... There's a sort of laziness that sets in, I guess. So I learned quite a few things by working outside of this bubble and looking at the world from a different perspective.

So you're having a naughty affair right now.
Yeah, in a way. And if it helps to kick the Stones up the ass, too, then that's fine. Then everything's been passed along as it should be.

Has Mick [Jagger] heard this record?
Yeah, Mick's heard it a couple of times.... [pause] Talked all the way through it, though. But then he talks all the way through anything. As far as I can gather, from what I hear, he likes it. Mick and I are still sort of testing each other out at this point. But I love the guy. I love to work with him. There are certain things about what he's done that piss me off, but nothing more than what goes down with any friends, really. If you can't lean on your mate then you're not really his friend, right? If you don't say, "I think you're fucking up, man," then you're an acquaintance, not a friend.

Any significance behind the tune "You Don't Move Me"?
Yeah. [laughter] I guess! To a certain point. It was a kick-off point, in actual fact, to write about Mick. As I got into writing the song it became about any situation where you're put into that sort of conflict. But it was a kick-off point.

So there is an underlying meaning here.
I can lie to you and say there's absolutely nothing to it, I never thought of that. But the honest truth is—of course. That was a kick-off point. But it's not solely about Mick. You know, when you're pissed off at somebody, you're pissed off at somebody.

How did he react to it?
I don't know if he's listened to it. I mean, he's heard it but I don't know if he's really listened to it. I'm sure he won't enjoy the actual meaning of it. But look, Mick and I go a little bit beyond just being able to insult each other. I mean, we've known each other for 40 years. It's not just two rich superstars indulging in a power struggle. It's not really about that at all. It's about us trying to find each other at this point. I think maybe what we found out is that without knowing it, Mick really needs The Rolling Stones more than actually The Rolling Stones need Mick. We all love the band and everything but I don't think Mick thought that he needed the Stones and he's probably just realizing that now, which is why we're putting the band back together—at his request, not mine. And I think it's a very astute move. But I do hope that it's not just a rescue attempt. I would hope that he wants to do it and realizes that he's gotta get back into it strong. See, this thing's gotta grow up. It can't just go backward and compete with some other new recording stars. It's got nothing to do with that. It's got to do with carrying on your life and growing up and making it work. And to me, that's the most interesting—the only interesting—thing about it: Can it be done? Can you actually be a rock'n'roller for this long? I played with cats who were just as powerful the day before

they died, Muddy Waters being one. It remains to be seen if that will hold true for either Mick or myself.

Most people don't know if you guys love each other or hate each other.
Nor do we. Mick and I have always been able to work together no matter what we thought about each other at certain points. To me, this is an interesting time. I'm 45 years old. There's a point in your life where you have to reassess things. It happens to everybody. It's happened to our relationship so now we have to see if we can get over it. Sometimes I'm not a great help, other times he ain't a great help. But we're still trying.

But for the moment you're making a break with the Stones. And in spite of what directions you might go in with the X-Pensive Winos, your signature sound still cuts through and is instantly identifiable. Maybe it's because you don't use many effects.
Maybe that has something to do with it. But I can pick up any guitar and immediately get that sound. I know it must be a particular way of striking the instrument, I guess. I call it heavy-handed when I want to be modest.

There's a lot of people like that.... Albert King comes to mind.
And somehow it always sounds like him. I don't know, there's just certain styles of playing that you do play in your own way. Maybe it's in the way your fingers bend, for all I know. And so whenever you pick up the guitar it's not so much the sound of the instrument itself, it's like the thing that you add onto it—the attitude.

Obviously the production values have changed a lot since the first Stones albums but your approach to the guitar is still the same. It's a direct and very intuitive thing.
Yeah, I wanted to keep it very basic. And I thought if I'm going to start doing solo albums I want to keep at least the first one very straight ahead—just get into it with a good band. To me, the most important thing is finding the guys to work with. That was far more important to me than the songs, at the time—to find myself a bunch of guys who can feel and sound like a band.

How did that come about, through intensive rehearsals?
Well, it happened in a very natural way—the beginning of '86, I suppose—whenever *Dirty Work* came out. I originally planned to take that out on the road in much the same way like *Some Girls* was done, for instance. *Dirty Work* was an album that was specially built for a tour, so it was a two-part thing. And when that didn't happen I suddenly found myself on the beach in a half daze, so to speak—nothing to do suddenly when I was expecting to do something. And at the same time [drummer] Steve Jordan found himself in the same situation. We've known each other for a few years and had gotten to know each other real well the year before. He just hit the same point—had left the David Letterman show for whatever reason and the Aretha Franklin track came up [a remake of "Jumpin' Jack Flash"]. They wanted to record in Detroit. Well, I know the song and I love Aretha, so I thought, "There can't be any problems doing that. It might be fun." So Steve came along and we did that together. That was the beginning of our musical connection. And after that we did the Chuck Berry movie together [a documentary, *Hail! Hail! Rock'n'roll*]. And throughout that period of getting to know each other I also got to know guys that he worked with like [bassist] Charley Drayton. And through doing the Chuck Berry movie, I met Jerry Spampinato, who is on a couple of tracks on this new album. Waddie Wachtel I always wanted to work with, for years and years. We had done a couple of sessions.... I don't think they were ever released. But we said, "Sometime we gotta do something serious together." That was a long-standing arrangement. And

Ivan Neville I've known for quite a while. He's played bass on Stones tracks before. He's such an all-arounder. So the challenge was to put them all together and make it feel good. Everybody just fell straight into it and within a week we had a real band.

I remember hearing over a year ago that you and Charley Drayton and Steve Jordan were jamming up new material together.
Yeah, we were rehearsing way downtown. I guess we started very early last year, February or March [1986]—somewhere around then. Just putting guys together and putting songs together.

You don't compose your stuff at a keyboard?
Naw! I can't walk into a place and say, "It goes like this." Songs, to me, they come through osmosis. The bass player will feed you something that takes the song in a whole new direction or you'll stop for a bridge and somebody will come up with a good idea. "Ah, hold on! That note there!" Or somebody makes a mistake and stumbles onto something new. To me, all the best songs were basically beautiful accidents.

I remember seeing Dr. John at a session where he was struggling to bring in a tune under four minutes. Finally they did a take and there was a lot of electricity in the room and they just took off. The song came in over eight minutes but everybody in the room agreed, "That's the one."
Yeah, that's the magic. It happens very suddenly and then it's a matter of just recognizing it, or having a good guy in the booth who recognizes it. I always leave the tape running all the time, just in case. Even when someone's taking a shit, I leave a two-track running all the time to get the odd ideas. And often in those bits you get an extension of a song that you wouldn't otherwise get if you were just sitting down and nailing what's on paper. I'm the reverse. I prefer to find the music by playing with the band. But now and again things happen the other way. I wrote "Satisfaction" that way. You suddenly wake up with an idea and there it is. So now I always have a guitar and a tape machine handy by my bed in case that happens again. And it doesn't happen very often. You wake up and you know exactly how it should go as long as you can put it down right there and then. It's like a dream, you know? Sometimes I'll come up with some brilliant song or melody while walking along and by the time I get home it's totally gone. After a while, it always comes back. Once it's in there... And sometimes it might be years, other times it might be a week or a day. You can never tell. Eventually, nearly all of them come back.

Did any of these tunes emanate from the lyrics or did most of them come from the music?
Luckily, most of them come in the way I like them to come—with the hook and the riff together, fill in the verses later on. A good example of that on this new album is "You Shouldn't Take It So Hard." That hook came at the same time as the riff. And invariably you'll find that when that happens the alliteration and the rhythm of the words is ten times better than if you try to force or wedge a line in there. If you have to think a line up separately to make a hook, it never seems to me—maybe because I'm on the inside looking out from the other way—but to me there's always a certain discomfort with that. Most of these hook phrases—"You Shouldn't Take It So Hard" or "It's a Struggle"—they're all very mundane slogans. They're the things that people say every day. You can hear "Make No Mistake about It" every time you watch a tennis match. Clifford Drysdale will always say, "That's a sure winner, make no mistake about it." I mean, I was starting to hear all these titles coming back at me from ads on TV and from the weirdest areas, just things that people say. You just give it a slight twist and you've got a hook. Working with Steve Jordan, we fell into that a lot. We didn't expect to write this thing together. I know that I need to work with somebody else. I'm not particularly interested in writing songs on my own. If one or two come like that, that's fine.

But I enjoy sitting around with someone, paper strewn wall-to-wall, kneeling down, scribbling away, and flashing off of each other.

And Steve served that function for you on this project?
Yeah, the more we got into it, the more we realized we didn't need a producer or anybody else. We didn't need to bring in anybody else to bounce off of. That was the way I wanted to do it. And I also did spend a few days with Tom Waits just knocking a couple songs together. I'm really interested in his work and it's fun to sit around and write songs with him. But there's nothing on this album connected with that process. It might be on his, for all I know. It's like, "Well, it's yours or it's mine." Whoever's got room, you know?

The production on this album is really loose.
It's all soiled by human hand, you know?

It's almost in defiance of what's happening in the industry now with all the technology taking over record production.
In a way it kind of is. There's a certain spirit to me that's lacking in an awful lot of what goes for rock'n'roll records these days. But then, I'm getting old so maybe I'm starting to get reactionary. I never quite trust my own judgment, especially when I just finished a record because you're so far into it that in a way you're too close. But the only thing I do know is I still... Even with most of The Stones' work, I don't remember listening to the music that intently in that gap between finishing a record and it coming out. I usually take a real breather from it. And actually with this one it's strange, maybe it's just because it's mine. I don't know if I'm vain or what but I find myself listening to it over and over again throughout the day. And it feels good. Usually when you've finished something, you gotta get away from it, no matter what you think about it. But Steve and I feel pretty good about this.

The cycle always changes. People eventually get sick of being inundated with over-produced albums. And if that's what is happening now, this album is going to sound fresh by comparison.
Hopefully, yeah. It's not something I planned on. It's not an underlying cause for this album. It's a hope for it. If it just persuades a few people, I'll be happy. We're just trying to make records with a bit more of the human touch rather than pushing buttons on drum machines and synthesizers. There are so many toys on the market and everybody's playing with them. But there's no dynamics in that. And, after all, rock'n'roll is really about interaction. It's got so much to do with that. Rhythm and dynamics are really the basis of rock'n'roll—the only two areas where you can really be interesting. It's not the actual notes and the chords. God knows they're simple enough, right? I mean, you have to keep the melodic content down to a minimum as compared to other kinds of music. Trying to be innovative in that area, coming up with a slightly new melodic twist in rock'n'roll—that's a very hard thing to do because it's very limited music in that respect. But in terms of rhythm and dynamics, all the world's wide open. And to me, that's what making records is about, that indefinable thing that you can't find on any meter in the studio. When you're making a record, it's about what's going down on tape. And really you're looking for that incredible thing that making records can do. You can actually put down a feeling that will come off, an actual spirit, an indefinable thing. There's no way it should be able to get on there but it can and it does. It's an incredible medium.

All the albums that you've been involved in where there's another guitar player, whether it's been Brian Jones or Mick Taylor or Ron Wood, have this quality of production where the guitar tracks are so intermeshing that it's hard to separate them.

That's what I've always liked about guitar records—when they start to go through each other to the point where it's not important who's playing what. There might be an interesting tension going on from one guy to the other and that goes straight to the people, in that respect, if you've got it on tape. And it's those moments that are worth capturing, not these set up poses. That's what I've always loved about early rock'n'roll records, that tension and energy that came through those speakers. Before I was into it that much in terms of who was doing this and who was doing that, I was just affected by that overall sound. Just what you can put out of that speaker has always been fascinating to me. Now if you say... Alright, I happen to write songs, make records, and I happen to play guitar. But to me, what I really do is make records. That's what I enjoy doing and what I think I'm probably best at. And that's a combination of all those things but it still fascinates me. In fact, more and more. I suppose it's easy to get blasé making records for all these years already. But now I find it even more fascinating than ever.

And you mentioned that in the process of making this album, these musicians really kept you from being blasé.
Oh yeah. And also I realized that even though you try to remain as fresh as you can, inevitably... I mean, 20-odd years with the same band, you do fall into certain ruts and certain habits of working. And one of The Stones' habits was that if I'm knocking out a riff and it's really working and then I get stuck somewhere for a bridge or something, I'll stop playing and everybody'll stop playing. Everybody'll put their instruments down and go off. This is one of the things The Stones—one of their luxuries. If I stop they all stop and that means time for a break, knock off for maybe half an hour before you can get 'em back together again. You can't rush that thing. That's the way The Stones work. But these guys just keep playing. And if I get lazy they'll say, "Pick it up motherfucker!" And nobody says that to me, you know? [laughter] But then you gotta pick it up so you just keep playing. So instead of... I'll have my guitar half off, ready for the usual break and it'll be like, "No way! Let's play!" It's great. I enjoy it.

You sound a lot more confident about singing on this album.
Well, I'm getting there. You'd never guess that I was soprano until my voice broke when I was about 13. I was a prized possession for a while—me and two [of the] other worst hoods in my school. We had these angelic voices. But I didn't realize really, until I started doing this stuff, how much I had retained from my old choirmaster some 30-odd years ago, all the things I had learned from him about singing. But the voice has changed a lot since I sang in Westminster Abbey. I didn't really enjoy singing for a long time, but I'm getting the hang of it again now.

What kind of things have you been listening to lately? Are you a record buyer?
Occasionally I go on binges and buy every blues reissue I can find. They're putting out a lot of good stuff now, all the early Chess recordings. They've cleaned it up a lot and I'm not sure if I really like that or not. Sometimes I think I'd like to hear the old hiss along with some of those blues tunes. You've got to pick and choose with that. And, of course, the whole CD thing is fairly new. I'm sure they're going to improve the sound even more in years to come. DATs are already happening. A lot of new technology is being developed and I presume this isn't the end of it. Hell, I started recording on two-track. Now look at it. But I think there's so much stuff that it's kind of overwhelming for musicians and listeners alike a bit in the last few years.

So you're still a blues fan.
Always. You can never get enough of the blues—or Mozart, or great reggae. Although you don't hear great reggae anymore because they're caught up in pushing buttons too nowadays. It really

takes all of the expression out of it. I'm more interested in human expression and how it affects people. To me, that's the beauty of music. I think it might be a romantic notion, but to me music is passed on and on and on through word of mouth. Anybody who plays something knows how much they owe to the guys who went before. And it goes on and on and on, way back to the beginning of time. There's probably only one song, really. Everything's a variation on it.

Finally, what would be your choices for desert island discs?
"Little Queenie" by Chuck Berry, "Key To The Highway" by Little Walter Jacobs with Jimmy Rodgers on guitar, "Still a Fool" by Muddy Waters, "Reach Out [I'll Be There]" by The Four Tops," "Mystery Train" by Elvis, "That'll Be the Day" by Buddy Holly. Then something by Segovia, something by Mozart, something by Bach, and anything by The Jive Five.

CARLOS SANTANA

GUITAR HERO CARLOS SANTANA and his band rocked Woodstock in 1969 with an electrifying performance of "Soul Sacrifice," one of the most exhilarating moments of the festival, captured on the documentary film that helped define a generation while catapulting the group to international fame. Nearly 30 years and several musical phases later, Santana still plays with the same soul-searing intensity and bent-string conviction. His guitar signature, a warm-toned long sustain that affects a singing quality, is instantly recognizable and never fails to connect on a direct emotional level with listeners. At the time of this interview for *Guitar World* (June '88 issue), Carlos was in transition, between bands and on the verge of transcending to a new peak in his ongoing exploration of the music. The following year he would charge his creative batteries by joining forces with jazz legend Wayne Shorter and embarking on a triumphant worldwide tour in a band that included bassist Alphonso Johnson and drummer Chester Thompson. By 1985 Santana would eventually realize another one of his dreams—recording with blues master John Lee Hooker on his album *Chill Out* (Pointblank, 1985).

A collection of Santana's greatest hits, along with choice cameo performances with John McLaughlin, Vernon Reid, Weather Report, and John Lee Hooker, was released in 1997 as the three-CD boxed set *Dance of the Rainbow Serpent* (Columbia).

FEBRUARY 4, 1988

He's sitting on the bed of his hotel suite, playing his Paul Reed Smith guitar, staring out the window on a rainy day in New York City and thinking about where his new direction might take him.

"I know I'm not the kind of person who's gonna wind up being a walking jukebox, like many rock-'n'roll artists," says Carlos Santana. "They just play their hits and that's it. That doesn't appeal to me. I don't wanna just go out and play 'Black Magic Woman' and 'Oye Como Va' all night, because that was part of the '70s and my watch says it's 1988. So I wanna get into '88 and not look back."

A little over a year ago, I chided Carlos in a *Guitar World* review of *Freedom*. "Scrap the sappy, safe, predictable, slick pop arrangements and get back to playing the guitar, man," is what I said, or words to that effect. I don't know if he ever saw that review, but he must've been thinking along the same lines himself when he recorded his recent *Blues for Salvador,* his 22nd album for Columbia. There is killer guitar on every track. Eight of the album's nine cuts are instrumental, featuring Carlos' signature singing/stinging guitar lines. For guitar fans, it's a dream come true—easily his most exciting, most scintillating, most inspired display of ax magic in over a decade. *Ah, welcome home, Carlos!*

Drop the needle anywhere on *Blues for Salvador* and you get the real deal. The man redeems himself for any past lapses, like the horribly saccharine radio-play hit "Winning" from a few years back and other hook-laden wimp fare he has dabbled in of late. "Bailando/Aquatic Part" revives memories of "Soul Sacrifice." The lyrical ballad "Bella" is played with a soulful Wes Montgomery tone that allows the nuance of Carlos' expression to shine through beautifully. And the sheer conviction that he displays on the title track, a duologue with keyboardist Chester Thompson, is positively Herculean.

And there's more. Carlos stretches like in days of old on the live jamming vehicle "Now That You Know," recorded during his band's '85 World Tour. He burns red-hot on the Latin percussion workout "Hannibal," which segues to a loose, bluesy swing feel at the tag. He cranks out some vicious wah-wah licks reminiscent of Hendrix in all his glory on the funky "Deeper, Dig Deeper." And he unleashes with a vengeance on "Trane," which is powered by drummer Tony Williams.

There may not be any trendy displays of two-handed tapping, wang bar theatrics, or scalar pyrotechnics on *Blues for Salvador.* Nevertheless, it gets my vote for Top Guitar Album of the Year. [It won a Grammy Award later that year.] It's a strong statement from a national treasure.

It seems a lot of young guitarists today are missing something in their playing—that whole depth of feeling in music that you represent.
You see that guy who does those Federal Express commercials and speaks real fast? It's funny but after two seconds, whatever he's saying doesn't hit you. Whereas, if you have somebody like Richard Burton delivering the same words or, say, an old black man from Mississippi just sitting on the porch—the way they talk, they pause a lot because they are allowing you to digest what they are telling you. A lot of musicians today or aspiring musicians, they play a lot of notes and it's all just technique, it's an intellectual thing. You can practice and develop this side, but it's still a surface thing. What they need to practice to be completely rounded is the stuff that Jimi Hendrix was doing, or Otis Rush, or B. B. King, Albert Collins, Buddy Guy—playing with feeling. With one note, you can shatter a thousand, especially if you know how to get inside the note. A lot of these guitar players today, they don't know how to get inside a note so they're always playing over it.

It also seems like there's a dependency on equipment today.
Too many guys are using the same gadgets, they all sound generic. After a while they lose their identity, which is the most important thing that they have been given in life. They also lack vision.

Hendrix is someone who had vision. Some people have talent, some people have vision. And vision is more important than talent, obviously.

There's a whole new movement known as neo-classical, spearheaded by Yngwie Malmsteen.
Yeah, he's really good. So is Al Di Meola.

But a lot of young wanna-be players are just following in their wake, just skimming off the top of some of the flash techniques that they have developed without really understanding the depth of their musicality. Consequently, kids are playing so fast they never come up for air.
It's like Miles said—they need to go to Notes Anonymous, you know? My nephew does that a lot. It's a different kind of vocabulary and some of it can be really nice. But it's like playing with one hand. I like to play with the whole deck of cards. If you play too many notes you're going to run the risk of not reaching the listener long-term. Kids are in awe of speed, but hopefully they grow out of that phase. After a while the same kids who liked Kiss or Peter Frampton or even Journey, they'll say, "Please don't tell anybody I used to like those guys." They take the posters off their walls and grow out of that phase. But the things that last are like the Wes Montgomerys, B. B. Kings, T-Bone Walkers. Those are the things that are going to last until the end of time. This other kind of stuff is gonna come and go like Freddie & The Dreamers, as far as I'm concerned.

That's why your new album is an important statement right now. In the face of all this technical obsession comes a guitar album that is full of conviction and feeling.
Well, teenagers don't necessarily like to show their emotions. They don't like to cry in front of people. They like to show off but they don't like to show their innermost emotions, which is what real music is about. As long as there's balance, it can all play a part. If I were a gardener, I would want to see as many colors and textures and aromas as possible in my garden. One wouldn't be enough.

Is there any reason you decided to put this album across with such heavy emphasis on guitar after a number of albums with more of a vocal emphasis?
I'm planning to do more of this from now on. I have come to the conclusion—and I don't know what took me so long but nevertheless I am here now—that it's time to let the guitar play the melody, let the guitar be the singer. And it feels really, really good. I've been saying real musicians are like snakes, they're constantly shedding their influences. For example, when you practice and you tape it, in 45 minutes you're gonna hear yourself getting rid of people that you love—T-Bone, George Benson, John McLaughlin, B. B.... Entering into an hour, you start hearing yourself because you cast off everybody that you love. And that's what's really most important to me now. I have come to a place where I'm not afraid to be the main vocal in there no more. You know, if Herbie [Hancock] and Wayne [Shorter] can see that I can cut it, I guess that I can cut it. So it gives me a certain kind of confidence to be able to play with musicians on the level of a Tony Williams. And it's easier for me now to embrace this vision, with the guitar being the primary vocal.

At what point in your development did you feel confident enough to take that stand?
I had confidence since I was a child but I lost it when I came to America. Seeing Jimi Hendrix live and B. B. King live I said, "Man, I don't know anything compared to these guys." So it took me a while to regroup again. Not until I jammed with John McLaughlin [*Love, Devotion, Surrender,* Columbia, 1973] did people start acknowledging that I also had something to say. That gave me a certain confidence. But you know, every day you wake up and you transcend. You can't rest on your laurels. Every day you have to wake up to attack the note differently. There's only what— seven notes? So it's how deep you get into it. Make each note like a deep blue sea. So you gotta keep

transcending. Every day you wake up is another opportunity to go beyond. That's why I let my band go. For the first time in my life I'm just roaming around now and I'm excited by the challenge of starting up something fresh. We're planning to get a band together for the summer with Wayne Shorter and Tony Williams. I'm just jamming a lot with different people now and it's good because if I had my band I would've missed out on a lot this year already. So I feel good because I don't have the responsibility of maintaining a group now, being a babysitter and psychologist and all the things that you have to be to be the leader of a band. So it's a good time for me. I can afford to go out there and really learn. If I want to take some time and learn theory or learn how to sing or learn harmony and voicings on the piano, then that's what I need to do, because I want my vision to be more expanded.

What would you want to study?
I need to know the architectural order of Wayne Shorter's music. In my opinion he transcends the stuff that Gil Evans does. Gil is incredible but the order of Wayne Shorter is different. It's not comparing apples and oranges, but again, listening to Wayne's music, it makes me feel like a two year old. And I need to crawl out of the crib and find how that order relates, how he puts it together. I guess what I'm saying is I have to learn more cycles. Everything is a cycle of music anyway. You go around and you come back, and as you go around you tell the story differently. I'm more interested right now in taking more time to learn more cycles, learning more voicings and stuff like that.

What things have you learned from Wayne Shorter that translate onto guitar?
You know, I can't really put it into words because I must confess I'm really ignorant when it comes to naming chords—flatted fifths and ninths and all that kinda stuff. I've played 'em a lot but I don't know the names of 'em. I'm not saying ignorance is bliss but that's how I learned. My father taught me the basic chords on guitar and violin. From what I understand, neither Louis Armstrong or Wes Montgomery could read. Sometimes when I get cocky I feel like people who need to learn how to read are those who don't know how to create, so they just interpret stuff. But now I see the importance of learning more chords and learning to read, definitely, because I have exhausted this as much as possible now. I have taken it as far as I'm gonna take it. You can only dive into your subconscious for so much and put it all together—what you know and what you don't know. But now, again, I feel like it's time for me to really, really do some woodshedding and learn a whole bunch of different chords and inversions and stuff like that. Melody is still the house. Theory is just the interior decoration. So I wanna learn just enough theory to make the house look nice. But, again, the main thing is the melody. I always go back to the melody. If you tell a melody soulfully, sincerely, you're gonna get 'em. It's like Eubie Blake used to say, "If they listen, I got 'em."

Sounds like you're ready to jump to a new level.
I don't know if I'm gonna succeed or fail but I'm definitely hungry to move forward. I'm very much antsy about it. Right now America's in the '60s with the Grateful Dead and the Beach Boys. They just wore out the '50s with "La Bamba" [a reference to a remake of the '50s Ritchie Valens hit by Los Lobos]. I went to Jamaica about a week ago and they're in the '70s there. I went to Mexico and they are in the '30s, '40s, and '50s there. Nostalgia is fine but that doesn't turn me on as much as moving forward, going out there and being able to play with Herbie or Miles or John Lee Hooker. There are very few musicians who can do that, you know? Go to any part of town and play with anybody. Most musicians, they're very insecure, they only stay in their little ponds—heavy metal with heavy metal, blues with blues. And to me, it would be a curse to stay in one place for too long. Some people like to get a PhD in one subject, but people who I love, they got a PhD on life—like Jimi or Gil Evans or Miles. So that's what turns me on the most—music. Not just one facet of it. It's

more challenging and you do get scratched when you go jam with other people. That's part of it, but you have to be bold enough to go out there and complement what they're saying and not be hot-doggin', showing off how fast or how loud you can play. So I'm learning all this language.

You've been jamming with Wayne Shorter?
Yeah, we just jammed with Jerry Garcia, Wayne Shorter, Tower of Power, Cuban All-Stars, and Chester Thompson. That was a week ago. Then last weekend I played a benefit for Jaco Pastorius with Peter Erskine, Hiram Bullock, Marcus Miller, Victor Bailey, Terri Lynne Carrington, Don Alias, Herbie Hancock, Wayne Shorter. We all jammed together and it all fit. I was in a trance. I found myself directing the whole thing and Herbie came up to me afterwards and told me he appreciated me conducting the flow. He trusted me and he liked the way I was conducting traffic. So it shows me that all music can come together. I never liked the term "fusion" but I liked the slogan from the '60s, "bringing it all back home." Fusion sounds like microwave food. I like when people spend a whole day cookin' in the kitchen, man. So at night when you sit down it has a different flavor than somebody just putting Stouffer's in the microwave. That's what fusion is to me. It has no love behind it. But "bringing it all back home" has more meaning for me.

Your music, though it has Latin influences, is indelibly tied to the blues.
That's the real deal. To me, music has to be deeply rooted in the blues. That's where jazz came from anyway. The blues is a foundation from the old world music, whether it's African or Spanish or whatever. If you can play the blues, you can play with anybody because the feeling will be there. Otherwise, you can have a nice voice but you're not gonna give people chills. Their hairs are not gonna stand up. They're not gonna walk away pregnant. I get letters from people saying, "When you guys come to town, after they unplug the amplifiers and the trucks drive away with the equipment, we're still hearing the music." It registered with them in a deep way. So there's music and then there's entertainment, you know? That's what I would suggest the youngsters take notice of. Because entertainment is very fickle. I'd rather listen to real musicians in front of Macy's in the cold at Christmastime than a lot of the MTV stuff that I'm hearing. Because those guys outside Macy's can play! They're hungry and they can feel it. So those are my priorities—naked feeling. I think teenagers need to make that bridge. When I was a teenager I didn't want to explore my feelings either. You wanna be macho or cool. But if you wanna take the long term as far as being a musician, you have to learn to cry. Not whine, but cry.

Your association with Wayne Shorter now sort of relates to your ongoing interest in John Coltrane's music?
Right. Except that Coltrane's was more modal music. It seemed that he was deeply rooted into Afro-Indian music so it was like a drone. Wayne doesn't do that. Wayne has different drones—every four bars is a different drone. In other words, he's more architectural in the harmonic content. Miles and Wayne are the main people for that. So I want to learn that order. Because I understand the order of Otis Rush and all that cut-and-shoot music, as I call it. Now I wanna learn this other kind of music that Miles and Wayne represent. It's kind of like Tiffany. It's very elegant and very, very elite. It's not from Woolworth's, you know?

You mentioned the Jaco tribute. Did you know Jaco well?
I knew him well enough to talk to him a couple of times and let him know that it was important for him to pace himself. I told him... My father used to back up Lester Young, Charles Mingus, Billie Holiday, people like that. He was good friends with T-Bone and Charlie Christian. And he told me that he wished he could've said something to Charlie Christian or Billie Holiday about the way

they were living their lives—very seldom sleep, a lot of drugs, a lot of party, a lot of booze. It's like burning candles from the both ends. And I was telling Jaco about that. I said, "You know, Jaco, it's important to look at the other side of things. Look at the Duke Ellingtons and Eubie Blakes, people who went the long distance." But he wouldn't listen. I think he was like Jimi Hendrix. He had his destiny cut out for himself on this planet. He wasn't satisfied with things that normal people are satisfied with. He was looking for something else.

I was one of the few people who saw him the night before he got beat up at that bar in Florida. He came to our concert in Fort Lauderdale at the Sunrise Theater. Alphonso had taken an incredible bass solo and Jaco jumped on stage and held his hand like he was the champ. People didn't know who he was. The bouncers wrestled him out. They got into a scuffle and took him outside. I usually wait 'til everybody leaves—an hour and a half after the concert—before I go out. There were still people there wanting autographs or whatever and Jaco was there, too. And he told me, "Man, you played your ass off." Then we started talking about Jesus and that's the last time I saw him. One of his friends gave me a card—'cause he was hanging around two big goons. It was weird. And one of these big muscle guys gave me a card and said, "Listen, Jaco's gonna be in this club later. If you want to, we can send a limousine for you and there's gonna be some blow and the Miami Dolphins players are gonna be there." And I just don't like that kind of life anyway. Never did, you know? I didn't go. And within three days I heard what happened. There was nothing you could do, man. From what I understand, he had a history of walking that death wish. But we're gonna remember him for his music.

Does your current interest in stretching make you want to explore a new voice on your instrument? Is that gonna change as well?
No, very little. The more I fool around with guitar synthesizers, the faster I wanna come back to my regular guitar. One time I read this interview where Jan Hammer said that the end of guitar had come because synthesizer was going to take over. And I said, "Then how come you trying to sound like a guitar?" To me, the most beautiful sound to this day is the sound of T-Bone Walker and Wes Montgomery. So unless somebody's gonna sample that, I don't see no point. I could fool around with Roland guitar synths so it sounds like cellos. It's amazing because you can play certain things that almost sound like Pablo Casals because sampling is really good nowadays. You can do piano samples and almost feel like you're playing Art Tatum kind of runs. But again, it's like the faster I leave America, the faster I wanna come back. To me, America is what's happening in sports and in music. And when I leave this country and go to other countries, as beautiful as they are, I can hardly wait to get back. Same thing with my guitar. Every time I fool around with something new I can hardly wait to put it down and come back to my guitar. Because when a guitar is played, especially by the people who I love, like Otis Rush, it's very hard to beat it, man. The way he bends a note, it's like sucking on a sugar cane. He gets all the juice out of it. And that comes across to the listener. I like all the other instruments, but the guitar for me, especially because we get to bend notes, it's easier to pinch the listener into really listening to it, which is ultimately the goal.

Do you ever play much acoustic guitar?
Not really. I love John McLaughlin's acoustic work. Also Bola Sete. But that doesn't really appeal to me as a player. I like the voice of the electric guitar. After hearing T-Bone Walker, I got spoiled, you know? I like the single melody note to electric guitar. That appeals to me the most. It's hard for me to wear it out. Some people get bored so they learn a lot of chords. Well, I haven't gotten bored yet playing mostly single melody notes.

And you haven't ever played much with effects pedals?
No, I get lost every time I try one of those effects pedals. It feels really foreign to me, like Saran Wrap

on your teeth or something. I don't even like to play with one of those cordless gadgets. As soon as you plug in it sounds like you're playing through half an amp. You lose all the bottom. It's like white wine. I like red wine. I like plugging straight into the amp. That way, the sound is in my hands. It's pure. Just a Paul Reed Smith guitar and a Mesa-Boogie amp is all I need to get that sustain.

Aside from this new band with Wayne Shorter, do you have any other projects on the horizon?
I'm doing a special one-time thing with John Lee Hooker and the Berkeley Symphony Orchestra—if you can imagine a symphony backing up John Lee Hooker doing a boogie. It's been one of my dreams for about two and a half years now to put the blues with a symphony and have Herbie and Wayne in there, too, just to show how it can all work together.

I heard you were also interested in jamming with [cuatro player] Yomo Toro?
I'd love to. I love the way he plays. It would be nice. I'm looking forward to playing with a lot of musicians still, from Jimmy Cliff to Jimmy Page to everybody. I'm not looking forward to playing with George Michaels, to be polite, but I am looking forward to playing with musicians. There's a lot of musicians yet to get involved with and see what kind of chemistry is in there.

© ALDO MAURO

STEVIE RAY VAUGHAN

HE WAS PERHAPS THE GREATEST blues guitarist of his generation, a Texas tornado who scorched the fretboard with blistering, note-bending intensity, gut-wrenching vibrato, and a deep blues feeling. His all-too-abbreviated legacy—five albums as a leader and a handful of sizzling cameo appearances on other albums—was rounded out by three posthumous releases, including his soulful collaboration with older brother Jimmie Lee Vaughan on the aptly titled *Family Style* (Epic, 1990).

Born on October 3, 1954, in the Oak Cliff section of Dallas, Texas, Stevie Ray first picked up a guitar in 1963 at the age of eight. Recordings by Lonnie Mack and Albert King shaped his aesthetic and in 1968 he joined his first band, an R&B outfit called Blackbird. Shortly thereafter he formed The Chantones with schoolmate Tommy Shannon while occasionally playing bass in brother Jimmie's band Texas Storm. He dropped out of high school in his senior year and moved to Austin in 1972, taking up with bands like Crackerjack and the Nightcrawlers. In 1974 he joined popular Austin band The Cobras and in 1975 formed his own blues–R&B revue, Triple Threat. When that group disbanded in 1978, Stevie Ray and drummer Chris Layton recruited former Johnny Winter bassist Tommy Shannon to form Double Trouble, named after the classic Otis Rush recording of the '50s. The burgeoning reputation of the group led to an invitation to play the 1982 Montreux Jazz Festival, where

Double Trouble "reduced the stage to a pile of smoking cinders," according to *People* magazine. In that Montreux audience was David Bowie, who promptly recruited Stevie Ray to play on his *Let's Dance* album (EMI, 1983). Vaughan and Double Trouble were soon signed to Epic Records by legendary A&R man John Hammond, and their debut album, *Texas Flood,* was released in the summer of 1983 to critical raves. Vaughan's meteoric rise to guitar hero status was undercut by his own self-destructive excesses. After entering a rehabilitation hospital in 1986, he endeavored to turn his life around and get back on the good foot. His first post-rehab statement, *In Step* (Epic, 1989) was the strongest of his career, showing renewed powers and a more in-depth approach to songwriting. At the very height of his admirable comeback, Vaughan's life was snuffed out in a helicopter crash on August 27, 1990, just 36 days short of his 36th birthday.

The following interview, conducted in Orlando, Florida, for *Guitar World,* was the first major sit-down that Stevie Ray had had with the press since getting out of rehab. I saw him soon after that cathartic interview came out in September '88. He looked me deep in the eye backstage after a gig, shook my hand, and said, "Thanks for what you did."

A P R I L   1 9 ,   1 9 8 8

He strode into the room looking sharp as usual—snakeskin cowboy boots, blue jeans, a "Late Night with David Letterman" T-shirt over which he had draped a cool black jacket with the face of Dr. Martin Luther King, Jr., boldly emblazoned across the back. On the lapel of the jacket, inconspicuous by virtue of its size, was a tiny white pin with the familiar frizzy-haired visage of Jimi Hendrix.

As we sat down to chat I immediately sensed a new vibe to Stevie Ray Vaughan. The first time I had interviewed him for *Guitar World* back in 1983, he seemed shy and tentative in his answers to my questions. He was clearly new to the game and perhaps a little insecure about his communication skills. He gave one- and two-word answers and rarely offered eye contact as we sat there in his tour bus outside the Beacon Theater in New York, just moments after sound check. But on this day at the Omni Hotel in Orlando, Stevie Ray was a different man. There was an openness and expressive quality that wasn't there five years earlier. He seemed more confident, focused, and introspective—a bit wiser for the wear. His intense gaze grabbed me and he spoke with a kind of urgency and clarity that was lacking in our previous conversation. He was a man on a mission now, eager to get something off his chest. Little did I know how revealing this interview would be.

You're back touring again after being off the scene for a while. How's it been going?
I'm just doing the best I can to keep doing this—trying to grow up and remain young at the same time. I got a lot of paradoxes in my life.

It is a paradox—living on the road, being open to the child in yourself, while still taking care of business. How do you deal with it?
Well, I try and stay sober nowadays. For a long time there... The whole trip started before I was playing, but I can't blame the music for what I got into. I can only realize that a lot of it came out of insecurities. So I'm trying to cope with this and that.

What... Alcohol?
Yeah, alcohol and drugs. I did many years in a career with it—a career of its own. And finally I'm realizing now that I was scared. I started with drugs and alcohol young enough to where I finally did stop that I was a 33-year-old with a six-year-old kid inside me, scared and wondering where love is. Some of the questions I had were, "Why me and not somebody else?" Some of us make it,

some of us don't. Some of us can be examples about going ahead and growing. And some of us, unfortunately, don't make it there and are examples because they had to die.

So you were struggling with that question of having fame thrust upon you?
Well, I don't know if it was thrust or if I really asked for it and got what I asked for and then didn't want to deal with it. But through the whole thing... I can't regret it all because there were many good times. And there still are. There were a lot of mistakes made and now I can try to learn from those. And it took—for me at least—it took all the crap I went through to come out on this side and learn why not to do those things. And one thing I found out was if I stayed loaded all the time my ego got patted on the back and I didn't have to worry about the things I should be thinking about, you know? It was a lot more comfortable to run from those responsibilities. However, now it's a lot more fun to try... It makes a lot more sense to try to stay honest. While I have made mistakes in the past, I can use those mistakes as lessons and straighten those things out wherever possible.

How did you break through to this point of realization?
I had to give up to win, 'cause I was in a losing battle. I knew that I had a problem with a lot of things for a long time while I was still going full force with it.

Was it affecting your playing?
I'm sure it was. Of course, to my ears a lot of times it was, "Boy, isn't that great!" And there were some great notes that came out but they were not always necessarily by my doing. It was kinda like I was getting carried through something. And I dunno... There's just a lot more reasons to live now. And not just like "live it up," you know?

So you appreciate your life more.
Yeah, from day to day. And one thing I'm trying to learn is that just because there were a lot of mistakes made, it doesn't mean that the person making the mistakes is really a bad person. I just had kinda misplaced what was going on, kinda separated from it. That's really what goes on with anybody who makes a mistake anywhere at any time. And really, everybody's got a lot of good in 'em. A whole lot of good. In fact, the core of them is really good. Mistakes and wrong paths that we take are just diversions—kinda like strange-looking learning devices, you know?

When did all this go down?
Exactly 16 months and six days ago. That's when I went into rehab. I collapsed, I believe, on September 17, 1986. Actually there were several levels to it. When I fell off the stage in London... I had an Indian headdress that I wear sometimes and I didn't look where I was going and stepped off the side of this walkway between the stage and backstage. And I fell. That wasn't so much because I was loaded, it was just that I wasn't looking where I was going. However, at that time I had gotten to the point where no longer could I have any idea what it would take to get drunk. I passed the stage where I could drink whatever I wanted to and hold my liquor, so to speak. One day I could drink a quart and the next day all I'd have to drink was one sip and get smashed.

That sounds like Jaco Pastorius. He'd get totally nuts on one beer and people started figuring, "Hmmm... There's something chemical going on here."
Yeah, it is a chemical thing. It's an actual disease. And I know that a lot of insurance companies are trying to figure out how to not call it that anymore, 'cause it's costing them too much money. But it is a disease and it's three-fold: it's mental, physical, and spiritual. And it takes rehab in all those areas.

So you must've gone through a whole period of denial.
I will for the rest of my life go through the recovery from that. Of course there's a lot of denial. There still is. It's like a process of breaking through waves of it. Every time I finally become able to open up my mind to solutions to some of the problems, every time I take another step out of my own way, I grow a little bit and then have to begin again and realize a little bit deeper. Because alcoholism—the alcohol problem, the drug problem, and the fear—all those are symptoms of an underlying problem that's called lack of love. There are holes in our perceptions of what we're doing and what's going on in our whole life. And we gotta fill those up with outside things—other people or other things. It's one thing to be able to depend on someone and trust them and say you love 'em. And that's a lot of what this problem is. Trying to fill up holes that we really don't know where they are. We just know that if we don't feel good we can take a drink and feel better for a few minutes, until we realize what we've done. I tell ya, sobering up really screws up your drinking. And for that I'm real grateful. And I can honestly say that I'm really glad to be alive today because, left to my own devices, I had too many vices and I would've slowly killed myself. I just didn't have the nuts to do it all at once. There were a lot of things there I was runnin' from and one of them was me. But you can't run from yourself. Everywhere you go you take yourself with you. That sounds like, "No matter where you go, there you are." But it really is true.

You mentioned that you had a breakdown just before that incident in London when you fell off the stage.
Well, everything fell apart. I had gone to Europe and I hadn't done any drugs for two, three weeks before I quit drinking. Partially because, for whatever reason, I couldn't get a hold of any drugs in Europe. At that point I had decided... I had to surrender to the fact that I don't know how to go without this stuff. In my mind I had kind of envisioned just staying high the rest of my life.

What were your drugs of choice?
I was in some ways a trash can, you know? Whatever I could put in there. But at that point it was mainly cocaine. I was addicted to cocaine. I was addicted to, for lack of a better word, disposable people—people that I was using. But I didn't realize it. I was also addicted to alcohol of any kind and every kind at once. At any rate, I hadn't been doing any drinking around the time of this breakdown. And I finally realize it now but part of my collapse was actually secondary withdrawals. But it had gotten to the point where when I woke up in the morning I would try to say "Hi" to somebody and would just fall apart, crying and everything. It all felt like solid doom. I had been trying to pull myself up by my bootstraps, so to speak, and they were broke, you know? And what I ended up doing was, when I would wake up just to try and get rid of the pain I would guzzle something. Whatever was by me—whiskey, beer, vodka, whatever. And I'd sit there and try to talk to somebody until they got me calmed down. They'd say, "You're not really going crazy. There's just some problems that we gotta work out." And finally I went to see someone in London, Dr. Victor Bloom. And he filled me in on the disease of alcoholism and filled me in on the fact that I'd been drinking since, no telling—1960, '61, '62 maybe. That's when I first started stealing Daddy's drinks. Or when my parents were gone I'd go find the bottle and make myself one. And I thought it was cool, thought the kids down the street would think it was cool. And that's where it started. Anyway, he had made it clear to me that I had been doing this, depending on it for all these years, and that it wasn't really feasible or realistic that I was just going to feel like I could just not take another drink. And he gave me four, five days. He said, "If you really feel like you need a drink, go and have one but have somebody with you so that you don't go off the deep end." He put me in a private clinic there in London. I had torn my stomach up real bad by drinking because part of my deal was I would make drinks and put cocaine in it, so it would last longer. I didn't realize that it would crystallize in my stomach and make cuts inside there.

How long were you in that clinic?

I went in in mid-September of '86. They let me out of the hospital to go and do the gig, the one where I fell off the stage. Anyway, I went back to the hospital right after the gig. I stayed there for a few more days and then came back to the States and went straight into a treatment center in Marietta, Georgia. And to show you how crazy this disease is, before I got on the plane to come back, I borrowed ten dollars from my mother—who was doing her best to keep her eye on me—told her I was going to buy some duty free cigarettes, and went straight to the bar and spent all the money as quick as I could on double shots of Crown whiskey, because I realized I had never been on a plane sober that I could think of. Here I'd just come out of the hospital, had some information on what was wrong, what the problem was, and how to deal with it. I was on my way to a treatment facility and had a quick thought of, "Hey, wow, I've never done this straight before." The old thinking came back. And that's what we have to have a defense against. And when I say "we" I mean alcoholics and addicts. We remain that way the rest of our lives. However, that doesn't mean we have to be active. I went through the treatment program there and fortunately I had great counselors. There was a lot of people that really wanted to get sober there. And they based their treatment off of a 12-step program. And not trying to make a commitment for the rest of your life but for just today. Take care of today. Tomorrow comes and it's today.

Each day is a victory.

Exactly. And as I came out, I had a tremendous amount of support. Still do. Other people in the band, the road crew, my mother, my girlfriend—lots of people and real friends, most of whom are in the program themselves. And we watch out for each other. If one of us is isolating or if they say "I'm fine" too many times with the wrong look on their face... That's one of the problems that we have. Somebody asks us how we're doing and we feel like shit but we say, "Oh, great, man!" You know, just trying to hold all of that in. There's no sense in running through life trying to act like everything's just groovy. It's one thing to take it like a man, but that doesn't necessarily mean not letting anybody in. But we all try to look out for each other and just do this thing one day at a time.

Are you still attending meetings?

Yeah, I just got back from one. They help—a lot. And if I don't take a drink, nothing got worse than it had to be. Nothing's so bad that getting drunk or getting high is gonna make it any better—period.

And what are you focusing your energies on now?

The music. All along there's been good reasons to play. I like it, a lot of other people like it. It's fun. It can help us out in all kinds of ways. I mean, this would be a pretty weird place without music or art of any kind, because it really is a way to reach out and hold onto each other in a healthy way.

Sounds like you've been through some personal, spiritual growth in the past year.

Yeah, and it's paid off in all kinds of ways. And the easiest way that I can see that it pays off is that I've learned to give it away. Not keep it.

I understand that John Hammond had been helpful during your recovery.

What a wonderful man that guy was. [Hammond died a few weeks before this interview.] As far as I know, he was the first one to open up a rehabilitation center for musicians in the '30s. He's a real sweet guy who quietly cared. At one point he had walked in on me in a hotel room and I was crashed out in bed with tea bags over my eyes because somebody had told me that it would get rid of the bags under my eyes. I was trying to look real good for the next denial role. "Who me? No, man, I'm fine." He didn't mention anything to me then. But the next time we really sat down and talked I got a chance to tell him that I had been sober for a while, and he was happy about that. He gave me that wonderful smile of his, because he cared. He was real old school. He didn't necessarily go for modern recording techniques. He just figured you recorded a record and just played it back, you know? Like... "Mix what? That's how it sounded, right?" But what he really cared about was what you played. And this world needs more people like that.

When did you get out of rehab?
I got out on November 31, 1986. So it was a little more than a month that I was there. And I went straight back to work, pretty much. And now I realize that it's a wonderful world out here. I just have to open my eyes to it. And I'm gradually trying and getting somewhere with learning how to meet life on life's terms. There are people that I've hurt and there are places that I got hurt myself. However, that doesn't mean that I have to go on and continue that process. I can try to make amends wherever I can and somewhere along the line I'm learning that I have to learn to forgive myself.

What about your brother Jimmie? Did you confide in him at all?
Not as much as I probably could've. Of course, in a lot of ways it was another case of trying to show I could handle this and I could handle that. I didn't really isolate from certain people, I isolated from everybody. And I would take a break from my isolation every once in a while to go off and do some recording or touring. And at one point it got real nuts. For a long time we had a schedule that was just completely out of hand. And the only reason it was humanly possible was because we were trying to think that we were superhuman. For a while there, before the breakdown, we had been touring and recording everything as we traveled, getting material for a live record. And that got real complicated. We were mixing and fixing in the studio during the day and gigging at night. It got crazy. I would stay there all night long in the studio, come back to the hotel room, take a shower, go to the concert sound check, play the gig, come back to the studio, and stay there all night long. For about two weeks I did that routine—trying not to sleep, taking lots of vitamins. And our attitude was, "Oh, you tired? Well here, snort this." And eventually I noticed that I was running out of gas. It was getting to the point where, you know, you can't give somebody a dollar if you ain't got one. You can try all you want but if you're out of gas you just cannot give anymore.

What were those performances like?
Some of them were OK, some of them sounded like half-dead people. We had made a point of pulling off things that we shouldn't have been able to pull off, and we were cocky about it. We just weren't thinking about the fact that you have to take some time and be real. And eventually we were beginning to see that the strain was taking its toll.

And that led to this breakdown?
Yeah, we were exhausted. And also during this time I was trying to run from some responsibilities and work out some realities in my life—personal relationships. Some of those are still unresolved, some of them are growing immensely. Nowadays I care about making a commitment to relationships and myself. It just really is time to grow up and realize that I can take responsibility for a lot of things. I cannot run the whole show, I don't run the world, and it doesn't revolve around me. And yet, you walk on stage and the whole deal is you're up there bigger than life. People idolize you. You let it go to your head and you believe it, then you're in trouble. So you have to keep these things in perspective. My talent is a gift that I have and I have to give it back all the time or it goes away. If I start believing that it's all my doing, it's gonna be my undoing. And I'm committing myself to doing the most I can with the gifts I have so that they do as many people good as possible.

Sounds like you've reached a new plateau in your life?
Well, I'm a real confused person. However, there are some focused parts. And I'm trying to put the pieces back together. But I'm finally realizing that fear is the opposite of love. And I've been scared all my life. I was walking around trying to act cool—no fear at all. You know... "Scared of what?" And that's why I stayed scared. I was scared that somebody would find out I was scared. But it's not so big a deal to be scared, to let somebody know. You tell 'em and they say, "It's OK, man. No problem."

Were there any other key figures who tried to help you out during your recovery?
Albert King. I remember one time we were doing a show together and I was just sitting there trying to act cool as usual, putting up this front like, "Ain't nuthin' wrong, man. I'm leadin' the life, you know?" And he just sat there watching me. A few minutes later he calls me over and says, "We're gonna have a heart to heart. I been watching you wrestle with that bottle three or four times already. I tell you what, man. I like to drink a little bit when I'm at home, with a woman or something. But the gig ain't no time to get high. You have too much fun at the gig and you don't know who's fuckin' ya outta money." He was trying to tell me to give myself a break. And I have to realize now, although I was trying hard not to realize then, that the truth is this: I don't drink because I have all these problems; I have all these problems because I drink.

How did you take Albert's advice?
I listened to him. However, I was hooked. And I had to reach the bottom before I would act on it. That's usually the case with an alcoholic or a drug addict. You gotta get down to the point where the only way to go is up. And I felt better soon as I gave up. And I hadn't felt that good in years and years. It's a strange thing to say but you really have to give up to win. I lost the battle but I won the war. A lot of us end up in jail or out of our minds or dead. And part of the problem is that alcoholism is so accepted. "Gee, he sure is screwed up, but he sure can play good." This is a destructive lie. The lie is that it's OK to go out in flames, but that really doesn't do anybody much good.

The case of Hendrix comes to mind.
I may be wrong but I think Jimi was trying to come around. I think he had gotten a glimpse of what he needed to change, and I found myself in a similar position. And it just took me hitting bottom before I took action. Thank God my bottom wasn't death.

Did people come to see you in the rehab hospital?
Yes, Jackson Browne. Eric Clapton came to see me and he was real calm and caring about it. He let me know that he had gone through it and was trying to just lend support. When I first met him, years earlier, he was sober and he just sat there watching me down two, three, four shots of Royal Crown. And how he looked at it was, "Well, sometimes you gotta go through that, don't you?" He said, "I did." And he understood that I wasn't ready to stop then. You can tell when somebody is not ready to quit. You can try, you can let them know what's going on, but you just can't make 'em quit. Because they're going to resent you for it. You can offer help and if they accept it, fine. But once you really become an addict or alcoholic, the drink and drugs just take the place of the people you care about and those who care about you. You start forgetting about those people because you can't face 'em. And one way to do that is to act tough, to convince yourself that, "Oh, they don't know what they're missing." And you die inside that way. When a person is in that spot, it seems like those people really don't care, because all they want to do is take this away from you. And what they're really trying to do is give you something instead. A lot of people wrote, called, and otherwise gave support to me that way. All those things helped save my life, man. And every day

that I live now it never fails, somewhere along the line in the course of the day, I get reminded about people like that. And now I realize that if somebody is in a similar spot and if I can reach out and help them, then it's my responsibility. Hell, if it hadn't been for people reaching out to me, I may not have made it.

DR. JOHN

I WAS 18 AND WORKING AT A TACO BELL in Milwaukee when "Right Place, Wrong Time" (*In the Right Place,* Atco/Atlantic, 1973) came out. It was my introduction to Dr. John, the trippy/funky persona that reached out beyond the bayou and grabbed middle America with swampy-ass tales of voodoo and gris-gris and goin' to the carnival and walkin' on gilded splinters and all those colorfully decadent images. I remember seeing him for the first time on Don Kirshner's "Rock Concert" and thinking about this whole other mysterious, forbidden world that existed down there in New Orleans, light years away from my own safe, Midwestern experience. Of course, I had gotten my first taste of New Orleans years earlier from Fats Domino and Ernie K-Doe records. I mean, absolutely everybody in America, no matter what isolated berg or bustling metropolis which they happen to inhabit, was hip to Fats' "I'm Walkin'," with that great Earl Palmer signature N'awlins parade-drumming lick at the intro, and K-Doe's "Mother-in-Law." I had the advantage of having a brother four years older than me with very discerning tastes in music. He had been cueing up Fats records from the time he was four years old and he passed that passion on to me, thankfully.

But Dr. John (aka Malcolm "Mac" Rebennack) was my own personal discovery. I guess it was the allure of the dark side—the spooky hoodoo/gris-gris vibe combined with the obvious lysergic nature of his psychedelic grooves—that first grabbed my attention. And the power of the music eventually took hold. I got to see the good doctor on several occasions after moving to New York City in 1980. There was one memorable double bill in the early-1980s with the Sun Ra Arkestra at Irving Plaza. Both bands did a second line through the audience that night. After putting together his own Social & Pleasure Club band, Mac held forth on a regular basis at the old Lone Star Cafe on 13th Street with cats like trumpeter Lew Soloff and baritone sax burner Ronnie Cuber. He would do the occasional showcase at Carnegie Hall during the JVC Jazz Festival or the Benson & Hedges Blues Festival and there were rare week-long engagements at the Blue Note nightclub in the heart of Greenwich Village. And they were some cool gigs. But there is really nothing like catching Dr. John down in his native New Orleans on a hot and humid night at Tipitina's—the house that Fess built—when the sweat is pouring and the Abita beers are flowing and the whole audience, en masse, is raising their butts to the sky as he pumps the piano and growls on about "Such a Night" or "Iko Iko" or "All on a Mardi Gras Day." It is then that you truly become one with the funk—N'awlins style.

The following interview was conducted in Mac's New York City apartment for a May 1997 cover story in *Fi* magazine. The good doctor has since released two albums—*Trippin' Live* (Surefire, 1997) and *Anutha Zone* (Pointblank, 1998).

JANUARY 13, 1997

Mac Rebennack's beloved Crescent City is long gone. It ain't quite the same down there no how, not like how it used to be back in the day. The once-bustling all-night music scene that he was such a part of is a thang of the past. The faint hope of resuscitating that scene with a thriving gambling industry—one that might help create more lucrative playing opportunities for local musicians—fell flat on its face when Harrah's Casino declared bankruptcy and closed its doors just a few months into its eagerly anticipated run. Meanwhile, Bourbon Street has been taken over by lame cover bands playing "Proud Mary" and "Meet Me with Your Black Drawers On" to German tourists and overweight conventioneers from Dubuque to Dallas, Peoria to Little Rock. They got a Planet Hollywood in the French Quarter now, just down Decatur Street from the Hard Rock Cafe. Across the way is the Fashion Cafe. Sure, the House of Blues is bringing in some good acts but the pseudo-hip trappings of that joint disguise the fact that it's really nothing more than yet another corporate trough catering to no-hearing *turistas* who wouldn't know what time it was if they had Big Ben strapped on their backs.

The real heroes and legends that the city has produced over time are vanishing one by one—Fess, Booker, Danny Barker, Melvin Lastie, Jessie Hill—and nobody's coming along to replace them. It's a sad situation. One thing will never vanish from New Orleans, though—the fonk. Now you know that's right. It's in the air down there. You can't escape it no how. Give me three hot, humid days in August, a bowl of gumbo, some red beans and rice with a generous dose of Trappey's hot sauce, some of Mother's finest jambalaya with a side of grits, a few pitchers of Abita beer, and a continuous flow of "Ooo Poo Pa Do" and "Mother-in-Law" on radio station WWOZ with the second line rhythms in the street and I could make Don Knotts a funky cat. And once you've got all of that in your system, you don't get rid of it so easy. You keep coming back for mo'. As Dr. John himself put it in his "little book of rememberations," *Under a Hoodoo Moon: The Life of the Night Tripper* (St. Martin's Press, 1995): "No matter how far away from New Orleans I've gone and what I've done, sooner or later I always want to come back to my hometown for a roots recharge. L.A. and New York are cool, but neither holds the spell for me that New Orleans still does."

So while Mac currently makes his home a short strut from Grand Central Station in the Big Apple, he does make regular pilgrimages back to the Big Easy. You can generally catch him around Mardi Gras time (mid-February) or Jazz and Heritage Festival time (late-April/early-May) and a few other random hits throughout the year. You might spot him at the Botanica on Broad Street where he stocks up on Santeria candles or at Gene's—the all-night donut and po' boy joint that Earl King frequents in the Ninth Ward. You might notice Rebennack at a funeral or at one of the Sunday afternoon practices of the Mardi Gras Indians up in the 13th Ward.

Though Mac has moved a long way from his old Third Ward neighborhood, he's still very proud of his Crescent City roots. As he wrote with the slightest hint of chauvinism in his audacious autobiography: "New Orleans remains its own strange self, and more than a little bit out of synch with other places in the United States. This is one of its charms, but also a curse."

As a teen, Rebennack went from playing guitar with Sister Elizabeth Eustace, a sanctified zealot, to running scag for his junko partner Shank. He was part of the vital scene happening at Cosimo Matassa's studio on Governor Nichols Street, participating as a guitar-playing sideman on several significant sessions there during the '50s for the likes of Huey "Piano" Smith, Lee Allen, Eddie Bo, Paul Gayten, and a dozen others. An ugly incident in 1961 nearly ended Rebennack's guitar-playing career. As he recounts in his book: "On Christmas Eve my little band and I took a gig at a joint in Jacksonville, Florida. We was getting ready to go to the gig when we realized that Ronnie Barron, who always took forever to do hisself up for gigs, had disappeared. I went to look for him and found him being pistol-whipped by the motel owner, who'd caught Ronnie with his old lady. I went to get the gun out of the guy's hand. We wrestled for it. I thought my left hand was over the handle but I was actually grabbing the barrel. We started in Ronnie's room and ended up outside in a brick garden. I beat the guy's hand against the bricks trying to get the gun away from him, and the gun went off. I looked down and saw the ring finger of my left hand, my fretting hand, hanging by a thread."

Following re-constructive surgery and long bouts of physical therapy, Mac switched over to piano and continued to make a living by playing behind the dancers at strip joints like Madame Francine's and Poodle's Patio in the French Quarter. But it was at after-hours jam sessions at Papa Joe's that he began to develop a sense of showmanship. As he recounts: "Those sessions were the first times I had to sing and work a house. When the regular singer got too hoarse to do it, I'd take over and handle the lyrics. By popular demand, I'd get up and sing long-ago-and-far-away standards like 'How Much Pussy Do You Eat' or 'Dope Fiend Blues.' Along with the regulation standards like 'Junko Partner' and 'Lush Life,' this was the stuff this crowd liked to hear. And they was the best-tipping audience of the night."

By 1967, after hitting it hard with his band, Mac was ready to reinvent himself. As he writes: "For many years I had nurtured my little idea of forming a musical group around the personality of Dr. John. Through my contacts with gris-gris and spiritual-church people and by reading New Orleans history that my sister and others had turned me on to, I had begun to dig the importance of Dr. John as an early spiritual leader of the New Orleans community. But it was when I read a piece by the 19th century writer Lafcadio Hearn that my head really got turned seriously around. In Hearn's story I found that Dr. John and one Pauline Rebennack were busted in the 1840s for having a voodoo operation and possibly a whorehouse. I don't know for sure, but there's a strong chance that Pauline Rebennack was one of my relatives, so I feel more than an incidental sympathy for the man whose name I took as a stage name in 1967."

Though he's long since ditched the greasepaint and gris-gris dust on stage, Mac Rebennack still shakes his funky butt and turns out quintessential Crescent City tunes like "Iko Iko," "Mama Roux," "Junko Partner," and his breakthrough hit from 1973, "Right Place, Wrong Time." Less the psychedelic Night Tripper–Pied Piper and more of a cleaned-up ambassador for New Orleans–style music, Mac is the living embodiment of the spirit that flowed through Tuts Washington and Professor Longhair and James Booker and Jessie Hill and Joe "Mr. Google Eyes" August and a whole lineage of eccentric, charismatic entertainers to come out of the Crescent City.

At a recent week-long engagement at the Blue Note, Dr. John appeared sans horns with a four-piece band that highlighted the guitar work of Bobby Broom. Feeling the financial strain of his costly tour last year with a full-scale big band (as a means of promoting his last album, *Afterglow,* Blue Thumb, 1995) he's scaled down his working band and is focusing more intently on funk rhythms and Fess–styled piano work than the elaborate Ernie Wilkins–styled arrangements of *Afterglow.* We began by talking about our mutual love/hate relationship with the City that Care Forgot.

Yeah, Mac, I just moved back to New York a few months ago after living down in New Orleans for the past three years.
Did you have a good time?

Oh yeah, you know how that goes. It was a groove, but it's also good to be back.
Man, I get so depressed down there. I love it and it's my hometown but they just gutted it and fucked it up. It breaks my heart. What really pisses me off is they not getting none of the local musicians enough gigs out of whatever is going on. I mean really... The gambling joints aren't hiring anybody and on and on.

Well, Harrah's going bankrupt was a big blow to that whole industry.
Well, you know, if they did that shit 20 years ago it might've meant something. They were talking about doing it [legalized gambling] since '69 or '70. Twenty-six years it took 'em to do that. I mean, they should really be embarrassed. Typical New Orleans crap—several years late and a whole gang and a half of money short.

Do you notice a lot of changes when you go back to town?
Man! If I ride out to when I was a little bitty kid—the pad's gone, the neighborhood is bad, bad. It wasn't that good when I lived there but it's real bad now. It's just depressing. All the neighborhoods all over... Oh man! I get to reminiscing about how it was when I be there. And I notice that all friends that lives there, they be reminiscing about how it was, you know? That ain't no way to be. You gotta figure something to do *now*, figure some way to change that shit for the better.

When did you first notice things changing in New Orleans?
When air conditioning came in. It helped eliminate street life. People used to sit out on the porch to get cool, and they'd socialize. I remember when I was a kid, people used to take a big block of ice and put a fan on it, and that was an air conditioner. But you had to keep the windows open to let the air flow in. And as a result, you was in contact with all your neighbors. People would hang out the windows and talk so there was a flow of ideas along with the flow of air. I remember in the Third Ward, one of the main forms of communication was leaning out of windows on both sides of an alley and people talking across. It's kind of a lost art. That whole communicational thing turned very sideways. It's like the fear that people have in the streets today—it got worse as a result of people not being outside. The more people don't hang out, the more bad things happen. And the more bad things happen, the more people don't wanna hang out.

So you still go back to visit?
Oh yeah, we went down there and hung with my grandchildren for Christmas and all. It was cool. I went fishing.

Seems like people keep trying to make a scene bubble up in New Orleans and it just hasn't happened, certainly not to the extent that it did in the '50s.
Man, there's no strips left and that aggravates me to my heart. You think they'd have one strip of music for local people. It just aggravates me when they just shut everything down. It just spreads

crime all over the city instead of it being in little pockets, you know? It's one thing to contain some-thing in a little pocket, but when it's all over the place... Things spreading into areas that was cool and really ain't cool now. It's real sad. They got people that's still living in the same place they were living 40, 50 years ago. And I don't know how some of them do it.

They're prisoners in their own home because of the high murder rate down there.
Well, a lot of them died, man. That's really pathetic. You know how many of the Hills and Lasties have died just being in the way of bullets and shit? Way, way too many. That little trombone player that got killed in the Treme... It's a shame, man. Jessie Hill, before he died he had lost like eight or nine children and grandchildren in one year. In one family! Man, that Lastie family... They've watched as all but one of their children died. Joe Lastie is the only one of them left. And it's just sad. I mean, here's the people that actually made a neighborhood good and they're all getting vic-timized. They was like saints, them Lasties. They like a part of some history to me. Somebody oughta write the real history of that family. You hear about the Marsalises and the Nevilles, but the Lasties are so much a part of New Orleans history. Like, Frank Lastie put sidewalks up in his neighborhood and got running water hooked up. He wasn't no politician. Here's a guy running the Guiding Light Spiritual Church, Deacon Frank. He got everything done in the neighborhood. That was country, man. I mean, they didn't have a paved road out there. And here's a guy who got all that done.

It was sad to hear that Jessie ("Ooo Poo Pa Doo") Hill recently passed.
Man, I had people calling me three weeks before he passed telling me he was dead. We got some very idiotic rumor-mongers down there who got nothin' better to do than call me up and tell me somebody's dying. That really gets me salty. I called his family and they said, "No, he's in the inten-sive/critical care ward. He's not dead." I mean, somebody just called my sister and said *I* was dead! Just a week ago! I think it's the same old rumor-monger who spread the rumor about Jessie. Also, I got a call that Norman Harris got murdered and it wasn't true neither. Is that all these people got to do? It was on the radio that Jessie died before he died. It was in the newspapers.

You were down in New Orleans for Jessie's funeral?
The last funerals I went to was Jessie and his brother-in-law Frank Lastie. That family, man... They was always so good to me as a kid. The music they played in church was something special. Their family was just all beautiful people. It's really sad that as you losing them kinda people there ain't nobody replacing none of them.

Can you talk about your relationship with Jessie?
Well, I first got tight with Jessie Hill when he was playing at a joint called Shy Guy's next door to a joint called Natale's out on Chef Menteur Highway. And he was playing "Ooo Poo Pa Doo" on the gigs at that time. I was working [as an A&R man] at Ace Records and I told [label owner] Johnny Vincent that I wanted to record him doing that tune. Johnny knew Jessie from being Huey Smith's drummer at the time but he ixnayed the whole thing without ever hearing the songs. Next thing I know, Jessie had a deal with Joe Banashack and Larry McKinley and Allen Toussaint to do the song for Minit Records. And it turned out to be a big hit. I knew the song was good because of the crowd reaction that he was getting at the joint where I first saw him. After the Minit shit all went dead, I saw Jessie out in California. We started a publishing company called I Found It. It was Jessie, Alvin ["Shine"] Robinson, Dave Dixon, and myself. We wrote a million songs for Shine, Junior Parker, and whoever we could write songs for. But I always wanted to get a good record on Jessie because he had some kind of different energy. And unfortunately, it just never happened. Even

right to the end, after he had his heart attack and emphysema and everything, he was still writing good stuff. I got some tapes of him and me, the stuff we was writing—it was seriously bad stuff! The sad thing is, I don't know who could cut it. Maybe somebody in his family might want to. Maybe Trombone Shorty's band or one of them little bands in Treme might cut it. But now that Jessie's passed and Alvin Robinson's passed and Dave Dixon's passed, I don't even know where some of our stuff is. It's stuff that we wrote and Jessie was trying to find before he passed. I was trying to find some of it, too, but I think his family's gonna get a little money off of it pretty soon.

Allen Toussaint was saying that the spirit of Fess was living on through Jessie.
Yeah, I related Fess and Jessie. There was a certain group of guys that had that special thing. In fact, one of the last songs that we did was Jessie's version of "Her Mind Is Gone," Fess' old tune. I had brought the tapes to some people at Atlantic [Records] and they just got lost in some shuffle somewhere. But we tried a lot of stuff, man. I remember when we had our little label and production company and all that. We came up with I Found It publishing and we came up with this little label called Free Records, which was a bad name for a label. We wound up giving them all away, never sold two records. But it's funny, all the songs that we had got covered... Cher covered one of our tunes, Aretha [Franklin] covered one, Wilson Pickett covered one, Brooke Benton covered one. So we had the right idea with something.

That was out on the West Coast? When you left town in the '60s?
Yeah, it was basically me and Shine and Jessie. And Dave Dixon was doing all the writing. But Harold Batiste was doing all the business. When Mercury hired me I told them, "Well, I'll take the gig, but only if you hire Harold." You know, Harold was like the guy we always looked to be the *bidness* guy. He was really an arranger. To us he was a business guy because we had no clue what a business guy was. And it's weird because when I was out in California, Harold was working for J. W. Alexander, who was a way better business guy. I mean, he used to manage Sam Cooke and all that. He at least knew something. But we never thought of people like him because he weren't from New Orleans. Obviously, we wasn't the best thinking guys back then.

You still reminisce about your early days in New Orleans?
All them days is real fond in my heart, you know? Like the day that Papoose [Nelson] told my daddy he couldn't teach me no more and wanted me to go to Roy Montrell for guitar lessons... That changed my life all over again. So many things happened in my life to do with that family in weird ways. I feel like my life is connected to them, like it wouldn'ta been what was good about it if I hadn'ta met them. It wouldn'ta happened for a lot of reasons. And a lot of stuff went down in the days when there was a lot of race weird stuff going on in New Orleans. At the time I didn't understand it. I guess I was too stupid to understand what was going on. But I was also caught dead in the middle of it between the unions and stuff. I didn't understand it but I had a bad attitude toward both of the musicians' unions, black union and white union. They give me so much grief. So anyway, Melvin Lastie—back in that family again—became a union rep. And I thought, "Wow, now it's gonna be OK." And it wasn't no different. I mean, one guy can't make no change, even if he was from that family. But it's like, we were all trying to do stuff. Like when AFO Records started happening, when they signed up Barbara George, they were bringing Jessie in to audition. That's how AFO Records got their start—from two artists that they got, Prince La La and Barbara George, who had a big hit with "I Know." Again, it's connected to that same Lastie family. I mean, that coronet solo that Melvin Lastie played on "I Know" changed the whole structure of trumpet to this date on record. That was 1960-something and here it is 1990-something and they still playing that way.

There are so many vivid images in your autobiography. I like the story about Roy Montrell taking an ax to your guitar back when you were taking lessons with him.

Oh yeah, I bought this stupid Harmony guitar because it was green. Then Roy took an ax and broke it up and I was scared. I said, "Man, I still owe my daddy money on this thing." He calls my daddy and says, "Mr. Rebennack, I'm gonna go and get your kid a real guitar." Roy was a good con artist but he was also a good cat. I mean, I loved the guy. No matter what he ever did in his life, I loved the guy, you know? But he just had his own way about things that was off-the-wall. You don't meet many people like that.

Seems like New Orleans turned out a lot of unique characters like that.... Booker, Fess, K-Doe.

Yeah, we were looking at a picture of Booker yesterday, it just cracked me up. I got that one picture of Booker when he was younger, before he had the patch. I don't know, I think I lost most of the pictures I had of everybody—or somebody stole 'em.

I like that story about Booker calling some guy over to his piano at a gig.... Guy comes over and Booker's got all these joints rolled up and stuffed between the keys. And at the end of it all, lying on the keys, is a syringe.

Oh, Booker was a kick! He was the most heartbreaking guy when I used to have to fire him out the band. There was three guys I always had to fire. One of them was Booker, one of them was Ray Draper, one of them was Didimus.

For what, showing up late or...

Oh no, man! Every time somebody died Booker would flip out. Like when his mama died, when his sister died, when Melvin Lastie died... He'd do weird things. The night he found out Melvin died he left his works and his cooker in the hotel room with the door open. He had dropped acid and was dressed on the gig like Cleopatra from the Nile. He came out with the background singers and when they announced me he comes out doing a thing like Cleopatra dancing. And later he was trying to run some kind of scam on the pay table. I said, "Booker, I can't front you no money. You already drew up two weeks of money. I can't even afford to fire you." So he conned me out of two weeks more money and took off in a plane. I had to fire him after he took off, *after* I gave him the money. Then he had went to Marvin Gaye and got two weeks money out of him, went to Fats Domino and got two weeks money, went to Joe Tex and got two weeks money, then goes home and gets busted. Then he conned the sheriff at parish prison to let him do a record—in the parish prison! Aw... On and on, man. But I loved Booker. So much stuff happened between him and me. It's all confused in my head but I remember some things clear.

You've just ended a relationship with GRP. How did that work out?

Alright. I loved working with Tommy LiPuma. Tommy and me have been friends for more than 30 years. He worked on *In a Sentimental Mood* [Warner Bros., 1989], *Afterglow* [Blue Thumb, 1995], *City Lights* [Horizon, 1978], and *Tango Palace* [Horizon, 1979]. But we did a lot of other stuff, too, over the years. We sold masters way back in the game. Tommy used to help me sell a lot of masters to people that nobody in their right mind would've bought. But Tommy had the heart and the class to take chances with them. And he suffered a lot of bad consequences from helping us a lot of times.

He seems to be widely liked by musicians.

That's because he's a musician. And it's also 'cause he understands and cares about musicians, unlike a lot of people in this business. Considering that we're in the music business, somebody got the priorities reversed so that we at the bottom of a ladder that we should be at the top of. It's not a good feeling.

And that situation seems to be getting worse.
It's been like that. You know, it's a long trail of funny money and strange change. I been in this business 42 years and it ain't changed. Not that part of it. The one thing that changed is the guys that used to beat us for money at least used to like the music. Now the people who are fuckin' us don't even like the music. So the few that do care about it, like Tommy, we treasure 'em.

What was the last thing you worked on with Allen Toussaint?
He produced *Right Place*. But we've done some stuff since then. We did that *Crescent City Gold* album a few years back [for Windham Hill Records, 1994]. But I thought the best thing we was thinking to do never came out. We did some stuff for United Artists right before they dropped me from the label. We actually cut the stuff but when I got to L.A. with the tapes I found out that the guy who signed me, Al Teller, had been fired from UA and the guy who took over immediately dropped me from the label. He never even listened to the stuff. But that was some killer stuff, man. It always feels good together with Allen. I guess when I first started doing sessions back at Cosimo's—that's how I met Allen, through James Booker. He sent Allen to sub on a session a long, long time ago. I don't think either one of us was in the union. And later Allen started doing all of Booker's dates. He took over where Booker and Huey had been. And one thing he taught me was to watch the piano player on a session. I always set up playing guitar where I could watch the piano player to make sure what the chords was so that you didn't mess up. We was only recording one-track so there wasn't no fixin' nothin' back then. When we finished cutting the song, it was over. So watching the piano player was a good thing for me to learn how to play on the date but it was also a good thing for me to learn how to play piano. Allen was way more than anybody else so far ahead of his time. And because he could do Huey Smith and Fess and James Booker, he was the most valuablest guy in the studio.

He talked a lot about you and him just coming out of Fess and how much you two loved Fess, as a player and as a man.
Well, you know, in between takes, that was what we did on the dates—do something that Fess was doing at the time. That was like the code between us all. We might start something else but we'd slide into a Fess thing. There was something about Fess that connected everybody. All the cats coming up, we knew that what Fess was doing was leading toward something. Even the drummers like Earl Palmer and Hungry Williams and James Black and Zigaboo [Modeliste] was all in some way connected to Fess' stuff. It meant a different thing to us at different times.

What is the thing that made Professor Longhair so unique, from a piano player's perspective?
For one thing, Fess didn't even think of the piano like it was a piano. He looked at it for what it really is, a percussion instrument. But he looked at it like he was playing all the Caribbean stuff in one thing. There was something real magic about his concept. When he would sit down and play medleys of Caribbean music, it was amazing. I got him to record one of them once. But there was stuff I remember him doing when he used to work at the One Stop record shop. That was a side of him that a lot of people didn't ever hear. All the way to the end I was trying to get him to remember some of that stuff, but it was all stuff that he had forgot. When he got sick and his health wasn't that good no more, he hung with what he could remember. It was like people saw a piece of Fess, but didn't really know what he was all about.

But I loved Fess. When my father passed away, Fess became like a father figure to me. He was a lot of things. He was a good man. He taught me about how to make a band frolic. That was one of the main things he always wanted of us. When he said, "Let's frolic, boys!" he wanted us to get behind the soloist and kick ass. It was about keeping the groove right there but kicking behind that soloist. And man! That's the thing what Allen used to do—he did it for his first album, the one he did for RCA Records, *The Wild Sound of New Orleans* [1958]. There's a tune on there, some race horse name—it's so Fess! Behind the soloist Allen starts frolicking just like Fess. But those little moments—that was the deal. All the piano players around New Orleans knew Fess' stuff to some degree. Fess inspired all of us. I used to love to hear Huey Smith do Fess and it was completely Huey Smith. It was Fess' notes but it was in Huey's lazy vibe of it. That used to tickle me. And I used to hear Allen do the way Huey would do Fess. That's a magical thing. He had that vibe you could feel. Just, different people feel stuff totally different. Booker would do the same stuff but he would do it much more precise-like. Allen had a looseness with it.

Allen talked about seeing Fess for the first time and being in such awe that it had such an impact on him as a young man. Sounded like a lot of alto players I've heard talk about hearing Charlie Parker for the first time.

I was a little kid when I first heard Fess. I wasn't 10 years old.... Maybe I was way younger, I don't even know. What I do know, he left an impression on me. I used to see posters of him and I heard his records before, but after hearing him on the gigs... And what I remembered was it was just him and a guy who didn't even have a set of drums. Guy had something he played with one foot and something else.... It wasn't a snare drum. It wasn't a kick drum. I don't know what he was playing, maybe a chair. I don't know. And Fess would keep kickin' the piano like a bass drum sound. And then they had a trumpet, and that was it. And I thought, "What the hell is that?!" At the time I was really into Pete Johnson. When I was a little kid I used to love listening to Big Joe Turner records because I liked the way Pete Johnson played. But when I heard Fess on that gig... It must've been like when guys tell me when they heard Art Tatum, like they're looking at God or something. That thing was so different. Everybody who heard him at the time was blown away, had no idea what the hell he was doing. Paul Gayten, for example, was never a great piano player, he was a record producer. But he told me one day, "See, what Fess is to you, he doesn't mean the same thing to guys in my generation. But we love him because he's changing things that y'all don't even see." Paul was real aware of stuff. I didn't know what the hell he was talking about. Course, I didn't know what the hell anybody was talking about. But Paul knew stuff. He was real educated. But I later saw how it changed the music. It changed stuff with everything—the way people felt grooves, the way people just moved to the changes. And I used to ask Fess, "Where did your thing come from?" And he'd tell me that he learned stuff from Tuts Washington, Little Brother Montgomery, and guys I never heard of like Kid Stormy Weather and Piano Blue. But he was a dancer, he did tell me that. He was a hoofer and that is what he did. And he said he learned stuff from Champion Jack Dupree, who didn't know anything on a piano except some real gutbucket stuff. I think the closest one that had something that reminded me of Fess, and then very little, was Tuts Washington. And they didn't get along from the day I met either one of them, so I didn't know how. Maybe way back in the game they got along. Who knows? It was before my time.

So Fess was a revolutionary figure in the music?

Oh yeah, he'd just mix all that Caribbean music up with that New Orleans parade thing and made it one kind of music. Then he'd mix up Mardi Gras Indian music with Caribbean music that set a trend, in a way, for the Indians without them even knowing it. But it was like a big thrill in my life just that the guy would even let me hang out with him. And Fess in some way encouraged me. He was always saying, "Don't just talk about it. Do it." He was that kind of thinking guy.

How does one go about learning Fess style? Is it something than can be transcribed or does it merely have to be soaked up?

I don't know. I use a lot of Fess' fingering, I know that. Between him and Huey is who I got from. Booker played much more correct fingerings to what that is. If you want to learn wrong—like that Homespun stuff [instructional tapes] that I done and some stuff I got coming out on a CD-ROM—show somebody how to learn wrong like I did from him. But it just is what it is, you know?

And the spirit in his playing comes across on every recording.
Actually, I never thought his records was up to par with what he did on gigs. I'd say that the early records on Atlantic were good examples, around the time he did "Big Chief," all them.

And he came back later [1980] with that great live recording, Crawfish Fiesta, *which was his last album.*
Yeah, I played guitar on that one because Snooks [Eaglin] couldn't make it. That was the record I was trying to get him to remember the Caribbean tunes in the studio. But at least I got him to cut "Rum and Coca-Cola." He couldn't hardly play that anymore. He used to do this one thing, he always called it "Swannee River" but it wasn't. I don't know what it really was. And it was something that he did that was like parts of a lot of famous Spanish songs all rolled into one of his things. But it was a different bunch of things from that "Rum and Coca-Cola" stuff. I used that name for the album because I knew that when he started gigs he'd always say, "We're gonna have a little crawfish fiesta tonight. Want y'all to bring your owns along." And he used to do all this crazy stuff.... I remember him at a gig, he'd be eating at the piano with gloves on, eating chicken or whatever you have. He'd take these gloves off and play the gig. He'd be talking to the people while he's eating before the band hit. I never saw nothin' like that before. And I remember him wearing a tux with a turtle neck shirt with some kind of dog tags and some kind of brand new outfit with tails—totally unique.

I understand that you never intended to be a front man of your own band, that originally you were thinking in terms of Ronnie Barron being the Dr. John character while you remained behind the scenes.
Well, I wanted Ronnie Barron to do that record and people told me it was a bad career move. So I hired Ronnie to do background on the record and I did it myself. Not that any of us cared. But I just always was picturing the idea of Dr. John and I was thinking Ronnie could do it because he was the singer in the band. I didn't want to be no singer. All I wanted to do was produce another record. I used to come up with a lot of album ideas to hustle the label into a deal. Somewhere along the line I figured I'd better figure out how to keep doing this—learning how to sing in tune and learning how to do this. So from the beginning [*Gris-Gris,* Atco, 1968] I had the attitude that, "Well, this is a one-off deal so I'll go back to producing records when it's over."

And this Dr. John thing just sort of evolved over time.
Or maybe it devolved. Whatever it did, it did that.

You wrote in your book about your interest in wanting to expand beyond funk and go into more so-called jazzier, sophisticated areas of music, which is what led into In a Sentimental Mood *and* Afterglow.
To me, it wasn't even that. It was just an interest in making different kinds of records. When I came up playing it was like, you just played music true to that music. All of that music is part of what I came up doing. I don't look at anything and separate it from something else. But I never read that book to know what the hell I said anyway. But I do know that when I writ that with the guy [Jack Rummel] I didn't know I was in the middle of being poisoned from being on lithium.

At the time you wrote the book?
Yeah. They thought I was a manical depressive and I was just probably depressed being off of nar-cotics or whatever the hell. That's when I wrote that book, and it's probably somewhat in some ways cockeyed behind that. I also just got out of rehab—a psyche ward and a recovery house—looking within so different than I had ever done before.

So you haven't even read the book to know if it's accurate or not.
No. One day I might. I don't have a copy of it no more but one day I might.

So how are you doing right now? You cool?
I've been clean seven years and change.

I think people have been fascinated over time about how drugs and an altered state of consciousness are connected with musical expression. Like Charlie Parker, Jimi Hendrix, Jaco Pastorius—different people who were notorious drug users and maintained a high level of musicianship at the same time.
You know, it's part of a lifestyle. When I was coming up it was just a common thing. We didn't even think about it.

Well, you know, when Bird came up so many people thought, "If I shoot up too, maybe I can play like him."
I'm sure that everybody had a lot of other false notions, too: "Well, if I steal some licks from so-and-so I'll get gigs like him or something." I don't know. The world's loaded with opinions that's bullshit. That's what the world's about.

So how do you feel about your own playing being clean?
I'm digging it. No question now, my brain works better. I enjoy little things in life today that just went by me before. It's not like the things I do every day are different from before. It's just that now it's like someone has turned on the lights, so I can see the many little details I missed out on. And I'll tell you what... One thing I know—when I was on narcotics I played a lot by remote con-trol. Now I just be looser and have fun more. That's what life's about. If it ain't fun, what the fuck are you living it for?

What is the origin as you know it of the word "funk"?
When I came up, man, cats always used to use that word. Studio band in New Orleans used to call themselves The Funk Clique, and that's back when the word "funk" was not fashionable. In the '50s, funk meant, like my grandma used to say, "I'm gone spank yo' funky go-go, boy." And that's what it meant—something that stunk. The word has become fashionable and cats now want to use the word "funk" because the general public claimed it.

Like the term "bebop."
Same thing. People takes what musicians do and they run with it so it comes out meaning some-thing else. At one time "uptight" meant nervous. Then Stevie Wonder made that tune "Everything Is Uptight, Out of Sight," and the general public learned the term from that record. Then later musicians turned it backwards again and the general public always stayed one step behind. I think it's just so we musicians can feel special about little things, like a secret code or something. We com-municate but it might really mean the opposite—like how musicians use "bad" to mean really good. But if you know the cat, you know what he's saying.

Where did funk rhythms come from?

Some people see it coming from James Brown, others see it from Little Richard, some see it from somewhere else. I personally think maybe someone like [New Orleans drummer] Paul Barbarin might've invented some of the funk beats. Earl Palmer sophisticated them up and put 'em on records [by Fats Domino and Little Richard]. But then New Orleans drummers like Charlie "Hungry" Williams, James Black, John Boudreaux, and Smokey Joe Johnson took and made their own styles of funk. And later cats like Zigaboo took a piece of those cats' stuff and took it to where the Meters went with it. Everybody takes something from somewhere. I think Memphis funk came by Al Jackson trying to play a version of Charlie Williams' stuff, and he played it how he played it, which was not a New Orleans style. But because the records was real successful, people accepted that as a form of funk. And then later James Brown had some good ol' funk drummers in his band. And what they did, which was off-shoots of other cats, led to people like George Clinton and Sly Stone. Any of them cats, they came out of some other cats and that's how things happen. But New Orleans funk always was a little subtle—too much for the masses in some kind of way. It's a real inside thing, what funk's about in New Orleans. But it opened a lot of cats' noses about playing funk. I mean, like, where did a guy like Horace Silver learn to play so funky? The cat just plays so funky! Where did Les McCann get to play so funky? Ramsey Lewis... Lot of cats did some funky shit at one time, and maybe they heard of Allen Toussaint and maybe they heard of somebody else, so forth and so on. But I particularly asked Horace one day, "When you was coming up, did you ever hear some New Orleans music?" And he said, "I remember this juke box at this joint we were working in Connecticut. It had Fats Domino singing "Goin' Home" on the juke box. And it was the first time I heard blues in that kind of bag." That wasn't the answer I was looking for, but it didn't matter. Everybody perceives something different, gets something different out of different things. Years ago when Art Blakey cut that Monk tune "Bye-Ya," the groove he played on that was so New Orleans. When I first heard that record I thought it was a New Orleans record. Here's a guy from Pittsburgh, Pennsylvania, playing Latin music funky. It all comes from somewhere and goes somewhere else.

What do you think of contemporary funk played with drum machines?

I call it comatose Muzak funk. It's for people that like to be in a coma state. It don't ever make you shake your ass for real. It just stays on a thing. I know kids who love that shit. I listen just to see what it is they like about certain things. What is it about that? And one of the things I notice, the machines that is programmed off of good funky drummers seems to be the ones that I likes better. But the rest of that shit, I don't even connect to it. I can't figure out what it is and they love it. It just don't move me. It leaves me very cold, man. It don't feel like fun in the music to me that way. I don't get it. But in this *bidness*, man, we don't know from day to day. Funk changes. Music changes. Everything changes. We change as people. The changes we go through, the changes the music goes through, come back to haunt us sometime. Sometime that's the one blessing it has, 'cause if Miles hadn't shifted gears 14, 15 times in his career, we wouldn't have forms of music. Had he not hooked up with Gil Evans at one point to do some records and then later hooked up with some other cats and went a lot of other places, there wouldn't be a lot of music that you hear today. Same with Trane—so many other cats. Those key cats did numbers on us all. And we need cats like that today to take it to the next thing. And there might be a few of them around. There's some fine young players out there right now. Real fine. It's just what they decide to do.

JOHNNY WINTER

LIKE MANY MUSIC-HUNGRY and culturally-curious white boys coming of age in the '60s, I was turned on to the blues through Johnny Winter's self-titled debut on Columbia in 1969. His scorching licks grabbed my rock-fed ears, just as Hendrix and Clapton had done a couple years before. But it was his soul-stirring vocal performance on "Drown in My Own Tears" (sans guitar) that really reached down inside and opened me up to a whole new world. Sure, I had heard The Rolling Stones and Yardbirds doing their Brit takes on Howlin' Wolf and Jimmy Reed, but this seemed much closer to the source. My appreciation of what Winter was doing on that debut showcase triggered a furious hunt for the real deal, which led me to a treasure trove of blues on the Chess Records label. I continued to follow Johnny Winter's career through his various flirtations with rock, notably his Johnny Winter And band featuring guitarist Rick Derringer and his post-rehab comeback phase marked by *Still Alive and Well* (Columbia, 1973), his return to hardcore blues via a series of late-1970s albums with his hero and mentor Muddy Waters on the Blue Sky label, his mid-1980s "tattoo phase" with Alligator Records, and subsequent projects in the 1990s for the Pointblank label. I've watched his whiter-than-white, spidery visage stalking the stage at least a couple dozen times over the years and he's never failed to spark a thrill.

I finally got a chance to meet Johnny, nearly 20 years after I began worshipping him as a blues-hungry adolescent, for an interview that ran in the May 1989 issue of *Guitar World* magazine. The following is a composite of material from that initial interview and from a later one conducted for the December 1991 issue of *Guitar World.* Winter's most recent release is *Live in NYC '97* (Pointblank, 1998).

NOVEMBER 14, 1988, AND AUGUST 5, 1991

Johnny Winter is an American music legend. A recording artist for 30 some years, he emerged from the Texas bar scene in the late-1960s to become an archetypal blues-rock guitar hero. Born in Leland, Mississippi, on January 23, 1944, John Dawson Winter III grew up in Beaumont, Texas, surrounded by the sounds of blues, country, and Cajun music. His brother Edgar was born three years later and the two brothers showed an early inclination toward music, singing in the church choir from the time they were youngsters.

Johnny began playing clarinet at age five and switched to ukulele a few years later. Johnny and Edgar began performing as a duet in an Everly Brothers vein, eventually winning talent contests and appearing on local television shows. When Johnny was 11, the Winter Brothers traveled to New York to audition for "Ted Mack's Original Amateur Hour." Soon after, they got their first exposure to rock'n'roll through the music of Little Richard, Fats Domino, Carl Perkins, and early Elvis Presley records. Around the same time, they also began listening to R&B on Clarence Garlow's "Bon Ton Show" on station KJET out of Beaumont.

At age 14, Johnny organized his first band, Johnny & The Jammers, with Edgar on piano. A year later, after winning a local talent contest, they cut two songs at Bill Hall's Gulf Coast Recording Studios in Beaumont. The single "School Day Blues"/"You Know I Love You" came out a month later on Pappy Daley's Houston-based Dart Records label, earning the Winter Brothers some local notoriety. Also around this time, Johnny began sitting in with radio host Clarence Garlow, who performed around town and had a regional hit with "Bon Ton Roulet." Garlow was responsible for introducing Johnny to Beaumont's all-black Raven Club, where the young albino guitarist got to see his heroes like Muddy Waters, B. B. King, and Bobby "Blue" Bland for the first time. In the early-1960s, Johnny cut singles for regional labels like Frolic, Diamond, and Goldband. In 1963, he went to Chicago to check out the blues scene. Upon returning to Beaumont, Johnny cut "Eternally," a pop tune with horn arrangements by Edgar. Atlantic Records licensed that single and the tune became a big hit around the Texas-Louisiana area. With the success of "Eternally," Johnny soon found himself opening area coliseum shows for big-name acts like The Everly Brothers and Jerry Lee Lewis. His regular band at this time featured Johnny on guitar and vocals, Edgar on keyboard and sax, Ikey Sweat on bass, and Norman Samanha on drums. That group, which changed its name from month to month, was alternately known as The Crystaliers, The Black Plague, and It & Them. After two-and-a-half years of playing constantly around the Deep South, the band settled in Houston where they spent most of 1967 as the house band at the Act III club.

In 1968, Johnny began playing in a trio with bassist Tommy Shannon and drummer Uncle John Turner. Their gigs at places like Austin's Vulcan Gas Company and Houston's Love Street Light Circus attracted the attention of a *Rolling Stone* writer who had been working on a piece about the Texas hippie scene. The author devoted three paragraphs to Winter, referring to him as "the hottest item to come from Texas since Janis Joplin."

Johnny had been investigating the blues scene in London, England, at the time the *Rolling Stone* story came out. Upon returning to Texas, he immediately became the focus of a fierce bidding war between major labels. Columbia Records executive Clive Davis eventually ended up signing Johnny to a million dollar contract, which created quite a stir in the industry. His excellent debut album, *Johnny Winter,* was released late in 1968 to wild acclaim. Also that year, Imperial Records released *The Progressive Blues Experiment,* a collection of straight blues tunes that Winter's trio had recorded live at the Vulcan Gas Company for Bill Josey and Rim Keeley, initially released on England's Sonobeat label.

There followed a series of classic hard rock and blues albums for Columbia—*Second Winter* (1969), *Johnny Winter And* (1970), gold-selling *Johnny Winter And Live* (1971), post-rehab effort *Still Alive and Well* (1973), and *Saints and Sinners* (1974). In 1975, Johnny jumped to the CBS affiliate label, Blue Sky, which was founded by his manager Steve Paul. His debut for the new label was the very rootsy *John Dawson Winter III.* Then in 1977, he fulfilled a lifelong dream by producing Muddy Waters' comeback album, *Hard Again,* which won a Grammy Award. Johnny and Muddy made a great team and they followed up that success with *I'm Ready* (1978) and *King Bee* (1980). As Winter said of that fertile period, "Working with Muddy made me feel like people were finally realizing that I'm not faking, that I really can play blues. I felt like those albums helped me to establish my blues credibility."

Johnny's final solo projects for Blue Sky were *Nothin' but the Blues* (1977), *White, Hot & Blue* (1978), and *Raisin' Cain* (1980). Following a four-year hiatus from recording, he returned with *Guitar Slinger,* his fine debut on the Chicago-based blues label, Alligator Records. He followed that up with *Serious Business* (1985) and *Third Degree* (1986), both excellent roots rock and blues albums. Winter's debut on MCA Records, *The Winter of '88,* was an attempt at appealing to younger rock fans with a more contemporary, commercial product. It was a disappointment to longtime Winter fans and was even dismissed as a failed project by Winter himself. His 1991 debut on the Pointblank/Virgin label, *Let Me In,* was a return to form and was followed by the equally fine *Hey, Where's Your Brother?* in 1992.

I spoke to Winter in the Manhattan studio of photographer Michel Delsol. I brought along a rare vinyl copy of *Johnny and Edgar Together,* the 1977 roots rock album with the striking Richard Avedon cover photo and the collage of nostalgic, hand-tinted family snapshots on the inner sleeve depicting the siblings in more innocent times.

Aside from these great pictures of you and Edgar as kids, this album features covers of tunes associated with Little Richard, Chuck Berry, Elvis Presley, and even a version of the Righteous Brothers' hit, "You've Lost That Lovin' Feelin'." What did this project represent for you?
That was just a lot of fun, just a lot of old rock'n'roll songs that we had done together over the years in clubs. I guess it pretty much represents what we have in common musically.

And what are your differences?
Well, I tend to like things that are kinda out of left field, things that are pretty raw and spontaneous. I think that's the big difference between me and Edgar. He enjoys playing with a lot of musicians and having things written out, where everybody knows what everybody else is gonna play. And he, of course, would rather be the person to write it out and tell everybody what to play. I enjoy playing with a smaller group, where you don't really know what's coming. Drums, bass, guitar, and maybe a keyboard—that's really what I like. You just count it off and if it's a good group, the guys just fall in behind you. It's real important that it's spontaneous, where the same song might be different every night you play it. That way, it doesn't get boring. But if you have five or six horns and a couple of rhythm instruments, which is how Edgar prefers to work, you really have to tell everybody what's going on.

I know you two have had disagreements about the merits of certain blues artists.
Well, I'd play him stuff by John Lee Hooker and Lightnin' Hopkins and he would hate it, just because they weren't in perfect tune and they would change wrong, like on eleven or fifteen. And

that just drove him crazy. But I always loved that. He'd play me stuff by John Coltrane and Art Blakey and all the jazz guys and I'd play him John Lee and Lightnin'. We definitely had Ray Charles in common, and James Brown and Little Richard, too. But I guess we really parted company when he started playing sax and got into horn arrangements. He loved big horn sections, where the parts are worked out cleanly ahead of time. And I didn't like that.

When you get into jazz, you're dealing with advanced theory and harmony. But it seems the further out you go—Archie Shepp or Rahsaan Roland Kirk—you come right back to the blues.
That's what I always thought. I always liked Ornette Coleman for that reason. He'd just do that super far-out strange stuff and, to me, it was the same thing as what John Lee Hooker was doing. John Lee can't tell people where he's going 'cause he don't know himself. But John Lee's stuff is just as weird as some of the avant-garde jazz, to me. As little kids, Edgar and I used to have these big fights about "Is Lightnin' Hopkins better than Ornette Coleman?" And I figured, being bigger, I could beat some sense into his head. If you look closely at some of those snapshots of that inner sleeve [of *Johnny and Edgar Winter Together*], you'll notice that I'm attacking him in at least a few of the shots, hitting him in the head with a block in this picture, slapping his head in that picture.

That's what little brothers are for. I'm sure Jimmie Vaughan was beating on Stevie Ray when they were growing up.
Yeah, classic sibling rivalry. In fact, we actually started off playing the same instrument—ukulele. But it seemed like when I went to guitar and got into it, Edgar decided he would play everything else. That was the only instrument he didn't mess with.

What's this picture of you and your young buddies posing with B. B. King?
Oh, I remember that really well. It was an all-black nightclub in Beaumont. I remember pestering B. B. and asking if I could sit in, but he didn't want me to sit in at all. He really didn't like that a bit. But we bothered him about it so much that he just kinda had to after a while. It was great, and the crowd seemed to be on my side.

What was the club scene like in Beaumont when you were growing up?
It was strange. The only way you could hear the blues was by going to a black club. It was something that your peers didn't do in those days. Only a few of my very close friends liked that kind of music. We'd go to clubs and there'd be two thousand black people, just three or four white kids. And you never imagined it being any different. I always figured that the blues was the kind of music I did for fun. I'd have to play something different when I was playing for white people and getting paid for it—rock'n'roll, country, New Orleans R&B, pop... And finally, when The Rolling Stones and bands like that started making it—all the English guys—it was hard to believe that these young white kids from across the ocean were playing the same kind of music that me and my friends were digging down in Beaumont. Then, when guys like Paul Butterfield and Mike Bloomfield started making it, I really realized, "Boy, it's definitely time. You better make it now 'cause now is when things are happening for you."

You met Bloomfield before then, didn't you?
Yeah, I spent some time in Chicago in 1963, when I was playing in a top 40 band called The Gents. I met Mike at the Tuesday night jam sessions he ran at the Fickle Pickle. But it was strange, man. Before I met Bloomfield, I was asking about Jimmy Reed and Muddy Waters and Little Walter and nobody knew what I was talking about. People just looked at me and said, "We don't know nothin' about those people." And it was like that all over Chicago until I met Bloomfield and he told me

where everybody was playing. But I'd meet musicians on the North Side who had no idea who Muddy Waters was. That amazed me.

Are you still in touch with the blues scene in Chicago?
Yes, that's one of the reasons why I liked recording there for Alligator. Chicago has some great blues radio stations. One of the legendary DJs in town is Big Bill Collins, who plays a lot of local and regional stuff you'll never hear anywhere else. And, of course, there are several real good blues clubs around town where you can hear great music. I really enjoy being there.

What were the radio stations like when you were growing up in Beaumont, Texas?
When I was coming up it was easy to hear good blues shows. There was XZRF in Mexico. Wolfman Jack used to be on that station and do blues stuff. And there was WLAC out of Nashville, Tennessee; KWKH in Shreveport, Louisiana. And blues record shops would advertise on these stations. You could mail order for the records you would hear on these shows. So if you didn't have a record store in your town that had good blues, you could get the stuff through the mail from one of these 50,000 watt stations that you could hear all over the South. It was easy to hear blues then. Now it seems like it's a lot harder.

Did you ever as a kid want to be a DJ?
Yeah, when I was a kid all the musicians I knew were people who had a day gig and played music at night. And some of them were also DJs. Clarence Garlow, who was a mentor of mine, was a musician and a disc jockey. B. B. King was a DJ. That's where he got his name. I understand that on his radio show out of Memphis, he actually played guitar along with the records sometimes. I wish I could've heard that.

I understand that you have an impressive blues record collection.
Oh, I love records. I must have about 10,000 albums in my collection. I've got most of them in New York but I keep the rare 45s at my parents' house in Texas.

What do you think about the CD reissues of old blues recordings, like the Robert Johnson boxed set that Columbia Records recently put out?
Well, to tell the truth, I still don't have a CD player. At first everybody was saying how great they were, but now I keep hearing that they're a little tinny or brittle-sounding. Tom [Compton], my drummer, said he had The Beatles' *Sgt. Pepper's* on CD and he heard things on that that he never heard before. I guess it's good for hearing layers and subtleties, but with a three or four piece blues band recording live in the studio, you don't get all those subtleties. I may be old-fashioned, but I just hate seeing records being phased out the way they are now. CDs are small and pretty but I like albums. I like seeing the picture nice and big there so I can read everything. Having bad vision, of course, I can't even see what's going on with the CD. Trying to read the liner notes on a CD or a cassette is almost impossible for me.

What were some of the first records you bought as a kid?
The first couple of things I heard were by Howlin' Wolf and Muddy Waters. I can remember hearing "Somebody in My Home" by Howlin' Wolf on this station from Shreveport, KWKH. I ordered the All-Star Blues Special and got a Howlin' Wolf record and a Muddy Waters record and a Bobby Bland record through the mail, all 45s. The very first blues album I ever got was called *B. B. King Sings the Blues*. It was a collection of some of his singles on the RPM label. And it's funny because a lot of those old records on RPM sound like he was playing a Fender Stratocaster. This was long

before he started playing his Lucille guitar. The sound of his guitar on those RPM sessions is very trebley. I kind of like it. He played different, too, in those days. Check out "Days of Old" and "Troubles Troubles Troubles" and "Be Careful with a Fool." That stuff is real trebley. After that, I started buying some of the Chess "Best of" series with Muddy Waters, Little Walter, Bo Diddley... I can really remember those first few albums I bought because there just weren't any blues albums out at that time. In those years, I really had to hunt for blues records.

You, along with people like Mike Bloomfield and Paul Butterfield, were really instrumental in getting young, white America interested in black blues.
Looking back on it, I guess it was kind of that way. I didn't think about it at the time, but there were not that many white people playing that kind of music back then. And in those early days B. B. King was playing almost exclusively for black audiences.

But at some point, he started doing big rock venues and outdoor festivals and the audiences became more mixed.
And once that happened, it made a big difference. They started playing a lot more guitar as soon as they got the white kids coming out. Before, Muddy didn't play any guitar at all and B. B. would do his vocals with the guitar hanging around his neck. He'd do the guitar leads but he didn't answer his singing the way he does now. When they were playing for black people, a lot of those guys felt that it was cooler to have somebody else play their guitar parts for them so they could just sit there and look sexy and mess around with the mike. Once they made it with white kids, though, the guitar became prominent. And it made a big difference to me because I had always thought of myself as a singer who backed himself up with guitar. I didn't really think of myself as a guitar player. But once I realized that people were thinking of me more as a guitar player than a singer, I gradually changed in my head the way I thought of myself. I began concentrating more on the guitar from then on.

People got very guitar-conscious by the late-1960s.
They sure did. And they also got hungry for the blues. It was a great time for music and I just saw it getting better and better. I couldn't imagine it ever slackening off at that point. You really couldn't see an end to it back then. Bloomfield and Elvin Bishop and Steve Miller were all doing their thing. There was Jimi Hendrix, really doing exactly what I had always wanted to hear somebody do. And it was all on the radio. It was blues everywhere. In fact, I guess so much blues was happening during the late-1960s that people just overdosed on it—because by 1970–1971, nobody wanted to hear it.

That was right around the time you formed your Johnny Winter And band with Rick Derringer and started going for a heavier, rocky approach to the blues.
Yes, that was closer to heavy metal, I guess. But it still had those blue notes in there. That's what is important to me. No matter what kind of beat you put to it, it's still those blue notes that make me feel good when I hear it. To me, "Johnny B. Goode" is a blues song. So I really hate to draw that line between blues, rhythm and blues, and rock'n'roll. I grew up on everything. You had to be versatile playing in Texas bars because everybody wanted to hear a different thing. So I got really freaked out once I had "made it." Before that, everybody wanted you to play everything. Once you made it, they wanted to figure out which category to put you in and they'd never let you do anything that was out of the ordinary. You were supposed to be either a blues player or a rock player or a country player or a jazz player. And I think that's what really hurt Edgar, being able to do so many different styles of music well. People just kinda quit buying his records because they didn't know if it was gonna be a jazz, rock, or funk record. And that's really crazy. If you can play several different things, why shouldn't you?

Did Edgar go through some kind of schooling that you didn't?
Nope, he just loved that kind of music. He really didn't have to, he just picked it up immediately. Musically, he was always ahead of everybody else and everybody knew it. In a month or two he would pass up guys six years older than him who had gone to Juilliard. He was always one of the musical geniuses. He could always get a horn section together even if he didn't have enough money to pay them because they were excited about being able to play with him.

You featured him a lot on Second Winter, *probably your jazziest album.*
Yeah, what we were trying to do was put Edgar into the music scene there and try to figure out stuff that we could do that would kind of suit both of us. That's why we called it *Second Winter.* It was the second winter we'd been up in New York and Edgar was the second brother. We were just trying to do stuff that wouldn't be too out of the ordinary for me but also sneak Edgar in there and let people know who he was. I'm sure we'll always do stuff together like that. In spite of our differences, we're still brothers. We got that tight connection.

Can you set the record straight about that infamous bootleg album with you and Hendrix [Sky High, recorded from a jam at The Scene in New York City]?
That wasn't me on it, as far as I can remember. I played that record and I don't think it's me on it. There were a lot of strange things on there—Jimi Hendrix and Jim Morrison jamming. I never met Jim Morrison, so I know it wasn't me playing. I did jam a lot with Jimi at The Scene. My manager at the time, Steve Paul, had that club and it was a great place. Everybody would hang out there—Hendrix, The Rolling Stones, Janis Joplin... It was just a tiny little basement place in the worst part of town—didn't hold more than 200 people. I heard some of the greatest jams there, some of the worst too. But there is one thing that Jimi and I did there that I heard somewhere. It was the Guitar Slim song, "The Things That I Used To Do." I'm playing slide guitar with Jimi on that. That's the only thing I've heard that is definitely me and Jimi together.

How did you feel about all the hype surrounding your signing with CBS in 1968?
It was really strange. When that *Rolling Stone* story came out [a feature story on great, unsigned Texas musicians, with prominent coverage of the albino guitar slinger], I went from nobody even wanting to talk to me in the States to people calling me and offering me all kinds of big advances, just overnight. I didn't believe it. I knew it wasn't real. I had been trying to talk to all these record company people for years and they wouldn't return my calls. And then all of a sudden, overnight, the same people were calling *me.* And I thought, "What is this? This doesn't have anything to do with being good." You know, it just didn't make any sense. And the further I went on into it, the less sense it made. I really did realize after a while that talent was a very small part of the whole thing. It also made me realize how ridiculous the record business was.

Did it change you?
It still hasn't changed my music, I don't think, but I guess it has changed me. I'm not nearly as innocent and naive about everything now as I was then. In some ways, I wish it hadn't changed me. I liked the old me better. But you know, you have to be suspicious of people. You come to realize that the whole thing is so ridiculous and so stupid and has so little to do with how good you are as a player. You either have to just laugh it off and decide, "OK, it's ridiculous, but I'm gonna keep trying to do it anyway." Or you get mad at it and say, "I'm gonna quit this and do something else." The whole thing made me a little bit more angry, I guess. And it's actually made me more aggressive in wanting to stay with the blues and making sure that people are aware of it. The only thing that's gonna work is just commitment to something. If you just try to follow whatever is happening at the

time, you're just gonna keep being blown around in the wind from one thing to the next. You really have to decide what it is you want to do and not be changed by the ridiculous stuff. There ain't that much money in the blues so the only reason you stay in it is 'cause you love it. And I really believe it's important to keep it going.

Right after you formed Johnny Winter And, you had your biggest selling records and toured more than ever before. Then in 1972, you folded the band and checked into a New Orleans hospital for nine months. What happened?
It just got to be too much for me to handle. There was so much pressure on me then to do good. I had this constant fear of failing. People were always telling me, "This is your only chance. If you don't make it now you're gonna be a has-been." I had been working hard on the road for two and a half years without any time off. The only time I had off was to go into the studio. It was so lonely. I never had any time to myself or to spend with friends. It was really an impossible situation. And when you're doing what's impossible to do, you tend to look for some way out of that kind of pain. So I kept working way beyond the point I should've, and I was really losing touch with reality. It was all a blur after a while—hotels, airports, arenas... And once the glamour wore off it just became a grind of nonstop gigs. The music was always cool but the traveling was the killer. And the only way I could get temporary relief from that whole grind was through drugs. At the time I thought, "Well, I just gotta get through these few more shows so I'll just do this for a while, get over this hump, and then I'll stop." But you get over the hump and find out you can't. I never thought I would become addicted to anything. And once I realized what was happening, I put myself in the hospital, went into intense psychotherapy, and completely quit taking every kind of drug. When I got out, I knew there were a few rules I had to follow: Never stay out on the road for more than six weeks at a time and never do more than five nights a week. I've followed that since 1973 and things have been pretty damn good ever since.

I read recently that The Progressive Blues Experiment *has been reissued on CD.*
Yes, that one seems to get reissued pretty regularly. I'm glad they keep putting the old stuff out, especially the things that I like. The stuff that I really don't like is another matter. Anything that Roy Haines has anything to do with, you can't trust. He keeps putting out the same songs with a different picture on the album cover and calling it something different. Or he'll change the order of the songs around and make it look like a whole new record. He has done that so much now, it's a crime that he gets away with it.

Is this stuff that you recorded in the early-1960s?
Yes, all kinds of different things. Back in the early-1960s I was still trying to find an audience, so I did my Bob Dylan imitation on a few tunes, my Beatles imitation on some others, my Rolling Stones imitation. My manager wanted me to copy whatever was popular at the time and I just did whatever he said. Nobody wanted anything original. So with a lot of that old stuff from about 1960 to *The Progressive Blues Experiment* in 1968, you're liable to hear just about any kind of music. It could be straight blues or it could be rock'n'roll or R&B or English Invasion. And Roy Haines keeps releasing this old stuff. I don't know how this guy keeps putting out the records. But he did it in Europe and now he's doing it in Japan. He will even find sessions that I did as a sideman and put that stuff out with my name on it and a new picture on it.

This was material originally recorded for regional labels?
Yes, and a lot of the stuff was just demos. But he always tries to make it look real modern, with an up-to-date photo, so you don't really know what you're buying. I guess my advice to readers is, if

it's got Roy's name on it, don't mess with it.

Well, people should know that when they buy your new album, Let Me In, *they will be getting the real deal.*
Exactly. It was one of my favorite records that I've ever made. We weren't trying to make a record that would be played on the radio, we were just having a good time in the studio. I really like going at it that way a lot better—trying to make good music instead of trying to figure out if each song is gonna be able to get airplay. I don't know what's popular now. I don't watch MTV. I know what I do is just not tailored for radio. I hope it does get some airplay, but that's not what we were thinking when we made the record.

One of these days you'll break down and get that CD player.
Yeah, and it's gonna have to be pretty quick, too, because now I'm getting my own stuff where there's extra cuts on a CD, and I can't hear 'em. Guess I really need to buy one.

BOOTSY COLLINS

MY FIRST ENCOUNTER with the extended family of P-Funk happened in 1977 when Bootsy Collins came to town with his Rubber Band. I reviewed the show for *The Milwaukee Journal* and wrote enthusiastically about this black superhero with the star glasses and star bass and a legion of rubberfans and funkateers. He called himself "a rhinestone rock star doll, baby bubba." His slogan: "Wiiiiiiiinnnnnnnnddddd-me-up!" Little did I know then that this costumed character was the same funky cat who pumped the groove on James Brown's "Sex Machine," a tune that had gotten me in trouble on the dance floor on more than one occasion. So my experience with the P was through the back door, so to speak. First I dug Bootsy, then I found out about George Clinton and "One Nation under a Groove." No matter how you enter into the kingdom, it's all on the one once you get there. Bootsy still prescribes to the Pinocchio Theory: "Don't fake the funk or your nose will grow." This interview was conducted for a story that appeared in the January 1989 issue of *Guitar World*.

SEPTEMBER 29, 1988

He is the Grand High Exalted Mystic Ruler of funk bass. A mythic, cartoon figure, larger than life and funkier than anything, he is back on the scene like a sex machine, funkin' up the place with his trademark star bass. He is William "Bootsy" Collins (aka "Caspar," "Star Child," "Bootzilla"), the proud purveyor of uncut funk, the bubbling bass pulse behind early-1970s James Brown, the man who put the P in P-Funk and the snap in Bootsy's Rubber Band. A true original, a bona fide bass hero, Bootsy is currently riding the crest of a new wave in funk, the likes of which have not been seen since the mid-1970s. "Yeah, it's all headed back that way," says Bootsy with an all-knowing grin.

New young funksters like The Limbomaniacs have gone out of their way not only to pay homage to Bootsy, but to feature him on their debut album as well (*Stinky Grooves,* In-Effect Records, 1988). The popular retro-1970s house music act Deee-Lite recently shanghaied Bootzilla for appearances on an album (*World Clique,* Elektra, 1990), as well as an accompanying video and tour. On New Year's Eve they threw it down in loud, funky fashion at the Palladium in New York City before departing for similar bashes in L.A. and Rio de Janeiro. A month later they were back in New York on "Saturday Night Live."

Bootsy has actually been back in circulation for the past few years, making guest appearances (Keith Richards' *Talk Is Cheap,* Virgin, 1988; Herbie Hancock's *Perfect Machine,* Columbia, 1988; Ryuichi Sakamoto's *Neo Geo,* Epic, 1988; and David Sanborn's TV show "Night Music"), producing other artists and working on his own projects (*What's Bootsy Doin'?,* Columbia, 1988, and the slamming *Jungle Bass,* Island, 1990). But the best is yet to come. Bootsy and the whole P-Funk mob are gearing up for a Second Coming of the funk that promises to rock the heavens.

"We're gonna have a reunion. A real P-Union," he explains. "Me and George [Clinton] are talking about putting a major thing together, a big scale tour. But until then we're going to do these paid rehearsals in smaller venues, just to get it together and build it back up step-by-step, the way we did in the beginning. Because the more we do it, the better it's gonna get. And then when James [Brown] gets out [of prison], we'll be ready to *really* throw down."

A Parliament-Funkadelic reunion tour with James Brown as special guest looms in the not too distant future as a funk fan's dream jam. And given Bootsy's past connections to both P-Funk and J. B., he would seem the most likely candidate to pull this sucker off.

"Yeah, I'm on a mission," says the funky catalyst, grinning behind those ubiquitous star glasses. "And it ain't just to go out and play. It's to try and keep this funk together. I feel like I'm just being used—whatever the forces are—to mediate on behalf of the funk. Just like a [Henry] Kissinger, you know what I'm saying? Come in and mediate this thing, get this thing happening. I know what I'm being used as, and I like it, because it's my turn to contribute to bringing the family back together. Whatever it takes."

The current family includes Bernie Worrell on synthesizers, Gary Shider and Mike Hampton on guitars, Gary "Mudbone" Cooper on vocals, Roger Parker on drums and the original Horny Horns— Maceo Parker on alto sax, Fred Wesley on trombone, and Richard "Kush" Griffith on trumpet. In a recent series of gigs at nightclubs around Manhattan, this funky family brushed off such P-Funk classics as "Give up the Funk (Tear the Roof off the Sucker)" and "Maggot Brain" along with familiar Bootsy tunes like "Rotor Rooter," "Friendly Boo," and "Munchies for Your Love."

It was roughly 15 years ago that Bootsy first played those tunes to adoring, funk-hungry fans, affectionately referred to as his Funkateers. Now he's back on the good foot, mixing in house music rhythms to appease a new young crowd while holding onto his old Bootsy fans with his patented Mu-Tron-inflected popping bass lines, perhaps the most instantly recognizable sound in the short history of the electric bass guitar.

After one of their recent Rubber Band reunion gigs, Bootsy commented on how easily the funk fell into place, how it felt like they had never stopped playing together, even though the last time they had actually assembled on the same stage was back in the late-1970s. "We're the ones that got the real P-Funk," he maintains. "Can't nobody else funk like that. Everything else is just an imitation of it." (A check of the latest rap and house albums indicates that Bootsy and P-Funk are still very much in vogue, via sampling. Everyone from Public Enemy and X-Clan to Young MC, Queen Latifah, Digital

Underground, The Jungle Brothers, M. C. Hammer, Ice Cube, ad infinitum, has copped those classic P-Funk strokes, going directly back to the mothership connection for their funky inspiration.)

"In order for us to jump back on and start doing it ourselves," says Bootsy, "we had to realize that the real force is with *us,* the real force is being together, the real force comes with being that family that we were. And to try to make that happen again."

This Disciple of the Funk looks forward to that challenge.

"It's like a whole new ballgame," he laughs. "We just want to really get back on it and do what we do best. So now, it's about going out there and getting in people's faces again, like we did in the old days. And I don't care if somebody's saying, 'Oh, that can't be done,' or 'Y'all won't never.' I ain't in it for that. I'm in it because I know what I gotta do now. 'Cause this is the only thing that we got. It's the only thing we represent that people can have fun with, that's not destructive. It's like a drink of water on dry desert. Not only to us, to the people that's in it. What more can you ask for? That's why we're gonna come on with it."

When the mothership touches down, when the joint is packed and the groove is throbbing, when the band is vibing off each other and the crowd is vibing off the band, when the funk floods the room and the crowd comes alive like a Pentecostal church service, shouting in unison, "Shit, goddamn, get off yer ass, and jam," when bodies are sweating on the dance floor and the band is digging deep—that's when the power of the funk really becomes apparent. You can feel it, you can smell it, you can almost taste it.

It's uncut funk, straight up, and strictly on the one. And the bass player? Ah... The name is Bootsy, baby!

How did you arrive at the Bootsy persona?
It was something that was inside of me all along, I just had to let it come out naturally. I had never looked at myself as being out front. George Clinton kind of brought that out in me. And it really came about—the Bootsy voice and the whole Bootsy vibe—from joking around in the studio with George. Late one night I began doing my imitation of Jimi Hendrix—that kind of talking thing he did on tunes like "If 6 Were 9" and "1983 a Merman I Shall Turn to Be." It started off as a joke. The very first time I dealt with that Bootsy voice was on a Funkadelic tune called "Be My Beach" from the album *Let's Take It to the Stage,* which came out in early 1975. It was just a one-off joke but George dug it and said, "Yeah, man, we should do a whole record with that character." So that's how *Stretchin' Out* was born [his solo debut album, released on Warner Bros. in 1976]. And I had the whole image in mind. All these things—the star bass, the star glasses, the red leather outfit with stars—all of it was Bootsy. I knew what I needed and I was just reaching for everything, trying to make it happen.

How did you get your signature bass style together?
That came about just because I didn't want to sound like no other bass players. At that time, bass players were coming in strong. Larry Graham, Louis Johnson, and Stanley Clarke were poppin' and pullin', putting the bass up front like a lead instrument. I think I was a part of that but I wanted to break away from the crowd, so I had to find my own sound. I began by playing the Big Muff fuzz and the Morley wah-wah on the live shows, though never on record. An then around 1975 they came out with the Mu-Tron. I was in a music store and checked it out and thought, "Damn, you know, this could be me!" It had that underwater vibe that I dug. It seemed to be the thing I needed to create my own sound. So I played it on my first album, *Stretchin' Out,* and I really liked it because it was so different. There was just something about that sound—it just seemed to be talking my kind of language. So without that Mu-Tron, there ain't no Bootsy.

What are the origins of your famous star bass?
I designed it but a guy named Larry Kless from Detroit was the one who put it together for me. I had this idea of a bass that was shaped like a star but I couldn't find anyone who could make it for me. I

came to New York and went to all the guitar places on 48th Street with a drawing of the star bass and everybody turned me down. They'd say, "No, it can't be done. Star? No, it'd be too heavy, the sound would be all messed up." But I didn't care about the sound. I just wanted a star bass. So it took me about a year of goin' around trying to find out who was gonna make this bass for me, and I finally found a guy in Detroit, where I was recording the *Stretchin' Out* album. Just on a hunch I stopped in this little music store called Gus Zuppi Music and I showed Gus the sketch. He laughed and said, "Well, there's a young guy in the back who might be able to do something with this," and he introduced me to Larry Kless. He took one look at the sketch and said, "Man, this is incredible. Let me try it."

So he drew me up a professional actualized sketch of the star bass. I saw it and flipped. I gave him $250 to get started and it took him about three weeks. But meanwhile, Warner Bros. was calling me 'cause they wanted a picture of the star bass on the album cover. I told Larry and he said he wasn't finished, so I asked him to just fix it up so it looked cool so I could use it as a prop for this photo session on the West Coast. He spray painted it white, put Plexiglass on it, and some strings. It didn't actually play—weren't no pickups in it yet. But it was perfect for that photo session. So I took it to the airport and people were staring at it like, "God, a star bass!" I didn't even have a case for it. I just took it straight onto the plane with me. And the pilot comes by and asks what it was. I told him I was an up-and-coming young artist and I was flying to an important photo session in L.A. and he said, "Man, you just sit right here and we'll put that star bass in the cockpit." So it rode all the way from Detroit to L.A. up front with the pilot and they seated me in first class. I was nobody, you understand, but I had a star bass. So they thought I was a star.

And you added star glasses and a white leather outfit to complete the look.
Yeah, I came to Los Angeles and walked up and down Sunset Boulevard lookin' for someone who could make these star glasses for me. I didn't know nobody out there. I didn't know nothin' about L.A., but I knew I could find it all out there. And somehow I just happened to run into these young guys who dug where I was coming from. They was tired of doing things the same old way and they jumped at a chance of doing something creative. So I got my star bass for $500, my star glasses for $150, and my leather outfit for $500. I was ready.

How did you get the gig with James Brown at the age of 15?
I was working with my brother Catfish and with our buddy Frankie "Kash" Waddy in a band around Cincinnati [The Pacesetters]. We were backing up singers around town and we landed this job as house rhythm section at King Records, cutting behind singers like Arthur Prysock and Hank Ballard. And James was recording at King with his own band around that time. We used to watch him and his band drive up to the studio. Man, they were jumpin' outta Cadillacs with fur coats on and here we were with these scruffy jeans and T-shirts, looking real crazy with these granny glasses and every-thing—'cause that was the time of peace and love, you know. But these cats wasn't into that. They looked at us and said, "What are them mugs? Get them boys outta here." They was like doggin' us and kickin' us out of the studio whenever we tried to sneak in for a closer look. We just wanted to hang out and hear them, but they didn't want nothing to do with us. Only ones who would talk to us were Maceo Parker and Fred Wesley. They talked to us like musicians but the rest of the guys in the band didn't wanna know about us. They'd close the door on us and we'd have to listen from outside.

But eventually you got in somehow?
Yeah. During a break, James came up with this great idea for a groove and wanted to try it out immedi-ately, but there was no bass player around [King Records session bassist Tim Drummond had apparent-ly split to get a bite to eat]. So finally one of the cats sticks his head out the door and says, "Bootsy, Bootsy, come on in, man. James needs you." And I'm standing there like, "Who... me?" So I got on in

the studio and James says, "Alright, it goes like this," and he sings the bass part. I pick up on it right away and he shouts, "That's it! Roll tape... Hit me!" And... Bam! Next thing you know, man, we had cut it. We finished and I was still in a daze. So when I got back outside, Catfish says to me, "So whatchadoo, man?" But I really wasn't sure. I actually didn't know that the tape would start rolling every time James said, "Hit it." I didn't realize that we had cut it until the next week when I heard it on the radio.

What tune was that?
"Lickin' Stick." So that was my first experience with James and it sure wasn't my last. I was still playing around Cincinnati with The Pacesetters after that but gigs started dropping off so we started doing benefits, just to play. We'd be lucky to make gas money during that period. So one day we get a call from Bobby Byrd [James Brown's keyboardist and backup vocalist]. He said, "Bootsy, we need you and the boys to fly down to Columbus, Georgia, right *now*! We're doin' a gig here and the band done quit on James." So we didn't even hesitate. We were supposed to play a benefit that night but we just told the club owner, "Whoever the benefit is benefittin'... Cool, but it don't benefit us. We goin' down to Columbus." So we go out of there, took a cab over to the airport, and jumped on a plane, still in a daze. And we ain't never seen a jet in our lives. We ain't never even been in a propeller plane. So, it takes off straight up in the air, 40,000 feet up and we ain't never been no higher than ten feet off the ground before in our lives. We get to the club, wearin' our old jeans and T-shirts, and the people are hollerin': "James Brown! James Brown! James Brown!" It's almost a riot, and we done walked right into the middle of it. We didn't know what was goin' on. So we went on back to the dressing room and there's an ugly scene goin' down. We see James' band over there yellin' at James, arguin'. He's got one mug up against the wall by the collar and we're thinkin', "What in the world is goin' on." We didn't know what we were walkin' into.

Finally, the band sees us and they looking at us like, "Whatchy'all doin' here?" It was like, they were on strike and we were crossing the picket line. And we had always wanted these guys to be our pals. We looked up to them and everything but they really didn't like us then. Finally James comes out and says to us, "Alright, let's hit the stage." We didn't have no rehearsals, no time to say "Hi" or anything. We hit the stage, plugged up and he calls off "Cold Sweat." And we hit right into it, man. We knew all the songs. That was the onliest thing that saved us. And the fans didn't know no difference. All they wanted was James Brown, and they got total James Brown that night. I think he performed more that night than he ever did before. I mean, he just wore it out. And I guess we brought a fresh new vibe with us, too, 'cause James really seemed to dig it. We were so excited just to be on the same stage with James Brown that we gave him everything he needed, and more."

Then after the gig we snuck backstage and James' old band is there. Man, they was through with us! They had those evil faces on. No smiles. But James took us aside and gave us his vote of confidence. He said, "Alright, what y'all want? How much do you want?" And we didn't know what to say. Five or ten dollars apiece was cool with us. But we decided to negotiate for something bigger 'cause he was gonna be takin' us out on the road, workin' every day, and we'd need to cover hotel bills and food and send some money home. So Catfish and Frankie put me up to it. I goes up to James and say, "Well, Mr. Brown... We think... $200... You don't think that's too much, do you?" And he says, "Fellas, I'll do you even better than that. I'll do you $250 a night. How's that?" Plus, he ended up coverin' all our hotel bills, which he didn't do for the rest of the band. And when they found out, they was *totally* through with us.

You remained with James Brown from 1969 to 1971. What events led up to you leaving James and going your own direction?
We started getting ideas about developing our own identity when we did a trip to London with James in '71. We get over there and the girls are all wearing hot pants and fishnets. They weren't doing that over in the States in 1971. And not only that, they had disco coming on strong. We went

to a discotheque to check out what was happening. The guy was playing records and lights was flashing on the floor and people was out there dancing. But we didn't like it because there was no live bands. We did like the fashions though. They was wearing all kinda crazy things over there and it gave us ideas. We wanted to dress up and be wild, but we knew we couldn't do none of that with James. That was a strict gig, man. And it was great for us at the time because we learned from him about being professional, about showing up on time and taking care of business. It was good training and it carried over to whatever we did from there on. But it was, like, time for us to move on, and James knew it. James knew we were young and reaching, so he was prepared for us not being around that long no way. We wanted to be wild and crazy, so we took our leave.

At that point you formed the House Guests. How long was it before you eventually hooked up with George Clinton?
During that time we was doin' all this crazy, wild stuff on stage, people kept telling us, "Aw, man, the onliest people we know that's as crazy as y'all is Funkadelic." We'd hear that in every town we went to but we had never seen them. We'd come to a town and miss them by a few days. And we really wanted to get on the same bill with them somehow 'cause I was really into blowing everybody away. That was our vibe at the time. We was cocky—real cocky. So we finally met up with George in Detroit. He was having problems with his band and wanted us as replacements but without our lead singer, Phillipe Wynne. Meanwhile, The Spinners wanted Phillipe *and* us as a package deal. It was a big decision we had to make. Two major bands that were happening at the time both wanted us. We had to figure out which way we were going. So what it came down to was, we went with Funkadelic as a complete rhythm section and Phillipe went with The Spinners. It turned out to be the best thing for everybody concerned.

On the inner sleeve of your album What's Bootsy Doin'?, *you list James Brown as #1 God of Funk, with George Clinton #2, Sly Stone #3, and yourself as #4.*
That's it. Ain't nobody else.

In 1982 you went on a five-year hiatus. Now you're back with a renewed spirit. What happened?
I had fallen off the scene for a while. What happened was, I had stopped reaching for things in the music. I got bored. I had just gotten to that point in my career where it was not fun anymore. It was like... Hit the stage, play the gig, get off the stage, drive in a limo to the hotel, wake up, go to the next gig... I was getting into a rut and I found myself hiding a lot from my fans. People would be waiting outside my hotel room door at night, and they'd be there again when I woke up in the morning. And the more that happened, the more I began to hide. I started feelin' funny inside. I didn't feel like that was me no more. So I just dropped off the scene 'cause I had lost that original feeling of reaching for something. When that star-time thing hits, you get too comfortable. And I lost all my drive. I got so wore out with taxes and the road.... I was just burnt.

How were you able to come back?
It was people like [producer] Bill Laswell who sparked me back to wanting to do this again. By working with him [on *What's Bootsy Doin'?* as well as on Ryuichi Sakamoto's *Neo Geo,* Herbie Hancock's *Perfect Machine,* and Sly & Robbie's *Language Barrier*], I got refreshed. Now my whole vibe is: Even when you're winning, you have to keep fighting like you're losing. You can't get too comfortable. So that's the way I'm going at it again. And if I keep that attitude, I'll be cool.

One final question. How would you describe to someone as white as Dan Quayle what the funk is all about?
The way I think I would try to explain it to him is... I would probably have to take him to the street

first of all, maybe go get some real fried chicken. And I'd show him the difference between Shake & Bake and real fried chicken, the kind you cook with lard where you end up with all kinds of grease on your hands. So we'd start off that way. Get him used to the food that the real funk people are used to eating. And that's the real fat food. Food that drips off your fingers. He wouldn't be down with that, so you'd have to let him experience those things first before you take him any farther. You couldn't just start in by telling him what funk is. But once he tasted the difference between Shake & Bake chicken and real greasy chicken, he might begin to understand the concept of what the funk is really all about. It's like the difference between a can of Coke Classic and a sugar-free Coke. It's like you got the real thing and then you got a cut on it. So once he understands those things, then you could explain to him that funk is a way of life. This is where we came from. It all started from the street and it kinda grew to this. It's how we express ourselves through music. I think he would understand it more from seeing what we dealt with.... It's a funky style, it's a way of life, it's the rhythm of things to come. So you'd have to explain it that way instead of just trying to tell him what the music was all about. He'd probably never get that one. I mean, can you see him trying to groove to some funk?

So I think the fried chicken route is definitely the best place to begin. Then I'd introduce him to some of the sisters on the corner to understand what that funk is all about. And then you can kind of step over into the music and play him some funk. "Now this is one of the funk records that we cut. Now check this out—this here other record that's *supposed* to be funky." He might hear the difference. He might get it then. But you can't depend on it. It takes a minute to get it. And if not this year, maybe next year. Who knows? Maybe after a while he'd even learn how to dance to it. Man, that would be deep. Dan Quayle dancing to some funk. That should be a video—explaining what the funk is to Dan Quayle. That's heavy, man.

© 1984 MARCIA RESNICK

ROBERT QUINE

HE'S A NOTED RECLUSE, a Downtown enigma and borderline misanthrope who can summon up contempt for a lot of music while remaining very passionate about a select few artists—Jimmy Reed, Jimmy Raney, Jack Scott, James Burton, Lester Young, Blind Willie Johnson, Harvey Mandel, Bill Evans, Gary Peacock, Charlie Parker, and Miles Davis. He's also something of a godfather figure for the so-called noise-punk-art-rock scene. Guitarists like Thurston Moore of Sonic Youth has sung his praises. And yet, Robert Quine is no random noisemaker. His guitar playing is deeply entrenched in the blues and rockabilly that he came up with as a young music enthusiast, though his gift for tasteful understatement and empathy in any musical setting reflects his love of jazz.

Quine's cathartic work on the landmark 1976 punk opus, *Blank Generation* by Richard Hell & The Voidoids, stands as seminal statement of over-the-top sickness. His more lyrical and interactive work can be heard in a series of '80s albums by Lou Reed (*The Blue Mask, Legendary Hearts,* and *Live in Italy*), Tom Waits (*Rain Dogs*), and Marianne Faithfull (*Strange Weather*). His ability to improvise tastefully-crafted, concise little gems in the service of simple pop songs has kept him active in the '90s as an accompanist to Beatles-esque singer-songwriters Lloyd Cole (*Don't Get Weird on Me, Babe*) and Matthew Sweet (*Earth* and *Girlfriend*). *Girlfriend* is perhaps the best distillation of Quine's genius since he played on Lou Reed's *The Blue Mask* (several of those tracks can be heard on the recently-released Lou Reed boxed set, *Magic and Loss*). For example, he provides sensitive accompaniment on "Winona," underscores the emotional content of Sweet's lamenting lyrics with a heart-wrenching solo on "You Don't Love Me," then turns around and rips the back of your head off with wretched excess on "Does She Talk?" Quine can have it both ways.

On *Weird Nightmare,* a Hal Willner–produced tribute to Charles Mingus (Columbia Records, 1992), Quine can be heard wailing on "Pitchecanthropus Erectus." He wrecks havoc throughout John Zorn's compilation *Filmworks 1986–1990* (Elektra Nonesuch, 1986), backs up singer Suzanne Rhatigan on *To Hell with Love* (Imago/RCA), and provides typically Quine-ian support behind ex-Bangle Susanna Hoffs on one cut from the soundtrack to *Buffy the Vampire Slayer* (Columbia, 1992). Quine is not obsessed with playing the correct notes. By Yngwie Malmsteen standards, his technique is brutal and stupid. But his playing is imbued with undeniable attitude and soul. The following interview was for a 1983 issue of *Guitar World.*

JUNE 22, 1983

Records are stacked to the ceiling of his cramped East Village studio apartment: Eddie Cochran, James Burton, Chuck Berry, Roy Buchanan, Jimmy Reed, Bo Diddley, Bill Evans. Every album ever recorded by Miles Davis occupies one whole shelf, right next to an equal supply of Charlie Parker and Lester Young albums. A dozen guitar cases are propped against one wall like soldiers forming a single file. Scattered throughout the joint are a multitude of opened and unopened effects boxes, practice amps, back issues of guitar magazines, bound copies of *Weird Science*... There's barely any room to sit, let alone live, let alone record. And yet, Quine wouldn't have it any other way.

This humble haven in the heart of hip bohemia is where Quine recorded his last two albums with cohort and Raybeats' guitarist Jody Harris—on a four-track TEAC Portastudio, no less. In this age of 48-track digital technology, Quine is clearly a throwback. But his aesthetic is equally clear.

"To me, nothing today sounds as good as the rock'n'roll records made in the late-1950s," he maintains. "And some of those records were made under the most atrocious conditions. 'You're So Fine' by The Falcons was recorded under grotesque conditions. So was 'Quarter to Three' by Gary U. S. Bonds. But both are magnificent recordings, in my opinion. There's something there that was caught—an energy, a feeling. You could never duplicate it."

He's on a roll now. "See, I believe the cliché: The music is the most important thing. Absolutely. My favorite Charlie Parker record is *Bird on 52nd Street,* which is the worst recorded record I've ever heard. It's got a wall of white noise over it. But I think it's his most inventive playing ever. It was just one of those magical nights and somebody happened to be there with a tape recorder. It happens to be one of the greatest jazz albums ever, and it also happens to be badly recorded. But that's irrelevant. I'd rather listen to that than a five-volume Keith Jarrett box that was digitally recorded on one of his eight billion dollar pianos. It's the music that counts."

I was honored that, for this interview, Quine removed his omnipresent and foreboding shades.

What are your early memories of rock'n'roll?
When I was about 12, that was in 1955, I got into rock'n'roll through "Speedo" by The Cadillacs and "Why Do Fools Fall in Love?" by Frankie Lymon. By about 1958 I gravitated towards the stuff on Chess Records and Vee Jay Records. I didn't know why. I didn't really know what blues was, but by 1958 I was listening to a lot of Muddy Waters and Little Walter and Jimmy Reed.

Were you playing at the time?

I got my first guitar that same year, 1958. I had taken piano lessons when I was a kid, coerced into it by my parents. And I must've gotten something out of it. But I got this acoustic guitar and loved the sound of it. The kind of things that The Everly Brothers were doing—"Bye Bye Love" and "Wake up Little Susie"—that's all I really wanted to do. But guitar lessons were ridiculous back then. If you didn't know somebody who could play rock'n'roll you were fucked. I had this guitar teacher who sent me home with a 1938 Gibson guitar instruction booklet so I was learning how to play "Yankee Doodle" on a single string. It was so discouraging that I just gave it up after about two months. But a year later, 1959, somebody showed me an E chord and things started to make a little sense to me. I suddenly realized that you could play most of these rock'n'roll songs with three chords, maybe four at the most.

When did you get your first electric guitar?
That was around 1960. It was a Danelectro. By then I wanted a Fender very badly but I couldn't afford it so I got the Danelectro and hated it. Now, of course, they're collectors items. It was a double cutaway two-pickup with gold finish. It came with an amp and the whole thing together was about $130.

What were your guitar influences then?
Well, The Ventures had just come out. But the big influence that made me want to switch to electric guitar was Ritchie Valens. He was in the famous plane crash with Buddy Holly and before he died he had a couple of singles out, like "La Bamba." I had never heard a sound like it before. That was an amazing little band. On drums he had Earl Palmer, who had done all the Little Richard and Fats Domino records. He had Red Callendar on acoustic bass and another guy named Rene Hall playing a six-string Danelectro bass—the first time that had ever been used. It was a very unusual sound. You had two basses going and this great guitar sound. There was a certain jazz-like phrasing in his style that intrigued me. And the tone he had was one of the nastiest sounds I've ever heard. Right after he got killed, at age 17, there was an album out with a picture of him playing a Stratocaster. Naturally, I knew that's what I wanted. I finally did get a Stratocaster around 1961 and actually started playing in some local bands then. That was the year I went to college and I immediately started a band. By then there was quite a guitar repertoire to work off of. The lead guitar player of The Ventures was not a great innovator, but he made it possible for a lot of bands to exist. You could just buy two or three Ventures albums and learn the songs and get a gig. I had a list from back then of the songs we played—about 35 Ventures songs, some Link Wray, some Shadows, which I was fortunate enough to discover.

When did you begin thinking seriously about a career in music?
Back then, never. I was raised to believe that it was always going to be a hobby. All through college and law school I always had cover bands. I went to law school in the late-1960s at Washington University in St. Louis, just out of a lack of direction. I can't imagine how or why I did it, just looking back. But I actually became a lawyer in Missouri. I passed the bar there but I never really practiced law. I came to New York in 1971 and wrote tax law articles for a legal publishing company. It was the most hideous boring thing you could imagine but it was a fortunate thing because after about two and a half years of that it was starting to drive me insane. So I started to think a little bit more seriously about trying to play music. I had assumed it would be impossible when I first came to town. I had an image of New York being full of session musicians. I just figured there was no place for me here.

You moved here from San Francisco?

Yeah, there was certainly no place for me in San Francisco either. I made some effort to get into rock bands there and just gave up. By then I was heavily into The Velvet Underground, which was a very unpopular thing to like then. They came out to San Francisco and played there for about three weeks and I went every night. I really believe they were the greatest rock'n'roll band to date but it was a very discouraging thing because they were being completely ignored at the time. I went every night and sometimes the place would be deserted. So while it was inspiring for me to see them, it was also heartbreaking. But that was a big turning point for me. Lou Reed was a big influence on my playing then. He was a real innovator on the guitar and was never appreciated at the time.

What was it that caught your ear about his sound?
Are you familiar with the album *White Heat*? There was a song on it called "I Heard Her Call My Name." And I had never heard anything remotely like that. By then there was some "out-there" guitar happening, like Sonny Sharrock. But it never really appealed to me. This was the first really surreal guitar I had heard that I could somehow relate to the rock that went before it, like Chuck Berry and Bo Diddley. It's all in there. It's not that obvious, but it's definitely in his playing. Just the feeling, the attitude behind it.

And this came after your blues phase?
I got into blues around 1958. But then rock'n'roll was so happening. For me, after 1959, rock'n'roll has never been the same. There's been a few good years now and then, but nothing like the excitement from 1955 to 1959. And, of course, by 1961, there was very little happening in rock. Things were getting into Bobby Vinton, Bobby Rydell, and all the Bobbies. And by then I knew enough about blues to keep going back farther and farther. And about that time, about 1963, that's when the folk boom hit. And as an indirect result of that, people started digging up rural blues—Skip James, Mississippi John Hurt, John Lee Hooker. They would start showing up at folk festivals and I got very heavily into it. And I went to college at a place called Erland College in Richmond, Indiana, which in the '20s and '30s and '40s was a very big center for music, oddly enough. There was a record company near there called Gennet Records which recorded everybody from Bix Beiderbecke to Louis Armstrong and Blind Lemon Jefferson. So it was a good place to dig up old records. I used to go around the ghetto there and people would come to the door and I'd say, "Do you have any old 78s in your attic?" And they were usually more than happy to get rid of them. I have a lot of great records somewhere out in my parents house in Ohio—Leroy Carr, Ma Rainey, a lot of those original 78s.

What blues artists affected you?
Jimmy Reed was always my biggest influence then. If you were to say Muddy Waters or Howlin' Wolf or whatever are much greater than Jimmy Reed, I wouldn't argue with you for a second. But something about Jimmy Reed really transfixed me. Most people who will put down Jimmy Reed will say, "Oh, you hear one record, you've heard it all—just the same boogie beat underneath." But in fact, there are a lot of subtle things going on in his records. Eddie Taylor is playing that boogie beat in the records and Jimmy Reed is doing very strange, subtle things on top of it. And a lot of times he doesn't even get credit for it. A lot of times you'll read these blues magazines like *Blues Unlimited* where they'll credit some session musician. It's Jimmy Reed! You can immediately spot him. The mood, the feeling of those records, I never get tired of him. I still have his autograph somewhere.

I once hitchhiked out to Dayton, Ohio, to see him play. This was around 1962. I was playing with an all-black band at the time in Richmond, Indiana, so we all went out there and they wouldn't let us in the door. The place was segregated. They started to let me in, then saw these other guys. It was very hypocritical of me, but I was such a fanatic that I went back three days later to see him.

Morally, I don't know what I can say about that, but I just had to see Jimmy Reed. He was playing with a house band and was relatively sober that night. I've heard so many stories about Jimmy Reed being drunk and falling into the audience, off the stage, smashing his guitar. But anything he did for Vee Jay from 1953 to 1960 was great. I've always been a sucker for any kind of repeating riff, like the ones he does. Another record that had that same hypnosis-through-monotony effect on me at the time was Muddy Waters' "Still a Fool." That was a real breakthrough for me, hearing that record. I was about 15 and I said, "Wow, this is a real weird record. The chords don't change. It's just the same riff over and over and over." At first it was annoying but it goes past that point. I just played it for days on end. So gradually I realized that you don't necessarily need to have those chords change. That's something that has stayed with me.

Was this around the time you had your radio program?
That was 1961 or 1962 at Richmond, just a local campus station. It was called "House of the Blues" and I had a great theme song, "Odds and Ends" by Jimmy Reed—just an instrumental where they use this really psychotic electric violin. One of the most surreal things I've ever heard. Great mood to that.

What were your earliest memories of jazz?
I had always listened to jazz because I grew up with it. My father was very much into basically Benny Goodman stuff, but through that I got turned onto Charlie Christian when I was about 11. My parents were cool enough. They even gave me a Django Reinhardt record for a birthday present when I was about 11. I mean, you can't complain about that. That was a pretty nice present to get. I loved that from the beginning. The Charlie Christian... Well, you could hear the connection immediately to Chuck Berry—that repeated riff, which is actually from Lester Young, which is how Charlie Christian learned. But Django... That music is so sweet. He has so much soul. And it's very rare that you can spot someone instantly on the guitar, no matter what guitar he's playing. A horn is a very different thing. It's much easier to have a distinctive voice on a horn. But Django, you could spot his sound easily.

When did you start getting heavily into jazz?
By 1964 I started getting a little bored with blues and made a conscious effort to start listening to jazz. I loved Skip James but after hearing six Skip James records, you got the idea. And, in fact, I already owned most of the great blues records by then and I was ready to stretch my ears a bit. By 1964 there was nothing really happening in rock for me either. The Beatles were interesting but they didn't really do much for me. The Stones were also interesting. But from 1964 to 1970 I was really devoted to jazz and I built up a gigantic record collection. I started out with whatever was funkiest, coming out of blues—Kenny Burrell, Ramsey Lewis—and in a couple years I had gotten into Bill Evans, especially his stuff from around 1959. His record *A Portrait in Jazz*—that's a record I wore out. I had five or six copies of that thing.

So you weren't specifically listening for guitar?
I started off with guitar. That's what I was going to relate to. But I was also interested in whoever was playing the best solos. So ultimately I was able to appreciate Charlie Parker, Lester Young, the early Louis Armstrong stuff from the early-1930s. His two takes of "Stardust" are incredible! Eventually I discovered Jimmy Raney. I rank him up there in the same category with Tal Farlow and other bebop guitar players, but he went past that. His lines are much farther out than is immediately apparent. You slow those lines down to 16 rpm, he teeters right over the edge into atonality the way some of the people in the Lennie Tristano school did. Apparently, he was influenced by that to a certain extent. I was actually able to play some of his solos at one point, slowing the record

player down to 16. That's one way to do it, because it stays in the same key. After I came to New York in the summer of 1971, I met Jimmy Raney. He lives in Louisville but he came in for the Newport Festival. He was playing at some local club and I did take a couple lessons from him. Basically, I don't know what I got out of it, but it was a real opportunity just to talk to this guy. There's not too many geniuses around. I rank him up there with Miles Davis, Charlie Parker, Lester Young, and very few others.

So going from Jimmy Raney to Lou Reed must've been extreme culture shock.
Well, Jimmy Raney influenced me before Lou Reed. Then after the Lou Reed influence I took lessons with Jimmy Raney for a while. But he wasn't in town for that long. There are a lot of weird varying influences that come into play.

Do you see a common thread here through all these influences?
It's just that they are all geniuses and they're great. I'm very pessimistic about the music scene in general, especially in the '70s and '80s, but I think it's a remarkable thing that I can walk around the corner and have my choice of 25 or 30 Charlie Parker albums. If somebody who has never been exposed to jazz can walk around the corner and buy a copy of *Kind of Blue,* that's very hopeful to me. I mean, when I came to New York in 1971, I was heavily into Lester Young and at the time there was not one Lester Young album in print. And as of a few years ago there's about 20 or so albums out. But I've already got my stash. I rarely buy anything that's been recorded in the last 20 years. Generally, I'm scrounging around in specialty stores looking around for strange R&B reissues, imports, rockabilly stuff. Starting around 1970 I just don't listen to the radio very much. Around '67–'68... That was a very exciting time for radio. But I've stopped listening.

Did you get into Eric Dolphy or Coltrane?
Yeah. The interest in bebop led to that. Eventually I bought *Ascension* by Coltrane when that came out and eventually I got into that stuff very heavily. And that affected my playing. I guess in that school Cecil Taylor was the one who interested me the most. Out of those people—Dolphy, Coltrane, Ornette Coleman—he was the one I related to the most. Some of the Coltrane things—like *Om*—to me was just an extension of the blues. But Cecil Taylor's *Looking Ahead* on Contemporary was a revelation to me.

You saw Trane live?
Yeah. One of the most powerful things I ever saw. In 1966 I saw Coltrane with Pharoah Sanders, his wife, Alice, on piano, Jimmy Garrison on bass, and Rashied Ali on drums. I was sitting in the front row and they really got into a scream. Both those horns were right in my face, and that's something you're gonna remember for the rest of your life. If you sit and try to analyze that stuff and try to understand it the same way you try to understand bebop, you're not gonna go anywhere. I couldn't. What is there to understand? You just feel it. And that's how I came to understand Ornette Coleman, as much as I do understand him. I'm not that much into his concept. The way I hear him is some kind of really twisted R&B with some bebop elements in it. His fans, I'm sure, would disagree with that. But that's how I hear it and it's the only way I can relate to the records of his that I do like—that rawness, that R&B element of it.

Do you analyze your own playing?
Definitely not. What I'm doing is pure instinct. I think I probably have my own style at this point and people tell me that I do. But one thing I don't believe in is someone who says, "I want to be completely different than anybody else." If they put that over the music, the feeling, they're gonna

end up with something less than if they just relaxed. If I'm playing a solo, no matter what context it's in, it's just possible that maybe some tired old blues cliché, maybe in the wrong key, is gonna work better than some precious original line of my own. I've never been afraid to try to copy whatever I could off of records. That's the only way to learn for me. That last couple of years I got back into James Burton, for instance. He was an influence on me in the '50s and recently, through the lack of anything else happening, I started scrounging up various things he did session work on—really obscure, awful things like Dino, Desi & Billy records. But he plays brilliantly on everything. I try to copy his stuff as best as I can. I can't really. It's never gonna come out the way he played it. How many people have you heard play "Johnny B. Goode"—the Beach Boys, The Beatles, ten thousand garage bands. It never sounds the same. Maybe all these people were trying to do it exactly like Chuck Berry did but they can't. For one thing, he put his guitar out of tune in a really weird way. I didn't discover that until 20 years later. You can't possibly sound like somebody else, even if you try.

How do you categorize yourself as a guitarist?
I would categorize myself as a blues guitar player. People generally laugh when I say that because I've never done it on a record yet. But I have that quality, and I think having that helps give a lot of validity to a lot of the other things I do. No matter how weird it is, the blues is in there somewhere—the phrasing, the breathing, stopping, not playing ten million notes per second. I started trying to play weird about 1967 from listening to these outside jazz records and it came out pretty worthless. I'd be playing a blues scale in the wrong key—it wasn't happening. But there was a breakthrough one night in 1969. I had been listening to "I Heard Her Call My Name" by the Velvet Underground and was also copying Jimmy Raney solos, then I went and played this gig. We were doing "Eight Miles High" and I had a very long guitar solo on that. And something snapped. I was playing strange and they weren't wrong notes. Suddenly, I was in control. It's a wonderful feeling when it happens. It doesn't happen that often. When you suddenly... You're somewhere else. You're transported. I have a tape of it somewhere. It actually sounds pretty good. That was a real breakthrough.

The last other major breakthrough I had came around 1973 when I started listening to electric Miles Davis. I was playing around with a song from *Bitches Brew* called "Pharoah's Dance." It's a modal song but the key is ambiguous. I wasn't copying solos, just playing along. You could play almost anything you wanted over it and I started using basic scales I had learned along with blues licks—putting it all together. And it all seemed to fit. And by the end of that summer, what I was doing was a little more defined. It made a little more sense. Another significant thing that happened that summer was hearing *Raw Power* by Iggy & The Stooges (Columbia, 1973). The guitarist on that record, James Williamson, took one aspect of Lou Reed's style and went on with that. He was coming more from Keith Richards than a jazz background but he ended up in the same area. I think his guitar playing on that album is really important historically. It still isn't appreciated very much but that's what, in fact, encouraged me to push the envelope on my own playing. I was already playing somewhat like that already so I thought, "This guy can make a record. Maybe there's some hope for me."

How did you connect with bands in New York?
I didn't really know anybody who played music, so the only thing I knew how to do was start answering ads in the *Village Voice,* which was really a disastrous experience—very discouraging, to say the least. I tried that very briefly and without exception the bands were horrible and they really hated me. I'd last about one song before they would tell me to hit the road. I had never done anything like that before. It was very unpleasant. So I got very discouraged but I kept playing. Finally, by accident, I was working at The Strand bookstore where Richard Hell and Tom Verlaine and Jody Harris were also working. And I got to be friends with Richard Hell. He had just left Television and

formed a group called The Heartbreakers. One night in early-1976 he was over at my house and I was drunk enough to play him some old tapes of stuff I had done. He had heard my weird stuff but he didn't realize that I could do the other stuff too. These were tapes from the '60s of me playing "Johnny B. Goode" and "Louie Louie." He didn't realize that I was, in fact, a rock'n'roll guitar player. So he asked me to join his band [Richard Hell & The Voidoids] and we did one album, *Blank Generation* [Sire Records, 1977]. The band lasted from early-1976 to late-1979. We got together for a little reunion and made a second album in 1981 [*Destiny Street*, Red Star, 1982], which was not as successful artistically as *Blank Generation*. I suppose if someone had never heard me before and wanted to hear typical guitar solos in a rock context of mine, there's some good ones on that album *Blank Generation*. But I think the best album I ever did, though, was [Lou Reed's] *The Blue Mask*. I wouldn't recommend that to anyone as my typical playing. I only play one guitar solo on it, on "Waves of Fear," which is not a typical solo. It's basically a Fernandez guitar going through an Electro-Harmonix Deluxe Memory Man analog delay with the chorus effect on a fairly extreme setting. I discovered this particular unit when I played very briefly with Robert Gordon and he turned me on to that for that slap back effect you need for rockabilly. In terms of effects, that's generally about all I use now. I'm never without it. I even practice with it. I just can't play without it.

So you're not that keen on technology.
No. As far as technology goes, the most exciting thing I've found is this Electro-Harmonix 16-second digital delay. I turned Brian Eno onto that. He, in fact, used it a lot on the last two records he did—*Mission Apollo* and *Music For Films, Vol. 2.* Basically, this little unit allows you to set up loops that last for 16 seconds. And it's very smooth-sounding, no glitches. Some delays have an audible click, but this one is smooth. And you can overdub infinitely on it—150 guitars, if you want. Obviously after about the tenth guitar the first one starts receding into the background a little. You can flip a switch, play what you've got backwards, then record forwards over that. Or you can cut the speed in half. It's really a remarkable machine. I plan to use it on the next thing I do. I did a record about three years ago with another guitarist, Jody Harris, called *Escape* [Infidelity Records, 1979]. We did it in my apartment, just a four-track recording. Just two guitars and a rhythm box. It was pretty primitive, but it came out pretty well. We're talking about doing another one together this summer. And for that I'll use this 16-second delay pedal to get those hypnotic riffs going. There'll be some kind of market for it. At this point I have enough of a name so I'll be able to sell the tapes to somebody. I have enough musical drive, but I don't have a lot of career-oriented ego drive. I'd like to make a living at it, if possible. But I don't have these visions of Robert Quine albums flooding the stores. It'd be nice, but I just don't expect it. I sort of operate on pessimism. It's how I seem to work best. It gives me room to relax. And the more relaxed I am, the greater the possibility that something great will creep out of my subconscious and onto the record.

You played with Eno?
I met him about five years ago. Then in late-1980 he called me to work on one of his records, which I thought was strange. He had just finished working on *Remain in Light* and *The Bush of Ghosts* and this was going to be his fifth pop album with a lot of funk rhythms in there somewhere. We actually went into the recording studio for a week—me, Fred Maher, Bill Laswell, and Eno. There was some pretty cool stuff. But what happened was, things got more and more ambient as they continued to work on the album until Eno started realizing that he did not want to do this pop stuff at all. So what he eventually ended up with was *On Land*. I'm not even on that. It was all stripped away. But it was really an education being in the recording studio with Eno, watching him work in the studio. It's a real cliché, but he really does use the recording studio as a musical instrument. That's his real genius. *On Land* is really a great record and easily the best thing he's ever done. That record

really influenced me. I think it's a revolutionary record. And he knew that the record would be more or less ignored. "Oh, another drone record." But in fact, it's totally revolutionary. The way it's produced, the way it's mixed. Apparently, he was influenced very much by this record I gave him, which was a big influence for me in jazz in the '70s—a track called "He Loved Him Madly" by Miles Davis from his album *Get up with It.* When I first heard it I thought it was the most boring thing I had ever heard. It's a slow dirge-like thing. I thought it was easily the worst Miles Davis ever. It took me about two years to get over those feelings, then I played it incessantly for about three months. And apparently, what Eno got out of that was something in the production. The understanding that the space itself, the air, the space between the instruments—that's part of the music.

What got you the gig with Lou Reed?
He had seen me with Richard Hell & The Voidoids in 1977 and talked to me then, although he did not remember me from years before when I saw The Velvet Underground in San Francisco. But he was raving about my playing. That was nice to hear. He wanted me to join his band but I said I would not play with him if he were not also playing guitar. That would be too sick because he was too big an influence on me. And to some extent anything I'm playing is coming from him. And for me to be playing all the guitar solos in his band and for him not to—that's way too sick. I just would not do it. So he really had to be goaded into playing guitar again. The live thing was very gratifying because he really stretched out and took some great solos, which in fact have been preserved for posterity on a video they made of it at the Bottom Line. There's a solo he does on "Kill Your Sons," which is a real vindication, I think.

Do you think of yourself as an influential guitarist?
Well a lot of guitar players on the street come up to me and tell me I've influenced them a lot. And a lot of critics tell me that I've influenced so-and-so. But I'm not that aware of it because I don't listen to much contemporary music and I just don't know.

© 1998 NEIL ZLOZOWER

JOE SATRIANI

I FIRST INTERVIEWED GUITARIST Joe Satriani in the kitchen of the China Club back in 1986. He was relatively unknown then, except to the staff of *Guitar World* magazine and a cult of other six-string fanatics who had picked up on his self-produced solo debut, *Not of This Earth* (which was financed on a credit card in 1984 and was re-released by Relativity Records in 1986). That night at the China Club we witnessed the coming out party of a bona fide guitar hero. A year and a half later I was sitting down with Satriani again, this time for a March '88 cover story for *Pulse!* magazine. Satch was big news by then. His album *Surfing with the Alien,* released by the fiercely independent Relativity Records in 1988, was surprisingly zooming up the charts. Something about this album with its cartoon superhero cover caught on with the record buying public, resulting in two million in sales. And a star was born. Satriani would release a string of excellent albums for Relativity before jumping to the majors. Last year, Satriani joined fellow guitar slingers Steve Vai and Eric Johnson for a whirl-wind tour, resulting in *G3 Live in Concert* (Columbia, 1997). His latest solo release is *Crystal Planet* (Epic Records, 1998).

I had the occasion to meet up with Satriani again in the winter of '96. I was producing the Blue Note debut of legendary jazz guitarist Pat Martino and Satch agreed to participate in this project. He found a window of opportunity in his busy touring schedule and met us on a weekend at the Marin County home studio of guitarist Michael Hedges. Joe, who was a huge fan of Pat Martino, proved to be a facile and daring improviser at this casual, extemporaneous session. He and Pat sat face-to-face and jammed for 40 minutes, just feeding off of each other's energy and ideas. We later cut and pasted together two tracks, "Ellipsis" and "Never and After," which appeared on Pat's *All Sides Now* (Blue Note, 1997). Hedges, a gentle soul and inspired artist in his own right, not only donated his own personal recording space for this intimate session, he also engineered and played percussion on "Ellipsis." We were all shocked to hear of the tragedy of Michael's death by car accident in December of '97. I still have a vivid memory of Joe, Pat, and Michael jamming in the studio between takes on a Rolling Stones tune. That image will remain with me for a long time.

JANUARY 27, 1988

It's a frigid evening in New York City but inside The Bottom Line, that Greenwich Village showcase club, things are heating up to a boil. Guitar fanatics are packed in shoulder-to-shoulder, standing room only at the bar. It's like a rush hour subway ride to Penn Station, but no one's complaining. They stand on tiptoes to get a glimpse of the guy on stage. The one who, as legend has it, taught Steve Vai how to play guitar.

The place is filthy with guitar press. Every national guitar mag is well represented for this special occasion. Normally, you couldn't pry these smug scribes out of their homes with a crowbar on a cold night like this, especially on a Tuesday night. Not even with a three-drink tab, courtesy of the record company. But they've all come down en masse to see a certified Next Big Thing.

And Joe Satriani does not disappoint. His dazzling array of tricks—left-hand fretted arpeggios, right-hand tapping, whammy bar theatrics, uncanny displays of precision speed picking—leaves these obsessed-with-technique types gasping for breath. But beyond the obvious flash, the daredevil feats of fretboard fantasia, there is undeniable musicality. It's in the way he phrases a line, the way he spins melodies, the manner in which he has arranged these pieces. Sure, he's a monster. But the guy also exhibits uncanny taste when he's not killing you with legato runs and frantic whammy bar dive bombs. The guitar scribes seem impressed. I'm impressed. And the crowd's going berserk. There's something very special about this Satriani dude.

Backed by the drummer Jonathan Mover and bassist Stu Hamm, the hulking presence onstage who had earlier stunned the audience with his solo slap bass rendition of Earl Scruggs' "Foggy Mountain Breakdown," Satriani stalks the stage with his white Ibanez screaming on "Lords of Karma." Next, the band kicks into a rocking version of "Crushing Day" before taking it up a notch with the frantic "Satch Boogie." The set ends. They're screaming by the bar. Even the jaded scribes are on their feet applauding for an encore. The trio comes back to a thunderous ovation and launches into the rocking title track from Satriani's second Relativity Records album, *Surfing with the Alien*. The fanatics in the house are hoarse from shouting all night, and now *this*? Too much.

Then right when you figured things had peaked, Satriani approaches the mike and announces, "We'd like to bring out a special guest vocalist and do some blues." The curtain parts and out pops Mick Jagger. Pandemonium! Satch and the band jump into Jimi Hendrix's "Red House" and Mick takes heed, struttin' and posturing like a proud aging whore on a hot Saturday night with the entire Navy fleet in town on leave. *There's a red house over yonder/That's where my baby stays/I ain't seen my baby/in 99 and one half days.*

Satch is smiling like a kid on Christmas morning, wailing on his six-string in heartfelt homage to Hendrix. Mick's turning it on now, even blowing some great blues harp. He's in fine form. No doubt about it, there's a lot of life in the old boy yet. They finish to howls of delight. A night to remember.

I met Satriani the next morning at the Parker Meridien Hotel. He spoke about his sudden rise to guitar hero status and the Jagger connection.

I had heard that Mick might sit in last night, considering that you're in his band now. How did you get that gig?
A few months ago I heard that Mick Jagger was putting together a band for a short tour of Japan. They had originally called Steve Vai and he declined, but he recommended me. So my name got passed around a bit and I think it wasn't until probably last week that Mick really heard me for the first time. So anyway, I got a call last week that he definitely wanted to bring me to New York for rehearsals. He had gone through everybody there who wasn't already gigging at the moment. So I jumped on a plane and the next day, there I was at the rehearsal. And it turned out to be a great audition. I was so impressed by Mick. He came walking into the room smiling, walked right up to the mike and started singing great stuff. And when the song ended he shook my hand, just like a regular guy: "Hi. How ya doin'? Sounds great. Let's do another song." And we played on and on for about four hours—Hendrix songs, old blues songs, Jagger songs, Stones songs. It was pretty intense.

So now you're The Guy Who Replaced Jeff Beck in Jagger's Band.
Well, it's just a three-week tour in Japan. Mick just wants me to do what I do. I mean, he could hire anybody. There are plenty of guitar players out there who can imitate Keith Richards or Jeff Beck or some other guitarist that Mick's played with. But he doesn't want that. He wants *my* sound—at least for those three weeks. After that it's anybody's guess. Just one step at a time. I'm very fortunate. Things just happen that way—all through chance.

Are you surprised by the great success of Surfing with the Alien?
Absolutely. In the beginning, the record company kept telling me, "Joe, you know, we love your record, we love you as an artist, but we wanna tell you that breaking an instrumental record is gonna be hard. So don't be disappointed." Now every week they call me up with, "Joe, you're not gonna believe this, but your record just went from here to there on the charts. What's happening! Why is this working this way?!" So it's been this celebration going on every week as the record creeps up another notch or gets added to another playlist somewhere. And I visit some of these radio stations that are playing the record. Apparently, people are really getting into the record just because it's different from everything else they've ever gotten. And the record is not surrounded by huge record company hype. Relativity is a bunch of really nice guys who work hard. It's not this huge corporate thing by any means. And I'm really a nobody. I'm just a guitar player. So this success is all very mysterious to me, but I'm loving it.

It's a far cry from where you were at ten years ago.
I can't deny that it was depressing at times. People would tell me, "You gotta use a vocalist or nobody will want to listen to it." Or they would say, "It's not fusion. It's not metal. What the hell is it?" But I never got so frustrated that I put my guitar on the shelf. I just kept working on it. And I thought, "One of these days people will like it. They'll be ready for it." I just really believed all along that it would eventually happen. I'd say, "When the time is right and the world is ready to listen to what I'm doing, I'll be ready." And now I'm noticing that it might be the right time. Why? I can't really put my finger on why. Maybe people like the new album because it's really different or weird. Maybe they like the idea that I'm using the guitar as a voice rather than hitting them over the head with the same old clichés that they've heard again and again. Maybe they hear some of the Chuck Berry licks I throw in here and there. I mean, it's fun guitar music. It's not heavy pretentious I-Am-God-Worship-Me kind of guitar, you know?

You have great facility on the instrument and yet you don't seem obsessed with technique.
Not the way some genres of guitar playing exploit technique these days. That's just completely boring to me. So many kids today can do all the scales and arpeggios and speed licks, but they can't phrase. So it all sounds very much the same until you learn about phrasing. It all comes down to editing and phrasing—what you choose to leave out, when you choose to enter and exit. I edit myself incredibly as far as melodies go. There's one song I do, for instance, called "Always with You," which is probably the most delicate thing I had ever set up before. It took me days to really lock into it, to where I thought I was approaching it the right way and not overdoing it. Just blowing chops all over it—that would've killed it. And it took a lot of care, a lot of editing, to make sure I didn't overdo it. Sometimes it helps to step back and analyze your performance. "Is this too much? Am I just showing off here?" It's like a painting or a novel or any other kind of thing you're creating. You have to think about balance and a lot of other things that come into play.

How did you formulate your aesthetic?
A lot of different things over time. I started off like most kids in the '60s, staring at my Hendrix records and Jethro Tull records and Jeff Beck records and listening to them in the dark thinking, "Wow! If I can play music and people would listen and feel the way I feel now listening to these records, that would be incredible!" And from there, I began practicing and studying the guitar. I had total support from my parents, who always said, "If you're gonna do it, then you gotta do it all the way." If they knew that I had made up my mind about something, then they wouldn't let me slack off. And my father taught me discipline. If he knew I didn't practice one day, he'd wake me up in the middle of the night and march me downstairs in my pajamas to sit there and practice. So that really helped formulate my aesthetic for discipline in practicing, which really paid off.

And there must've been some key figures along the way to inspire you to stretch.
Hendrix hit me in a sort of—I dunno—*religious* way. You know, people hear a calling—to be an artist, an architect, doctor, to follow a particular cause. When I heard Hendrix, it just clicked in me. He just opened up my head to that whole experimental point of view. I don't think that he ever failed in the studio to project a feeling of the notes with the sound of the notes, even given the primitive technology that he had at the time. All the things we have today are like a luxury compared to what was available during Jimi's time, yet he was able to overcome that and bring that sort of "sound of the world" to the instrument and project it out so that people listening could experience the feeling of the music as much as the notes.

I understand you studied briefly with [legendary jazz pianist] Lennie Tristano.
That was when I was just out of high school, around 1975. He really impressed upon me the idea of practicing scales and technique to a point where everything could truly be improvised. It was really an inspirational experience to study with Lennie. He taught me ear training by making me sing sax solos along with the records. And he had this great approach to practicing on your own. He'd say, "Practice with a nudity, a blankness. Have no style when you practice. And when you play, don't think, don't be judgmental. Go crazy. Do whatever you want." Or he'd say things like, "Never be in the subjunctive—I *could've* done this or *should've* done that. Just play! And when you go to practice, be maniacal!" And I took those words to heart. He was an amazing person, one of the world's greatest musicians. And that period of three months I spent with him was a real turning point for me in terms of understanding what you could actually do with yourself when you focus on something. That's what really inspired me to start reaching over with the right hand to fret notes, complete chords, extend phrases, and developing my own vocabulary on the instrument.

You ultimately became a teacher yourself in your hometown of Carle Place on Long Island.
Yeah, I taught a few kids, one of which happened to be Steve Vai. He was an excellent student because he was so dedicated and inspired. And, of course, he turned out to be an incredible musician.

You didn't exactly focus on a career in music at that time.
No, I wasn't too career-minded at all. So I just traveled a lot. I lived in Japan for about six months, kind of floated around and eventually landed in Berkeley, California, where I got involved with a writing partner, Neil Sheehan. We wrote a play or two together, did some songwriting together and eventually we decided to put a band together. It was a really energetic power pop band called The Squares, sort of like The Everly Brothers meets Van Halen. It was strictly radio-oriented and we were always just *that* short of a record deal. We tried really hard, but after four or five years it started getting old and depressing. That's when I decided I was going to start playing music that I liked playing, the kind I used to play when I wasn't serious about a career. So I checked out of that pop scene and figured I'd do something crazy like make a record, just as an exploration of things that I had picked up over the years—funk, two-handed tapping, melodic chord soloing. I thrive on that kind of diversity, as a player and as a listener. My record collection covers the whole gamut, from Charlie Parker to Prince to Asian music to whatever. And when I'm in the right frame of mind, when I'm playing naturally, all of those influences come out.

That first album was Not of This Earth, *which Relativity later picked up and reissued. What was your plan for* Surfing with the Alien?
Just to push a little further, with more emphasis on out-and-out crazy guitar playing. I didn't consider any kind of genre playing or anything like that. But I was surprised to learn after the fact that "Hill of the Skull" has entered the metal charts and "Rubina" has broken into adult contemporary. I actually heard that song in a supermarket. I was just shopping one day—and there it was! Apparently, some supermarkets on the West Coast pick up these sort of New Age radio stations. So that was an eye-opening experience. I can assure you, I never set out to make a New Age record or a heavy metal record. I've even heard a couple of things from the first record being used as background music for insurance company commercials in Los Angeles. So it's really weird. When you've gone through the whole process of experiencing the music, creating it, having it realized on tape, fretting over whether it was mixed and recorded properly, giving it to the record company, and going through the anxiety of whether or not it's gonna sell and whether or not you're gonna be able to continue as an artist making your music or will you have to keep your day job... And then to hear your music in a supermarket or some TV commercial—it all becomes very Vonnegut-like.

DANNY GATTON

THE WHOLE STAFF OF *GUITAR WORLD* magazine had been quite aware of six-string virtu-oso Danny Gatton long before he signed his major label deal with Elektra in 1991. Word had filtered into the office about this monster player in the Washington D.C. area, tearing it up at small nightclubs like Gallagher's and Club Soda. So in the fall of '88 they sent me and photographer Aldo Mauro to seek out "The World's Greatest Unknown Guitarist," the title of a feature which ran in the January '89 issue. Aldo and I drove out to Gatton's farm in the middle of Nowheresville, Maryland. There was a rickety ol' barn out there by the soy bean fields and a number of vintage Ford automobiles lying around in various states of disrepair on his property. And there, pounding nails into the new porch he was building, stood a short, powerfully-built man with Vitalis in his hair and a Telecaster insignia emblazoned across the back of his jacket. Hot rods and Telecasters, that was Danny Gatton, the world's most neglected guitar hero.

For the following interview, which appeared in a May '91 issue of *Guitar World,* I met Danny and his band at Bearsville Studios in the solitude of Upstate New York. He was working on his major label debut, *88 Elmira Street,* a triumph after a series of releases on the small, independent NRG label known only to his small, rabid cult following. Gatton followed that Elektra debut in '93 with *Cruisin'*

Deuces. Disappointed by record sales, Elektra later dropped Gatton from the label. In 1994 he recorded a blazing jazz-oriented project with Hammond B–3 organ star Joey DeFrancesco, the aptly-titled *Relentless* for the independent Big Mo Records. Tragically, in a fit of depression, Gatton took his own life on October 4, 1994, in the ol' rickety barn out by the soy bean field. But his legacy lives on in the memory of those who ever witnessed his incredible virtuosity and intense conviction on stage.

OCTOBER 6, 1988

Throughout the 1970s, Danny Gatton was known by a select few around the Washington D.C./Maryland area. Guitar enthusiasts would crowd into the small nightclubs where he played to marvel at his amazing technique. On that turf, he was the rival of Roy Buchanan, another amazing guitarist who had gained national recognition in 1972 with his major label debut on Polydor Records.

Gatton, meanwhile, remained relatively obscure through the '80s, releasing albums on his own small, independent label and eventually gaining a cult following in New York, where he began appearing on a semi-regular basis in 1987. Word quickly spread in guitar circles about this incredible guitarist who could play jazz, rockabilly, and blues with power and authentic feel. A typical Gatton audience was filled with aspiring guitarists who would squeeze up to the stage in order to get a peak at his busy right hand fingers, which flailed independently on the strings.

By 1988, on the strength of his excellent independent album *Unfinished Business* and his instructional video *Licks and Tricks for Guitar,* Gatton was being hailed by American guitar magazines as "the best unknown guitarist in the world," a label that Roy Buchanan had carried before his career finally took off.

Following a series of New York showcase gigs, which were attended by various major label representatives, Gatton finally signed with Elektra Records. His long-awaited major label debut for Elektra, *88 Elmira Street,* is a continuation of the jazz-rockabilly-blues formula that the guitarist has always favored. And being recorded at a prestigious studio like Bearsville in Upstate New York (where Todd Rundgren and Joe Satriani worked on their new albums), it naturally sounds better than the independent projects that he had been putting out on his own NRG label (named for his mother, Norma Ruth Gatton). I went up to Bearsville and talked to Gatton during the mixing of *88 Elmira Street.*

You must be pleased with the budget you got for 88 Elmira Street. *Sonically, it's a different ballgame from your previous recordings.*
It sounds like a competitive record, it doesn't sound like an independent record. The playing on *Unfinished Business* is fine but it's just not recorded as well as this.

Is there anything in particular that makes it more competitive?
The sound of the bass and drums, for one thing—the drums especially. That's all-important. It's not as hard getting a good guitar sound as it is getting a good drum sound. Their studio A at Bearsville is like the ultimate place to record drums because they have microphones all up in the ceiling so you get that big natural reverb. I was kind of skeptical about that when I first came up here, but I'm converted now. It obviously makes a world of difference.

At last, a Danny Gatton album with Jeff Beck production values.
Yeah, and it takes money to do that. You can't do it on an independent budget. This new album is just a superior product, compared to my other independent albums [*Unfinished Business,* 1988; *Redneck Jazz,* 1978; and *American Music,* 1975]. What can I say? This is a very competitive business. And if you want something that's gonna sound competitive, it's gonna cost you.

I notice you pull out the banjo on a couple of tunes.

Yeah, boy, I haven't played that thing in many a year. That thing was green when I got it out of the case. I'm not very proficient on that anymore and don't really care to be. I used to be pretty good at playing Earl Scruggs licks on the banjo but I really haven't done it in 15 years. That whole banjo style technique was the basis for my fingering approach on the guitar. The first time I ever played with a flat pick and fingers doing banjo rolls on the guitar was back in '71. I can remember when I switched over to doing it that way. Before then, whenever I would do some tunes that were like bluegrass tunes on stage, I'd put on the regular banjo finger picks and play guitar that way—tune it to G and the whole routine. But there was no time to be doing that in the show, so I just said, "Hell, I'll learn how to play without the picks." So that's how that started. And from listening to Lenny Breau is when I started using my little finger on the right hand, so now I've got them all going. I just started working the little finger in there about five years ago, and it makes a big difference in chord voicings because every finger gives a different tone. When I played with Lenny Breau a few times, I noticed his fingernails were real thick and long. And I saw that he was using that little finger in there a lot. When you're playing chords it really makes the top note stand out when you pick it with that little finger. So after I saw Lenny Breau I thought, "Yeah, it's time to grow some nails."

Is that why you put lacquer on your fingernails?

I put superglue on 'em. My nails aren't very thick and they tend to break, so I coat them with superglue and then I put this other nail stuff on top of that. And it works. This one's busted right now—broken right in half, but you can't tell. If I break a nail during a set, I'm in a world of trouble. This one [little finger] actually got real long—it was out there like that. And I thought it was cool, but then it was making noise on the strings. Just the nail just barely touching the string, you get these little bugs and snaps, so I had to cut it off. Plus, it was getting in the way of doing those Lenny Breau harmonic runs. It was too long for that so I had to cut it back.

Who are some of your other early guitar heroes?

Les Paul was a big hero of mine. His early records with multi-tracked guitars and speeded up guitars were so innovative. I did an homage to him on *Unfinished Business* with my version of "Cherokee," the way Les would've done it. It's even got some speeded up guitars flying through in the mix. I also admire so many other guitar players in other fields. Roy Clark and Joe Maphis had a very big influence on me. Thumbs Carlisle was a big influence. I got to play with him for a while when we both worked in Roger Miller's band. Thumbs got his name because he laid his guitar on his lap and fretted the notes overhand with his fingers and his thumb, just like this new blues kid Jeff Healey. I also loved Hank Garland's playing. In jazz I would have to mention Wes Montgomery, Django Reinhardt, George Barnes, Billy Butler, George Benson, and Charlie Christian. In rock it would be Carl Perkins, Scotty Moore, Lawrence Smith, and Johnny Meeks, who played with Gene Vincent.

But I would say that my number one main man on guitar would have to be Lenny Breau. Man, I loved him. He was the best guitar player I ever saw, in terms of being a complete musician. He was heavily into Bill Evans and McCoy Tyner and actually worked out ways of playing pianistically on the guitar, using unusual voicings on his seven-string guitar. He also elevated the technique of playing harmonics to a high art. He was a genius. The way his life ended up was such a crime. He was a heroin addict and died broke and nearly forgotten. I saw him playing once in the back room of a pizza joint in Nashville, making $25 a night and playing to about four or five people who had no idea who he was. That just made me sick. Some nights he would be so messed up he couldn't even tune his guitar and another night it sounded like God playing the guitar. He was my guitar hero, bar none.

There has always been the impression that you and Roy Buchanan were competitors for the same turf. What was that all about?
I met Roy in 1968 in Georgetown at a club called The Silver Dollar. We got off on the wrong foot from the first moment—not my fault, though. A guy named Roger McDuffle, who is now playing sax with Billy Haley's old band, The Comets, was the instigator. Roger told me about Roy so we went down to The Silver Dollar after our gig to check him out. And to me, it was so different from what I had been used to. I was really heavily into Howard Roberts at the time. When that whole British Invasion thing hit, I just kinda tuned out and went directly into jazz. And I thought that's what Roy was into. I had no idea. So we get to the club and here's Roy playing a Telecaster through a 4x10 Fender Bassman amp with the volume on 13, playing like Jimi Hendrix and doing all this wild feedback stuff. And to me it made no sense at all. I said, "Roger, what is this? I thought I was gonna see somebody do something?" And he says, "Ah, Roy's just messin' around." Then he says, "I tell ya what you do... Go up there and tug on his sleeve and tell him to quit fartin' around." I said, "Really? You sure?" And Roger says, "Sure, I've known Roy forever. He's a great guy—nicest guy you'll ever meet. He'll get a kick out of that." So my naive self goes up there, tugs on Roy's sleeve, and he looks down at me and I say, "Why don't you quit fartin' around and play somethin'?" And his eyes turn red.... The fire came out of 'em and he says back to me, "Well, who the hell are you? Do you play guitar?" And I told him, "Sure do." So he rips his Tele off and hands it to me and yells, "You're so damn good, *you* play it!" So right away we hit it off wrong. About a year later I straightened it out and we became friends. He came over to my apartment in Nashville and stayed with me for a couple days. He showed me some things and I showed him some things, then he went his merry way.

Shortly after that, Roy began putting on disguises and sneaking into clubs where I was playing. One time I caught him and said, "What the hell you doin', Roy?" And he said, "I just wanna see what you play like when I'm not around." See, he didn't have any competition for the longest time. He was *it*. There was nothing else like him around. And I didn't play like him, but I learned how to play like him because he was the thing. So there was a competitive thing going on between us. But we were also friendly towards one another. In fact, when my band The Fatboys would play a gig at some little place way the hell out in Virginia, Roy would call up the club on the pay phone and we'd leave the phone off the hook all night so he could hear the set. And I'd talk to him during the breaks.

Your version of "The Simpsons" on the new album continues your practice of playing familiar TV themes.
Yeah, and we've also got a real nice version of "The Untouchables," which didn't get on this album. We also do "Perry Mason" live. And every once in a while I'll throw in "The Munsters" and "The Adams Family" themes. And there's a couple of quotes from the "Dick Van Dyke Show" on "Red Label."

Covering that Beach Boys' ballad "In My Room" was a nice choice.
Ah, that sure was. Some of the people at Elektra suggested that I do something more contemporary. They actually submitted a whole bunch of top 40 vocal hit tunes from the past five years, which I got nothing out of because the lyrics meant a lot but there were no melodies. It sounds like Muzak when you try to make instrumentals out of vocal tunes, unless they have great melodies. Finally someone suggested an instrumental version of "Surfer Girl," which I thought was real hokey. Then I was set on doing "I Only Have Eyes for You" by the Flamingos until my singer Billy Windsor came up with "In My Room." We thought that up one night and cut it the next day. There's nothing too elaborate on that track. It's more of a groove tune than it is a flash tune. I've already flashed out on everything else on the record, so I wanted to keep that one nice and simple. I mean, you can only throw on so much flashy guitar before it starts getting tiresome.

The intro to "Slidin' Home" sounds like a Dobro.
It does, doesn't it? But it's not. It's really Billy Windsor's Fender flattop guitar with GHS silk and bronze strings on it. I played it with a regular flat pick and fingers and used an Alka Seltzer bottle for a slide. And the other guitar that's underneath it is a Martin D–28 played with fingerpicks and a thumb pick, doing a Fats Domino–styled piano part. And there's a third guitar just playing straight rhythm. I wrote that tune. That's my New Orleans contribution. Actually, this tune was inspired by Chuck Berry's "Deep Feelin'," which he played on pedal steel. And the tune "Pretty Blue" is like an old Bill Doggett tune "Honky Tonk." I just love those major sevenths against dominant changes. That's what "Pretty Blue" is—basically an E, D Major seventh progression. To me, that's the coolest sound in the world.

What happened to your old guitar, that great '53 Fender Telecaster that you played for years and years.
Well, Fender built me an exact duplicate of it so I traded my old Telecaster for a gorgeous '34 Ford Sedan. That's my other passion, vintage cars and hot rods. I work on cars all the time. In fact, I actually stopped playing guitar for a couple of years and did nothing but drink beer and work on old Fords. Anyway, I went to the Fender factory last year and brought my '53 Tele. And Mike Stevens, the head luthier at Fender, built this duplicate for me. Now Fender is releasing a whole line of these guitars. They're calling them the Danny Gatton Telemaster. It's a one-piece swamp ash body, a bit lighter than northern ash. The body weighs about four pounds and the necks come with no finish on them at all. I hate finish on a neck. I much prefer just bare wood. There's 22 frets on this new model, which gives me a high D. Most Teles only go up to a D flat. And they come equipped with Joe Barden pickups, which are side-by-side humbuckings. They have a tremendous capacity for power while still retaining the inherent integrity of the Telecaster tone. I mean, these are the Mercedes Benz of guitar pickups. So this Telemaster with these Joe Barden pickups is one hot guitar. The pinstriping makes it look like a Danelectro Longhorn. And for fret markers they've got cubit zirconiums, which are synthetic diamonds. They can pick up a candlelight from across the river, which is perfect for playing in a dark nightclub. Sometimes when you're on stage you can't see the fret markers, but you always see them on this guitar. This thing is really the finest instrument I've ever owned. They are all handmade and they're quite expensive. They list for $2,400.

Any other unique items on this guitar?
Yeah, the tone and volume knobs are unusual. The volume pot is even from zero to 10, the tone pot comes on at three, so you can get those great wah-wah effects by manipulating the tone pot with your little finger. And the toggle switches are bent over on purpose. Sometimes when you're playing fast and you try to reach the toggle switch, you might accidentally turn the volume knob down going for it. So with the switch bent over, you can reach it with the tip of your finger without turning the knob down.

Did you play your new Danny Gatton Telemaster on this album?
I used it on everything except the rockabilly tune, "Elmira Street Boogie." That's my '54 Gibson ES–295, which I think may be Scotty Moore's guitar, but I can't prove it. It's really old and beat up and sounds great for rockabilly. I used to use it a lot when I worked with Robert Gordon. [Gatton appears on Gordon's *Are You Gonna Be the One*, RCA, 1980, and *Too Fast to Live, Too Young to Die*, RCA, 1982.]

How did you get that cool slap-back sound on that track?
It's just a little Boss echo pedal. We re-did the guitar parts on the tune and I turned the volume control on the bass pickup down to 7½ because I was wanting a more authentic Scotty Moore kind of tone. So I got the sound that I liked on it, but actually it sounds more like a Telecaster than an ES–295.

Have you always played Fender Telecaster guitars?
No, I actually always played Gibsons up until 1971. I still have a '61 triple pickup Les Paul Custom, but I don't play it much. But I really admire the design of a Telecaster. It's like a Model T Ford, simple yet indestructible. I like to take guitars apart to see how they're put together. I get them from friends around the area. One of my neighbors down the road found a '56 Telecaster that had been up in his attic for decades. He knew I played guitar so he gave it to me to fix up. I do a lot of that. I fix 'em up, keep 'em, or trade 'em for car parts. I actually had a guitar repair business back in 1973. I did a lot of work on Roy Buchanan's guitars. I like to tinker with tools like that, either on guitars or cars.

How many cars do you have?
Seven, all Fords. I have a '32 coupe, a '34 half-ton panel truck, a '34 big truck, a junked '34 four-door sedan, a super nice '34 four-door sedan—the one that I traded my '53 Telecaster for. I also have a '54 coupe and a '56 Crown Victoria. Anything up to about '57 in Fords, I love. After that, they don't do anything for me at all. Chevies I like up to '63 and they don't do anything for me after that. I just like old things. I'm an old guy. I'm entitled to like old things. I live in an old house. I have old cars, got old guitars—except for that new one, but that looks old. People can't believe that neck is brand new. It already looks worn and the neck actually feels like an old neck. Edges are real sharp on new necks and they don't feel good. You have to sand them down a bit, so I round them off with a nail file.

What do you hope to record in the future?
Well, this first album was a sampler of different things that I do. I hope in the future to branch out and do a straight rockabilly record, a straight jazz record, a straight country record, and a B–3 trio album with Groove Holmes. But first we'll have to see how this one sells.

JAZZBOS

KEITH JARRETT

DAVID SANBORN

WYNTON MARSALIS

JIMMY SMITH

JOE HENDERSON

TONY WILLIAMS

STEVE COLEMAN & BRANFORD MARSALIS

LARRY CORYELL

JOHN MCLAUGHLIN

DAVID MURRAY

© 1986 EBET ROBERTS

KEITH JARRETT

MY FIRST PERSONAL ENCOUNTER with Keith Jarrett went well enough, given his enfant terrible rep and the fact that he had already dissed me 14 years earlier in a phone interview when I was a young pup reviewing music for *The Milwaukee Journal* back in 1976. Apparently, something I had said offended His Highness during that phoner. I think it may have been the second or third question. There was a pause on the line, then an exasperated, "I don't understand these questions! Are you really aware of my music!" Aware, yes. Worshipful, no. While many were believing the hype, buying into the whole touchy-feely aspect of Jarrett's arched-back, cathartic gesturing, and uninhibited moaning tendencies in performance, I always regarded such theatrics with a healthy dose of skepticism. Sure, sure, the guy was deep—dealing with the inner whatever in some attempt to dredge up the pure spirit of improvisation.... "Going into the cave to come up with the light," as he called it. But beneath that noble intent lurked an arrogant artiste with a huge sense of entitlement who was given to scolding audiences for coughing, though not above mewling or gurgling audibly (and disturbingly) during a particularly inspired passage, if the spirit so moved him.

And yet, there's no denying his prodigious output or his occasionally profound statements. So I took the assignment from *Jazz Times* as a challenge, if not a privilege. I remember riding out to

Jarrett's rural hideaway in the woods of western New Jersey, near Delaware Water Gap, Pennsylvania. It was at the height of Desert Storm mania and everybody (outside of New York City) was tying a yellow ribbon around some damn tree in hopes of "our boys" finally coming home. Jarrett was gracious and forthcoming, certainly unaware of any slight he may have dished me two decades earlier. And I entered into the spirit of the thing with an open mind and no personal agenda of my own, other than the task of gathering information and a few scenic tidbits. The piece came out well. It was only later when I wrote a scathing appraisal of Jarrett's *Bye Bye Blackbird*—making note of his rather annoying habit of singing-chirping-gurgling like Curly Howard of the Three Stooges as he played—that Keith started sharpening his ax. He and his manager, Stephen Cloud, barraged the magazine with hostile letters, inciting a bevy of rebuttals from readers who also found his "singing" to be rather disruptive of the fine music being made by the trio.

Oh well, add Jarrett's name to the growing list of musicians who hate my guts—Pat Metheny, Pat Martino, Ron Carter. But that's another story, or three.

MARCH 1, 1991

Like a musical chameleon, Keith Jarrett keeps changing his colors. He is constantly shifting modes, allowing different kinds of music to affect him, letting different disciplines emerge. Jarrett will jump from risk-taking, soul-searching solo piano improvisations (most recently *Dark Intervals*, ECM, 1988, and *Paris Concert*, ECM, 1990) to more methodical studies of Bach (*Well-Tempered Clavier, Book I*, ECM, 1988, and *Goldberg Variations*, ECM, 1989, are current examples). Then he'll shift gears again and come out swinging jazz standards with drummer Jack DeJohnette and bassist Gary Peacock (beginning with *Standards, Vol. 1 and 2*, ECM, 1985; followed by *Standards Live*, ECM, 1987; *Still Live*, ECM, 1988; and the trio's latest offering, *Tribute*, ECM, 1989).

And there are yet more sides to this complex and easily-misunderstood enigma. His recordings of organ improvisations (*Hymns/Spheres*, ECM, 1976, and *Invocations/Moth and the Flame*, ECM, 1987), clavichord improvisations (*Book of Ways*, ECM, 1988) and the sacred piano music of mystic philosopher G. I. Gurdjieff (*Sacred Hymns*, ECM, 1980) all reveal different layers of his musical makeup. Jarrett has also tackled such challenging projects as Arvo Pärt's *Frates*, which he recorded with violinist Gidon Kremer; Lou Harrison's *Piano Concerto*, written specifically for him and performed with the New Japan Philharmonic conducted by Naoto Otomo; and Alan Hohvaness' 1946 work *Lousadvak* for piano and orchestra featuring Dennis Russell Davies conducting the American Composers Orchestra.

But perhaps his most deeply personal work to date is *Spirits* (ECM, 1985), an intuitive musical invocation recorded by Jarrett alone at his home in which he plays guitar, saxophone, flutes, recorders, piano, and various ethnic percussion instruments.

This apparent jazz/classical schism has been a part of Jarrett's personality for the past 25 years. Born on May 8, 1945, in Allentown, Pennsylvania, he began playing piano at age three and undertook classical studies throughout his youth, appearing as a child prodigy in programs at Philadelphia's Academy of Music and at Madison Square Garden. He began formal studies in composition at age 15 before moving to Boston to attend the Berklee College of Music. While Jarrett was still in his late teens, arrangements were made for him to study in Paris with the great pedagogue Nadia Boulanger, but he passed on those plans in favor of moving to New York to play jazz.

After a tentative period of sitting in at New York jazz spots, Jarrett toured briefly with Art Blakey. From 1966 to 1969, he toured and recorded with the Charles Lloyd Quartet, a seminal crossover ensemble that drew on elements of blues, gospel, rock, and jazz for an appealing blend that won favor with audiences all over the world. In 1970, Jarrett joined Miles Davis' groundbreaking electric group, remaining for one year and appearing on *Live/Evil* (Columbia, 1970) and *Live at the Fillmore* (Columbia, 1970).

Around that time, Jarrett formed his own trio with Charlie Haden (Ornette Coleman's bassist) and Paul Motian (Bill Evans' former drummer), soon expanding to a quartet with the addition of tenor saxophonist Dewey Redman (another Ornette veteran). The group became one of the foremost acoustic jazz ensembles of the 1970s and was documented on the Impulse and Columbia labels. In 1971, Jarrett began his recording collaboration with producer Manfred Eicher and ECM (Editions of Creative Music) Records, the visionary independent German record label that brought an entirely new aesthetic to the recording of improvised music.

Throughout the '70s, Jarrett split his time between his American quartet and his Scandinavian quartet (with bassist Palle Danielsson, drummer Jon Christensen, and saxophonist Jan Garbarek). His landmark improvised solo piano recordings, beginning with *Solo Concerts* (ECM, 1973) helped to redefine the role of the piano in contemporary music. His big breakthrough album in that context, *The Köln Concert* (ECM, 1975), has sold several million copies worldwide, making it the best selling solo piano record ever released.

In 1984, Jarrett announced to a Boston audience that he would discontinue his solo piano concerts because he was discouraged that albums like *The Köln Concert* had inadvertently spawned the careers of such New Age piano tinklers as George Winston. To this day, Jarrett refers to New Age as "lobotomy music." As it turned out, it was only an idle threat. Jarrett has since returned to his solo piano outlet with the same passion and daring he exhibited in the mid-1970s.

I interviewed Keith Jarrett a couple of weeks after a solo piano concert at Avery Fisher Hall in New York. It was an unusually warm February afternoon. After a tour of his massive garage, which has been converted into a fully-equipped recording studio, we sat outside on the porch of his home, tucked away in the woods of western New Jersey near the Pennsylvania border. The sound of trickling water from a nearby creek and birds singing in the trees provided a pleasant backdrop to our conversation. I began with a reference to a 1988 piece in *Stereophile* magazine where Keith reviewed a recording of the Bach *Fantasias* by harpsichordist Igor Kipnis, who in turn reviewed Jarrett's clavichord project, *Book of Ways*.

I was impressed by the clarity of your writing in that review you did for Stereophile. *I thought that was an interesting concept, having each of you review the other's work.*
Well, I did, too. I wouldn't have done it otherwise. I'm generally disappointed in most reviewers' priorities. The things they choose to focus on are often not the things that affect the music. So I tried to do what I felt was missing in the world of music criticism.

I was amused by your reference to pianist John Lewis at the end of your review, where you wrote, "Don't ask me what I think of John Lewis' Well-Tempered Clavier."
Well, it just doesn't make a good name for the music to have people *dabbling* in things. Jazz musicians are often dabbling without knowing what they're dabbling in. When they get out of the field of jazz, all that does is hurt the serious intent of presenting Bach to an audience.

Oscar Peterson did a record where he played swinging interpretations of Bach [Oscar Peterson Live!, Pablo, 1986]. And then there's the Swingle Singers, who have done swinging renditions of Bach [Jazz Sebastian Bach, Philips, 1961].
Oh yeah, well, I don't even consider them jazz. [laughter] I don't know what I would call them. Clever singers, I guess. I think Bobby McFerrin did something, too—a jazz version of one of Bach's masses or something. To me, it's a waste of time, for one thing.

Ellington also did an album of swing versions of classical pieces [Three Suites, Columbia, 1960].
Yeah, but he didn't deal with something as serious as Bach. He used appropriate vehicles, things that

were already lighthearted and on the edge of being popular, like *The Nutcracker Suite*. So Duke could take that and make something that was a very original jazz album. But he didn't try to mess with Bach.

Is Bach sacred ground?
No, it isn't that there's anything sacred about it. It's just that it's all there. In fact, with Bach it's all there on the paper. You almost don't even need to have recorded versions of his stuff, you can just see the brilliance in the scores, although not everyone can read music. Everything that he wanted is so clearly portrayed on paper that to take it and modify it is like modifying a car to make it worse. It has the best of everything but you modify it because you want a custom car. So you start taking off all this perfect stuff and putting on some shit, you know? It doesn't make any sense. And that's my view of these takes on Bach. I mean, why modify something that's already perfect?

Did you record the Goldberg Variations *in your home studio?*
No, the recording of that was done in Japan in a beautiful, little, tiny concert hall in the mountains, not near any roads or anything. We had absolutely no problem with noise there. We could've recorded at any time of day. And it was winter so it was even quieter because the snow was all over everything like a blanket. That was a wonderful place to do that project.

When you undertake a harpsichord project like that does it require a certain amount of woodshedding to get used to the instrument? Is the touch very different than the piano?
It's so radically different that I consider them two entirely different instruments. There's no similarity between how you have to get the music out from harpsichord and piano. None. There's no touch control on a harpsichord, and that's the whole method on piano. There's no pedal on a harpsichord. There's really no ability to color the sound at all, except the instrument's own ability. You can't emphasize any notes. So we're talking about different universes instead of just different keyboard instruments.

Is the fingering on a harpsichord more physically demanding than on a piano?
In the sense that the keys go down very easily and when they pluck, they always pluck the same volume. In other words, you can't make a fluff on a harpsichord. It's a mistake, an outright error. It's never just something you can overlook. Because when you accidentally push down an unwanted key, that key is playing as loud as anything else you're playing.

It sounds kind of like a synthesizer in a way, in that there's no touch sensitivity.
The thing is, though, it's plucking a string. It's even more different than synthesizer and piano are. Because when you push the key down, you are literally ready to pluck a string. When you push it past that point, it plucks. You're not touching the end of something, you're plucking in the motion of the string. So it's closer to lute playing or guitar playing than it is to synthesizer. It's just that you're using a key to pluck the string. You can feel the tension of the strings being plucked. So you really do feel closer to the sound that you're making than even the piano. And a piano is closer than a synthesizer. With synthesizer, when you make electronic contact, that's it. You don't feel anything.

What type of preparation did you go through before recording the Goldberg Variations *on harpsichord?*
Well, I had been playing that music on piano since I was probably 20 years old, so I was very familiar with it. But the day that I decided I should record it on that instrument instead of piano, I stopped all piano playing and spent several months focusing strictly on the harpsichord, which is what I always do when I'm going to record a harpsichord project.

In fact, I just did another one last week. It's the second book of the *Well-Tempered Clavier*. I did the first on piano and the second one will be on harpsichord, which I guess is an historic thing in itself.

But we didn't think of that. My next harpsichord recording will be in the fall, which will be Bach's *French Suites* and Bach's *Sonatas for Viola da Gamba and Harpsichord.* So I'll spend from the end of July to the recording date, whenever that is, concentrating strictly on harpsichord and on Bach. And that project will be recorded here in my home studio.

The clavichord, which you played on Book of Ways, *is another unique keyboard instrument.*
Yes, the clavichord is entirely different. That is actually more touch sensitive than a piano. So on the touch sensitivity scale, the clavichord is on one side of the piano and the harpsichord is on the opposite end. The clavichord is a funny instrument. It's so soft that you couldn't hear it if you were sitting six feet away from it. I have one in the house that I play from time to time.

And on Hymns/Spheres *you played what sounded like a giant pipe organ.*
It was a small organ, believe it or not, in a giant church. The monastery is a big room and the pipes have a lot of room to make their sound. It actually was less than a full keyboard and the stops were all around both sides. They're all manual stops. With electronic stops, if you push a stop in or out, there's no halfway. You're just doing something mechanical. It's either on or off. But with these authentic baroque organs, they didn't yet get to that point, so you're pulling a mechanical lever that is gradually letting the air into different chambers. And that's what I like about those instruments. That's what makes the quarter tones possible.

When you come off an intensive period of harpsichord and go back to playing piano, does it require a lot of practice to get your chops back?
Well, if I were jumping from a harpsichord project of written music to a piano recital of written music, then I would have to do the same kind of woodshedding, just to get the music under my fingers. But if I'm jumping from harpsichord to improvising on piano, I can just get in gradually and let the music work its way into my fingers in performance, which is sometimes interesting. People don't know I'm using the concert hall as a practice room. [laughter] But sometimes that's the way it is.

Isn't that what Miles Davis said to his sidemen, "I'm paying you to practice on the bandstand."
Something like that.

Were you using the concert hall as a practice room at your Avery Fisher Hall performance a couple of weeks ago?
Well, that was the third solo concert I did in February. I did February 1 in San Francisco, February 4 in Calgary, and February 17 in New York. Before the San Francisco concert, I literally did not sit at a piano or touch a piano for two or three months. And I just went on stage, did the sound check for two or three minutes, had dinner, and went back and played a concert. So I had primed myself, in a way, for that New York concert. But it doesn't really work that way, musically. The music could've been better in San Francisco. There's really no rule how that works.

How did you feel about the New York solo performance?
It was good. I guess on a scale of one to ten I would say that was around seven or eight.

What about the two different halves, before and after intermission?
I don't remember clearly. I felt that the first 15 or 20 minutes of the first half was something very strong, but the problem was everyone was coughing. So my concentration was shaken somewhat. I don't understand why the coughing always happens during the most delicate spots. You never hear anyone cough during drum solos. [laughter]

There happened to be a virus going around at that time. I think a lot of people who came to the concert had colds.
Yeah, but still it happened in the very beginning, not in the middle or near the end. And the very beginning is the most critical part. If I needed the audience to choose a time to be quiet, I would say, "OK, I don't care what you do after the first 15 minutes. But the first 15 minutes I don't want to hear anything." Because I don't know what's going to happen anymore than they do when I sit down at the piano. I'm just working it out in the moment. So that first 15 minutes could've been a lot more intense, I could've gotten into that space stronger. And I don't mean play louder—just musically it would've been even better without that coughing. So I remember those first 15 minutes as being the critical time that determined whether the whole concert was going to be a 7 or an 8 or a 9.

How did the concert before that go?
Thirteen days before that, in Calgary, it was probably the best concert I had played in the last five or six years. It certainly was better than the Köln concert in terms of content. But you never know. I wasn't really primed for that as a pianist either. I hadn't really played much the previous week and I didn't sleep the night before the concert. I wasn't really in good shape at all but there it was, the music just said hello. It's not always under my control.

Do you feel like you've become more tolerant of these distractions, that you've mellowed?
No, it's not mellowing, but I know what you mean. It's actually... People used to think I was frustrated when I would stop. I would say that now I'm truly frustrated because I don't stop. It's the reverse of what people think: "Oh, he's in a better mood than he used to be in because he doesn't let this bother him anymore." But it never bothered me personally, I didn't have anything against the audience. I wasn't making enemies out of people making noise. I just felt that I needed to advise them that what they came to hear would deteriorate by their actions, not just by my inattention but *their* inattention. But at a certain point I must've said to myself, "Hey, this is just not working, talking to the audience." First of all, they don't want me to say a word. Secondly, I want to play the piano, I don't want to talk about this either. It's more of an existential frustration. So I've resigned myself to an attitude of just: "Hey, man, they're gonna cough and I'm gonna try to do my best here."

I've read that you are highly sensitive to the environment, that you can read the aura of a concert hall and feel the energy of the audience.
I wish I couldn't, you know? I'd love to be able to say: "No, I can't." [laughter] But it's true, which is why the coughing bothers me so much.

How do you assess the New York audiences?
The New York audiences, I noticed over the last three or four times I've played here, seem to be in some way deteriorating. I don't know how to explain that. I don't mean that I think they're bad audiences but there was a time when they were getting better and better at letting the space open up and the music happen. And it wasn't because the music was that much better or worse or different, it was *them.* And now I'm sensing this loss of identity or something, like they don't know who they are or what they're there for anymore. They hope something will distract them.... I don't know, it's kind of a nebulous feeling I'm getting. Avery Fisher is a tradition now for me. I play there every year, so I can kind of gauge the response. It's the same room, same piano often, so the sonics don't change. But I'm talking about this general open feeling on the part of the audience, the thing that can let the music really start to happen. That's deteriorating in New York. And it's not deteriorating, it seems, in any other city I play in. I just get this funny feeling in New York. And I don't just get it from the audience, I get it from walking around the city as well. There's a crumbling feeling that I've been sensing.

The last five years have been the beginning of the new Dark Ages in New York.
Yes, it's like they don't even know what they are hoping for anymore, what values they have anymore. And this is where progress has gotten us. That's why I'm out here in the woods. [laughter]

I was kind of surprised that you did two encores at the Avery Fisher Hall concert.
Well, one of the good things about doing so few concerts is that each one takes on greater meaning. You really feel like doing them when you sit down at the piano. I used to do 40 solo piano concerts a year. Can you imagine trying to come up with something totally fresh one night, flying to the next city on the tour, and having to come up with something completely fresh again? It gets very taxing. But pacing myself now allows me to get into each one on a much deeper level.

I was also surprised that you came out and played a real earthy blues for the second encore. It seemed to immediately change the environment of that very prestigious room.
Well, the blues is definitely good for that. The trio just played in Vienna in a hall that's considered to be one of the world's best concert halls. It was the first non-classical music in the 150 or so years this hall has existed. So we played a blues at the end of the thing, and it was pretty freaky to realize—the room is ornate and Mozartian and doesn't look like anybody should ever or had ever played the blues in it. The audience couldn't believe it either. It was really like being in a surrealistic movie.

Were people shouting out encouragement from the audience?
Yes, it was one of the best, most exciting concerts, the best audience reaction I ever saw for the trio. But I told the promoters, "Now, don't think that just because this trio played this room that you can get any other jazz group in this room, because it's not gonna work. If it wasn't for the flexibility of the guys in the trio, we would've bombed. We all had to play our dynamics way down and still get the intensity out of it. I think Jack will always remember that night because being a drummer he's used to occasionally having to be restrained, but this was a radical thing. We all had to be playing chamber music in there because the sound was flying all over the place. And because we had to do the whole concert like that, Jack really got into it. He started inhabiting this low dynamic range and he knew how great this was. He was hardly touching his drums.

Was he playing a lot of brushes?
No, he's just got a great touch, so he can pull back. It was the only room I ever played with the trio where I felt I was playing too hard and would have to pull back.

Were you pleased with the new trio album, Tribute?
Yes, but the trio is so much better than its recordings. Amazingly better. I can immediately play you one tune from the second last concert on the European tour, which was only recorded on cassette, and you'd see what I mean.... [laughter] Fucking burning! And not just burning, but full of ideas. I'm not putting down the albums we've done but I always feel—whoever I'm talking to, if they haven't heard the trio in certain concert situations, they haven't heard it at its best. So if you extrapolate from what you do know, you just have to add like another 90% onto it. It's kind of hard to imagine. I don't even realize how good some of the things are. I know how good *Tribute* is but I can go into my little cassette tape file and pull something out and I'll be sitting there thinking: "I don't believe that!"

So who decides what gets put out?
Well, we don't record everything professionally. These are documentary tapes I'm talking about, just cassettes. But there's sort of an unwritten rule in the music world that when the professional tape recorders are running, it's never the very best time.

It's true. I just saw Jackie McLean at the Village Vanguard recently and his new record doesn't even come close to what he did that night.
Right, and I think people ought to be aware of that. I mean, the average listener should know that. That's why I always say the trio is better than the recordings. Because people tend to look at the history of a musician through their recordings, which is not correct. If you didn't see them live, there's a big gap. And if you only saw them live once, it doesn't count. The records are important because they tell a story, but it's only one of the stories. And it certainly isn't the whole story of the trio. The story of the trio is also what was *not* recorded. Unless we capture one day on the exact moment when we play the peak that we've ever played, I'll always have to say that the trio is better than what you're hearing on records.

This whole concept for Tribute—*dedicating songs to particular jazz artists—was that something you had in mind before the recording or was it an afterthought?*
Definitely an afterthought. And this is not a list of my influences or any silly thing like that. Each tune rang a bell of either a player or a singer that I remember who affected me over a long period of time. I mean, Anita O'Day is not one of my favorite vocalists and yet her version of "Ballad of the Sad Young Men" is what I remember. I don't even know if I've ever heard it sung by anyone else.

When did you first hear it?
Oh, long ago, I guess when I was a student at Berklee. It was on a Gary McFarland big band recording.

So you have specific memories of all these tunes?
No, not all of them. There's a different kind of way each name popped up. I remember hearing Nancy Wilson sing "Little Girl Blue" when I was younger, and I always remembered that version for some reason. I think it was with George Shearing and strings. But, for instance, I never heard Charlie Parker play "Just in Time." It was just that our version, particularly the tempo, reminded me of how Bird would've done it.

Super up-tempo and swinging real hard.
Yeah, but we've played it five times as swinging as it is on that record. [laughter] So that tune wasn't a question of emulating some version of his. Just listening back to the tape, the tempo said Bird to me.

What was it about your version of "Lover Man" that brought Lee Konitz to mind?
That's a good question. I'm very familiar with the way Lee plays and I guess I could somehow imagine him playing "Lover Man" that way. As it turns out, he plays that song a lot but I didn't know that when I decided to dedicate this song to him. I didn't know it was a special tune that he likes to play a lot. In all of these cases, I didn't think about what was ringing the bells, and I didn't have a list of names that I wanted to pay tribute to. This version of "Lover Man" just said Lee Konitz to me. I think that Lee is somebody who deserves more credit than he's ever gotten. He's not one of the guys who comes up in conversation all the time, but his contribution to jazz is immeasurable. There's only a handful of guys who play ideas. And there's a bunch who play notes. Guys that play notes, I don't consider to be improvisers. They're playing finger patterns and habits and hip licks and things they heard. But Lee Konitz and that whole Lennie Tristano side of jazz was trying to bring out a way of playing ideas that didn't even always have to coincide with what the chords suggested. And that was a big innovation in those times. Lee was playing at a time when every other alto playing was trying to sound like Charlie Parker, and he was sounding like Lee Konitz. That's quite an accomplishment.

Two of the songs on this Tribute *album really capture the essence of the guys you have listed—Coleman Hawkins on "Smoke Gets in Your Eyes" and Miles on "All of You."*
Yes, but that was just a coincidence. I didn't have any plan to play those tunes that way. I wasn't thinking about Coleman Hawkins when I was playing "Smoke Gets in Your Eyes" or Miles when I was playing "All of You." Those names came to me later. There were reviewers in Europe who had this elaborate theory about how I did this album. They mentioned the theory to me in an interview and I said, "Oh, boy, I'm gonna have to tell you something. It was all casual, man. Nothing was planned ahead of time."

What about your version of "I Hear a Rhapsody" reminded you of Jim Hall?
Well, Jim and Bill Evans played that on their duet album, *Undercurrent* [Blue Note, 1959]. Jim Hall and Lee Konitz are two people I really admire. And I guess I was happy to be able to find a reason to put their names on this album. Jim's knowledge of the instrument, just his knowledge of all the possible voicings you can find, has always amazed me. And both those guys are not egomaniacs. They play with a kind of thoughtfulness that I admire.

Who came up with this concept for Tribute?
I just called Manfred [Eicher, founder of ECM Records] one day and told him my idea and he basically said, "Good, let's do it." And besides, we can't keep calling these trio albums *Still Live, Still Still Live,* or *Still Live Again* like it was *Rocky IV* or something. So I came up with *Tribute.*

What do you feel is unique about the trio?
I think this trio is unique in the sense that we don't consider ourselves a permanent band but we have stayed together. And the only reason we have stayed together is that every time we play a little bunch of concerts the music jumps to another level that it was never at before. Whenever that happens, it's a signal that we shouldn't disband. Each tour I'm thinking to myself, "This could be the last tour. We might feel like we did what we should do and put an end to it." But every tour we find some new dimension that we add to. It connects. And on the last tour it went like—*whoosh!* It took off and we didn't even know what to say. We were—flabbergasted. [laughter] At the end of the tour Gary and I were saying, "Jesus! I can't believe this." I mean, we're always aware that it's limited. It's just three guys playing standards, and yet the music is still going up and up.

Your relationship with Jack goes back to the Charles Lloyd band. When did you first start playing with Gary Peacock?
Well, of course, I knew Gary's playing from '64, at least. But Gary and I didn't play together until his 1977 album *Tales of Another* [ECM]. It was the first time Jack, Gary, and I played together.

And you felt the chemistry immediately?
No. I mean, I looked forward to the session and I liked some of the stuff on it, but it just didn't occur to me for a couple years after that that there was something to do with these guys. And then when it did finally dawn on me, that I should try that combination with standards, I was by no means thinking of making it a working band. Just recording, once. And then it just gradually insinuated itself into our lives.

Peacock is great, as a soloist and as a force for momentum in the band. I couldn't think of another bass player for this trio.
I can't think of another anything for the trio, that's one of the things that makes it so special. You can't imagine—maybe someone can—but I just can't imagine replacing anybody. It would work. I mean,

music would be made. But all of a sudden some giant change would come about, some compensation. People would have to start compensating, and we're not doing that at all. We're just playing. Another great thing about this trio is nobody in this trio is against doing anything. There seems to be less biases among the three of us than any other two people I've ever worked with. With the old quartet [Paul Motian on drums, Charlie Haden on bass, Dewey Redman on tenor sax], I had to write the tunes knowing Dewey was playing them, knowing what he liked and didn't like, knowing that Charlie didn't like to do certain things, knowing in Paul's case—Paul was cool but Paul still had his unique stamp that didn't change. And that was hard, man. To make sure everyone else was happy and still do something I wanted to hear? Very hard. With the trio, I know those biases don't exist. Because what happens when we play is whatever is happening happens. If something starts swinging, it starts swinging. If something gets free, everybody's hearing that and doing that.

Gary's never been in a band in his life that's willing to swing like this trio. And he's in heaven when we play funky. And yet, if someone thought about Gary Peacock's history they would not see him as a funky bass player. But it's only because the context that he was in demanded different things of him. Sometimes Jack and I have to actually slow him down, like, "Wait a minute! Not so soon! We just started the piece!" [laughter] But that's... I don't care. If something's going to be a problem, let it be a problem on the side of enthusiasm, not on the side of: "Hey, I don't do that." I had nothing but that sort of attitude from other musicians I worked with until we formed this trio. In Miles' band, Miles exerts a presence that's strong enough that everybody knows that they've got a role. They're flexible in it but everyone knows what Miles thinks about sound. But the trio is... Nobody's even putting that on anybody. There's no one will being exerted in the trio.

Does the fact that Jack also plays piano and you also play drums make it even more sympathetic?
Probably from Jack's point of view since that means he knows something about the structure of some of the tunes or the words to them, having also had to learn them the same way that anybody does. And it also makes him sensitive to ballad playing because that's important for a drummer. So many drummers think they don't have anything to do during a ballad, that they're just waiting for the up-tempo thing to come along. So they just cruise through the ballads. But Jack loves playing ballads.

Do you have any club dates planned with the trio?
No, it just doesn't work to do that anymore. This trio has pretty many fans now and if we play a club, we'd have to do a rather long engagement, two or three sets a night. And we put so much energy into each tune now, as you can probably hear, that it would be physically impossible to do two or three sets a night for five nights. But we did the club circuit for as long as we could. We did it after anybody else in our position had stopped. We were still playing the Village Vanguard as late as 1985. I love that place. But the last time we played there, it was winter and there was a line around the corner and people were—I was afraid they'd be freezing out there waiting. So it isn't practical anymore. Plus, it just isn't enough money for us either. And furthermore, one thing that makes the trio fresh is not playing. So what happens in clubs is you end up playing so much you don't have the time to digest what you've done during the week-long engagement and you end up coming out of it not knowing what the hell, if anything, happened. I'm finding that when we play less frequently we have more to say. If we hear each other all the time, we know too much about how we play together, and it gets hard to be fresh that way.

So you probably don't do much rehearsing before the trio concerts.
We never rehearse. I think we might have rehearsed three times because we had some special ending or something we wanted to do with a tune. But we never do arrangements. One of the *New York Times* reviews of the trio at Avery Fisher a couple of years ago said something about "the arrangements

weren't coherent." And I showed it to Gary and Jack and they were giggling because *of course* they weren't coherent. We didn't have any, you know?

Can you explain the significance of the name of your publishing company, Cavelight Music?
I thought of it as Plato's classic story about the cave, if you know that. It's just an analogy of the world living in a cave and people thinking they know what light is even though they've never really seen it. It's just a literary analogy making a metaphorical point about waking up, I guess. People thinking they're awake and they still haven't even opened their eyes. And light always plays a role in my music, if you look at the titles I've used. There's been a tendency to use the word "light" a lot. And that connects with Gurdjieff because one of his main statements is that man is asleep and you can only do anything of any value when you're awake. But people are going around acting the part of being awake and not being really there. So there's the cave analogy again. But I think the actual story was someone went out and saw that there was light. The world was outside this cave and he came back and tried to describe it, but no one believed him.

What do you think is missing in the curriculum of music schools today?
[laughter] Hmmmm... I think perhaps what's missing is non-musicians. There should be a connecting point between life and music. But music schools are craft schools and they base their rhetoric on the science of sound and notes. So there's a missing connection between life force and music. I guess there should be somebody in residence who is not a musician, who musicians would have to deal with somehow in a class or something and not talk music. Too many schools are caught up in the progress trip. Consequently, you're not ending up with valuable musicians, you're ending up with proficient musicians, clever musicians. That way, you end up with the Swingle Singers or something worse— Rachmaninoff or Liszt. To say something important takes only a few well-chosen words. And in music, to say something important very often takes only a few well-chosen notes. How do you know which notes are the ones to choose? Well you can't talk to a musician who is a music teacher about that, unless they are also somehow into philosophy. And I guess that's what I mean. There should be philosophers at music schools.

I just met a guitarist who is doing clinics in what he calls "guitar synergistics," where he's teaching people how to develop the inner musician by doing things away from the instrument like yoga, meditation, how to breathe when you play...
I used to give workshops that were often on nonmusical topics and completely crazy ideas about messing with the natural desire to cool out. At these workshops, each person would play for everyone else in the room. There would be the guys who could play a lot of notes and there would be people who weren't very good players, and it almost always turned out that the people who couldn't play very well were the ones who were truly making music. And so I would ask the people in the room, "What did you experience? Is there some way you can concretely describe the difference between hearing this proficient guy and hearing this young lady who was technically limited but at the same time very expressive?" For me, it was easier to see who she was than to see who this other guy was.

Because he was hiding behind his technique?
Right, but what this guitarist you mentioned is suggesting is that there are techniques by which you can de-technique this other thing. Like the technique of yoga, the technique of meditation or whatever. And I'm saying I don't think that's really true. In the end, that's a progress illusion. Let's say someone comes to you and asks, "What's missing in my playing? I know I can play well but there's something missing." To describe what's missing is still to miss the point. The point is that he knows there's something missing and no one else can supply it, and no other technique can supply it. It means that

he has to become, I would say, ferocious with himself. And if a teacher could be ferocious with him and deny him technique, deny him any access to a technique that would cool him out, it would help his music. Because the music is not going to come from yoga, it's going to come from whoever's playing it. It's gonna come from him with or without these other techniques. The work that needs to be done can only be done by that guy.

The last time I visited the Berklee College of Music, I noticed that many of the students seemed obsessed with transcribing solos as opposed to creating music.
Well, you know, the reason I didn't allow *The Köln Concert* to be transcribed since 1975 is because when you look at the notes on paper, you have the illusion that you're seeing the music. And all these guys were saying, "Why don't you transcribe this? There are so many pianists that would love to play this." No they won't love to play this. They will start playing it and they will hate themselves. Because what's on the paper... The notes are there but you were hearing *me* on the recording, you weren't hearing the notes.

What can you tell me about the reclusive pianist John Coates?
Well, I used to sit in with him at this place called The Deerhead Inn, located in the small town of Delaware Water Gap, Pennsylvania. In fact, I kept my set of drums there and used to play with him on weekends. People have come up with these elaborate theories about me and John Coates. I don't know if they don't have anything better to do or they're bored or something, but they say things like, "We've just unearthed the fact that Johnny Coates and Keith Jarrett were friends. And that explains where Keith got some of his phrases from because we heard Johnny and it's obvious to us." And what they're saying really is they don't have anything better to do than to think up things like that. I mean, why is that necessarily true? We were very good friends and we're both pianists, but that doesn't mean that we rub off on each other. I would be playing drums with him most of the time so naturally I heard him playing piano. And some people have come to the immediate conclusion that since I heard him play, I would've used some things that he used. I think that's ridiculous. People never heard of the guy, then when they found out that I used to play at The Deerhead Inn with Johnny, they constructed this weave of nonsense.

It sounds like a case of some critics trying to unmask the enigma of Keith Jarrett.
Yeah. I mean, when he was playing well, he was a very good player. Anyway, I used to go there and play on weekends, around the time when I was playing with Charles Lloyd, when I was still in my 20s. It was a thing where I'd take my drums there and leave them there the whole summer and just play every weekend for free. Then I fell into guitar and started playing guitar there. And one night Stan Getz came in, a little inebriated, and we played a set. Afterward he asked me if I would play guitar with his band in Martinique. I played the game with him for a minute but then I said, "By the way, Stan, I'm really not a guitar player. My name is Keith Jarrett and I actually play piano." And he said, "Oh, I think I've heard of you."

I didn't know you played guitar.
Well, I don't anymore but I did. Until a couple of years ago I was still fooling around. Now I'm too busy with harpsichord and composing.

DAVID SANBORN

ALTO SAXOPHONIST DAVID SANBORN first registered ticks on my awareness meter with his 1975 debut album *Taking Off* (Warner Bros.). There was a fusion band in my hometown of Milwaukee named Sweetbottom that covered just about all the material on that great album, including the super funky "Duck Ankles." So I was well acquainted with Sanborn's music back then. As a charter member of The Brecker Brothers band, Sanborn had been on the scene since 1974 but he didn't make a real national splash until 1976 with his brief but urgent solo on David Bowie's hit, "Young Americans." There followed a whole slew of high profile studio session work for the likes of Stevie Wonder, James Taylor, and Linda Ronstadt and a featured spot on Gil Evans' album *Priestess* (Antilles, 1977). The 19-minute title track was a virtual showcase for Sanborn's signature alto rasp and plaintive cry. By the mid-1980s, David Sanborn was a bona fide superstar, as visible an artist as there was in crossover music. His playing became so popular and identifiable, in fact, that it spawned whole hordes of Sanborn clones, all affecting that same plaintive cry in hopes of connecting with record buyers.

While the imitation was flattering, it caused Sanborn to re-assess just what he had created. At the time of this interview for an August 1988 cover story in *Down Beat*, he seemed in a period of transition—pleased with his success but anxious to break through into some new musical territory that would reinvigorate him. For a couple of years he hosted perhaps the hippest syndicated music show on television since "The Sound of Jazz" aired in the '50s. The late, lamented "Night Music" was a gathering of eclectic souls from Sun Ra to Bootsy Collins, NRBQ, Sonny Rollins, and Dr. John, interspersed with vintage film footage of Slim Gaillard, Thelonious Monk, Fats Waller, and John Coltrane. Far too hip for the commercial world, it played to a rabid cult following before finally being yanked by the network in 1990. Sanborn threw everybody a curve with his experimental *Another Hand* (Elektra, 1991) and by guesting in 1992 on a Tim Berne album of Julius Hemphill compositions, *Diminutive Mysteries* (JMT, 1992). His album *Pearls* (Elektra, 1995) was a lush treatment of romantic standards with strings arranged by Johnny Mandel. Sanborn continues to play with authority and with one of the most immediately recognizable sounds in jazz. Suffice it to say, Sanborn has managed to parlay his singular voice into a cottage industry.

MAY 4, 1988

You can recognize it in an instant—the Sanborn Squeal. Couldn't fool nobody on a blindfold test with that. Or could you? So many Sanborn clones have come down the pike of late, appearing on everything from pop-jazz fare to jeans commercials on TV, that it's getting harder and harder to tell the rip-offs from the real deal. If you take the time to really listen, you can hear the truth. But a cursory twirl of the radio dial or channel selector might suggest that every commercial musician and would-be alto star out there is aping Sanborn's signature sound.

This is a situation that both befuddles and frustrates Dave. Of course, it's happened over and over again throughout the course of music. There have been Bird clones, Wes clones, Charlie Christian clones, Trane clones. But the humble Sanborn refuses to think of himself in the same company with those jazz greats. In fact, he's not comfortable being called a jazz musician at all.

On the eve of his 11th release for Warner Bros.—the typically funky, hard-blowing, and eminently well-crafted *Close-Up* (produced by Marcus Miller and co-produced by Ray Bardani)—Sanborn seems confused. There are long pauses between his sentences, and occasional sighs. Clearly, the man is at odds with his current direction. What will come out of this sudden change of heart is uncertain. He hinted at getting away from the tyranny of drum machines and studio manipulation by embracing an all-acoustic context. Meanwhile, he continues to make regular guest appearances on "Late Night with David Letterman," featured in the house band alongside Paul Shaffer, Will Lee, Anton Fig, and Sid McGinnis. And he continues to broadcast his weekly program "The Jazz Show," which is syndicated on the NBC radio network. There are also plans for a TV show this fall, which Sanborn will co-host with "Saturday Night Live" regular Dennis Miller. [Miller actually never got on board this project. Sanborn's co-host in that first season was the wry British musician Jules Holland.] This music and comedy hour, to be seen on Sunday evenings beginning in late September, is tentatively called "Sunday Night." [Eventually it was called "Night Music."] Sanborn will lead a house band consisting of Marcus Miller on bass, Omar Hakim on drums, Hiram Bullock on guitar, and Don Grolnick on keyboards, while interacting with a wide variety of musical guests. But that's down the road. For now, Dave's got some other things to get off his chest.

We spoke in Sanborn's Upper West Side apartment in Manhattan, a day before he had to split for London to perform at a gala birthday bash for Nelson Mandela.

You've made a mark over the years in the sense that you have a sound that is immediately identifiable.
I guess I have. And I don't mean to be naive about it or humble, but I guess I have. It's a little bit uncomfortable for me to think about that because I don't think of myself as an innovator in the slightest. When people tell me that it's hard for me to grasp what that means. I think more than any-

thing else, I happened to be the only guy around who... I got a lot of exposure and I think a lot of it just happened to be luck. The fact is that I was an alto player playing mostly in a pop and R&B idiom, and there weren't a lot of people doing that in the early-1970s. And I think just because of the exposure that I got with David Bowie [*Young Americans,* RCA, 1975] or with James Taylor [*How Sweet It Is*] or with Stevie Wonder [*Talking Book,* Tamla, 1972], I was very lucky, because I'm not doing anything new. I never was doing anything particularly new or innovative. I was just distilling a lot of my influences. I was always trying to sound like Cannonball or Phil Woods or Jackie McLean or people that I was listening to.

But you have established a signature quality. That sax riff on "Young Americans" really stuck in my mind. Not the line so much as the pure sound of it.
Well, I think that is really what you try to do as a player, or in any kind of form of self expression, is that you find yourself. And then you refine your craft but whatever comes out is you. And you practice. When I said I was trying to sound like Cannonball, what I meant was I would listen to Cannonball but I wouldn't try to play those licks. I couldn't do that because that wasn't me. It's like the reason why I'm not a bebop player. I mean, I can affect some mannerisms of bebop and I relate to the time feel. And I understand a certain amount of it, but me trying to play that is like, "Why?" It's like what we were talking about earlier, when you hear Bobby McFerrin sing with a band—it's not that he's not great there, too, but what makes him distinctive and makes you really notice him is the stuff he does on his own, solo. You step out of your idiom—your area, your focus of expression—to learn and to grow. But what you come back to is your... I don't want to use the word "art" because I don't necessarily think of what I do as art.

It's your voice.
You come back to your voice. But what I'm trying to get across is that whatever your avenue is, whatever you have to say to the world, comes down to a pretty basic thing—it's your voice. As a painter, as a sculptor, as a writer. Hunter Thompson and John Updike—it's their voice, it's their point of view. And in a more abstract way that's true of music. It's somebody's point of view about the world. It's all their influences and you can maybe hear all those influences, but you distill all those influences and they come through, hopefully, in a very subconscious way. They make you what you are and they give you a connection to the tradition. But your voice is your point of view about that tradition.

So you're more interested in personal statement, whether it's coming from Albert King or Ornette Coleman.
Exactly. That's one of the great things about music to me is that it's somebody's personal statement. Ultimately, that's what you end up with. You refine your craft, but the object is to express yourself. And if you got nothing to express, if you got no character and no humanity to express, what good is all that technique?

How do you feel about yourself in that regard?
I have absolutely no technique and I'm rapidly losing my personality. [laughter] I don't know what's happening to me right now. I'm going through a transition that I don't quite understand. So consequently I can't articulate it right now.

It's a question of context. Where do you want to place your voice? You seem to like a lot of different types of music and your expression could manifest itself in so many different avenues.
It can be a trap in a sense. It's like what happens to a lot of sidemen or studio players when they

make their solo records. All of a sudden they say, "I can do this, I can do that, I can do this." Well, that's fine, but what about *you*? I know you can play jazz and rock'n'roll and R&B and everything else. But where are *you* in all this?" And so it's important, I think, to create the context, whether you actually create it physically or just generate it like what Miles Davis does. Miles Davis doesn't write music but he does create music. There was no doubt that during the period that Wayne Shorter was writing all that music for Miles, that was Miles' music. Even though Wayne wrote it and gave it the raw materials, Miles shaped the context. Miles is an arranger on a much more pervasive, ambient level. Gil Evans creates a mood. So in a sense when Gil did those arrangements with Miles for *Porgy & Bess,* that became Miles and Gil, even though in a lot of cases what he did was just orchestrate Gershwin's piano score. When he told me that I was shocked. But it's how he orchestrated and it's how he shaped the music, and it became a personal statement. And the fact that he chose that music—it's all of those things that go into it. So there's a lot more to playing than just playing.

And where does that leave you?
I think I'm having to re-evaluate the whole process for myself right now. Because I don't... I mean, I guess I'm gonna have to start writing again. I don't really feel the... I don't have a strong sense of direction right now about where to go. So basically what I'm doing—I'm going back to some basics. I'm going back through tunes, standards in the fake book, which is what I do from time to time— just kind of getting a sense of what I want to do for myself for now. It seems like what I'm doing has become very stylized. But as a result of my own actions and as a result of other people imitating me... I mean, it's a little disconcerting to hear that. In a lot of cases, these guys copying me play better than I do, with a lot more technical facility. I hear some people that sound like they have my sound with Mike Brecker's technique. I guess I should be flattered that people consider me an influence just in terms of sound. I think whatever influence I've had on players has been that—the sound.

But at the same time that you're flattered, you're wary of it?
Yeah, I don't wanna listen to that too much. It's a little distracting, sometimes. But I don't dwell on it. I don't try to say, "Well, gee, I've gotta sound different now." It's kinda funny to me, especially if I hear somebody copy my mistakes. There's a guy who I won't mention... I shouldn't even say this. Uh... I won't say it. I don't really know where I'm going with all this, what I'm saying to you right now.

There have been hordes of sax players who have imitated or tried to imitate John Coltrane or Charlie Parker.
Well, how can you be a tenor player and not be influenced by John Coltrane or be an alto player and not be influenced by Charlie Parker?

And, by the same token, how can you be an aspiring alto player in 1988 and not be influenced by David Sanborn?
Yeah, but the difference is that Charlie Parker was an innovator and a genius whereas I'm just... I have a *style* of playing. Charlie Parker was an innovator rhythmically, harmonically, melodically, sound-wise. He revolutionized the instrument. *And* the music. I just came up with an interesting sound and I was lucky enough to make a living at it and to have people wanna hire me so I could play and continue to learn how to play my instrument better. But I think it would be a mistake to... I mean, you can't even say those two names—Charlie Parker and me—in the same breath. Because there's an abyss there between what he did and what I did. I just have a pleasing kind of sound and a style that happens to be popular, but I'm not in any way an innovator. And I'm not putting myself

down for that because I don't think... That's not my karma, or whatever, to be a great innovator. I'd like to continue to play better than I play now but I also have to be realistic about what are the tools that I have to work with. I can operate in a certain kind of emotional area. But I get a little uncomfortable when people say that I'm an innovator.

I'm just suggesting that young kids emulate you....
Because I'm what they hear!

Right, but they might tend to emulate you....
Because that's *all* they hear. Not because I'm that great or I have that much to say. For a long time I was the only saxophone out there. There was a period in the early-1970s—I know it because I was doing all the work—if there was a saxophone solo needed for a Linda Ronstadt album or James Taylor record, they called me because I happened to do something on Bowie's record that somebody liked. I mean, there were not a lot of young jazz players being recorded in the '70s. It was all fusion music. There weren't a lot of saxophone players during the period. Mike Brecker is a notable exception. So he's the other guy that got exposure during that period. I got perhaps more exposure because I played in higher visibility pop contexts. And I got called a lot because the alto cut a little bit more than tenor and it fit with the context. So I was in the right place at the right time with the right instrument.

Sounds like you're confused about what's happening with your career?
Yeah. Well, I'm at a point now where I'm just kind of reassessing what I do and getting back down to... I don't know, I guess I'm just doing research, is what it comes down to. Listening to a lot of music, mostly. I've been listening to a lot of bebop, which is particularly easy now that all these classic bebop albums are being reissued on CD, even some of the more obscure stuff by Chuck Berry, Sonny Clark, Harold Land—all the great players who helped to build this music.

Jackie McLean.
His records had a really profound effect on me. There is an album that he did called *Bluesnik* [Blue Note, 1961], which was all blues tunes. I remember I even did one of them when I was in college—played it at the Notre Dame Festival. I came out of blues and R&B via Cannonball—tunes like "Dis Here" and "Work Song." That stuff and Jimmy Forrest and Gene Ammons, that big robust tenor sound, is what pulled me out of R&B. And then I heard Jackie McLean and thought, "Wow, this is great," because his alto tone would just cut like a knife.

You were in St. Louis then?
Yeah, Jimmy Forrest was in St. Louis at the time playing with Grant Green. There was also a group called The Three Sounds. A lot of the players who are in New York now are from St. Louis. Lester Bowie, Julius Hemphill, Oliver Lake, Phillip Wilson. I worked in an organ group in East St. Louis with Hamiett Bluiett. I just kind of played around. I remember once playing this little coffee house, about the size of this room. It was me and Oliver Lake and Julius Hemphill and Phillip Wilson and a bass player. That was interesting. So I guess there was a kind of nominal scene at St. Louis at the time but it was starting to die around the early-1960s. It wasn't as active as Chicago by any means, where there was a real active blues and jazz scene. I just don't think that the city had enough support for a real active music scene.

When did the Black Artists Group start up?
Late-1960s or early-1970s. I was long gone by then. I left town in '63 and never really went back. [Sanborn moved to San Francisco, where he hooked up with the Paul Butterfield Blues Band, appearing on the 1968 album *In My Own Dream*.]

Did you play with Albert King in St. Louis?
Yeah, that was actually my first gig. It was scary. Because...

He's such a mean old dude.
Yeah he is. A bit cranky. He's pretty formidable. Somebody told me that he was a part time narc for the State Highway Patrol. I kind of believe it, he had that vibe. But that was actually the first time I ever played with anybody professionally. I kind of sat in with his horn section. There were four horn players and a friend of mine had been playing with him at the time and invited me down. I had been going to see the band at these teen centers and community rec centers that would have dances on Saturday night. They'd hire Albert King and Little Milton and local bands like Jules Blattner & The Teen Tones. And I remember just sitting in with 'em doing "Crosscut Saw." I did a couple of gigs with them. I never got paid, but I was just thrilled to be there. And then I sat in with Little Milton, which was another real thrill. A friend of mine was playing drums and another friend of mine was playing piano with him. That's when I met Phillip Wilson. And Phillip actually as much or more than anybody was probably responsible for me being a professional musician. I hung out with Phillip a lot and we played together quite a bit in St. Louis. Phillip was always getting fired—for playing too much or for his attitude. But Phillip is a great guy, very generous of spirit.

I remember seeing you and Phillip playing at the old 55 Grand bar in SoHo back around '82–'83.
Yeah, him and Jean Paul Bourelly and Hiram Bullock. I used to jam there a lot with Jaco and Bob Moses and Mike Stern. It was a funny scene there, man. We called the place 55 Grams. [laughter]

I remember coming down there one night. It was you, Delmar Brown, Stern, Moses, and Jaco playing "All Blues" for about two hours.
And nobody realizing it was two hours. [laughter] That place was so wide open it was unbelievable. And the real party was in the basement. I mean, that's where the action was.

I know Jaco would go down there during a drum solo and...
Get whacked—completely whacked. He was unbelievable.

I remember him and Stern went down there one night during a drum solo and they came back with each other's clothes on—they had switched.
Yeah, Jaco was a fuckin' lunatic. I met him when he first came to New York when he was doing his first album at Bobby Columby's studio in New City. And he was real straight life then. Didn't drink, didn't do drugs. I think Joe Zawinul has told the story about giving Jaco a drink. "I want you to loosen up." And after Jaco took that drink, Joe said, "I've made a serious mistake." Jaco definitely had a chemical imbalance. It got so intense—pretty hard to handle. Don Alias managed to hang in there for quite a while, but even he found it trying. As long as he had the bass in his hands, he was incredible. The rest of the time was trouble. Yeah, there have been a lot of casualties. It's hard to maintain your equilibrium and keep moving forward and not let this shit drive you crazy. Because if you care about what you do, it can get pretty painful sometimes to deal with just the whole creative act.

And I would think that you're under a lot more pressure than most because you sell a lot of albums.
You're under a lot of pressure in that area if you let yourself, if you start thinking that there's something expected of you. I think the key to that is keep your expectations low and to not live above your means, so that that doesn't become a primary motive for doing what you're doing, either overtly or subtly.

Is there an implied pressure from the record company to sell more records?
It can get pretty frustrating sometimes, particularly if you're not selling a lot of records. You begin to say, "Gee, if I just did what this successful group is doing over here I could sell a lot more records and make my life a little bit easier so I wouldn't have to worry about running from the landlord every month."

That's why I was suggesting that young conservatory trained kids have one eye on the Billboard *charts, to make themselves aware of what's getting over commercially.*
Yeah, they look at me and they say, "Here's a guy who's really making it. So I'm gonna sound like him, so I can make a lot of money." Yeah, I think that's got a lot to do with it, too. And that's discouraging.

And they say, "Sure, Charlie Parker's great but where is he now? My rent is $800 a month. I need a gig!"
Yeah, and that's a little discouraging, which is why I think it's great that somebody like Wynton came along and said, "You can play this music and make a living." And [he] not only inspired a lot of younger players but also created that kind of reality for the record companies to acknowledge: "Well, people are listening to this music, people are buying this music." And they are, they do. But aside from that, I think it's really important for everybody to find their own voice, their own way of expressing themselves. And I think it's easier if you do it in a context that keeps the financial in a little bit better perspective, where that doesn't become the primary motivating force behind you doing what you're doing. That's not why I'm doing what I'm doing. I didn't go into the music business. I became a musician because I love the music. And the business is part of it, because you have to make a living like everybody else. And I got very lucky because I was able to make a good living doing what I'm doing. But, I mean, I don't have a mansion and a limousine. I don't sell millions of records. But I do OK. My rent is paid here, but this is not a palace. And I've been living here for 15 years so my rent is fairly low. But I have enough. I've got instruments and I have mobility. But the most important thing is that I can make records and I can have a band and go out on the road and play. I have opportunities. That, to me, is the great reward. That's the tangible reward of, you know, success—is being able to afford to go out and play music, being given the opportunity to go out and perform and play and make records. And everything else is nice. If you get a couple extra thousand dollars there for Christmas, that's great. Or if you wanna buy another instrument and don't have to think about it before you do it, that's great, too. But I've been doing this for a long time. I mean, I'm 43 years old. I didn't even make a record on my own until I was in my '30s, which is no big deal one way or another. But I haven't been doing it that long. And I haven't been really economically successful up until the last few years.

Are there a lot of misconceptions about what you're making?
People think... I get it all the time. I used to get it from jazz players who would have an attitude about me because they thought I was making all this money. Now it's from a whole other perspective. People think that I'm incredibly wealthy. I mean, Kenny G's got a lot of money, but he sold two and a half million records. I don't sell those kind of numbers, I don't make that kind of money.

People see a face on an album cover and automatically assume the guy's rich.
Oh yeah, there's that association. And if people see you on TV, forget about it. They'll say, "This guy's got a place in L.A., he's got a place on Park Avenue, he's got limos and bitches...." You know, the whole nine yards. But it's all fantasy. So a lot of what I'm going through right now is just rearranging my priorities and not getting caught up in the machinery of success. Because it's so

seductive to say, "Well, just do this and you'll make a bunch of money." But when you do that, you die inside. And the ironic thing is you die musically and then you die commercially. I believe that. Maybe I'm naive in that regard, but I really believe that the true sense of being commercial in the long run is to be yourself and hope that people will buy *that.* But if you go into it trying to calculate what people are going to like and then do that, then you're fucked.

And it'll change in two years anyhow.
Not only that but—why do that? Why not just go and be a commodities trader? If you wanna make a lot of money quick... Well, I guess there is a lot of easy money in music. It hasn't occurred to me that way because I've been a working musician for 25 years and I've worked a lot. And you know, I've been on unemployment a lot. I've had times where I didn't have enough money to pay the rent. I've gone through it. And it's definitely better not to have that pressure on you. But that doesn't necessarily make your life better. Sometimes if you're doing something you really love, that can be a minor inconvenience, the fact that you don't have enough money to pay your rent. Obviously, you gotta make a living. But you gotta do this because you love it. And you gotta play the music that you love or there's no point to it. You gotta care about what you do and it has to be more than some calculated way to make a lot of money. And I do enjoy it.

I have an early warning system. If I get to the point where I start to see that I'm going in the wrong direction, I put the brakes on. And so it's not necessarily something that I do that I'm dissatisfied with and think, "OK, now it's time to change." It's just that I sense, "Oh, oh, there's some rocks up ahead. I'd better pull off the road a little bit and think this over." Or maybe it's middle age crisis. It could be that, too.

So you're woodshedding now.
Yeah, in a roundabout way. That's what we're back down to, studying piano voicings, harmony, practical application of harmony, scale studies. I got the Nicholas Slonimsky book [*Thesaurus of Scales and Melodic Patterns,* Schirmer Books, 1987]. I got an Oliver Nelson book. I got the Joe Viola Berklee books. I got a couple of fake books, some stuff that Larry Willis wrote out for me, some Bach and Mozart flute duet books. I think voice leading is the key.

Do you think down the road you might do a standards album?
I don't think so. I think I may do an album that's all acoustic. But see, I don't think that my... That whatever I have to offer... My strong suit is not playing jazz, necessarily. It's playing whatever music I choose to pull together, whatever the context is, that has elements of jazz, that has elements of pop and R&B in it. If I can concentrate on anything it would be to develop a strong melodic sense. And, I think, for me it's important to start thinking of an acoustic context. It's easy to get lost. As a saxophone player it's easy to get lost in the wash of electronics. It's nice to hear the sound of the saxophone. It's nice to hear that woodwind quality. The brass aspect is nice, but if you lose the woodwind aspect then you're fucked. You might as well just sample it and do it like that. Because the only thing you're left with is the embouchure nuance. And that's what disturbs me about a lot of the saxophone players that I hear now—most of whom I don't know—is that—and I don't know if it's trying to sound like me or what—is that they lose some of the warmth and the character of the instrument as a result of playing hard, trying to play funky or rhythmic. There's another quality to the instrument that's really important—that warmth.

Wasn't sax the original rock'n'roll instrument?
Yeah, it was a great instrument for rock'n'roll, back when there was an acoustic bass. You listen to The Coasters' records—that wasn't about guitar, it was about saxophone and drums. And there was

acoustic piano. The solo instrument was saxophone. The guys back then played loud but they could develop a full sound—people like King Curtis and Illinois Jacquet and Arnett Cobb and the transition into Sil Austin and Earl Bostic. And those were the people that carried the tradition over into rock'n'roll. Then when electric instruments started coming to forefront, gradually the saxophone faded into the background until it got lost. All of a sudden it didn't cut through as much. It didn't have the power, it didn't have the presence. And when you had to play that much louder to cut over electric instruments, you started to get a more strident sound, you started to get less of the character of the instrument and more of just the bite and the brassiness—which for some things was OK, but that's not all there is to the instrument. And I think the fact that I play alto and I played fairly loud and I cut through maybe had some effect on me getting hired so much in the '70s, 'cause I started out playing with electric instruments. That was my context. That was my reality. Whereas, most sax players my age chose to be jazz players or started out in big bands. But I played in rock'n'roll bands and I played the alto. So I developed more of an electric rock'n'roll, R&B sensibility.

From what you're saying, you're not likely to jump into the EWI like some players are.
No, I like the sound of... I don't want to rule out all that electronic stuff, but I don't feel comfortable in that context. I like to listen to it and I respect somebody who does it well. Michael Brecker does it great. He plays the shit out of the EWI.

It's a whole woodshedding process just to get into the electric side of things.
Yeah, and I don't get any physical pleasure out of it, you know? It doesn't get me off. Playing acoustically... I mean, to me it's almost like the difference between seeing a beautiful car and a beautiful woman. Beautiful woman does something to you. Beautiful car does, too, but hopefully not in the same way.

WYNTON MARSALIS

SWING JOURNAL, JAPAN'S PREMIERE jazz magazine, has scrutinized and celebrated Wynton Marsalis' fabled career from day one. In 1992, the magazine invited me to interview Wynton on the milestone of his 10th year in the business, the anniversary of his self-titled debut album that was released in 1982. Wynton has been a controversial figure throughout his career, drawing the ire of critics who question his heart and his conservative aesthetic while acknowledging his obvious command of the instrument. Even fellow musicians have gotten into the fray. Keith Jarrett bashed him in a notorious *New York Times Magazine* article that he penned, at one point challenging Wynton to a blues standoff to test his authenticity factor. Wynton's cool response? "How can I respond to something that is obviously irrational?"

Whether or not his playing moves those who are still mourning Miles Davis' death, the fact is that Wynton Marsalis is a trumpet virtuoso and he remains the figurehead of jazz for his generation and generations that followed. And in his position as artistic director of the Jazz at Lincoln Center program, he has sought to elevate the art of jazz to its rightful stature alongside classical music. His latest release, *The Midnight Blues* (Columbia, 1998), is a Marsalis-with-strings affair that recalls his romantic recording *Hot House Flowers* (Columbia, 1984). A Pulitzer Prize winner for his oratorio on the three-CD epic *Blood on the Fields* (Columbia, 1996), Marsalis continues to represent jazz with dignity and class.

JULY 7, 1992

Ten years ago, Marsalis was a brash young upstart possessing maturity beyond his years, a gifted but outspoken heir to the trumpet throne. Through the summer of 1980 he had paid his dues in one of the finest institutions of higher learning in jazz, Art Blakey's Jazz Messengers. He also had gotten some invaluable experience the following summer on a whirlwind tour with the Herbie Hancock Quartet, garnering rave reviews for his immaculate execution and his bold ideas. As one critic proclaimed at the time, "Wynton has Brandenburg technique and a Ray Charles soul."

Then in 1982 came his self-titled debut on Columbia Records, heralding the arrival of the new Young Lion of jazz. In the ensuing years, Marsalis single-handedly galvanized an entire generation through his determined pursuit of excellence. Even his stage demeanor—natty suits and a classy carriage that recall the elegance of Ellington—has had an effect on his peers. As he told *Down Beat*: "I like suits. I like to be clean when I go to work, playing music that I think is important in front of people."

With the advent of this neo-conservative aesthetic, a new wave of young jazz musicians began dressing up in suits and ties and seriously dedicating themselves to the tradition, following in Wynton's wake. The list is almost too long to mention but includes such names as trumpeters Wallace Roney, Roy Hargrove, Terence Blanchard, Phillip Harper, Marlon Jordan, and more recently Nicholas Payton; saxophonists Justin Robinson, Donald Harrison, Todd Williams, Wes Anderson, and Ralph Moore; bassists Christian McBride, Charnett Moffett, Reginald Veal, Peter Washington, Bob Hurst, and Delbert Felix; pianists Marcus Roberts, Benny Green, and Cyrus Chestnut.

As Stanley Crouch, perennial chronicler of Wynton's career since 1982, wrote in his liner notes to that debut album: "Wynton Marsalis is one of the most remarkable young musicians to appear in jazz since the early-1960s. His arrival is especially important because there has been talk about the decline of jazz, and more than a few have sworn they've seen the art gurgling on its deathbed. The talk usually continues that all of the younger musicians are being lost to one pop fad or another, that the old hallmarks of discipline and adventure have been replaced by the slick and the predictable, and, finally, that most younger players have neither a sense of history nor a respect for the accomplishments of their predecessors. But Wynton Marsalis is a perfect retort to those misconceptions because he has everything—virtuoso technique, passion, intellect, curiosity, a sense of history, and enough humility to guarantee that he will continue to work hard and self-critically at his craft."

Wynton's virtuosity has also manifested itself in the classical arena. His *Trumpet Concertos* was met with great fanfare in 1983 and received a Grammy Award the following year for "Best Soloist with Orchestra." As Wynton said of his passion for classical music: "I studied classical music because so many black musicians were scared of this big monster on the other side of the mountain called classical music. I wanted to know what it was that scared everybody so bad. But as far as both musical idioms are concerned, it's harder to be a good jazz musician at an early age than a classical one. In jazz, to be a good performer means to be an individual, which you don't have to be in classical music. But because I've played with orchestras, some people think I'm a classical musician who plays jazz. They have it backwards. I'm a jazz musician who plays classical music."

Accolades and awards followed through the '80s as Wynton continued his prolific output in both classical and jazz idioms. In a rare Triple Crown sweep in 1984, *Down Beat* named him Jazz Musician of the Year, Best Acoustic Jazz Group, and Best Trumpeter. That same year he won the coveted Edison Award of Holland and France's Gran Prix du Disque. The following year he won jazz and classical Grammy Awards again for *Hot House Flowers* and his baroque trumpet works album.

But just as Wynton began achieving worldwide recognition as the top trumpeter in his field, a critical backlash unfolded. Some scoffed at his technical virtuosity, calling his precision trumpet playing cold, retentive, dispassionate. Others began to chastise him for bad-mouthing peers, colleagues, and elders, notably Miles Davis, whom he (and Stanley Crouch) accused of selling out to commercial pressures.

But Wynton made no apologies for what others perceived as his arrogant stance. As he commented: "I am the result of a great tradition and I'm trying to live up to the standards of that tradition. I have a long way to go but I'm going to do everything in my power to get the public to understand the real significance and beauty of the music, not by watering it down but by getting to such a place in my art that it will be obvious to all who listen that I'm coming from a great tradition."

By 1987, Wynton began viewing his position as top dog in the jazz world with the utmost responsibility and seriousness. He began doing clinics in earnest, stressing the importance of diligent study to the young musicians he inspired. "Study is the only protection against folly," he told *Down Beat* that year. And all the while, he continued his uncompromising artistry at an alarming pace, producing both classical and jazz works of undeniable quality and taste.

Wynton's 1988 double-album, *Live at Blues Alley* (Columbia, 1988), documented his quartet at the peak of its improvisational, interactive powers. As Stanley Crouch wrote in the liner notes: "Marsalis is now much more of a master of the instrument than he has ever been.... He rises to an intensity similar to that of John Coltrane, where virtuosity, passion and conceptual brilliance make for an aesthetic triangle of intimidating proportions."

The following year saw the release of Wynton's first important concept album, *The Majesty of the Blues* (Columbia, 1989). Rather than serving as a vehicle for his impressive chops, this album was an opportunity for Marsalis to flex his compositional muscles, expanding in a direction that alludes to some of Ellington's extended suites (as evidenced by the 30-minute suite "New Orleans Function").

As Crouch noted: "This album is a fresh start for Wynton Marsalis, but it is also a development of all that he has done on his previous records. We hear Marsalis coming in even closer contact with the wisdom of a music built on the rhythms and the colors of the blues."

By this time, even his staunchest critics began acknowledging that Wynton was beginning to "loosen up" on stage and blow in an uncommonly earthy fashion. At one memorable concert at the Bottom Line in New York, I witnessed Wynton go so far as to remove his suit coat and drape it over a chair, roll up his sleeves, and dig into a funky New Orleans second line groove while sitting in with the Elvin Jones Jazz Machine. Suddenly, his playing was imbued with more humor, more feeling and soul than ever before.

As Wynton himself noted at the time: "This direction I'm going in now allows me to address more of the fundamentals of the music and to dig deeper into my own experiences. This vision is more my own because I'm leaving the realm of just pure music and entering into the realm of experience and music. I'm not going backward in any way. I'm just seeking a much more comprehensive mode of expression."

Wynton took that notion of personal expression to a deeper level with *Soul Gestures in Southern Blue* (Columbia, 1991), a three-album blues cycle (*Thick in the South, Uptown Ruler,* and *Levee Low Moan*). Nineteen ninety-one also began Wynton's involvement as Artistic Director of the Jazz at Lincoln Center series, giving him a prestigious vehicle for his ongoing mission—the preservation and perpetuation of the jazz tradition and its rich legacy.

As he said, "We're still working to accomplish the vision of the program, which is to have an actual effect on American culture. We want to influence the younger generation to think about American music."

Last year's series included tributes to New Orleans legends King Oliver, Count Basie, John Coltrane, and Duke Ellington. This year's series included tributes to Thelonious Monk, Duke Ellington, Jellyroll Morton, Johnny Dodds, and Miles Davis. This year, the program will also make its initial forays into the national arena with a 28-city tour by the 16-piece Lincoln Center Jazz Orchestra and the release of the first of a series of commercial recordings documenting Jazz at Lincoln Center concerts. This season also marks the establishment of a series of Jazz at Lincoln Center Young

People's Concerts, hosted by Wynton, and the premiere of a ballet with music by Marsalis and chore-ography by Peter Martins, artistic director of the New York City Ballet.

This year also marks the release of Wynton's latest recording, *Blue Interlude* (Columbia, 1992), which he describes as "a contemporary romantic encounter set to rhythm and tune." The album is highlighted by the extended 37-minute suite "Blue Interlude (The Bittersweet Saga of Sugar Cane and Sweetie Pie)." The piece is preceded by Wynton's six-minute spoken "Monologue." In his liner notes, Stanley Crouch dubbed *Blue Interlude* a breakthrough album, adding that "it just might be a master-piece." I spoke to Wynton just prior to the start of this year's Jazz at Lincoln Center season.

It's amazing that you have squeezed so much expression into ten short years. There's a huge output of music here. Looking back on it, did you have a game plan back in 1982 when you released your first record?
No, I didn't know how it would evolve. I just knew that in 1982 I wanted to play jazz and not to be fooled into something else or succumb to the pressures that were around me—either pressures of commercialism or the pressures of a constituency, where you want to be part of something so bad that you'll compromise your real desire to learn and study music just so you can be co-signed by another group of people. I just wanted to have the strength, and ask the Creator for the strength, to continue to maintain a certain level of actual artistic integrity and ride out the bad times of playing and developing on my horn—ride out the bad times and keep faith in music, keep trying to develop and pay respect to jazz music. Because all through the '80s there was this big tremendous celebra-tion of pop music and pop jazz, all of this attention was going there and many times my band would be like the only band at a jazz festival playing jazz. And there was tremendous resistance from the jazz community to the ideas that I was presenting at the time. But these were ideas that I had overwhelming faith in. So I would have to ask the Creator for the strength to continue to have faith in these ideas, which was supported by this documentation.

When I started in 1982, I kind of had an idea.... I didn't know what my development would be like, but I knew it would be hard to stay out there and play, because Art Blakey made that very clear to me. To really want to be a jazz musician and to have that power that comes from really dealing with jazz music and being engaged with American culture on that level... He would always make that clear to me. If you want to stand out there, if you want that power—and I don't mean power in the sense of control over other people—it's like a spiritual power, a nobility. He said if you want that, you have to pay the price that it's gonna take to deal with that, because that's something that comes from God. It doesn't come from anybody telling you that you have it. And if you want it, you have to be willing to pay the cost. And the payment is strictly in my faith in the music, regardless of what I had to deal with.

Is that a lesson that you have passed on to other younger musicians?
Well, I don't know. Marcus Roberts is one of the few musicians I really feel has been influenced by me in any way.

What about Roy Hargrove or any of the countless young trumpet players out there right now?
Well, Nicholas Payton. He's the second person who I think has been directly influenced by me, in terms of believing in intellectual development, having faith in the music, having a certain amount of real integrity, and really studying and developing his talent. I think there are many other musicians who have maybe seen me and been influenced by the fact that I came to their school and talked to them. I've been in contact with many, many musicians, and maybe I was an inspiration from a dis-tance. I don't feel that really my actual music has influenced them, though, because I don't really hear that in their playing.

In the process of continuing to do your thing, you've become an elder statesman for a new generation of musicians who look up to you.
Well, a lot of those musicians came in contact with me when I visited to lecture at their schools. Like Roy Hargrove, Peter Martin, Herb Harris, Jeremy Davenport, Christian McBride. I went to their high schools and talked to them when they were just starting out. Christian McBride was at the Mellon Jazz camps when he was 14 years old. Walter Blanding is another one. It goes on and on. I have intimate contact with these musicians either from going to their schools or answering their letters. I know them. So it's really a different type of relationship.

Is this part of your mission?
I'm not on a mission. All I'm trying to do is deal with American culture and do something that represents what men like my great uncle stood for. He memorized the Declaration of Independence and the Constitution and the Bill of Rights. He was 90 years old when he died in 1982. As a young man, he would go down every year to the voting office and recite the Declaration of Independence and all of that, and they still wouldn't let him vote. He would do that every year for 15 or 20 years until they finally let him vote. So the type of people I'm trying to represent are the people who represent the finest that our culture has produced—people with a level of dignity and nobility. I'm out here to be against vulgarity and I'm for intellectual achievement. And I stand by that because that's really the tradition that I come out of, and that's what I believe in.

A lot of times, our music is not equated with that. So it's my job to make the public vision of our music congruent with what the music actually is—not to allow the music to be used to fulfill somebody else's adolescent type fantasy of escaping the middle class. And that's why I have such tremendous support from the older people.

I call it a mission because in your current record company bio there is a quote from you stating, "We are fighting for the survival of our art form in our generation." That sounds like a man on a mission to me.
I guess you could call it a mission, then. But this is what I'm representing. It's what I believe in and what I've always believed in. When I was 15 I believed in that. It's just that... A lot of times in public I have to make statements that are very unequivocal because I want to make it clear there is no amount of pressure that's going to cause me to bow down to any of that stuff that's out there. You know how it is with commercial pressures. I'm not bowing to that. I don't care what the cost is. I don't care what's said, what's written.... I'm out here to pay homage to the Creator, first of all, for allowing me to come out here and function on this level as a musician. And I'm paying homage to the people, the community—the actual people in America. Not just black people, all the people. I have many different types of students and they write me letters all the time, man. And that's the deal. That's my mission.

Tell us about the Jazz at Lincoln Center series that you are presently involved in.
Yes, we're developing a good program and we're lucky to have people like Albert Murray and Stanley Crouch aboard, as well as the support of everybody at Lincoln Center.

Considering how busy your schedule is, how were you able to fit this in and why is it important to you?
It's important because Lincoln Center is a great institution. And with the support of the institution we can have the kind of national and international impact for jazz that would be very difficult for us to have on our own. This is something that the conception of jazz has always needed. I don't really like to say jazz because jazz is just a word—it means records to some people, it means concerts to

others. But when I say jazz I mean the conception of jazz. And the thing that the conception of jazz has always needed was institutional support, support in the education system, positive publicity, to be marketed for what it actually is and be promoted for its strengths.

What had happened in the past is the weakest aspects of jazz is what received the most publicity and most marketing. Until 1969 or 1970, the music that was being called jazz then wasn't even jazz at all. And that is the ultimate disrespect. That's why I think my involvement with Lincoln Center has been a great step in a positive direction. And the fact that we have Rob Gibson as a director is a great plus for us, because he's a man of integrity and vision. He works hard and he understands what our objectives are. They're also his objectives.

How would you assess the whole climate of how jazz is perceived now as opposed to ten years ago?
I think it's come a long way, but we have a long way to go.

You have had a significant impact on how people perceive jazz, by your own example. In effect, you have been an ambassador for jazz over the last ten years.
Well, I love jazz music, and I just feel, had my image been more compatible with who I actually am, even in the beginning, then we would've gotten even more publicity. The image that was put on me by the media really had nothing to do with me. It was an attempt to try and once again denigrate what jazz music really is.

How would you describe this image?
You know, first I played classical music, which was considered negative—even though classical music is also a large component of the jazz tradition, because jazz comes out of ragtime and all the older musicians studied classical music. And being a first-class trumpet virtuoso.... I'm sure it's one of the first times in the history of the world that somebody's been denigrated for being a first-class virtuoso at something. Some people perceived that as a defect, which always seemed relatively humorous to me. And then just the whole animosity thing that the media built up between me and Miles, me and my brother [Branford] and Sting. All these things have nothing to do with ideas, yet they are put in front of the public. There's all of these battles that I get dragged into and it's always with some force that represents pop music in jazz. And the media or those who should be disseminating the information about jazz are always on the side of the pop musician.

So if we would've had more support for jazz in the beginning, then I think we would've had even greater impact. But seeing as how we didn't get that support... It's not that we're mad... And when I say "we" I mean all the musicians who are serious about playing jazz. I was one of the few whose name was being mentioned. I'm not mad or embittered that I was dealt that kind of hand, which is definitely wrong. Because that's what Art Blakey told me, man. He said, "If you're gonna stand for this music, you gonna have to stand against all this other stuff."

Now I'm just hoping that the jazz community can get its stuff together soon enough and realize that the fact that Roy Hargrove and them young cats have contracts, that's not what's keeping Ron Carter and some of those older musicians from getting contracts. Ron Carter and them's contracts is going to rap musicians. See, so there's always this thing that we just have to deal with in terms of realizing that we all have to work together. That's why the jazz festivals were having problems. And that's one reason why we were so successful with our jazz festival at Lincoln Center. When people come to our festival, they know that they're coming to hear jazz music. They're not coming to hear pop music or rock or fusion or European avant-garde music, they're coming to hear jazz—swing, blues, tunes by great composers of jazz. You know, we're not trying to present concerts to make jazz music less great than it is, to negotiate our way through a series of political moves and constituencies and all of that. We're here to play the music.

At the recent JVC Festival in New York, it was a real treat to see you playing alongside Nicholas Payton and Doc Cheatham. It was a joy to see the interaction and communication across the generations.

You know, the music has always had that. I can remember when I was 18 or 19, I was playing alongside Dizzy and Jon Faddis. And now Nicholas Payton is doing the same thing. That's how this music is. It endures through all kinds of adversity. And I'm just here to pay as much homage as I can to the nobility of our great jazz tradition. I want to see that our tradition continues to be practiced and treated with the respect it deserves.

Your new album, Blue Interlude, *is in some ways a departure for you. And yet you hinted at this direction on previous albums. Tell us about this evolution and the direction you seem to be going in now.*

I think what I'm doing now is writing more music that's reflective of the improvisational style that we had developed over all of the first seven or eight albums that we did. The conception that I use on all the songs that I'm playing now can be traced back to the first record, particularly to a tune called "Twilight," which is a 14-bar blues with a bass vamp going underneath. The horns work in a contrary motion, then there is a solo trumpet section over a vamp and the drums are swinging in a certain time while the bass is playing a vamp. And when the saxophone solo comes in, the rest of the band starts swinging a 14-bar blues. This conception of putting different instruments in different times and dealing with group improvisation based on the establishment of certain thematic dialogue is something that I had been working on from the very beginning.

And that conception has really come to fruition with the extended suite on your new album?

Well, it's just another step in the evolution of that original conception I had with "Twilight." For me, that concept was itself a breakthrough in terms of what was going on in my generation at the time. I was like 18 or 19 when I wrote "Twilight." So that tune was done against the backdrop of what was happening musically in 1982. And believe me, there wasn't anyone my age playing jazz in that way back then.

Can you expand on your comments about Live at Blues Alley *representing the end of a phase for you?*

Yeah, I was referring to the idea of a quartet stretching out for long periods of time, purely a solo conception. Those two nights at Blues Alley [a jazz nightclub in Washington D.C.] represented the highest development that we had been working in at the time. The rhythmic interplay and complexity we achieved on tunes like "Skain's Domain" and "Nosmo King" is a highpoint for that quartet [Bob Hurst on bass, Marcus Roberts on piano, Jeff Watts on drums]. So for me, *Live at Blues Alley* was about the whole chance-taking aspect of improvisation in the truest sense, in terms of having four people playing four totally different rhythms that are going to have to resolve in the form at some point, and we don't know what that point is going to be but we're making up our minds where we're gonna resolve it as we're going along. That's a type of very advanced rhythmic improvisation, the kind you hear with the Coltrane quartet or the classic Miles quintets.

So when I said I didn't think that we would be doing that anymore, I meant that I felt we had taken that conception as far as we could take it, without just going into pure energy type playing. And that's not anything that ever really interested me. I'm more interested in the most heroic aspects of jazz, which is to take something chaotic and make it coherent, which is what we were doing on *Live at Blues Alley,* particularly on songs like "Skain's Domain" and "Delfeayo's Dilemma." Those types of things had never really been explored to that level in jazz. The complexity of the trumpet lines that I'm playing on "Skain's Domain" and the difficulty of executing those

5/4 rhythms and swing patterns and all the different things we were doing... I didn't really think we could take that much further. So now instead of just playing purely in that kind of improvisational context, I'm trying to incorporate that same type of rhythmic sophistication in the context of structured, extended composition. Also, I have more people in the band now [a septet] so it gives us more personality to explore. To me, it's all just indicative of a general philosophy or direction for my music.

What can you say about "New Orleans Function," the extended piece on The Majesty of the Blues.
On that album I was trying to make, once and for all, the musical refutation to the concession of new and old in jazz. Which is to say, for me, the earliest music in jazz is still very modern because it's about the negotiation of group agendas, which is what the world is still trying to address. So I decided to put out a record where all the songs would be blueses. One side of the record would be an ultra-modern extended piece of music, which is what "The Majesty of the Blues" is. That song, in a lot of ways, is like "Twilight." It's a blues but it modulates in different keys. There are four saxophone interludes and each interlude takes the song to another key. At one point the saxophone is playing a part that is indicative of an exotic type of Middle Eastern sound. But it's actually the clarinet line of a New Orleans ensemble brought down an octave and played on the tenor saxophone. The song is in 6/4 against a steady vamp, and it grooves.

On the second side, it's a classic New Orleans funeral, which is "The New Orleans Function." So what I was trying to do with this album was just show the similarities, that you could put both of those things on an album and they would sound like they belonged together. So the New Orleans music on this album doesn't sound any older than the most modern music, which is "The Majesty of the Blues." And actually when it was recorded it was going to be released as two records. The other record came out later called *Levee Low Moan.* That's the record that was recorded at the same time as *The Majesty of the Blues.* So the two of them actually form one unit. The *Levee Low Moan* album is a lot of the same thing—songs modulate into different keys, they have horn interludes, and they deal with a contemporary conception of what the blues are, in terms of different harmonic structures, using that same conception of group and thematic improvisation that we had been working on since the very beginning. But it's really addressing a certain level of harmonic sophistication that wasn't there in my earlier works.

Was Tune in Tomorrow *[Columbia, 1990] any kind of departure from this conception?*
Yes, because that was a soundtrack. I was just fulfilling the requirements of the soundtrack. They wanted me to come up with something that had the feel of Duke Ellington's "New Orleans Suite," so that project gave me a chance to study that album. That's the kind of music they wanted for the movie. That's what I was hired to do. So that album definitely stands apart from my other albums. It's like the *Crescent City Christmas Card* album that we did [Columbia, 1989]. Those are just specific projects that we did for hire. We're still using the same vocabulary and the same type of improvisation, but a lot of the music on *Tune in Tomorrow* is descriptive music, strictly in the service of the movie.

I particularly enjoyed the spoken word intro to "Blue Interlude." It reminds me of Ellington's Orchestral Works *album, where he provided these poetic commentaries before "Harlem Suite" and "The Green Broom."*
Well, at first I wasn't gonna do it, but whenever I performed this piece live—and we had been performing this piece for about a year before we recorded it—I would do that monologue at the beginning. So my production manager David Robinson said, "Man, you should talk just because you always introduce that song in concert the same way. You always talk at the beginning of that song.

That's a part of that composition." So that's why I decided to include it.

Tell us about this piece you premiered earlier this year at Lincoln Center, "In This House, on This Morning."
Yes, there were two extended pieces that I wrote back-to-back. One is "Griot New York," a ballet that I did with choreographer Garth Fagan. It has three 40-minute movements. And "In This House, on This Morning" was an hour and 35 minutes long. It deals with religious music, trying to get everything in there from Gregorian chants to the music of John Coltrane. It's about all the different sounds of religious music with no overt references to any one particular thing. I tried to take the themes of various aspects of religious music and incorporate them into a piece with different movements. And it goes through the whole emotion of an actual church service—not necessarily a sanctified church or Baptist service, because I'm not from the sanctified or Baptist church. I've been in those churches and I wanted some of that feeling. But more than that, I wanted to convey the feeling of church services anywhere you go. They all have a certain level of introspection and reverence and exuberance. And they all have many different components.

It seems that you are more and more interested in extended works, long forms.
Just right now. But I don't go in one direction at a time. The records come out and they have one thing on them, but I don't have to stick to that as my only thing. It's like in life. Sometimes I talk in short sentences, sometimes I talk for a long time. Sometimes I eat a lot, sometimes I won't eat that much.

JIMMY KATZ

JIMMY SMITH

I CONDUCTED THIS INTERVIEW for *Jazz Times* (February '95 issue) on the phone from New Orleans. Jimmy was back home in California, no doubt watching cowboy movies on TV, a favorite pasttime of his. Our conversation was freewheeling and hilarious, and after it was over I realized that I had maybe five or six minutes of useable material. He did talk about the development of his trademark Hammond B–3 organ style and his current recording but the rest was a kind of stream of consciousness monologue that ran its own course. I remember thinking at one point during the interview, "This cat should be doing stand-up comedy albums." He was in that great X-rated party humor tradition of Red Foxx, Rudy Ray Moore, and Robin Harris—a born entertainer. At the end of our chat, I mentioned to Jimmy that I had just polished off a catfish dinner at my favorite New Orleans restaurant, Uglesich's. "Catfish? Ooooh, you dirty dog!" he moaned with envy. When I went on to describe the dish—chef Anthony's popular Muddy Waters catfish topped with jalapeño peppers and garlic—Jimmy made an unusual proposition. "I'll tell you what... Next time I come to New Orleans, I think I might suck your dick if you treat me to some catfish." Unfortunately, I moved from New Orleans the following year and never had the opportunity to follow up on Jimmy's generous offer.

SEPTEMBER 29, 1994

He is now and has been for the past four decades the king of the hill, the baddest of the bad, the undisputed heavyweight champion of the Hammond B–3 organ. When Jimmy Smith jumps on an up-tempo groove and lets his right hand fly or when he digs deep into a greasy blues with real-deal intensity, practitioners and connoisseurs alike can only sit back in utter amazement, shake their heads in disbelief, and mutter: *Damn!*, which also happens to be the title of his latest Verve release.

An all-out blowing session, *Damn!* (Verve, 1995) confirms Jimmy Smith's status in the B–3 world—still the organist that everyone is chasing. For this fiery session, Smith's inimitable B–3 burn is highlighted alongside some of the hottest young horn players on the scene today. Challenged by Young Lions like guitarist Mark Whitfield, trumpeters Roy Hargrove and Nicholas Payton, saxophonists Tim Warfield, Mark Turner, Ron Blake, and Abraham Burton, Jimmy rises to the occasion and wails with abandon. Teeming with energy, *Damn!* harkens back to Jimmy's landmark session from 38 years ago with a young Kenny Burrell, Lou Donaldson, Hank Mobley, and Donald Byrd, recently compiled and released by Mosaic Records as a three-CD boxed set entitled *The Complete February 1957 Jimmy Smith Blue Note Sessions.* The same intensity prevails.

From funky throwdowns like James Brown's "Papa's Got a Brand New Bag," Horace Silver's "Sister Sadie," and Herbie Hancock's "Watermelon Man" to scorching bop anthems like Dizzy Gillespie's "Woody 'N' You" and Charlie Parker's "Scrapple from the Apple," the entire session is marked by scintillating interplay. Anchored by bassist Christian McBride and drummers Bernard Purdie and Arthur Taylor (in his last recorded performance), Jimmy drives the session from behind his hulking B–3 like a seasoned quarterback taking his team downfield for a last minute touchdown in the Super Bowl. Simply put, the sparks fly on *Damn!*

James Oscar Smith was born on December 8, 1925 in Norristown, Pennsylvania. Both of his parents were pianists and his father was Jimmy's primary teacher. At the age of nine, he won first place in a talent competition playing boogie-woogie piano. At the age of 12, he teamed with his father in a song and dance act, performing at various clubs and on radio shows in and around Philadelphia. Following a stint in the Navy, he used the GI bill to attend the Ornstein School of Music, where he studied bass and piano. It was in 1951, while playing in Don Gardner's Sonotones, that he became interested in organ. Soon after acquiring a Hammond B–3 organ, he went into a self-imposed period of intensive woodshedding that lasted nearly a year.

Since the release of his 1956 Blue Note debut, *A New Sound... A New Star... Jimmy Smith at the Organ, Vol. 1,* few organists have received as much attention. A perennial poll winner since the late-1950s, Smith redefined the cumbersome instrument while opening a new door in the process for generations of players to come. As the late Leonard Feather wrote in his *Encyclopedia of Jazz*: "The first attempt to bring the organ into the orbit of contemporary jazz was undertaken by Jimmy Smith, an extraordinary musician who makes fuller use than other jazz organists of the variety of stops at his disposal. Smith plays fast-tempo jazz improvisations in a style that would have blended perfectly with Charlie Parker's combo, had Smith risen to prominence during Parker's lifetime."

With swagger and sass, Jimmy took the cumbersome 400-pound instrument to a new level beyond where B–3 pioneers like Milt Buckner, Bill Doggett, and Wild Bill Davis had gone before him. Smith's new sound utilized the first three draw bars and the percussion feature of the Hammond B–3. He also cut the tremelo off and began playing fluid horn-like lines with his right hand, inspired by players like Coleman Hawkins, Don Byas, and Arnett Cobb. As he once explained, "I copped my solos from horn players. I don't listen to keyboard players. I can't get what I want from keyboard players," although he also admits that Bud Powell, Art Tatum, and Erroll Garner were important influences.

Jimmy, in turn, has influenced generations of musicians. His inspiration has been acknowledged by countless other organists including Brother Jack McDuff, Jimmy McGriff, Booker T, Billy Preston, Larry Young, Lonnie Smith, Richard "Groove" Holmes, Georgie Fame, Joey DeFrancesco, Barbara Dennerlein, and John Medeski. His continuing influence is reflected in today's acid jazz scene via sampling by groups like the hugely popular Us3, who regard Jimmy Smith as the godfather of soul-jazz.

Perhaps Clive Davis of *The London Times* put it best when he wrote: "Smith continues to extract an awesome degree of power from his keyboard. The slick walking bass lines laid down by the pedals and the cluster bomb explosions of blue notes from his right hand have been copied by admirers across the generations. His ability to build to a dramatic gospel climax remains undiminished."

That testimony rings true on *Damn!*

You recently opened for Horace Silver at the New Orleans Jazz & Heritage Festival. Later Horace was overheard saying, "I'm not gonna let anybody ever book me to follow that crazy Jimmy Smith. He didn't even leave a piece of stage for me to play on. He burned the place down!"
I didn't even know what I was doing. I was under a spell—my mojo spell. You know anything about voodoo? I spread it all around the bandstand before I go on. Then I spread just a teeny bit around my organ and I let my tenor player step on just a little bit of powder. That's to keep his ass hot. And that's how come he burns so much. When he plays, he plays! The rest of the stuff, the aroma just goes all over the bandstand.

So you got your mojo woikin'.
I gotta keep it woikin'.

Did you do the same thing down in Osaka when you made that live record last year with Kenny Burrell?
Hey man, we had it working there, too. And the drummer Jimmie Smith—I had to spread a little bit around the drums 'cause he sound scared of me. He never played with me in his life. He played with Jimmy McGriff, but he never played with me. And he told me, "It's altogether different when you're playing with Jimmy Smith. Everything—all my life has changed." He said, "Jimmy Smith will rejuvenate you, change your stuff around." 'Cause I had to teach him how to play with me. A drummer can't just jump up and play with me, not just any drummer. 'Cause I'll lose him. Oh man, he'll get lost in the shuffle—dropping sticks and everything.

And that mojo dust works.
Hey, motherfucker, if I come down there to New Orleans again to play, I'll put a spell on you. You won't know your way home. You be driving on the wrong street somewhere.... "Damn, I thought this was Rampart."

That live album is great. Sounds like you were all in a good mood that night, playing some blues in Japan on the night before Christmas.
Oh man, we had champagne and Kentucky Colonel chicken. Yeah, we had the Colonel in Osaka, man! That's the day we went on top of the Hilton, the penthouse.... Man, they had a nice buffet up there. Kenny took his bear with him and I had my wolf with me.... Uh, well, Lola's a lion.

Your wife Lola says all you wanna do is eat and look at the cowboy movies.
That's right.

And never gain a pound.
You got that right. And I'm almost 66 years old, you know.

It's great to hear you still playing with Kenny Burrell after all these years.
And he don't look too old either. He's getting gray but the face is still young.

Elvin Jones is another guy who looks eternally youthful.
No, well, Elvin's too ugly to look old. That's an ugly man. You know what happened, when we first met it was Haight-Ashbury in Frisco, and man.... I was off on Monday.... I was playing at the Jazz Workshop and he was playing at the Blackhawk. So anyway, I wasn't working on this Monday and he was on. So I walk in the door to catch Elvin's gig and the guy says, "Jimmy Smith, come on in! Elvin Jones is here, man. I hope you guys can hook up tonight, man." And here comes Elvin, "Hey, man, we're gonna get into something tonight, OK?" I said, "What? I ain't never played witch you, man." So he just grabbed me, and he's strong anyway.... I had to put all my little karate shit on his ass. I grabbed his dick. He say, "Turn my dick loose, motherfucker." I say, "Man, don't fool with me, boy." Everybody say, "Jimmy Smith is crazy, don't fool with him." 'Specially when I'm not playing... And I'm "off," I'm really off. It's what the black people call you. It's not o-f-f, it's o-a-f. They say, "The nigger's oaf." That's from the South. Say that. It sounds good. It's got a ring to it. So anyway, we play. Elvin broke the sock cymbal right off, man. He done broke that sucker, 'cause he's so strong, man. And when we got done, I was soaked, he was soaked, our socks were wet. I'm serious, Bill. Our socks were soaking wet. I messed that suit up—you know, all that salt you get from sweating. You ever see a musician with those white armpits? These motherfuckers with all that salt beadin' their ass up?

Just like race horses?
Exactly.

I just got this Mosaic box in the mail...
The what?

Mosaic Records just put out that boxed set of your stuff from 1957.
I never heard of Mosaic Records.

All your Blue Note stuff from three days in a row in 1957...
Oh man, I don't know about that. It's probably sitting back there unopened with a bunch of other records I ain't never had time to get to.

You don't listen much to music at home?
Nope. But do you know I'm doing a rap thing with the Plus Three.

Plus Three?
We Three?

You mean Us3?
Well, somebody's damn three.

Yeah, it's Us3. Or as they say down here, Y'all Three.
[Laughter] Yeah, goddamn! You got that sucker on the head, boy. Y'all Three. Whatever the fuck they are. Well, you heard about the three little monkeys, right? Hear nothin', see nothin', fuck nothin'... That's them. But we played together over in London. Man, them kids was going crazy! I mean, I never heard young people holler so loud. It's not like when the girls used to holler for Frank Sinatra, right? It's not that kind of holler. This is like a violent, exciting, stomping their feet

kind of holler. We did four nights, had 600 people every night in this small club. They just jammed 'em in. And the only thing about it, buddy... My wife got a contact high. They had some reefer, some hash.... I mean, smokin' in the club! My wife came past them going up to the soundboard so she could hear what it sound like, you know. And by the time she got to the dressing room she be sayin', "Whoooo! Jimmy-Jimmy-Jimmy-Jimmy! What are they smokin' out there?" And I say, "Oh shit." And I stepped out the dressing room door and the shit hits you right there. And she came all the way through that whole crowd that was smoking. Man, she stayed in that dressing room the rest of the four nights. She didn't move nowhere. She was really high. And her eyes was all funny look-ing and shit. Man, that was a wild gig. Of course, I also played Carnegie Hall twice this year. Did you see me on there, Bill?

I was there [Verve Records' 40th anniversary celebration]. Yeah, that was a good show.
Why didn't you come back and say something?

They had such a tight security thing happening it was hard to get backstage.
It was, it was terrible. They were putting all the managers out. They actually were gonna put Lola out until one of the fellas said, "You gonna put Lola out? Then Jimmy's not gonna play." And the other fella said to Lola, "No, no, no, I better let you inside because I understand Jimmy has a temper."

So tell me about Babs Gonzalez?
That nut! That damn nut! Oh, Bill, man... Did you know him?

No, but I loved his records.
Yeah, but damn, man, he was a nut. I met him in 1957. We were in the studio at 70 Broadway with [Blue Note founders] Alfred Lion and Francis Wolff. I had Eddie McFadden on guitar and Donald Bailey on drums. And, you know Babs, he lets everybody know when he's making his grand entrance. He used to wear a cape. He was like Batman and shit. Ask anybody about Babs Gonzalez. He wore a cape and all that kind of shit. And he thought he was gonna be my manager. He was telling people he had discovered me but I was discovered already. Blue Note had came down to Philadelphia and they heard me play there. Babs said he brought them down, you know, like he's my manager. So I had to deck this motherfucker, man. Did you know about his red pepper he'd throw in your eyes? Oh shit, he'd keep that in his lapel pocket. He wouldn't fight. He couldn't fight. He'd just throw pepper in your eyes, then he'd whup yo' ass. So this man... He say, "I'm your manager, motherfucker...." And he put that forceful voice shit on. And I say, "Oh, no you not." And you know, I been in the Golden Gloves since I been seven years old. In Philadelphia you got to be able to pug. You don't pug, you get your ass kicked too much. So I pugged my ass over. I was knockin' suckers out that were damn near 195 pounds, when I was in the Golden Gloves. You know what I mean? I decked them suckers, man. And when I hit Babs, he laid out so pretty like he was going to a funeral or something. I hit that motherfucker so hard. See, I forgot 'cause I lost my temper. He went out so nice, laid on the floor, and Alfred Lion is running around screaming, "Oh my god, Jimmy's killed the man!" And all this shit. Frank Wolff be coming around with his camera and everything. It was chaos in that fucking studio.

I know you got into some kind of karate.
Yeah, for 25 years now.

I've seen your album Respect *[Verve, 1967], where you got your kung fu robe on the cover.*
Not kung fu, motherfucker. That's shotokan. And that means sho-kill-yo'-ass. I studied that

particular method. Shotokan is when you go to the diaphragm and pull out the fucking food, show him what he ate for dinner, you understand? And I mean that shit. Go in there, pull them fuckin' greens out, put 'em right in his face, and watch him faint. You know what I mean?

Yeah, that would come in handy on the subway.
Hey man, shit, you don't need no damn gun. Pull them fucking intestines out—and they be movin', you know, like worms. That shit be running all over my damn hand.

OK... Switching topics here, how about telling us something about your early development on the organ.
Well, I wanted to learn fast, you see. I'm self-taught, you know. I left my organ in the warehouse where I supposed to pick it up and take it home. But I didn't want people to know I couldn't play that sumbitch. 'Cause I couldn't play it at first. So I left it in the warehouse and then... Incidentally, the warehouse that I left it in, my daddy had plastered this particular warehouse. I'm a plasterer by trade. My dad taught us, me and my brother. So it was right on time. My daddy was nicknamed Mr. Blue Jimmy. Anyway, I asked if I could store my organ in this little room and practice, and the warehouse guy said, "Do anything you want." So I stayed in that warehouse a year. I'd take my lunch, I'd take three sandwiches. And what I did, I had a guy make me a chart on the wall of the pedals, so I would look at that chart instead of looking down at the pedals to see where you was putting your foot. You look at the chart—that's how I taught myself from the chart so I wouldn't have to look down. You can't be looking down at the damn pedals on a gig. You wanna get the people's attention. So I taught myself my damn steps and I had to find my own sound. I kept pulling out stops until I lucked up on these three damn flute things. Then I cut my tremelo off to give it a big sound, and that sounded good. And that's where I got my sound. 'Cause I can put my tremelo to fast or medium or whatever to get the sound you want, see? So when I came out that fuckin' warehouse, man, I was ready for anybody.

So you still play the same type of instrument?
Yeah, same one, Hammond. Forty years and those motherfuckers never gave me one. They never gave me shit. I'm still mad at 'em. So anyway, I stayed in the warehouse for about a year—got a down payment from a loan shark, Mr. Goldstein. And he told me, "Now Little Sonny, I'm gonna have a man collecting every Saturday night." And man, this motherfucker Bob would come in to the club—he'd be half tanked anyway—and he always carried that damn piece with him because if you didn't pay, he'd blow your ass away. So I made sure I had that motherfucker's money, you know? Hey man, I *paid* for my organ. Anyway, I got to playing some blues one night and people be shouting—you know how black people holler, like they in church. Piercing sound—it hits you. Well, Bob was getting into it. He had been drinking and he got excited and puts up his hands in the air and yells out, "Yeah!" And his piece falls on the floor. Somebody shouts, "Man got a gun! Lord have mercy, man got a gun!" Cleared the fuckin' bar. And you know how black people are—they can move, boy. Now there's a spiral stairway in this club. Can you imagine a bunch of black folks trying to get up a spiral stairway—crawling all over each other, ladies got their dresses up, their bloomers showin' and shit—and I'm lookin'. It's hard to get past somebody on a spiral stairway, but niggas can tiptoe past each other, man, doin' 'bout a hundred mile an hour. Man with a gun... You kiddin'? They were *flying* up that damn staircase—like a black Batman or something. And the poor little Jewish club owner comes out in the middle of all this... "Vat iz goink on? Ver de people go? Vat gun? Ver iz de gun? Who's got de gun?"

Sounds like a scene from a movie.
Yeah, man. We had some fun back in the day. Still do.

JOE HENDERSON

I FIRST MET SAXOPHONIST Joe Henderson at a 1992 session he did for Verve, a tribute to Miles Davis entitled *So Near, So Far: Musings for Miles* (Verve, 1992). On the date were guitarist John Scofield, drummer Al Foster, and bassist Dave Holland and all seemed in a particularly inspired mood that day. The perennial Grammy winner and poll winner has since recorded a successful tribute to Antonio Carlos Jobim (*Double Rainbow,* Verve, 1994), an album of expanded arrangements of his own original material from the '60s and '70s (*Joe Henderson Big Band,* Verve, 1967) and a lush version of Gershwin's *Porgy & Bess* (Verve, 1997). The following 1992 interview was for the prestigious Japanese jazz magazine *Swing Journal.*

NOVEMBER 27, 1992

Born in Lima, Ohio, on April 27, 1937, Joe Henderson grew up listening to his brother's jazz records and was finally given a tenor saxophone at age nine. As he told *Down Beat*: "I listened to Lester Young, Flip Phillips, Stan Getz, Charlie Parker, all the people associated with Jazz at the

Philharmonic. This stuff went into my ears early on, so when I started to play the saxophone I had in my mind an idea of how that instrument was supposed to sound."

He studied for a year at Kentucky State before spending four years at Wayne State in Detroit, where he often gigged alongside Yusef Lateef, Barry Harris, Hugh Lawson, and Donald Byrd. In 1960, he was drafted into the military. During his two-year stint, he spent some time in France, where he met jazz expatriates Don Byas, Bud Powell, and Kenny Clarke. Upon being discharged from the service in 1962, he settled in New York and quickly hooked up with trumpeter Kenny Dorham, one of the most important creators on the scene at that time. Henderson's first recording date came with Dorham in April of 1963 (*Una Mas,* Blue Note). Two months later, he was given his own Blue Note debut as a leader, *Page One,* with Dorham, McCoy Tyner, Butch Warren, and Pete La Roca. He soon became an in-demand player in the Blue Note stable, appearing on important records that same year by Andrew Hill (*Black Fire*), Lee Morgan (*The Sidewinder*), and Grant Green (*Idle Moments*).

In mid-1964, Henderson replaced Junior Cook in the Horace Silver Quintet and appeared on Horace's very popular Blue Note recording *Song for My Father,* to which he contributed to the composition "The Kicker." The following year, he contributed the original "Mo' Joe" to Silver's follow-up album, *The Cape Verdean Blues.* In the liner notes to his adventurous 1964 album, *Point of Departure,* Andrew Hill is quoted as saying: "Joe Henderson is going to be one of the greatest tenors out there. You see, he not only has the imagination to make it in the avant-garde camp, but he has so much emotion, too. And that's what music is—emotion, feeling. Joe doesn't get into that trap of being so technical that the emotions don't come through."

Joe's playing on those early Blue Note sessions is marked by a blistering, big tone that recalls Sonny Rollins and Ben Webster while also moving skillfully in and out of the freedom bag. That chameleonic quality was perhaps best demonstrated on Larry Young's album *Unity* (Blue Note, 1965), with Elvin Jones and Woody Shaw. As (esteemed jazz critic) Nat Hentoff wrote in those liner notes: "By now it's an established fact that he is one of the more original and persistently evolving of the new tenor saxophonists. He has also proved more than equal to a wide variety of Blue Note settings—from basic blues to the most advanced, exploratory jazz." And in the liner notes to his 1967 Blue Note album, *The Real McCoy,* Tyner was quoted as saying, "If I had to use one word for Joe's playing, it would be 'mature.'" During the latter part of the '60s, Henderson moved to the Milestone label and released a number of revelatory albums, including *The Kicker* (Milestone, 1967) and *Power to the People* (Milestone, 1969).

In 1969, the saxophonist spent six months working with the pop-jazz band Blood, Sweat & Tears. Though it brought him more money and notoriety than he had seen before, that gig proved to be ultimately frustrating. Through the '80s, Henderson's growth was documented in a series of live trio recordings including *The State of the Tenor, Live at the Village Vanguard, Vols. 1 & 2* (Blue Note, 1985), and *An Evening with Joe Henderson* (Red Records, 1987). His first of several projects with Verve was *Lush Life: The Music of Billy Strayhorn* (1992), a collection of solo, duo, trio, quartet, and quintet performances featuring trumpeter Wynton Marsalis, pianist Stephen Scott, bassist Christian McBride, and drummer Gregory Hutchinson. *Lush Life* was a certifiable jazz hit, topping the *Billboard* jazz chart for seven weeks. In his 4½-star review of the album for *Down Beat,* Owen Cordle wrote of Joe's tenor playing: "His sound is at once sturdy, lean, overtone-conscious, and hard-hitting. Rhythmically, he leaves mortals in the dust at every turn."

In 1963, at age 26, Joe Henderson was listed in *Down Beat* as a tenor sax talent deserving of wider recognition. Twenty-nine years later, *Down Beat* paid Joe the singular honor of naming him a Triple Crown winner—Jazz Artist of the Year, Jazz Album of the Year (*Lush Life*), and #1 Tenor Saxophonist—in its 40th annual International Critics Poll. He also won similar Triple Crown honors that year in the 57th annual *Down Beat* Readers' Poll. The last artist to win in three categories on both polls was Duke Ellington in 1969. As Joe told *Down Beat:* "I think playing the saxophone is what I'm supposed to be doing on this planet. It's the best way I know that I can make the largest number of people happy and get for myself the largest amount of happiness."

For Henderson, the question became: "What next?"

Verve executive Richard Seidel provided the answer with *So Near, So Far: Musings for Miles,* a collection of tunes associated with the late, great Miles Dewey Davis, III. Performing alongside the #1 Tenor Saxophonist on this date are three excellent musicians who have all had some personal history on the bandstand with Miles. Bassist Dave Holland followed Ron Carter in the lineup, coming aboard in August of 1968 and remaining with Miles through the fall of 1971. Holland appears on such pivotal albums as *In a Silent Way, Bitches Brew,* and *Live/Evil.* Guitarist John Scofield played with Miles from 1982 to 1985 and appears on four albums—*Star People, Decoy, You're Under Arrest,* and *Siesta.* Drummer Al Foster joined Miles in 1971, replacing Jack DeJohnette. He was with the band through its most psychedelic phase, including such electrified albums as *Get up with It* (Columbia, 1972), *Dark Magus* (Sony, 1974), *Agharta* (Columbia, 1975), and *Pangaea* (Columbia, 1975). Foster remained close to Miles during the trumpeter's period of self-imposed exile from 1976 to 1980 and re-emerged as the drummer with the comeback band on *The Man with the Horn* (Columbia, 1981), *We Want Miles* (Columbia, 1981), *Star People* (Columbia, 1983), *Decoy* (Columbia, 1983), and *You're Under Arrest* (Columbia, 1985).

Over the years, Al Foster has remained a quiet, mysterious figure who shuns publicity and avoids interviews. Not surprisingly, he was unwilling to speak about Miles for this story, explaining only that the sense of loss he felt after Miles' death cannot be put into words. It was quite revealing, however, that during this session Foster had a photograph of Miles taped to one of his cymbals. "It was a picture of Miles with the words 'Blue in Green' written on the picture," says Richard Seidel. "He played the whole session looking at that picture."

It was with genuine feelings of love and respect that these four master musicians came together at the Power Station in New York City on three consecutive nights in early October 1992 to pay tribute to Miles. Seidel and Don Sickler, the trumpeter and arranger who had previously prepared a book of Joe Henderson solo transcriptions, got together and chose the material for this session. As Seidel pointed out, "I did not want to do tunes like 'So What' and 'All Blues,' which have been recorded over and over again. Because I think one of the things that works for a musician like Joe Henderson is to stimulate him with fresh material and in that way hope to inspire even greater improvising."

Seidel and Sickler put together a demo tape of Miles tunes and submitted it for Joe's approval. Sickler then went to work transcribing the music and rearranging it for quartet. This was a particularly tricky situation considering that a tune like "Miles Ahead" was originally scored for 19 pieces and the remainder were written with a piano quintet in mind. On "Flamenco Sketches," for instance, Sickler actually transcribed Bill Evans' voicings at the beginning of the piece and submitted the charts to Scofield to use as a jumping off point for his chordal work on that delicate ballad. As he explained, "I basically wrote down what I heard, putting down on paper as much as I could just to get the chords right. Bill played so delicately on that piece, using so very few notes in the chords. I also wrote down what Miles played but, of course, Joe just interpreted it his own way. That is always extremely interesting to notate something and then have a great artist like Joe Henderson take it in a different direction while still maintaining the melodic contour."

On the first night they cut "Swing Spring" (recorded by Miles in 1954 for Prestige), "Joshua" (recorded in 1963 on *Seven Steps to Heaven*), and "So Near, So Far" (also from *Seven Steps to Heaven*). On the second night, which I attended, they cut "Pfrancin' (No Blues)" (from the 1961 album *Some Day My Prince Will Come*), "Flamenco Sketches" (from the landmark 1959 album *Kind of Blue*), and "Milestones" (the mellow original from Miles' 1947 debut as a leader for Savoy, *Miles Davis All-Stars*). On the final night, they tackled more open-ended vehicles like "Circle" (from 1966's *Miles Smiles*), "Teo" (*Some Day My Prince Will Come*), and "Side Car" (from the 1968 recording

Circle in the Round) along with the challenging big band chart "Miles Ahead" (from the 1957 Columbia album of the same name).

The musicians shared a close feeling of camaraderie on the session and often spoke about Miles during the breaks, reminiscing about the man behind all this great music. I spoke to Joe Henderson at length later in his hotel room.

Both your Billy Strayhorn songbook and Miles Davis songbook have a very live quality to them.
Right, we tried to go for first takes in the studio on both of those records. That is basically the way that I am, a first take kind of person. If something goes down on tape that is going to cause one of the players some sleepless nights, then we'll do another take. But basically, there are mistakes that sound good and mistakes that don't sound good. And sometimes you have to leave the good ones in there.

Miles was especially good at that.
Right. It is possible to make a mistake on a note but you might be able to justify that note within the next group of notes, like Miles often did. It is a mistake only when you tell people it is. Left to their own ears, they wouldn't know the difference. So I, too, sometimes use a mistake as a jumping off point into some new idea. I'm not overly concerned with getting everything just perfect. I prefer going for the first take where you have the excitement of unfamiliarity kind of nudging you on. You are not as familiar with the piece of music on that first take as you would be on the third take. But it starts to get old fast. You start to lose a little of that freshness. I like dealing in that area where you don't quite know what it is that you're after. I will always go for that first take over one that is almost planned out to a point where you know it too well. There is a big difference there.

It's the difference between jazz and chamber music.
In a way. And on that level, I'll try to go for the first takes. On this Miles session, on the first day we went from one tune right to the next and ended up keeping a lot of first takes. On the second day we had a couple of tunes that we had to do again. And on the third day we did more takes. And they're all different takes, in terms of solos, feelings, stuff like that. I remember the first recording date that I did, a Kenny Dorham album for Blue Note called *Una Mas*. We made a few takes on some of the tunes and Kenny noticed that I was playing different stuff on my solos every time. I have always done this. I just grew up with this notion that you do not try to repeat ideas. You try never to play an idea that you know that you already played. That is the worst sin that you could possibly commit as a creative musician. Once you have played those ideas, then you bury them. You go on to the next set of ideas within the same parameters. And when you try to do that often enough, as I have over the last 30 years, that becomes a way of life.

The material on your Miles tribute album covers a lot of periods in his career.
That was the idea—to try and span as many decades as we could. Not all, of course. But I think there are four decades represented there. The earliest piece we did was "Milestones," the latest thing was "Side Car," which he did in the 1970s with George Benson.

This album carries the spirit of Miles but it also has your own unique stamp on it.
Right. A friend of mine kept telling me, "Joe, be sure that they don't make this a Miles Davis album. This is your album without a doubt." But I think we struck a delicate balance. We are definitely paying tribute to Miles in doing tunes associated with him, but we did them the way we would play them. I felt that Miles' spirit was very much in the room on those three days we recorded, but we were very careful not to just do a repeat of a Miles album. Having guitar instead of piano was just

one way of making a fresh statement on these old themes. On this album we are definitely paying homage to Miles, but it's not just a repeat or re-creation of what Miles had done. I don't think it would've been fair to do that. We played the tunes the way we play them and I think it worked, if I'm allowed to advance an opinion. This was a way of putting something back in the till, so to speak, by way of acknowledging one of the greatest musicians that has been on the planet in my lifetime.

A little-known fact about your career is that you actually played for a short period on the same bandstand with Miles Davis. Tell us about that.
My time with Miles was the shortest of anybody on this session, but I am sure I enjoyed it just as much. Actually, it was far too short. It was a brief period in 1967, just about four weekends, really. We played one weekend at Leonard's in Boston, we played one weekend at the Opera House in San Francisco, one weekend at the Village Vanguard in New York, and another weekend somewhere in Philadelphia though I can't remember the name of the place. And the time that I was there, the only constant in the band was me, Wayne Shorter, and Miles. I never knew who would be playing bass, drums, or piano from night to night. Herbie Hancock would show up one night, Chick Corea would show up the next night. Miroslav Vitous would be there one night, Eddie Gomez would be there the next. Jack DeJohnette would be there one night, Tony Williams the next. I think Miles was evolving in some kind of way. It was fun playing on the same bandstand with him but since the lineup kept changing so much, we were never able to really develop anything as a band. We never found a direction because the rhythm section never had a chance to gel. Plus, this gig came along at a time when I had already started to find my own way as a leader. I must have had seven or eight albums out on Blue Note by then and must have recorded on about 20 others as a sideman. So it was kind of an anti-climax for me at the time that it happened. Actually, Herbie told me that I was supposed to be in the band before Wayne got there. Apparently, my name came up as a replacement for John Coltrane in the Miles quintet. I had met Trane in Detroit and he ended up recommending me to Miles when he was getting ready to leave the band. But I got drafted into the army in 1960 and ended up doing my stint in the military, so I never got the gig. But the military was a good experience for me. I served in Europe and had a chance to meet a bunch of expatriate jazz musicians in France like Don Byas, Bud Powell, and Kenny Clarke. And I learned to speak French and German at that time. So even though I didn't get the gig with Miles, the military turned out to be alright for me. Fate has a way of dealing our cards to us. We just have to pick them up and follow on through with life.

Another little-known fact about you career is that you spent some time with the group Blood, Sweat & Tears. Tell us about that experience.
That was around 1969–1970, after I had played with Miles. I was there for about six months. It was great money coming in but I just couldn't imagine playing these songs over and over and over again. Finally I said, "Look guys, I can't take it anymore." I had to split. It was a disappointment for me. I had looked forward to doing some writing for the band and getting in and playing soprano and flute more. I just wanted to be broadened. When I joined Sweat, I got so many telephone calls from around the world, "Why did you do that? How can you leave jazz like that?" Then when I left the band, I heard so many comments like, "Well, at least you could've stayed long enough to get you some money." You can't win. But you have to understand, I had gone through a history of recordings with Blue Note where you rehearse some things for a couple of days, then go into the studio and make a record. And then to get thrown into a situation where the idea was... Well, there was so much money around and I'm going to rehearsals in a chauffeur-driven limousine—that just wore me down. I just am not made that way.

Where did you go from that gig?
I went back to doing what I had been doing previous to Blood, Sweat & Tears. Life just got back to normal again. All that press and stuff, that was highly unusual to me. Jazz artists weren't used to getting that kind of exposure. So I just got back to what, for me, was kind of a normal life, and I was pleased to do so. I liked the guys in Sweat but I had just hoped that opportunity would've gone so much farther than it did. I had been so much into this first take zone, I had been trained to do an album in three days at Blue Note. So the whole idea of taking a few months to put an album together was a little strange to me. I mean, why burn people out? Why play a thing to death? Nonetheless, for the little bit of time I was there, I did have fun imagining what it was gonna be like. We did four tracks, kept going back to square one with overdubs until I just couldn't take it anymore.

Do you feel like with this Verve relationship that you've entered a new phase in your career?
I kind of think so. This is the first time I've been with a big company that seems to care as much as Verve does, and that's a great feeling. It's not that Blue Note or Milestone didn't care, but they showed it in a different way than Verve does. They seem to believe in me here and I believe in them. It's almost an unreal marriage here. It's almost too right. But it seems to be working well. I think the companies do have to get behind the artists and do what they can to promote a product when it's a worthy product. And I'd like to think that a lot of those things I did for Blue Note were worthy products that could've just as well reached the kind of ears that *Lush Life* has reached and, I hope, this *Musings* album will reach as well.

Were you surprised by the success of Lush Life?
Naturally. I am not used to that sort of attention. But it's great because I think it's a nice record. So I am really pleased by the success of that album. It lived in the top zone of the jazz charts for nine weeks. In fact, it is still up there. That is a great feeling. And it could not have happened to two nicer entities—myself and Verve Records.

How do you react to all the critical acclaim that you have gotten lately, particular the Triple Crown awards from Down Beat?
Well, my immediate reaction is that this very well could have come 20 years ago. The records that I made 20 years ago or more are out there, so it is possible for comparisons to be made. The critics can go back and check the records and see amongst themselves that this could have been said about me 20 years ago. Now, that might sound kind of arrogant of me, but I have heard this so much in Europe. My fans over there are angry at *Down Beat* for taking so long to recognize me. "They wait 'till this guy's 55 years old—this is something they should've told him 30 years ago." They think I should be beside myself with anger, but I'm not. I'm just continuing to do what I do with or without this acclaim. That is the story of my life. I do not need these critics to tell me that what I have been doing is worthwhile. And if it makes *Down Beat* feel better to lay it on so thick now after ignoring me for so many years, well, that's fine.

To tell the truth, these honors really do nothing for my ego. The things that really give my ego a boost is coming up with a new tune or forging ahead with a new set of practice études and getting deeper into playing the saxophone and coming up with new things on the instrument. Those are the things that really excite me, not these honors, because honors can be fleeting. Next year somebody else walks away with all the honors. It is a bit questionable.... I mean, why now? Almost at a time when you don't give a shit about that kind of stuff, then here it comes. I've never been in that zone where I didn't care, but I never sought it out either. I've never been out trying to get that top trophy. That's not what I'm about. I'm about playing ballads, playing the blues, dealing with chord changes, coming up with different lines every time I'm up at bat. This time the ball gets knocked over the left field fence, next time it may be an inside the park home run, just as long as I make a good showing of it. And I have to please myself as well. So the acclaim... It's bittersweet, but so much more sweet than it is bitter.

What are you about at this point in your career?
About growth. I like to think that I have grown, that I continue to grow every day because I consciously try to do that. I think that is a responsibility that I owe to the art form, to the profession that I am hooked up with. I have gotten a lot from this music and I believe that it is up to me and to other people like me to add to it and evolve with it. That is my mission.

It is somehow fitting that success finally caught up with you rather than you trying to chase it down, as some have.
Exactly. I have seen some hardcore jazzers make a hard left turn and start chasing the dollar down. And they fell right on their faces doing it because it didn't work. I don't go in for jumping on any bandwagons. That, to me, would be living a lie.

How do you feel about the success of the so-called Young Lions?
Well, on the one hand, I am glad to see that a new generation is interested in getting serious on their instruments. That is always encouraging. But on the other hand, what do they have to say? Some of these kids are just out of college and they already have record deals and are leading bands. They haven't had any kind of apprenticeship. They haven't been on the bandstand with an elder, someone who has lived this music their whole lives. These kids go to music school and come out and start making records. Something is missing in that process and you can hear it in their playing. And that something is called life. But I believe you can hear the difference in a young player like Kenny Garrett. Here is a guy who has paid dues on the road and lived with this music. And I believe you can hear the difference in his playing as opposed to some of these so-called Young Lions.

You seem to be very committed to growth and change as an artist. Is the term "jazz musician" too confining for you?
I didn't ask to be narrowly defined as a jazz musician. I think of my own musical tastes as being more broad than that. I have listened to a lot of folk music through the years, I have played a lot of classical music, and I have very true feelings in those directions as well. There are impulses that I have that would surprise you. There is a part of me that just loves James Brown, and it has always been there. But other people have kind of defined me over the years as this jazz guy. And there is a large part of me that gets an awful lot of good feeling from being in that area. But that is not all that I am.

TONY WILLIAMS

IT IS SIMPLY ASTOUNDING to consider that drummer Tony Williams was a mere teenager at the time he joined Miles Davis. And yet, the rhythmic innovation and sheer command of his instrument that he demonstrated on '60s landmarks like *E.S.P., Nefertiti, Miles Smiles,* and *Sorcerer* still boggles the mind. While moderating a panel discussion on Tony's contribution to jazz at the 1997 *Jazz Times* convention, I was struck by the unabashed reverence that drummers Carl Allen, T. S. Monk, and Lewis Nash had for the man. And listening back to some of those great tracks like "Dolores," "Agitation," "Pinocchio," and "Footprints," we were all taken aback by how fresh and ferociously full of conviction it all sounded. Tony was the catalyst of Miles' second great quintet, pushing Herbie Hancock, Wayne Shorter, Ron Carter, and Miles himself to unprecedented heights in the annals of jazz. As Miles wrote in his autobiography, "I could definitely hear right away that this was going to be one of the baddest motherfuckers who had ever played a set of drums."

In the limelight from the time he was 17, Tony Williams grew up under close scrutiny from critics and colleagues alike. Consequently, not all of his musical choices—leaving Miles to form the seminal fusion band Lifetime, for instance—met with approval from the "jazz police." A proud, strong-willed individual all his life, Tony was blessed with extraordinary gifts and a hunger for learning. Like his mentor Miles, he kept moving, right up until the end. His swan song—*Wilderness* (Ark 21, 1996) featuring saxophonist Michael Brecker, guitarist Pat Metheny, bassist Stanley Clarke, and Herbie Hancock on piano—is a grandiose orchestral work that highlights Tony's composerly vision rather than his mighty chops behind the kit. I last saw him perform in mid December of 1996 at Birdland in Manhattan alongside pianist Mulgrew Miller and another former Miles quintet band mate, bassist Ron Carter. Though seemingly in good health and playing as strong as ever on that rare trio gig, Tony died only a few months later in the hospital following complications from routine gall bladder surgery. Speculation about hospital negligence and an impending lawsuit have flooded the jazz community since his death on February 23, 1997.

Although my final interview with Tony was conducted shortly after the release of *Wilderness,* the following interview (for a July '92 cover story in *Modern Drummer*) took place in Manhattan around the time of his fifth Blue Note release, *The Story of Neptune* (1991). I met Tony at the studio where he was presiding over a final mix. We walked Uptown to his hotel and chatted over cognac in the hotel bar.

DECEMBER 3, 1991

Pacing around the control room with a fat cigar jutting out the side of his mouth, Tony Williams is a portrait of swaggering intensity, Edward G. Robinson playing Little Caesar as he supervises the mixes of his new Blue Note album, *The Story of Neptune.* Working closely with engineer Bob Brockman, he listens intently to playbacks of a brisk, driving Latin number, "Neptune Overture: Creatures of Conscience." With Tony's keen ears and Bob's quick fingers at the board, they make a fast, efficient team as they hone in on the ultimate blend. "A little more in the toms," Tony commands like Captain Kirk at the helm of the Starship Enterprise. And when Bob suggests that they bring up the bass drum just a bit, Tony nods in agreement, as if to say, "Make it so," in the manner of another captain of the Enterprise, Jean-Luc Picard.

Satisfied with the mix, they move on to the luscious ballad "Neptune Pavanne: Never Fear." Wallace Roney's muted trumpet work here conjures up haunting memories of Miles Davis—shades of *E.S.P.* Tony feels it, too. He takes a deep puff on his cigar and gazes at the ceiling. An audible sigh escapes his lips. The melancholy mood is suddenly broken by "Crime Scene," a jaunty funk-swing number in the Horace Silver/Art Blakey tradition. Tony breaks up the beat in odd, unpredictable ways, coaxing the other musicians with assertive bursts from the snare before unleashing on the kit at the tag. He hears the sizzle and seems pleased.

Tony's signature ride cymbal work sets the tone for a unique rendition of the Beatles tune "Blackbird," a pleasant ditty done up with a swinging new suit of clothes. As the tune fades, Tony turns to me and says, "Get ready for this next one." A sly smile breaks across his face as the tune begins. It's "Neptune Finale: The Earthling," a mind-blowing showcase of the drummer's legendary chops, guaranteed to leave aspiring drummers gasping in awe. Switching gears, he moves from polyrhythmic bombast to sublime lyricism on a velvety smooth rendition of "Poinciana," a piece further distinguished by Tony's rare use of brushes. The album closes on a rousing note with Freddie Hubbard's "Birdlike," a supersonic 4/4 romp paced by his inimitable high hat/ride cymbal pulse. A flurry of double bass drums and crashing cymbals at the tag puts the finishing touches on this latest Tony Williams project, his finest effort as a leader since signing on with Blue Note back in 1985.

A boy wonder with Miles Davis more than a quarter of a century ago (he came aboard at age 17 and makes his first recorded appearance with Miles on the 1963 quintet album *Seven Steps to Heaven*), Tony has attained sage-like status in the jazz world. A world class drummer, venerated bandleader, and respected composer, he has become a mentor figure to his young sidemen—trumpeter Wallace Roney, pianist Mulgrew Miller, bassist Ira Coleman, and saxophonist Billy Pierce. His torso may be thicker, his butt wider, his demeanor a bit more judicious and professorial, but at 47 he still plays with the burning, youthful enthusiasm he exhibited through his groundbreaking work with the Miles Davis Quintet (1963–1968) and his own revolutionary fusion band Lifetime (with organist Larry Young, guitarist John McLaughlin, and later bassist Jack Bruce).

Anthony Williams was born in Chicago on December 12, 1945. The son of a tenor saxophonist, he grew up in Boston and began studying with Alan Dawson at age nine. By 13, he was sitting in frequently with organist Johnny "Hammond" Smith, an experience that later served as a role model for his guitar-organ-drums trio Lifetime. Tony worked around Boston as a teenager with multi-reedman Sam Rivers and worked in the house rhythm section at Connelly's, where he backed visiting headliners. One such headliner who came through town was hard bop alto sax great Jackie McLean, who was amazed by the 16-year-old's drumming prowess. Tony eventually moved to New York in December of 1962 to work with McLean. In May of 1963, he got the call from Miles. Tony's volcanic drumming style—a bridge between the complex polyrhythms of Elvin Jones and the free floating pulsations of Sunny Murray—became a catalytic force in the second great Miles Davis Quintet.

As Miles himself mentions in his provocative book, *Miles: The Autobiography* (Simon & Schuster, 1991): "Just hearing that little motherfucker made me excited all over again.... He just lit a big fire under everyone in the group. Tony was always the center that the group's sound revolved around. He was something else, man."

During his tenure with Miles, Williams moonlighted on a number of important Blue Note sessions, including Herbie Hancock's *Maiden Voyage* (1965), Jackie McLean's *One Step Beyond* (1963), Andrew Hill's *Point of Departure* (1964), Wayne Shorter's *The Soothsayer* (1965), and Eric Dolphy's *Out to Lunch* (1964). He debuted as a leader on Blue Note in 1964 with *Life Time* and followed that up the next year with *Spring,* both albums serving as a showcase for his budding compositional prowess while also revealing Tony's connection to the avant-garde. In 1968, he left Miles to blaze a new direction in music with Lifetime. Their initial offering, *Emergency* (Polydor, 1969), is considered a fusion classic. Its bristling energy predated Miles Davis' own experiments in that direction with *A Tribute to Jack Johnson* (Columbia, 1971) by two years and spawned such off-shoot projects as John McLaughlin's Mahavishnu Orchestra and later John Abercrombie's Timeless trio with Jack DeJohnette and Jan Hammer. A mid-1970s edition of the band, dubbed New Lifetime, featured the incredible guitar pyrotechnics of Allan Holdsworth but was considered less successful than the earlier outfit.

In 1977, Tony moved from New York to his present country home in Marin County, just north of San Francisco. That year he reunited with his Miles Davis Quintet band mates to form V.S.O.P., an all-star acoustic jazz quintet named after the finest cognac money could buy. It was an appropriate name for a group that also boasted such names as Wayne Shorter, Ron Carter, Herbie Hancock, and Freddie Hubbard, who filled Miles' spot in the quintet.

Tony broke a long recording dry spell as a leader in 1979 with *The Joy of Flying,* a hastily thrown together project for Columbia that featured an all-star cast including Cecil Taylor, Tom Scott, George Benson, Michael Brecker, and Herbie Hancock. Switching gears in 1981, he went back out on tour with V.S.O.P. In 1982, he appeared on the self-titled debut album by 19-year-old trumpet sensation Wynton Marsalis and in 1983 V.S.O.P. continued to tour and record with Marsalis replacing Hubbard.

Tony entered into his second phase with Blue Note in 1985 with the release of *Foreign Intrigue,* an album that blended in his brilliant kit playing with DMX drum machine and Simmons electronic drums in a modern mainstream setting. That debut album featured veterans Ron Carter and vibist Bobby Hutcherson and it also marked Tony's initial contact with up-and-coming stars pianist Mulgrew Miller and trumpeter Wallace Roney. With *Civilization* (1987) Williams hit on a new formula with Roney, Miller, and saxophonist Billy Pierce. Their chemistry became apparent on *Angel Street* (Blue Note, 1988) and they took it up a notch the following year with *Native Heart.* Now with

The Story of Neptune, the Tony Williams Quintet has cohered into an incredibly interactive unit that stands as one of the finest acoustic jazz groups on the scene.

Following the intensive mixing session at the studio, we cabbed Uptown to Tony's hotel. At the bar, the conversation flowed as freely as the V.S.O.P.

The last time you did a major interview with Modern Drummer, *you were just beginning your second phase with Blue Note. So much has happened since then. You have a whole body of work with this new band.*
Yeah, these five years for me have been an incredible learning experience and something that I hadn't foreseen. It's afforded me the opportunity to work with a bunch of excellent young musicians that have given their all to this project. When it started out I didn't know how long it would go. And the reason I started the band was first I wanted to see if what I had been studying in the years previously would take hold. Basically, I wanted to see if I had learned anything from the composition classes I took. *The Joy of Flying* came up so quickly. Columbia said, "Make this record." But I didn't have anything prepared and I couldn't write quickly like a composer should be able to. I realized then that I had to acquire some tools that I didn't have. So I set about gaining those tools, from '80 to '86.

It sounds like a different kind of woodshedding.
Yeah. I had other types of bands and I had been in bands like this but I had never put a band together like this myself. So it was kind of scary to try it. I didn't know if there was an audience for it, if the music that I was going to write was viable for me, if I could write the things that I like to play. So these past five years, from '86 to '91, have been very gratifying. This new record sounds better than I had hoped it would. And I like that experience because it comes from being able to let go of things. There's a bunch of ideas that I had for this latest project that didn't make it on the record. In other words, I didn't force something. I just let myself be open to things or just let things happen. And the results were even better than I had planned them to be.

How were you composing pieces like "Hand Jive" and "Pee Wee" back with Miles in the '60s?
I was composing those things the way I still compose now. Those things just came to me. I'd sit down at the piano and play these things out and they'd come up.

So you always had keyboard knowledge.
Yeah, I have harmony knowledge and theory. I could always read. But composition is different. You know, really knowing how to structure things. Those other things just came to me. But actually sitting down and saying, "I want to form a tune like this." Not just happenstance, not just, "Oh, that sounds good, I'll use that." Where you actually say, "I wanna do this and I wanna do that." That's when you're a composer, when you can actually take something and direct it the way you want it to, working with the logic of harmonic rhythm and melodic cohesiveness. And the other part of it is, back with Miles it took me ages to write things because I'd agonize over them. If I had an idea, I wouldn't know how to develop it. Now through taking composition classes, I know how to take three notes and develop it into more, to take an idea and develop it. Before I would take an idea and say, "Gee, that's a nice idea, but what comes next?" And that was the thing about becoming a composer. I can write fast now. I can take something and build upon it. You know, those tunes like "Hand Jive" and "Black Comedy" and "Pee Wee," those are only three tunes in the midst of, what—six years of working with Miles. Those took me a long time to put together.

*What about the stuff on your first two Blue Note albums [*Spring *and* Life Time*]?*

Those are in another vein. Those are more sort of free playing, avant-garde kind of things. And they came out really well.

Is that kind of coming out of your experience with Sam Rivers in Boston?
No, those were coming out of my experience with a lot of things—my love for Ornette Coleman's music at the time, Cecil Taylor's music, Eric Dolphy, all the things that I had heard that I was really involved in. I was listening to a lot of Bartók at that time, every day, Stockhausen and a lot of Stravinsky. So it was wide-ranging influences. And you have to remember, the times were different then. The times you live in have to do with what you produce, and you can either control that or not. The '70s for a lot of people were a reaction to the '60s. And if you didn't live in the '60s, then you didn't have to react to it. So I get a little upset.... I think it's funny to hear people talk about the electric music that jazz went into in the '70s, especially from guys who were toddlers in the '60s, you know what I mean? And they start passing judgment on music that bands came out with, either jazz-rock or fusion music. But they didn't have to deal with the times. I was playing music in the '60s so I had to think to myself, "What am I gonna do next?" But if you didn't have to do that, of course, you can sit back on Mt. Olympus and pass judgment on what other people did in the '70s.

You've written some tunes in the '80s, like "Sister Cheryl" and "Angel Street," that will stand up over time.
Yeah, well that was one of my goals, even when I was a youngster—to write music that other people would want to play. Not just to hear people say, "Wow, you can write music." That wasn't necessarily enough for me. I wanted to be able to write music that other musicians could play. That's important to me. There's a lot of things I want to do in this genre of acoustic jazz with the classic setup of two horns, piano, bass, and drums—the quintet sound that I grew up with. I want people to hear it and to know that it's a living language. This is not some museum stuff. It's not Latin or Esperanto, something that isn't spoken anymore. And I also wanted to give it some of the power and some of the other things that you don't generally hear in this genre. And the way I record the drums has a lot to do with the bigness of the sound.

You didn't have that kind of presence in the Miles quintet.
Right, you didn't have that back then. Again, that was a different time and those records sound great. But these are my records now and I want my drums and what I have to say to have a real presence. And I take pride in the fact that I do have a recording concept. Working in the studio is a whole other discipline and process that has to be learned. Just playing an instrument is not enough. You have to know how to play that instrument and you have to know how to record it, how to put it on tape, how to make it sound good. And I like that. I like the process of recording, which is different than performing, which is another discipline again from writing music. Writing music is a very solitary, lonely process. I sit in a room with a blank piece of paper in the morning and hopefully by five o'clock that afternoon I've got some stuff down on paper. So the recording process is another process that has to be really studied and appreciated. And the things I've learned about what I wanna do, even through just hearing the music of today, I can bring some of that bigness and power to a group that's just acoustic and make it work. And you don't hear that with other bands.

How would you compare yourself as a bandleader to the way Miles ran his bands?
Well, because I'm a drummer, I do things differently than somebody else would do it. See, I don't play piano or saxophone or what normally would be called a scale instrument so I have to pay a little bit more attention to detail than somebody else might. They can do a lot of things quicker than I can. So I take a little more time and I listen to rehearsal tapes of the band a lot to make sure that

certain things are the way I want them to be. Because I'm the one that has to take either the credit or the abuse if it's good or bad.

Sounds like you're more of a perfectionist in the process than Miles was.
Yeah, I have to be because I'm a drummer, and a drummer's role is different than a horn player. And secondly, drummers aren't thought of as having these abilities that other people have. So I've had to also work very hard at not having a chip on my shoulder. I try to have that not come across in my music or in anything I do. Because, you know, people kind of look down on drummers.

You really think so?
Sure. Well, when I grew up, that's the way it was. There's a joke: What do you call people who hang out with musicians? Drummers. And so the drummer was always the least paid.... I remember people telling me that I couldn't get as much as the other guys in the band because they had to pay to get the drums to the job. So immediately you're penalized for playing the drums. And people think of the drummer as the least educated, the most uninhibited, you know, like a wild man. All those kinds of things. So that's what I've been dealing with throughout my career and I try not to wear that as a defensive thing. I don't go around saying, "It's because I'm a drummer." But I know that it's still there. So I have to make sure that the records don't sound like a drummer's record, that they sound like music.

So basically, drummers can't get no respect.
Well, everybody knows that. It's not something that's unique to me saying that. I mean, the drum set is an American invention, it's an American treasure, but it isn't afforded the dignity that people will afford, say, harmonica. That's just a fact of history. And it's just not drummers, it's the whole concept of the drum set itself. It's the only instrument that people play around the world that is like that. The drums of Africa and India and Japan—they don't sit down and play with their feet and their hands at the same time. This is a very unique configuration in the musical history of the world. And it isn't really—by Americans, where it was invented—afforded the kind of dignity that it should have. But that's a whole other article.

But there's a whole legacy of drum royalty, from Baby Dodds and Big Sid to Art Blakey and Max Roach and beyond.
Yeah, I'm not questioning that. Of course there is. I'm talking about how the drummer is perceived in people's minds. I mean, do you know that there is a fear of drums?

What is it based in?
It's based in myth and folklore and stuff like that. I mean, I had some woman at a Hertz counter ask me one time, "Why do drummers take drugs?" She didn't ask me is it true that drummers take drugs. To her it was a fact and a natural thing. Drummers have been perceived since the beginning as the crazy person in the band, the wild man, the least educated. I can't go into why and the whole chronological order of how it came to be that way. But we all know it's true.

Can you relate the story of when you first saw Miles play and how you got the gig with him?
I first saw Miles in Boston in 1961. It was the band with Paul Chambers, Hank Mobley, Wynton Kelly, and Jimmy Cobb, who I had met a year earlier. I asked Jimmy if I could sit in and he said, "You'll have to ask Miles." Being a brash kid with no fear, I actually went right up to Miles and asked him and all he said was, "Go back to your seat, sit down, and listen." So that was the first time I met him. A couple of years later he saw me play a gig. I had been in New York about four or five months,

working with Jackie McLean. Miles came in with Philly Joe Jones to check me out. I think Jackie had been telling him about me. About a month later, Miles called me from California and asked if we could get together when he got back to New York. We rehearsed at his place with Ron Carter and Herbie, and that turned out to be his next band, along with George Coleman on tenor sax.

That group, and especially the lineup with Wayne Shorter, had an incredible chemistry.
Yeah, chemistry is everything. And I have that same kind of chemistry with my band now. I really can't deal with some guy who has the attitude that he is just temporarily in the band because he's just waiting to be a big star. I had somebody like that for a brief time but he's not in the band any longer. Hasn't been for a while. I need people around me who are committed to the band, who like the music, who want to play this music. Same thing with the booking agency and management. They have to be clear-minded people who don't get crazy over the littlest things. That's been my goal, and now I have that. Now I'm surrounded by nice people who aren't out to prove anything. I just wanna make music, I wanna play the drums, and I wanna get better and play better dates. That's it. I'm not trying to beat anybody over the head with political things and I'm not a purist. And I don't need people around me telling me that I'm a legend and that I should be only doing this and this and this, and that jazz is this pure music that... I don't know, I don't wanna say anymore. I'll get in trouble.

I'm interested in your decision to include a Beatles tune on this new album. I've heard "Blackbird" done a couple of times before but I've never heard it swing like that.
Really? Thank you. Well, it's because I'm a real big fan of The Beatles. And when I say that, people get nuts. I had this Beatles poster in my apartment and people would come to visit and they'd see this poster and say, "Man, why you got that on your wall?" You know, here I am supposed to be this "jazzer" and I'm listening to The Beatles. But the thing is, it's the context that people don't wanna deal with. When The Beatles hit, I was still 17, 18 years old. That was part of my generation's music. So why wouldn't I like that music. When I was a kid, my dad was listening to Basie and Gene Ammons and I was starting to listen to Miles and all the jazz stuff. But I was also hanging out with kids my own age who were listening to The Everly Brothers, Frankie Lymon & The Teenagers, The Flamingos, and that kind of music in the '50s. So I'm a person of my generation.

Yeah, even Leonard Bernstein was checking out The Beatles when they came out.
Right. And so was I. I liked them. I said something to somebody in a clinic once. He said, "You liked the Beatles?" And I said, "Yeah." And he said, "You mean Ringo?" And I said, "Did I say Ringo?" It was the tunes that I liked. None of them were great players. It's the tunes, the music, the whole thing, the times. And as a young person—even now when I listen to some of that stuff, it connects with me. I recently picked up that complete package that they were selling about a year ago. It's got all the albums that they ever made. It's part of our culture. I also got into Jimi Hendrix and Cream and that was some of the stuff that influenced me when I decided to leave Miles in 1968. I decided to leave before that, but then I left at the end of '68 and got the first Lifetime band. I wanted to create a different atmosphere than I had been in. So I said, "What better way to do it than to go electric." And the other influence I had from my youth was organ trios—Jimmy Smith kind of stuff. I used to play in bands like that in Boston when I was a kid. I used to play a lot with Johnny Hammond Smith. He really liked the way I played and I did a lot of gigs with him. So then later on I said, "Gee, that would be a nice way to do it—organ, guitar, and drums. But do it real aggressive, with a lot of rock'n'roll kind of feeling, energy, power.... BAM!! And when we did it—it started in 1969—there was no thing called fusion music. We called it jazz-rock.

The music was so raw and outrageous it was threatening. But the so-called fusion movement at some point got too polite.
Yeah, and you can't be polite about it. Now the guys you hear now is like stuff you hear in restaurants and in elevators. And they call that fusion music.

It's interesting because there's a whole new audience of people who are hearing Lifetime records for the first time and they're inspired by that raw energy.
Yeah, I'm glad. Lifetime was something that had to be done at that time. And certain people hated it. But I'm so used to that [criticism]. I have to do things and I know that there's going to be a certain level of people that are going to cry out, "Why did you do that? Why did you have to do that?" And it's very curious to me.

You recently did a tour with Jan Hammer and Fernando Saunders.
Yeah, we did a brief tour of six cities. That kind of music was not about subtlety at all. It was slamming all night. It was fucking great. We did three of my tunes, the ones I did at the Herbst Theater thing with Herbie. And then the rest of it was Jan's music, stuff he had done with Jeff Beck years ago and some "Miami Vice" stuff. It was thrilling. And it was not fusion, it was rock.

Was it reminiscent of your second Lifetime band with Allan Holdsworth?
Not at all. That was the second edition of that band, it was called the New Lifetime. I wasn't really happy with that, but I learned a lot from that experience. The guys were great but the band had a different attitude. It just wasn't the same without Larry Young. He was the heart of that original Lifetime band. And that band fell apart, unfortunately.... I think the beginning of the end was when Jack Bruce came in the band, not because of Jack but because everyone started to have their own idea of what it should be. And it was a big lesson and a big learning experience for me because I realize, looking back on it, that if you don't have a vision then you can't tell people what it's supposed to be. So everybody in the band started having their own vision of where it should be. And I was very young at that time. But that's why I left Miles. I left him because I had been with him six years and his band was changing and I felt that I wasn't needed any more. So I said, "Well, if I'm gonna be on the road and writing music and playing drums for the rest of my life, I should get out here and make all the mistakes that I'm gonna make early while I'm still young because when you're that young you have the resiliency to bounce back from your mistakes." So that's what I did. Maybe at the age I'm at now it's harder to bounce back, but that's what happened back then. I was always young enough that I could learn from those mistakes and bounce back.

Did you play at that Paris concert with Miles last summer? [An all-star tribute concert in which alumni from various Miles Davis bands appeared on stage with the maestro to re-create tunes from yesteryear.]
No, no one called me.

I saw him at Montreux the day before playing the music of Gil Evans with Quincy Jones conducting a huge orchestra.
Yeah, Wallace was there. He told me about it. I don't wanna spend too much time on this, but Miles' passing is really hard for me. It's something I still can't believe and I don't think I ever will. I just think that... You know... It's just, ah... I mean, he was a...very significant person. Just a... It's not supposed to be this way.

It was really wonderful to see Wallace playing right alongside of him. It was like the father and the son. They really had a close rapport. And sometimes on your new record when Wallace puts the mute

in sort of conjures up that image of Miles.
Yeah, the reason Wallace is great to me is because he plays on the edge. He's always on the edge of making a mistake. A lot of trumpet players right now play too perfect—these young guys that are in the news—we won't mention names.

I know who you're talking about.
And they just... I can't play with that. I don't like it. It's just... I like that edge feeling and Wallace is the only guy around who plays like that, of the young guys.

That's interesting, because Miles said in his autobiography that you play on the edge, that you fired up the band.
Yeah, I never read his autobiography. But Wallace plays like that, too, and that's important. I hear a lot of guys playing—really I don't because I don't listen a lot to the radio.... But from what I've heard, these guys are playing and instead of getting all this press... It's real boring, really fucking boring shit! This real controlled kind of focused kind of trumpet sound, it's just some very retentive shit. I'm not into that museum shit at all. And I don't want people around me who wanna just do that.

It's like hanging out with undertakers.
Yeah, that's a good phrase. I don't hang out with no fucking undertakers. 'Cause I'm still a young man and I'll always be a young person at heart. I mean, life is too short to hang it up and settle. I don't want to settle for anything. And I'm not afraid. I don't live in fear. And I'm tired of people telling other people what they should listen to. I'm not into naming names only because that's not the point of the conversation. I'm not into making controversy about "So and so said this. What do you think about this?" And you say, "Well, I think he's full of shit." And then they take that back to the guy, "So and so says you're full of shit." So, you know, I'm not into creating this back and forth thing in the press. All I'm saying is, people who have this thing about music who want to tell other people that this music here is not good and this music over here sucks, you should only listen to this.... That to me is musical fascism.

I agree. Some of my colleagues are like that.
Right. And they don't wanna let people... It's like the issue of pro-choice or pro-life. See, I don't believe in abortion. But, I do believe in a woman's right to choose. People lump everyone together. They say, "Well, if you're pro-choice, that means you're pro-abortion." That's not true. I'm sure there are many people like me who say, "No, we don't believe in abortion. But I'm not a woman and I'm not the State. And I'm not gonna tell a woman what she has to do. And I don't want the State to tell a woman that she doesn't have the right to choose." I think that's very important. And that's what's happening in music. There's a bunch of assholes out here—writers and musicians—and there are writers who are mouthpieces for other musicians. And I'll name a name for you—Stanley Crouch. He's a mouthpiece. And I don't know if you saw his article in *The New Republic* on Miles. That shit is so fucking disgusting!

He was talking more about himself than about Miles.
Exactly. He's trying to let people know how much he knows. And he's a mouthpiece for somebody else, this other trumpet player who has no talent and who will never come close to making a great record. And then the other thing that pissed me off was the contribution that Miles has made to American culture, to American society—not musically, I'm just talking about culture and society, as a person, as a man. It's scary. Why trash him? I mean, what good does it do? Of course, there are certain things that Picasso wasn't, that Beethoven wasn't, that Edison wasn't. Edison didn't invent

this, Edison didn't invent that. But who fuckin' cares? What they did do was so important that the only reason you would trash them is for your own benefit. And then the other thing is, a guy like Miles was a man. And he did things—it sounds kind of trite—manly, forthrightly. The only reason a man like Stanley Crouch would do that is 1) to make himself look important, 2) for money, or 3) it's like a little kid, a little boy... You know like when a little boy goads his parents to see how far he can push them? That mischievous kind of attitude. Like a little boy testing his own power. It's not adult, it's not manly. It's like a brat attitude, like how far can I push the establishment? You know, because he likes being disliked. He likes putting himself in the position of saying, "Well, I'm saying something that nobody wants to hear." It's like when you're a little kid and you tug on your mother's dress and she says stop it, you keep tugging because you know that she's getting mad. You know what I mean? That kind of fucking adolescent bullshit. And Miles is too important to do that to. Why didn't he do that to fuckin' Stan Getz? There's a million people he could've written that thing about, man. And Miles is just too important to just—never mind.

I know what you're saying. I was really angry when I read that article.
Yeah, man. I was just so fuckin' mad, because it had no rhyme or reason. It had no reason to be. And Miles was like a father to me! I mean, he meant so much, you know? I wouldn't be the person I am, whatever that is, if it weren't for him. And for a know-nothing like fuckin' Stanley Crouch to use that now just for his own—anyway.

Some used-to-be-a-drummer telling Miles what time it is.
Right. And you can print what I just said. I mean, I don't give a fuck about Stanley Crouch. In fact, I would like that to be printed. He's just... It's just an adolescent attitude and he's just a mouthpiece for this other jerk who can't hold a candle to Miles. And it's easy to understand what he'll say: "Well, Tony says that because... (whatever)."

Changing the subject, you play brushes on "Poinciana" on this new album. That's pretty rare, isn't it?
Well, yeah, I played brushes with bands when I was younger and on other people's records. But this is the first record of my own that has my name on it and my band where I played brushes on a track. Basically, I'm not that fond of brushes but I think it's a nice touch on this record. I get criticized because in live performances and maybe even in records people say, "Well, you play real loud." But my response to that is that it's a conscious decision on my part. It's not like I don't know that I'm playing loud. I mean, that's drumming. If you want polite, go listen to the MJQ. If you want soft, listen to Sergio Mendes. See, the drums to me... That's part of the ethic and the whole world of drumming. It's like, if you don't want drums to be loud, then it's like telling a piccolo player, "Don't play high." It's like telling a trumpet player, "Don't be so brassy." It's like telling a bass player, "Don't play low." That's part of what the drums are about. Volume and physicality and aggressiveness. That's drumming, to me. The drums are real important to me. Part of the character of what I've always tried to do is make the drums sound good to people. And that's why I play the way I play, to wake people up and make people think, "Oh, the drums are more than just bang-bang, crash-crash." I play loud because it's part of the vocabulary of the drums. But then I also play other things. I play soft, I play medium, I play almost loud, I play real loud. If you look at the body of my work or on many different albums of different people, you have a whole gamut of dynamics. I can play whatever you want. But when I do play loud, it sounds good, I think. I'm not just thrashing around.

That must've been frustrating to you as a kid growing up listening to records when drums were not recorded so good.
Well, not really. Actually I heard more good than I heard bad. I remember one time when I was a

kid coming to tears because Art Blakey sounded so good and I couldn't duplicate that on my drum set in my bedroom. And I didn't realize that it was because he was in a studio with microphones and everything. Here I was in my bedroom playing my tinny drum set and I didn't sound like Art Blakey. And I was so broken by that: "Oh God, I'll never be a good drummer." Blakey sounded so good.... The way his high hat sounded in combination with the cymbal, the press rolls. And here I was 13 years old, totally broken.

Too many young kids today think that drums started with Dave Weckl.
Right. I know the name and I've met him and I know he plays with Chick, but I've never heard a record. I like to stay away from these guys. He came onto me one time, like a lot of guys do—they come onto me like they're the "new thing" and I'm the old guy. You know? Lenny White did that to me years ago. And what is Lenny White doing today? And Dave Weckl, he's playing with Chick and that's great. But I stay away from these guys, specifically. Their playing is more about style than substance. And style is not important, style is not music. Anybody can get on the drum set and play real fast. I saw a kid four or five years ago at the NAMM convention.... He must've been five or six years old and he was playing all this solo stuff. And people were amazed. But who is he gonna play with? I mean, solos are one thing. Playing fast around the drums is one thing. But to play music, to play with people for people to listen to, that's something else. That's a whole other world. And if you think you're more important than the drums are, you got another thing coming. You gotta make the drums sound good. You're not sitting back there to make you sound good. You're sitting back there, first of all, to make the music sound good. And then to make the drums sound good and to be a drummer. Not to make people say, "Oh man! Can that guy play!"

You've accomplished so much in your career and yet you feel that you're still learning.
Of course. Learning is something that I really enjoy. I'm always taking lessons for something. Since I moved to California in '77 I've gone to cooking classes, I've learned how to swim, I've taken up tennis, I took an intensive course in German, I'm dealing in the stock market. I have a subscription to the *Wall Street Journal,* I look at it every day. It's fun. The next thing I'm gonna do is scuba diving. I'm always trying new things. I feel like an eternal student. I'm always trying to learn something new and it's a great feeling.

You can't sit still.
No, I sit still a lot. I'm a couch potato. I watch a lot of TV.

Your mind can't sit still.
Right, I need stimulation—to learn, to keep feeling like I'm going somewhere emotionally.

© TERI BLOOM

STEVE COLEMAN &
BRANFORD MARSALIS

IN THE FALL OF 1991, *DOWN BEAT* magazine was intrigued by the notion of getting alto sax-ophonist and bandleader Steve Coleman to sit down in a freewheeling conversation with tenor and sopra-no great Branford Marsalis, who at the time was touring with his hard-hitting, interactive trio. It seemed a natural pairing. Both are musical renegades pursuing strongly individualistic visions. And both are out-spoken in their own ways—Coleman against musical conservatism and edicts from "the jazz police," Marsalis against ig'nance in general. The following interview took place in haste, backstage at the Joyce Theater just moments before Coleman's band went on. Both musicians were in good spirits and into the spontaneous flow of our backstage chat. The resulting interview appeared as a January '92 cover story under the heading "GANG OF 2: Branford Marsalis and Steve Coleman—A Wild, Free-form Session!"

Born in Chicago on September 20, 1956, Steve Coleman, co-founder of the Brooklyn-based M-Base collective, continues to explore his ongoing fascination with rhythm with two bands, Five Elements and his 21-piece big band, The Council of Balance. Some months after this interview, Branford took over the job as musical director for "The Tonight Show" with Jay Leno. However, being cast as Jay's sidekick rubbed Branford the wrong way and after two years on the show, and the celebrity that came with it, he bailed. In 1995 he began combining jazz and hip-hop elements in his rock-funk band Buckshot LeFonque, which recorded two albums for Columbia and toured extensively. More recently, Marsalis returned to the jazzy side of things with a quartet featuring longtime associates Kenny Kirkland on piano and Jeff "Tain" Watts on drums. Branford, who was born in New Orleans on August 26, 1960, also happens to currently be heading up the jazz division at Sony-owned Columbia Records, where he is putting his strong opinions to good use on the executive side of things.

SEPTEMBER 15, 1991

The posters were splashed all over town: BRANFORD MARSALIS with very special guests STEVE COLEMAN and his Five Elements. DON'T MISS THIS EXPLOSIVE SAX SHOWDOWN. FIVE EXTRAORDINARY PERFORMANCES ONLY!

While it wasn't exactly a cutting contest on the order of Flip Phillips and Lester Young in one of their classic JATP battles, the two did mix it up a little bit during their recent week-long engagement at the Joyce Theater, a prestigious concert hall in the Chelsea section of Manhattan that ordinarily showcases up-and-coming dance companies.

Coleman and his Five Elements opened with an electrified, rhythmically charged set, serving as a visceral counterpart to the acoustic intimacy of Branford's trio (with bassist Robert Hurst and drummer Jeff Watts). Steve exuded a funky Brooklyn street vibe with basketball shoes and colorful, loose-fitting garb. Branford dressed strictly *GQ*. Coleman danced openly to the groove, his unbound enthusiasm at times causing him to leap off the ground, à la Pete Townshend. Branford played it cool.

Seemingly polar opposites—one an upstart on the cutting edge, the other part of the jazz establishment by virtue of his family name—and yet beneath the surface the two saxophonists have much in common, not the least of which is a wicked sense of humor and their mutual disdain for critics. The week-long engagement at the Joyce gave audiences a chance to hear for themselves what they have in common musically. I spoke to both saxophonists backstage just minutes before their final night together.

This is kind of an unlikely double bill. It sort of implies the two of you are kindred spirits.
Branford Marsalis: Is that true, Steve? No, not us, man.
Steve Coleman: We supposed to hate each other.
BM: He's with the M-BASE clan and I'm with the neo-classicists. [laughter] The two shall never mix, man.

Where's your tux, Branford?
BM: I'm wearing it. Not a tux, but my obligatory suit.
SC: [laughter] My obligatory suit... I like that.
BM: Wall Street, man. It's part of the thing.... So I've heard.

Well, I didn't know that neo-classicists could play on a Gang Starr album.
BM: Oh, that's right. I forgot about that. Uh... That was an aberration, man. Don't mind that.
SC: On that stuff he doesn't care. That's what that's about.
BM: [laughter] No, they played on *my* album, I didn't play on their album.
SC: Sting, Grateful Dead, all that shit... He don't care about that.

A neo-classicist with no conscience.
SC: [laughter] No conscience.
BM: Yeah, an eye on the market always, babe. That's why I play jazz. [laughter]

When did you start knowing about each other?
SC: When did you play that place...20/20?
BM: Possible 20 on 55th Street? You were there?! Get the fuck outta here! You were there? Holy shit, that's funny man. That was 1982! That was with Lew Soloff's band. Wynton was on tour with Herbie Hancock, so I played this gig with Lew. It was basically Wynton's whole band fronted by Lew Soloff. And it was supposed to be a fusion club, I think, but Soloff threw 'em for a curve.
SC: I remember a friend of mine saying, "Have you heard Wynton's brother?" I said, "What brother?" Weren't you playing alto then?
BM: No, that's when I first started playing tenor. In fact, that was my first week.

Can you remember your impression of Branford then?
SC: I thought he could play. The thing is, when you first hear cats when they first come to town... When I listen to people, I listen for not only what they're doing but the potential of what they might become. He was pretty young then. At that time I was pretty young, too. I could hear what his basic influences were but I really didn't get a good listen to him until I heard him with Art Blakey and a little after that with Wynton. I heard you with Blakey on alto. Man, I saw this funny video of you with Blakey. You were playing these hybrid funk-bop licks. Just watching y'all was funny. I mean, Wynton was little, skinny and shit. And you had all this big hair.

What was this, your Artis Gilmore phase?
BM: It was never that big, but I just never got it cut—just a lot of out-of-shape hair. Looked great with a tuxedo, though.
SC: It was coming out of the '70s, that whole period. Before his Magic Johnson look.
BM: I prefer the neo-classicist look. [laughter]

Branford, when was the first time you heard Steve?
BM: It was one of the early Five Elements records, I think. And soon after that we did *Scenes in the City* together [Marsalis' 1984 debut as a leader for Columbia].
SC: When was that?
BM: Eighty-three, man. Right after I came to town. I was real scared when I first got to New York. You know, this was supposed to be the place where the bad motherfuckers are. Then I heard them and I wasn't scared no more.
SC: [laughter]
BM: But the thing that was very apparent to me was... A lot of the people that I met in New York were primarily concerned with the perpetuation of their own egos. And the thing that struck me about Steve was—everybody thought he played "out," I guess. But when I heard Steve play, the first thing that came to my mind was Charlie Parker. And although I had never played like Bird on a record, I had listened to Bird a lot. And when I heard Steve I immediately thought, "Man, that cat's been checking out Bird." So when I did *Scenes in the City*, people were saying, "Who you gonna get?" I said, "I wanna get Steve Coleman." But they all said, "Steve Coleman??!!" I said, "Yeah, Steve Coleman!" See, most people can't hear but they have good memories. They memorize sounds like how you memorize a photograph. But they can't hear for shit.

Are you talking about audiences or musicians?
BM: Both, and critics, too. For instance, when I was in Wynton's band I was playing like Wayne [Shorter]. And the writers said, "He plays very much like Wayne." So then I go on a gig and start playing verbatim Sonny Rollins solos and these writers would say, "Wow, man, I hear a lot of Wayne in your playing."

SC: [laughter]

BM: And cats that were hearing you playing Five Elements shit, they never dug the cross reference. They couldn't really hear where that shit was coming from. They wrote all this bullshit about obtuse meters and all this, but they never heard Bird.

SC: See, jazz musicians have this thing about whether you can play changes or not. Ain't that right? It's like, "Can he play? Can he play *changes*?" You heard that shit all your life, right? "He can't play no changes." That kind of thing. I know what they mean—I understand, basically. Personally, I always thought one of the most important things was phrasing, not being able to play the changes. Like, I really notice a big difference in phrasing in cats who checked out Bird and transcribed solos and whatever—just went through a whole thing with Bird. And with Branford, I heard it immediately the first time I heard him play. And to me, it's not about whether you play the shit verbatim or not, it's about hearing a certain lineage in a cat's playing, in his phrasing, his form, how he gets in and out of things, his sense of balance in the music. You can hear all that in the music and you can hear a big difference in different people's playing because of that. A lot of cats who come straight out of Albert Ayler, they're gonna have a different sense of balance and resolution and phrasing and everything than a person who comes out of Newk [Rollins] or Bird.

BM: The bottom line is, jazz has an underlying logic that can't be denied. I started reading *Down Beat* in the '70s and in interviews that I read there had been those people who constantly tried to pretend as though the lineage didn't exist. They always used the coinage "new" as in the "new sound," which in previous generations has come over a cumulative period of time. But because we are signing record contracts much earlier than the previous generation, we are expected to play with the technical fluidity and melodic innovation of people in their early '30s when we were like in our early '20s. For instance, I was a history major in college and I never once heard a history teacher who said in order for us to progress as a nation we must destroy the past. Nor were historians ever labeled neo-classicists. But it seems in jazz the obsession with new vs. good... It seems like new is much more important than being good.

Isn't that more about marketing?

BM: I'm talking about interviews—critics, musicians themselves. Steve and I were talking today and he said something that I've always believed. The fact is, I once said in an interview that there's freedom in structure. There's really no freedom in what they call freedom. If a cat is playing a certain style of music and that's the only style of music that he can play, then he's not free. He doesn't choose to play avant-garde or whatever they call it—open sky music, all these fucked up names. He ain't got no choice. He has to play that because that's the only thing he can play. That's not freedom, that's slavery.

SC: It's like only knowing one way to get to your house. And you don't have any other way to get there.... If that way is blocked off, then you can't go home.

BM: You know what I mean? You only have one way. And you have a slew of musicians who are getting tumultuous amounts of credit and they only know one way to their home. And they make fun of the people who know five or six ways instead of trying to learn other ways themselves. Well, most of them don't have the musical ability to learn five or six ways.

SC: It's hard, too, because once you start getting placed for something, that's when it becomes even harder to learn—because you're getting all this shit now and you have to live up to this big image, you know what I mean? And then, it's like, you can't admit that you don't know anything. It gets even worse. When nobody knows you, it's much easier to learn, I feel. But getting back to when I first heard you... Around that time, I read this thing you said in an interview about originality and you said, "I'm too young, I got time to get my own sound. By the time I'm 30 I'll have my own sound." And then recently, I talked to somebody.... Not one of your...

BM: One of my dear friends. [laughter]

SC: [laughter] Yeah, right. And he was saying, "Well, I read this article where Branford Marsalis said that he was gonna get his own sound and I don't feel like he's done that." But I feel like I hear a big difference between your playing then and your playing now. And it's not... You know, critics look for this.... I don't know what they look for, but they're always wrong.

BM: Most of 'em can't hear, first of all.

SC: But I'm sitting here listening to him [Branford] this week and I'm hearing a lot of shit. There's a depth there, a certain kind of detail that was never there before. And it's funny because I hear some of that same thing that I hear in you and my early recordings in some of the younger guys now. I mean, I don't wanna name names but there's a whole lot of cats out there—some of them are getting recognized right now but they really don't have any experience, they haven't played with anybody, and they're getting this kind of hype heaped on 'em now. And I just hope it doesn't stop them from learning because recognition has a tendency to just squash that.

BM: Well, that's really up to them. I feel there's a lot of hyperbole that influences reality. Like if somebody's gonna do an interview and tell some writer that I'm the saddest motherfucker that's come down the pike... If I believe that, that's my problem. And if the interview comes out and says I'm the baddest motherfucker... If I believe that shit, that is also my problem. I think that every artist of every kind in any idiom, be it a writer or a musician or a dancer, you have to know when you're good and when you suck. And you have to get into yourself and you have to do what you have to do to improve. So all of the other stuff is all periphery. It doesn't even matter anyway.

*So you must be satisfied about your new record [*The Beautyful Ones Are Not Yet Born, *Columbia, 1991]. It's like an incremental leap from the first three records you did.*

BM: Oh, hell yeah. And I expected it to be this way. It's just been a logical progression. I turned 30 right when *Crazy People Music* [Columbia, 1990] hit. Not like 30 is a magical number but around there—29, 30, 31—something happens. Because I had been doing research all along but there's a point at which, with all deference to the people I love and respect, you have to say, "I don't want to play like them anymore." And for me, the big step was saying, "I can't stand playing standards."

SC: You knew that would come one day?

BM: Hell yeah, it's bound to come if you gonna play anything worth a damn. You know what I mean? Like Bird and them did to the standards what we'll never be able to do to the standards. So the only thing we can do is do our thing, you know? I mean, there are certain standards I don't mind playing, and most of them have never really been standards, per se—Monk tunes, Wayne Shorter tunes, Herbie tunes, shit like that. But standards in general, man... I'm like... That's why when we did *Trio Jeepy* [Columbia, 1989] and it was considered like this landmark record—that was very amusing to me. Because *Trio Jeepy* was just a record... I had to do a record before I went out on tour with Sting. *Royal Garden Blues* [Columbia, 1986] was disastrous because I did it after Sting's tour and I need at least six to eight months to get my jazz chops back. And that would've meant a two-year lapse again. So I recorded the record right before I went on Sting's tour.... I didn't have a band so I called up Milt [Hinton] and we went into the studio [with Jeff Watts] and did some standards. And it was hailed as this really modern-day landmark, but we just went in and had a jam session, essentially.

It sounded like it.

BM: You know, that's what it was. And people were saying, "This is great!" But that wasn't my idea of a great record at all.

Mine either.

BM: Good. I'm glad you agree.

SC: [laughter]

But this new one, as I say, is an incremental leap from Trio Jeepy.

BM: Yeah, it is. This is what I would've done as far back as '87, except one thing that is often over-looked in terms of development is personnel. Don't nobody play the drums like Jeff Watts. And very few play the bass like Bob Hurst. But neither one of them was available in '87. So I had to go with what was available—not trying to be mean to the cats I was playing with, because they're great musicians. I mean, Lewis Nash and Delbert Felix are definitely great musicians. But *Random Abstract* [Columbia, 1988] was a compromise record. Because when we started rehearsing, I brought out all of this material that wound up being a part of *Crazy People Music* and it couldn't be played, so I had to shelve it.

SC: And it's also the rapport you have with Tain and Hurst. 'Cause that's what I'm hearing.

BM: Yeah, there are very few people I can have that kind of relationship with though. The shit is all about music for me. And that's what I love about Steve. It's all about music for Steve. Steve is one of the few musicians I can talk to where when we talk we don't have to deal with each other's ego. We have a conversation. I don't have to say... Like if Steve is playing next to whoever and I say, "Yeah, man, that motherfucker played a great solo," I don't have to dance around and go, "Yeah, and *you* sounded great, too." We don't have to deal with any of that ego-pampering. We can just talk to each other. We can talk about Bird or talk about Sly Stone or James Brown or whatever the fuck you wanna talk about, and it never has to become a debate on personal taste. Like if I ain't into the shit, I ain't into it, and it ain't no thing. With everybody else, it's a thing. You have to like the person that they like or you're indicting them.

SC: A lot of times in interviews, interviewers try to get you to go at each other. One guy did an interview with me once and wanted me to come down on Kenny G. And I mean, Kenny G's music is not my favorite type of music, true. But I'm not gonna sit there and rag the cat, because I've got better things to do. Kenny G should be allowed to play anything he wants. It makes no difference what I like and what I don't like. And they try to underscore this big thing between me and Branford. I mean, it's obvious that we have different tastes, just by listening to us play.

BM: But then again we don't.

SC: What they miss is the connection. I really think it's maybe because what you said, they can't hear.

BM: Oh, they can't, man. I mean, the shit they be writing!

SC: I think that when I started my band, I could've told interviewers anything about my influences or whatever, and they would've believed me. Some of the early gigs I got... I remember one time I went to this punk rock place and I asked the cat for a gig. Cat say, "What kind of music do you play?" I say, "What kind of music do you have here?" He tells me they book punk rock so I say, "That's what we play." So the guy says, "Gimme a tape." I gave him the tape and next day he say, "Well, sounds great. There's one tune in here that sounds a little bit like jazz, but the rest of it sounds good." And that was it. We just went in and played it the way we played it. And the only reason I did that was because I knew club owners, for the most part, can't hear.

BM: That's right.

SC: Same with critics. If I tell them I'm influenced by music from Siberia or whatever, they'll write that shit and then the next interviewer will copy that and it goes on and on. That shit has happened to me. People have called me up and said, "Well, I don't know much about you so could you send me some materials, some interviews." So they copy from those interviews to write their interview, you know what I mean? Or sometimes you'll say something and people will make mistakes. Geri Allen did something in one of her interviews where she said M-BASE meant Basic Array of Structure... And she fucked up the last word and said "Experimentations" instead of "Extemporizations." And I saw that same mistake in 20 interviews after that, just from that one time she said it wrong—which to me just proved that cats just get other interviews and copy the shit down. They have no idea themselves what's going on.

BM: I had one interview in *Down Beat* [November '89] where I made a reference to Nicholas Slonimsky's *Thesaurus of Scales and Melodic Patterns* and it came out as "Leo Sherminski"! Then some guy sends me a letter saying, "You oaf! It's not Sherminski, it's Slonimsky." Well, no shit, but I didn't say that.

Sounds like lazy-writer syndrome—too many writers doing the equivalent of learning on the bandstand.

SC: Well, they get a gig.... Some editor says, "You have to write about so-and-so" and they might not know nothing about it so they just copy the clips. They never ask the musicians. Record reviews, too. I was telling Branford this morning, you get good reviews, you get bad reviews and it don't seem to matter. They good for the wrong reasons or bad for the wrong reasons.

BM: All I know is, the first person who ever decided to describe music with adverbs should be shot in his ass.

SC: [laughter]

BM: I have yet to hear a "thundering drum" or a "lachrymose saxophone." I'm still waiting to hear that shit. I mean, you know? It worked in Walter Mitty, but I haven't seen it work since. I have yet to see onomatopoeia be effective to describe any kind of artistic performance.

SC: And you have to understand that most critics and writers... They're usually people who tried to be musicians and didn't make it so they turn to some music-related job. So here's a cat who couldn't play chords on a guitar telling you who's playing changes and who ain't. And here's some cat who couldn't make it as a drummer telling you who's swinging and who ain't.

BM: With extremely weak-ass writing skills. I mean, go to school, man! Go to fucking school like I'm going to school! Go learn how to speak English!

Some critic who couldn't make it as a drummer... You wouldn't be thinking of anybody in particular now, would you?

SC: [laughter] Naw, that was just off the top of my head. But there's a lot of critics out there like that. The record company executives are the same. I was up at a record company office the other day and the guy was trying to tell me, "Yeah, I'm hip. I transcribed Clifford Brown solos." Some young executive at a record company and he's trying to tell me, "I'm hip, I'm one of you guys. I went through that. I know what it's like." I mean, what are you gonna say to that?

BM: Nothing. Just keep playing.

SC: [laughter] That's really all you can do. You just play and you have to ignore it. I've read stuff where they shit on Trane, man. Called him anti-jazz—talking about air leaks and this and that, talkin' about [how] his tone sounds like sandpaper on a turtle's back. And this was like during his classic shit, you know? People are writing stuff like that! Same people who turn around and later call him a genius.

Maybe it's an impossible task. Maybe it's like what William Burroughs said: "Writing about music is like dancing about architecture."

BM: [laughter] That's well said.

SC: The best things that I've heard is what the musicians have said themselves—anytime where a person interviews a musician and just lets the musician talk. Those are the times I've been most informed. But when a guy is like throwing in his comments and trying to show how much he knows.... Or even if he's trying to like change your words around. Man, I stopped talking about music a long time ago.... They just fuck up. You could spell out all the words during the interview and they'll still fuck up. And then people read that and say, "Man, Branford don't know nothin'."

All the inaccuracies and misquoting, you know, after a while it just makes you...
BM: Yeah, it's tricky, man. But I think it's a necessary part of the business. I mean, that's the way the society works. You have people who do and people who write about the people who do.

Branford, do you find it liberating to play in a trio setting?
BM: It's always been easy for me to play in a trio setting. I've never had that problem. Like it's really strange to me that every time you say trio people say, "Man, you must've been terrified."
SC: I don't get that either, man. What is that about?
BM: I think somebody must've told them 20 years ago that it was terrifying to be in a trio setting.
SC: I think a lot of musicians who aren't good musicians believe that you need a piano in order to make music. But, you know, Branford can go up there and play solo.
BM: Well, I don't know about all *that* shit. [laughter] *You* can get up there and do that.
SC: But you know what I'm saying. They think that if the piano leaves, you can't hear no more music. It just gets like "out" to them.
BM: Well, most musicians, that's the way they are. They hang onto that piano for dear life, boy. But for me, if I couldn't internalize the song, then I couldn't play it. If I couldn't hear the changes go by in my head, I wouldn't play it. On all those songs, I can hear the shit in my head. And if I can do that, the piano's right here [points to his head].
SC: And you can get to the point where you hear the whole band in your head—the bass, the drums, the guitar, everything. And that's the difference between playing music and faking it. There's a lot of guys, for example, who can't even keep a form straight. I mean, they'll play and go to the bridge and generally get lost on normal shit, you know? And a lot of that's because when they practice alone they don't hear that whole thing in their head. Or else they just practice licks completely divorced from any kind of context. You hear guys running the scales in practice and that's what they play like on the bandstand.
BM: It also affects your ability to field a band, too. I think that once I could hear the shit in my head then I knew exactly the kind of sound that I wanted. So you know—like other notoriously famous musicians have done—I could take credit for the development of Bob and Jeff and say it was all me.
SC: [laughter]
BM: Yeah, I taught 'em everything they know. But no, they are great musicians and they have created the sound. And I knew that if I got them, then that's what the sound would be, which is why I wanted them or nobody.
SC: You can hear a big difference in Bob, too, man, since the trio thing. He's really opened up.
BM: That's a bad man, boy. And he gets like no dap—I'm talkin' about no credit.
SC: That's true, 'cause he's like a real quiet guy.

But he's bound to get some attention from this trio album.
BM: When we play trio, man, that shit is really happening. Because the pulse of that band comes from the bass, not from the drums. That's why Jeff can just break wild because Bob's holding the fort. And he does with serious fuckin' A-plomb, man. I mean, I got these two bad motherfuckers in the band, so it'd be crazy for me to allow them to just be a fulcrum for my shit. You know...
"Alright, man, 'Miles Mode,'" Then eight minutes of me soloing... "Thank you very much... Bob and Jeff!"
SC: [laughter] Mutt and Jeff is more like it.
BM: Like Hamp does... "Let's hear it for...uh...the boys in the band. They know who they are." Or like Howlin' Wolf used to say... He did this shit where he couldn't remember the cat's name in the band: "On guitar... The guitar player."
SC: [laughter]

BM: But this trio is three motherfuckers going for broke, not one guy and two backup dudes. Let's have the shit all loosey-goosey. Let's take the structure and destroy it.

What do you think is the fundamental flaw of music education in this country?

BM: I think the biggest problem is that the United States' societal norms are defined by Western European civilization. And the majority of American musical culture was developed by African Americans, who have a completely different sense of aural sensibility. That's a-u-r-a-l, not o-r-a-l. I specify because I've seen interviews where they've written it wrong. Anyway, that's where the school problem comes in. Because from the Western vantage point everything is written down, everything is understood through the literal text. Whereas, for the African sensibility, the tradition is passed down orally. There's a dichotomy there. There's a problem there. Because when you talk to a cat at a clinic about the way shit sounds, they immediately start talking about chord scales. And I say, fuck chord scales, because it's only a theory. It doesn't exist. I mean, we can burn all the sheet music right now and the only thing that that means is we wouldn't have a chance to butcher Mozart's music. Because Mozart's dead, we don't know how the shit was supposed to sound. Mozart wrote down the shit that he heard in his head, but there are people teaching where they make you think that Mozart wrote what he wrote because he could write music. But there are ways of knowing, man, that supercede writing. Louis Armstrong couldn't read music, didn't seem to hurt him none. I'll trade places with him right now. Shit, I'll play the fuck out of "Struttin' with Some Barbecue" and not being able to read. I love that. You know what I mean? But I think that a lot of times in the educational environment when it comes to jazz, it's just tough—everybody that's teaching the music was brought up to believe in the Western European philosophy. And in America it's a combination of the two, but the oral tradition is never really highlighted, they don't talk about it, it's never really brought into focus. It's all theory, chord scales, theory, chord scales. "This is what Bird played." It's never like *why* did Bird play this? And the why is the most important question to mankind.

SC: They don't know why.

BM: World War I started 19-whatever—14, 19, 11, whatever that shit was... Who cares *when*? Why? Why did it start? What were the ramifications of this? That's the shit that, when I listen to music, I ask myself. Why did Bird play what he played? What are the musical ramifications of him playing it exactly the way he played it? And that's something that a chord scale book can never teach you. I think that it is the logic of music in general that slips by most people. Education is almost a deterrent sometimes. And I'm not putting down education, because I was musically educated. I can read and all that shit, but I say fuck that because the weight of it is an overwhelming deterrent for a lot of people that play jazz. What do you think, Steve?

SC: I always say that about Western education.

BM: You supposed to disagree with me, man.

SC: I believe in knowledge and learning all you can and everything. But there are certain cats, like Branford, that come out of places like Berklee and have managed to—I don't know—wipe off the theoretical shit and get on to dealing with the music.

BM: Berklee was good for me because you had all of the book learning and that was nice, but at night the cats was all jamming in the E Room. And there was no bullshit, man. You know, Wallace Roney was there, [Marvin] Smitty [Smith] was there, Kevin Eubanks, Tim Williams, Tain. And cats were always coming to town. Kenny Washington would come to town, stop by, and be at those sessions. Ronnie Matthews would be at the sessions, telling me I wasn't shit and didn't know no music. That's why I love Ronnie. He reminds me of the folks at home, you know? Instead of just telling you you suck and throwing you away, he'd tell you you suck and then he'd pull you aside and show you the right way to do it. And I always appreciated that about him.

What kind of reviews have you gotten for this Joyce show?

BM: Man, this guy from *Newsday* was saying I wasn't shit and this and that. And upon further review of his writing skills... That's the shit that upsets me, that their writing is so horrible.

SC: That shit don't matter, man. When they was bothering Trane, Trane said, "I invite all the critics to come and talk to me and I'll explain the shit."

BM: He said the wrong thing. He shoulda said "I invite you motherfuckers on the bandstand with instruments, and I'll be more than happy to switch to the pen and we'll see who comes closest to which gig."

SC: [uproarious laughter]

BM: For me... I say, you give me six weeks with some Faulkner, some Shakespeare, some fucking James Joyce and I give you six weeks with a horn and some records and we'll see who comes closest to what. That's my challenge to the critics.

LARRY CORYELL

THERE WAS ONE MEMORABLE CONCERT I attended at the now-defunct Palladium in New York. Larry Coryell was playing solo acoustic guitar, opening for the great Trio of John McLaughlin, Al Di Meola, and Paco DeLucia. Di Meola came out and introduced Larry as "the father of fusion guitar," and the crowd gave him a warm standing ovation. Indeed, Coryell had been blending jazz harmonies and improvisation with a rock sensibility since the mid-1960s, paving the way for generations of slash and burn plectorists. I recall another memorable Coryell solo concert in 1981 on the campus of Hofstra University on Long Island. Coryell was opening for Pat Metheny's *80/81* band with Dewey Redman and Michael Brecker, Jack DeJohnette, and Charlie Haden. Again, he played solo, but this time it was solo electric.... What a subversive notion! He had his old Hagstrom Swede with him back then, and he ripped up the joint.

I have seen dozens of heroic Coryell performances since then. The guy is a fearless improviser who holds nothing back and often takes chances that seem beyond his grasp. You're on the edge of your seat wondering if he's going to pull something off or not—and he inevitably does. Not the most fluid and flawless technician on the instrument, but one of the most exciting. At age 55, Coryell's still generating heat and going out on a limb every time he hits the bandstand, no matter what the context. In the early-1990s, Coryell flirted (successfully) with smooth jazz for Creed Taylor's revamped CTI Records. His latest outing was strictly a player's vehicle—an ambitious updating of his landmark *Spaces* album on Vanguard from 1970 (which included McLaughlin, Miroslav Vitous, Chick Corea, and Billy Cobham). For *Spaces Revisited* (Shanachie Records, 1997) Larry went toe-to-toe with guitar virtuoso (and Coryell disciple) Bireli Lagrene. For that project Coryell was also joined by Cobham on drums and Richard Bona on electric bass. There have been many milestones in his fabulous career—a featured role on Herbie Mann's *Memphis Underground;* key contributions to albums by Chico Hamilton, Gary Burton, and Charles Mingus; duets with the late Emily Remler. But his work on *Spaces Revisited,* as well as with his current touring quartet, finds the great guitarist at the top of his game—still slashing, burning, and swinging after all these years. His latest project is a fusion power trio date with drummer Steve Smith and organist Tom Coster entitled *Cause and Effect* (Tone Center, 1998).

The following piece appeared as a May '84 cover story in *Down Beat.*

FEBRUARY 8, 1984

A Texas-born, West Coast–bred lad of 22 came to New York City in 1965, toting a Gibson Super 400. He dug Kenny Burrell. He loved Barney Kessel. His favorite album was *The Incredible Jazz Guitar of Wes Montgomery* (Riverside, 1960). "That album changed everything for me," Larry Coryell says. "As Ralph Gleason wrote in the liner notes: 'Make no mistake, Wes Montgomery is the best thing to happen to jazz guitar since Charlie Christian.' And he was right."

The kid had great taste and unlimited potential, plus chops to burn. But something happened. Culture shock set in and the would-be Wes disciple took off on the fusion trail (or "con-fusion," as many straight-ahead players of the day referred to it). "Everybody was dropping acid, and the prevailing attitude was, 'Let's do something different,'" recalls Coryell of those tumultuous times. "That spirit, that desire, that visionary thing is what was happening among musicians, and the results were great."

Coryell's contributions to that movement have been well documented by now. He trailblazed the scene with Free Spirits, a group of young jazz-trained musicians whose experiments with fusing jazz and rock pre-dated such crossover pioneers as Blood, Sweat & Tears, England's Soft Machine, Dreams (with Billy Cobham and Randy and Michael Brecker), or Jeremy Steig & The Satyrs.

Drummer Bob Moses, a member of that seminal fusion outfit (along with saxophonist Jim Pepper, bassist Chris Hills, and rhythm guitarist Chip Baker) says of his guitar playing colleague: "I have to give Coryell credit. He was the first musician that I met who was equally dexterous in both the jazz bag and the rock bag. He understood both worlds really well, and I think it took somebody like that to make the rest of us all appreciate rock'n'roll. I have to admit that I was a terrible bebop snob before I met Larry. I used to think that if you couldn't swing and make the changes and play bebop, you were bull-shitting. The very first time I heard Larry, he was playing bebop like Wes Montgomery and I thought, 'Wow, this guy's a great player!' Next time I heard him, he was playing a Chuck Berry thing, and real-ly playing it well. I think because I saw his jazz chops first and had the respect, it made me take the rock thing more seriously. So I started to listen to rock after that and found that there were things I liked."

Free Spirits released its debut album in 1966—one year before Jimi Hendrix would make his big splash with *Are You Experienced?* (Reprise, 1967), three years before John McLaughlin would come to America to join Tony Williams' Lifetime, three years before Miles Davis would release his land-mark *Bitches Brew* (Columbia, 1969).

Coryell later formed Foreplay with saxophonist Steve Marcus and in 1973 he formed The Eleventh House with drummer Alphonse Mouzon, following in the wake of the Mahavishnu Orchestra. It was at this point that Coryell put his Super 400 hollow-body guitar on the shelf and picked up a solid-body guitar. He began cranking out distortion-laced, lightning-fast rock riffs and quickly became one of the preeminent spokesmen for so-called electric jazz. Together with McLaughlin, Coryell influenced a generation of chops-conscious players. Included in the ranks of Coryell disciples was a 19-year-old speedster named Al Di Meola, who burst onto the scene in 1974 with Return to Forever. And the race was on.

When the fusion movement fizzled in 1976, Coryell turned to acoustic guitar as an antidote to those loud, electrified sounds that had prevailed for so long. For the next three years he would devote himself solely to acoustic work, performing duets with French guitarist Philip Catherine and with American guitarist Steve Khan. In 1979 he toured Europe in an acoustic trio with McLaughlin and Spain's flamenco master Paco DeLucia, and later began collaborating with Polish violinist Michal Urbaniak and his wife, vocalist Urzsula Dudziak.

A self-destructive period saw him slip into booze-soaked oblivion in 1981. But he cleaned up and courageously bounded back the following year to tackle what stands as the most challenging project of his diverse career—transcribing and recording three Stravinsky ballets for the Japanese label Nippon/Phonogram. He considers The Rite of Spring from those sessions as his crowning achievement to date.

Coryell's fall from grace in 1981 and his subsequent struggle with Stravinsky taught him some invaluable lessons about humility and about music. And he's emerged all the stronger for it. The following interview took place in Greenwich Village the day after his recording session for Muse at Rudy Van Gelder's famous studio in Englewood Cliffs, New Jersey [released later that year as the aptly-titled Comin' Home, Muse, 1984].

How did yesterday's straightahead session come about?
[Saxophonist] Ricky Ford had asked me to be on his record for Muse [Future's Gold] last year. And at that time Joe Fields of Muse approached me about the idea of doing something straightahead. I hadn't done anything straightahead for years, not since I played with Elvin Jones and Jimmy Garrison on my first Vanguard record back in 1968 [Lady Coryell]. So we went into the studio after a week-long engagement at the Village Vanguard, and we just did it.

So this is a return to your own roots.
What it was for me was going back, and through the inspiration of Billy Hart and George Mraz and Albert Dailey, they enabled me to bring out the roots that I brought with me to New York in 1965, which were buried underneath an avalanche of culture shock and all the political turmoil and everything else happening at the time. That stuff was buried but it was never killed off. And now it's coming to the surface. I had originally gotten interested in jazz because it was the hardest kind of music I had ever heard. I had originally heard it on the guitar, but I started to see that making up single note melodies and chord melodies on the instrument was a real challenge. And I became attracted to people who could do that well, like Barney Kessel, Wes Montgomery, and Kenny Burrell. But the idea was to do that well but also be different. I just don't want to imitate my heroes for two reasons. Number one, I can't imitate my heroes. And number two, I don't think I should. So the prevailing attitude of many of my colleagues from the '70s is now, "Let's relax and play what we had the ability to play all along but didn't because we were trying to stretch the boundaries."

How would you assess what happened in the '70s with fusion?
I just think it was a time when people with tremendous amounts of talent, who had the ability to play jazz or classical or any kind of music they wanted to—they were visionaries and they wanted to do something really special. And it was a highly competitive time. It was post-1960s. The more intelligent musicians were saying, "We can reach white audiences, too. Why should it just be The Beatles? We love The Beatles but we also love Coltrane. We love The Rolling Stones, but we also

love Miles." And out of that came bands like the Mahavishnu Orchestra and Return to Forever and Dreams and Foreplay, the band I had with Steve Marcus—all players who were capable of playing straightahead but who also had an ear for contemporary music and a desire to do that. Return to Forever was probably the best of the bunch—one of the most incredible groups I ever heard in my life. The discipline! And the virtuosity! Amazing.

What was the failure of the fusion movement?
What happened, in my opinion, was that guitar playing just got too fast. And it also got highly competitive. For years I thought, "All I want to do is become the number one rated guitarist in *Down Beat* by the time I'm 30." It was that whole adolescent attitude, placing more importance on the arriving than on the striving. That brought down the scene.

The thing about you that seems to cut through in just about every context of your playing is a blues feeling.
That's right, man. That's part of the roots. I don't think you ever lose your roots. I actually started off playing country and western and also got deeply into the blues. Wes was playing blues. And that had to be pointed out to me by another guitarist who was my age but was more into blues and rock than jazz. "Listen to that, man. He's playing blues." And I didn't realize it because of all those changes going on. But it's really basically blues. And then it hit me: "So that's what it's all about." Because my idea was: "Oh, jazz is playing on Cole Porter tunes." But the roots, the basic structure comes from the blues. It's just a process of sophisticating the blues thing. [Charlie Parker's] "Confirmation" is like a blues taken a couple of steps further harmonically. So I guess I've always related to that blues quality.

Are you pleased with the results of what went down in the studio yesterday?
Yes. It's as if everything that I've done all these years—with electric, with acoustic, with blues, with classical—was a lead-in to that session I did yesterday. It's remarkably reminiscent of *The Incredible Jazz Guitar of Wes Montgomery.* I got a similar sound and had a similar sounding rhythm section. Wes had Albert and Tootie Heath and Tommy Flanagan for that album—just guitar and rhythm section playing blues-oriented jazz. We do an up version of "Confirmation" that is killing. I was practicing that song every day before the Vanguard gig, playing that head over and over until I got it under my fingers. We also do a version of "Good Citizen Swallow," which I wrote for the Gary Burton Quartet back in the '60s and was recorded on *Lofty Flake Anagram* (RCA, 1967). We also did a minor blues that I call "No More Booze," which is pretty close to the way Wes would sound on a minor blues. Of course, I couldn't get a sound like he got because I play with a pick and Wes played with his thumb. The only other time I came this close to sounding like Wes was on a cut called "Treat Style" from the *Lady Coryell* album. But the difference between that and yesterday's recording session is that almost 20 years later I can play changes much better. When I first got to New York I was so intimidated by who was here that I stuck to playing very simple blues. The few times I would go out of the blues scale was to play avant-garde, because that was popular at the time. Now I'm very comfortably playing changes.

What inspired you to pick up the hollow-body again after not touching it for 11 years?
I have to credit that to Philip Catherine. I was heading in a rock direction when he turned me around to acoustic guitar. He came up to me in 1976 in Berlin and said, "Do you know [Django Reinhardt's classic ballad] 'Nuages'?" And I said, "No." Now there was a nice, simple tune with changes. And that was the beginning of my re-examination of the guitar. The acoustic guitar was sort of an antidote for the loud rock stuff I had been doing and it led to my rediscovery of the hollow-body jazz. And I tell you, for the three years that I worked on and off with him in acoustic duets, from

1976 to 1979, that tune "Nuages" went through my head constantly. It's a great tune to play on. So I have to credit any good things happening to me musically in the last few years on the instrument to Philip's influence. Not to say that I haven't been influenced by everybody else along the way, from McLaughlin to Joe Beck to Atilla Zoller. But Philip Catherine... There was a connection there. I taped everything that he and I and [bassist] Neils Henning Orsted Pedersen played on this tour in April, and what I noticed in him was a tremendous improvement in his time feel, which must've come from natural evolution and/or playing with Neils. 'Cause Neils has got the connection to Oscar. Let's face it, man... Nobody who loves the blues like I do can fail to love Oscar Peterson. You just cannot help but love that joy of life and that love of playing and the tremendous virtuosity. As a kid I had this record with Oscar Peterson on one side and the Modern Jazz Quartet on the other. And the MJQ always put me to sleep. But Oscar, man! I said, "That's the stuff for me."

So what happened on that tour with Philip Catherine to affect your own direction so dramatically?
I found that Philip was growing in a very good direction, just in terms of the quality and intelligence of his playing. I had forgotten what Elvin had told me in the late-1960s. He said, "This music is in the mind." And I know what he means. It's not so much in the technique or the lines, it's in the mind—and the soul. But what happened on this tour was that Philip and I had been playing Ovation acoustic guitars and suddenly he brought along his old Gibson ES–175, the original jazz guitar that he had owned for years and years. And it threw me off. He had a nice sound. It was smoother and he didn't have to hit the strings so hard anymore. But I was so uncomfortable during that whole tour, I was intimidated. And I didn't have the desire to ask him not to play it. When you respect someone so much, you don't tell them what to do. And I see now why it was such a very painful tour for me. It was rough, man. I started buying graphic equalizers and sound boosters and things to try and compensate. What it really was—my soul wanted me to play my Super 400 again. So when I finally picked it up in July of that tour, I experienced what Philip must've experienced when he went back to his ES–175. It was as if all that time on the acoustic had just been a preparation to go back to the jazz guitar. It's funny how blind we can be sometimes.

What did you learn about your own playing when you switched back to hollow-body guitar?
One thing that I learned when I picked up my Super 400 again was that you don't need to play that fast to improvise over changes. What you need to improvise over changes is an organized mind. And what you need to learn are not so much the rapidity of scales or the combinations of rapid scales, but you've gotta learn melody fragments. So that's what I set out to do in the Spring of '83. And it started to hit me that it's almost as if... I never should've listened to John McLaughlin. I never should've listened to anybody who's that advanced technically, because these guys pick every note. And the way for me, with the limits of my technique, to really get smooth... I can't pick every note. I don't have this ability to get this incredibly technically hard thing that's called cross picking, where you're doing a downstroke on a higher string and you're gonna come back and do an upstroke on a lower string. It's really hard to do. So I started listening to the cats who were able to really swing—guys my age, like John Scofield and John Abercrombie and Pat Metheny. But I didn't want to listen to them too much because I didn't want to start sounding like them. The one thing that all three of them had in common is that they didn't pick every note. They were doing a lot of stuff that I brought with me when I got to New York. And what I had to do to re-create the right feel, to reproduce the thing that I had back then was to go back and play the way I used to play on the instrument I used to play, the Gibson Super 400. So I had to learn how to play that guitar all over again, and it was hard.

What was the difference?
The first thing I discovered was that I had to develop a totally different touch. With the Ovation

and certain solid body guitars I could really whack away at it and it would work. There was a lot more power picking and strength involved, especially with the acoustic guitar. But with the Super 400 I had to develop a very light and sensitive touch. Now I have another important bit of information in my creative arsenal. I've learned that I cannot just play the same way on different kinds of guitars. I've got to really go with the way the instrument is to be played properly. With the way a Super 400 is set up, the rules change. I know for myself that if I play a solid body guitar with the thinner gauge strings, I have a lot more facility. But as it stands, within the limits of my technique, I've got facility to burn. What I really need to do is continue going in the direction of intelligent playing. And by intelligent, I mean soulful. That's the struggle.

So these past few years have been an educational process for you.
Absolutely. And I learned that it's really important to pay attention to details, because what this music is about is balance. You gotta be in tune, you gotta have a clear head, you gotta know the music. No more shuckin'. You can't shuck! What I found [was] that, for me, during the late-1960s and early-1970s with all this playing over vamps, you just shuck. If you can find one scale then fine, no problem, you can shuck your way through a whole gig. Just play as fast as you can on one scale. A lot of the tunes were constructed: "We'll play a C scale for eight bars, then a C# scale for four bars." Easy! No problem. And my re-examination of the guitar really began with the acoustic work with Philip Catherine. That was like the antidote to the electric stuff. Philip switched to an ES–175 in April of '83. I picked up my Super 400 in July of '83 when I did this guitar summit thing with Vic Juris, Chuck Loeb, and Rory Stuart. It was a fantastic gig and it was really important for me. What I've done is a very conservative thing—to go back to a hollow body.

And seek a balance in your playing.
Right. And there's something that Andrew White said that contributes to this idea of balance in my philosophy: "If it gets too good, it ain't jazz." It's good to get it as tight as you can, but you don't have to make it perfect. And this perfection is really something else that I discovered within myself that was going to kill me artistically. Until I was willing to take risks and make mistakes, I wasn't going to make any progress. But the key to my progress was taking my mother's advice and practice and work, work and practice, especially when you don't want to. The time off that I had, I forced myself to practice and I forced myself to compose. Now I don't like anything that keeps me away from the instrument. I forgot that that's how you get good.

What made you forget?
By the late-1970s, I had gotten successful. I did some big tours, did some television, *People* magazine stories and all that horse shit. I got arrogant. The grandiosity set in. I forgot how I got there. I had forgotten about the hard work, that struggling. I got lazy. But I came to realize that what I had to do was go back and do all that work again—practice constantly, listen to other people's music, study other people's phrasing, work on learning new tunes and old standards, work on horn lines and piano lines, practice scales. In order to get good, you gotta do all that stuff. My slogan became G.O.Y.A. (Get Off Your Ass). I had to work like a madman, especially when I didn't want to work. And it took a lot of humility. It was the beginning of the end of arrogance.

So that Stravinsky piece kicked your ass?
Yes it did. I learned a lot about music by playing Stravinsky.

How did the Stravinsky project come about?
Nippon/Phonogram had approached me to do Rimsky-Korsakov's *Sheherazade* in February of

1982. That was relatively easy, and it came out nice. Then the president of the company just figured, "Well, if Mr. Larry can do the Rimsky-Korsakov, why not take it to the next logical step and have him do Stravinsky?"

I remember hearing you do some classical pieces on your album The Lion and the Ram *[Arista, 1977].*
Yeah, I did a Bach piece and I wrote a piece about Stravinsky, based on the "Mass of 1948."

So you've been fascinated with Stravinsky for some time now.
Yeah, because I knew he was bad. There's a story that Coltrane went to his wife one day and said, "I found my universal musician." It was Stravinsky. And Coltrane was kind of like E. F. Hutton. When he said something, you listened.

A lot of jazz musicians have had an affinity for Stravinsky's writing.
There's also Ravel and Debussy and Satie and Manuel de Falla and Bartók. Stravinsky's not the only classical composer that jazz musicians love. But if you can tackle Stravinsky, you can do just about anything. It's like required reading. After it was all over, I realized that I had passed a milestone in my life. I would never hear music the same again. Since the Stravinsky, I found that when I play blues I don't play rock'n'roll blues anymore. I'm discovering that there's no end to the way you can improvise in a more or less accepted jazz approach on a dominant seventh blues or minor blues.

How did you get started on such a massive undertaking?
The plan was to do *The Firebird Suite, Petrushka,* and *The Rite of Spring. Firebird* is more accessible but *The Rite of Spring* is out there. So how it began was Michal Urbaniak brought me a score to *The Rite of Spring* and a tape of an orchestra playing it. And he said to me in that beautiful Polish accent, "Good luck!" Of course, I had interpreted this to mean: "You're never gonna play this!" That was in June of 1982, and I was so intimidated that I didn't make any progress on the Stravinsky project until Christmas Day of 1982. So for those six months or so, I would sit there and listen to it and say, "This is impossible," while Urbaniak's words would ring in my ear. And what made it appear impossible was that Nippon/Phonogram wanted me to record all three ballets in two days, digitally with no overdubs or editing. It was the hardest thing I ever had to do in my life.

What was the most challenging aspect of this project?
The technical demands. The shit was so hard to play. All of it was incredibly hard. The original plan was to go through the Stravinsky pieces, find a couple of chord changes and a couple of patterns and blow on 'em—forget it! As I started getting into it, I decided I might as well play the whole thing exactly as it was transcribed [for solo piano]. With the exception of a couple of places where I improvised in *The Rite of Spring* and a few liberties I took with *Petrushka,* I did the pieces as faithfully as I could. There are a couple of passages in *The Rite of Spring* that are just like jazz. It was the only part of the whole piece that I could relate to. The rest of it just sounded like music from Mars, especially when you get to the end of the piece. The finale of *The Rite of Spring* is so difficult. It starts out in more or less D tonality with a lot of dissonance, then goes through all this difficult stuff. Then, just to really get our goat, he takes it down a half step. Stravinsky is so clever. The end of the final movement is so chaotic. In the ballet, a dancer falls down and dies after doing this insane, furious dance. The music becomes very jerky and lurching and very emotional. It's the sound of somebody dying. Some of the chord jumps and movements of time signatures are so insane.

How did you prepare for the Stravinsky session?
For the three months prior to that record date, I was obsessed with the project. People from

overseas would come by my home in Connecticut to visit me, but I would always be practicing. In fact, I practiced so much that my hands broke out—sores and blisters. I got a callus on my left index finger from so much barring. But I think a lot of it was anxiety, too. I mean, nothing could ever be that bad again, as far as anxiety. It got to a point where the mere mention of the name Stravinsky would intimidate the shit out of me. Scared me to death. Three weeks away from the date I called up Teo Macero, the producer of this project and said, "Teo! I can't do this!" I was really faced with this mental block. I don't know if this is true of other artists but inside of me there's this voice, almost like a prosecutor, that says, "You can't do this." It just thrives on negativity. So Teo would call me over to his house and explain to me how he did certain things with Miles on his "Rodrigo" piece [from *Sketches of Spain*]. He's amazing. He'd look at all these fucking dots on the paper and just rewrite it. And in order to get through certain difficult sections, he had me slow way down and isolate on some double stops. And with his help I got through it. It so happens that I ended up recording *The Rite of Spring* on March 21, 1983, which is the vernal equinox. It was also the day that my car got towed away for not paying a bunch of parking tickets, so there's some kind of balance there.

You must have a feeling of great satisfaction now that the Stravinsky project is behind you.
I'll be honest with you, it was a tremendous victory to overcome my own insecurities.

Who were some of the other musicians that you've met and played with over the years who made a great impact on you?
Lots. From Dizzy Gillespie I learned about chords and a lot about history, a lot about taste. One of the most important things I got from playing with Sonny Rollins was the sheer love of music, and it shows in his playing. The charisma of that man! But what I got from working with Miles was just one word: Stop! When in doubt, stop. Don't finish that phrase. I'm one of those players who plays a lot of notes, it's true. That's me, I accept that. For years, man, I thought, "Well, if I take a lot of heroin I'll just play one or two notes per chorus and they'll love me." But what it is, the spaces are starting to open up in my solos. Even though I tend to be all over the instrument the spaces are opening up, and that came from just a few intense weeks of being around Miles where he said, "Don't ever finish a phrase." And that makes a lot of sense. Easy does it.

Did you record with Miles?
Yeah, but it was never released. We did a thing [in 1978] that was like jungle music. It was fantastic. It was just a riff, a bass line, two keyboards—Miles on one and Masabumi Kikuchi on the other. Al Foster on drums, T. M. Stevens on bass. It was like his idea of rock'n'roll. It wasn't fusion and it was fantastic.

What are your ongoing playing situations these days?
I've been doing this duet with Michal Urbaniak. He plays electric violin through all these toys and nine times out of ten the violin would be dominating the shit out of the acoustic guitar. So I brought the Super 400 up to this gig we did, played a couple of tunes on it and I realized all I had to do was play that guitar and I could be heard. It's almost illogical to try and match an Ovation acoustic guitar with the powerhouse electronics that he gets out of his violin. Although I will continue to play the Ovation with him and strive to get a better balance between the two instruments, I learned my lesson.

You recorded with Urbaniak?
We recorded three albums together for small European labels. And Michal is funny, man. He wants us to get over in the States so he came to me one day with a bunch of Windham Hill records and

said, "Larry, we got to get this sound now." So I checked out these records and I fell madly in love with Michael Hedges—fantastic. But it ain't jazz, it's not what Michal and I learned how to do. So I said, "Michal, we're just gonna have to wait for this shit to come around to what we do, man." You should've seen us trying to sound like Windham Hill. We'd fall on our butts, man. I learned that you can't fake it. You can be versatile and you can be a virtuoso, but you can't just decide that you're gonna sound like this or that. You gotta go with what you know. And what I did yesterday—this straightahead session at Rudy Van Gelder's studio—I believe, is a culmination of a long progression back to the thing that attracted me to this kind of music in the first place. And the reason it took so long is that it was supposed to take so long. I wouldn't have had it any other way. Even the mistakes in this tape are good because it's honest and soulful. But I'm not closing my mind to any other stuff. I want to continue exploring, continue working with Urbaniak, with Vic Juris, with Alphonse Mouzon, and also in the conventional format with Albert, George, and Billy. I got booked again at the Vanguard in April. That kind of music sounds good to me and after going through all the different paths to get to it I'm bringing a lot more ability to play it. I want to continue composing. It's a process. The whole thing is doing it, it's the process.

It's the striving, not the arriving.
Yeah, because you're already there if you're striving. You're in a process of becoming what it is the great force has in mind for you. And I believe the force is there for everyone to tap, but we have to do the footwork and we also have to have faith when we're not in touch with it. See, that was the hard part. I lost my faith. And it's a highly competitive business. I'll never forget when McCoy Tyner turned to me in 1981 when I was in very low spirits and he said, "After all, this is a business." And he's right. It's a business. You gotta show up on time, you gotta keep trying, and you gotta practice. That's the thing I learned.

JOHN MCLAUGHLIN

I FIRST SAW GUITAR GOD John McLaughlin back in 1973 when the Mahavishnu Orchestra came through Milwaukee as an opening act for Frank Zappa. My 19-year-old pals and I were heavily into Zappa at the time (circa the *OverNight Sensation,* DiscReet, 1973), so naturally we were all very excited to witness The Grand Wazoo in the flesh. We convened at Hoppe's Bar, downed a few brew-skis, and rolled a few doobies for the road, gearing up for an evening of "I Am the Slime," "Montana," "Camarillo Brillo," and various inspired and lengthy Gibson SG solos by Frank himself. I was, how-ever, in no way prepared for what I was about to experience when the Mahavishnu Orchestra took the stage.

I didn't know who they were. The leader was dressed in all white and had a spiritual demeanor about him. He put his hands together in a praying gesture before they lit into their first song and humbly asked for quiet in the auditorium. At that point, some moron in the back row let out with an inebriated, leather-lunged battle cry: "Booogeeeeee!!" John seemed a bit unnerved by that. But when drummer Billy Cobham, sitting behind an arsenal of drums and roto toms that looked as imposing as a battleship, counted off the first tune (from *Birds of Fire,* Columbia, 1973) and the band jumped on it, my hair stood on end. And when McLaughlin bore down on his double neck guitar during one solo, I practically fell to my knees with my teeth chattering. Challenged by Jerry Goodman on violin, Rick Laird on bass, and Jan Hammer on synthesizer, not to mention the precision power drumming and Herculean thrashing behind the kit by Cobham, John delved into some deep waters that night—and changed my life in the process. I knew nothing of John's work with Miles Davis or Tony Williams' Lifetime at that time. But following that memorable concert, I would make a concerted effort to find out. Over the years I would catch him in concert with a second edition of the Mahavishnu Orchestra, with Shakti, the One Truth Band, the Trio with Paco DeLucia and Al Di Meola; yet another edition of Mahavishnu, his acoustic trio with Trilok Gurtu and various electric bass virtuosos, his Free Spirits trio with Hammond B–3 organist Joey DeFrancesco and drummer Dennis Chambers; and his current The Heart of Things band with Jim Beard on keyboards, Mitchell Garrison on bass, Gary Thomas on tenor sax, and Chambers on drums.

I interviewed McLaughlin for the first time in June of 1978 when he came through Milwaukee with his One Truth Band. I was the arts editor and co-publisher of an alternative biweekly newspaper called *Cityside* back then, just getting my feet wet in jazz. I was green and gullible and John was very gracious, giving me a full hour on the phone and filling up my head with notions about Hazrat Inayat Khan's "The Sufi Messages" and other esoteric socio-political raps. I've interviewed John several times since then, including this August 1992 cover story for *Jazz Times*.

APRIL 13, 1992

The streaks of gray in his hair give John McLaughlin a distinguished, professorial look. The red bow tie adds a touch of Continental class. He wears it well. It's just hard for me to accept the fact that my boyhood hero has turned 50.

Twenty-three years have passed since he traveled from England to the United States to play with Tony Williams' Lifetime and Miles Davis. Those were trailblazing days. Miles, and Tony were leading the way down a new path, exploring a marriage between the language of jazz and the visceral power of rock—something that Jimi Hendrix had only hinted at. And John McLaughlin was a key player on that exciting new scene. Through his scintillating work with Lifetime, Miles, and his own Mahavishnu Orchestra, McLaughlin had become the living link between Jimi and John Coltrane. He stood as a towering influence on a generation of musicians.

Some people say the fusion movement fizzled by the mid-1970s. The once-dynamic genre reduced to a critical joke. But by then, John was into another bag with Shakti, an East-West amalgam that fused the structures and discipline of Indian classical music with jazz-like improvisation. Then it was on to his One Truth Band, followed by the great acoustic guitar Trio with Paco DeLucia and Al Di Meola, followed by an updated edition of the Mahavishnu Orchestra, and his current acoustic trio with the extraordinary Indian percussionist/drummer Trilok Gurtu and French bassist Dominique DiPiazza. Like his mentor Miles, he keeps moving forward, creating new landmarks along the way.

As I enter his hotel suite in Manhattan, John appears jovial and ready for his week-long engagement at the Blue Note nightclub. He is sitting on a couch, tuning his beautiful hand-crafted flame maple acoustic guitar, made for him by the great luthier Abraham Wechter, who also built his one-of-a-kind Shakti guitar back in 1976. As he rips off a few stunning licks, it's clear that John has fully recovered from the career-threatening, freak household accident that occurred in 1990. While watching TV at home in France, the guitar virtuoso got his fretting forefinger caught in the track of a swiveling television set. As he recalled at the time, "It was so quick, so fast. I heard it snap. I saw the end of my finger flopping around. It was just a nightmare."

Six stitches and a splint put that finger right, but the injury forced John to cancel a stateside tour with his trio. Now with the release of *Que Alegria,* his 1991 debut on Verve, the trio is out touring with renewed vigor. And John is once again playing beautiful music with, as Coltrane put it in his notes to *A Love Supreme*: "elation, elegance, and exaltation."

I'm fascinated by the transitional period in '68–'69 when jazz and rock started coming together. And to me, the first so-called fusion album that really grabbed rock fans was Jack Johnson *[Columbia, 1971]. Miles had certainly flirted with rock forms on* In a Silent Way *[Columbia, 1968] and* Bitches Brew *[Columbia, 1968], but there was something about the raw power of* Jack Johnson. *I mean, you're playing power chords on that album like Pete Townshend!*
Well, you know... That was Miles' favorite record. You know how the majority of *Jack Johnson* came about? The bulk of that record came out of some jamming we did in the studio. There was Herbie playing the most horrible Farfisa organ and Michael Henderson on bass, Billy Cobham on drums. We were all in the studio, just waiting for Miles. He was talking to Teo Macero in another room and that went on for 10–15 minutes, and I got bored. I started to play a boogie in E, just to have some fun, that's all. I was playing these funny kind of chords that later I used more to advantage in "Dance of Maya" [from *The Inner Mounting Flame*, Columbia, 1971]—kind of angular chords, but all really related to the blues. That's what "Dance of Maya" is, a blues in E, really, with some funny angular chords. And I was really hitting the strings hard, just going for it. Billy picked it up, Michael picked it up, and in a couple of minutes we were gone. So finally the door opened and Miles ran in with his trumpet. The [recording] light was on and he just played for about 20 minutes, which I had never seen him do before. It was a situation where he just walked in and everything was happening already. And he played so fine. It was so spontaneous, such a great moment. That whole record was.

It sounds like maybe you should've gotten a co-composer credit for some of that album.
No, there was no tune. Why even bother to discuss who wrote what? What happened with all the musicians who played with Miles in the studio was strictly Miles' doing. Let's make that perfectly clear. Miles' records were always quite carefully directed by him, orchestrated in a way that was not quite obvious. Because he had that thing, that ability to be able to make musicians play in a way that they would not normally think of. He had a way of pulling things out of them that they were unaware of. He certainly did it to me. So it was absolutely Miles' vision—the way the concepts would go. I think we have to put the credit on Miles. We all had ideas. Everybody would come up with things—a riff or a motif. But they were all really in the function of Miles and his music. We were only concerned with what we could do to contribute to what he was playing. And I think everybody more or less had that same idea. So it's a kind of useless question: Who wrote what? Because the concept and the way the music grew and was recorded was truly, absolutely Miles. And I think that was true even in the latter days, when he got more into funk and hip-hop. I know a lot of people mocked Miles for that, but not me. To me, Miles could do no wrong.

What was your impression of the Miles tribute concert you attended in Paris last summer [July of 1991, just weeks before he died].
I was very moved, personally. To see Miles with all those people representing all those years of music—to see him walk on stage with Wayne [Shorter] again, to see him playing with Jackie McLean again—it was something else. And of course, the *In a Silent Way* band was a highlight with Joe [Zawinul] and Chick [Corea]. Actually, I didn't play in that band. I played on two pieces, "Jean Pierre" [from *We Want Miles*] and "Katia" [from *You're Under Arrest*]. Darryl Jones was on bass, Al Foster on drums, John Scofield was also playing guitar. The way Miles set it up, each tune—as was Miles' wont—had a kind of opposition element happening. He would pair up players—Scofield and myself, Wayne and Bill Evans, Jackie McLean and Steve Grossman, Herbie and Chick—so that there were always two soloists on the same instrument, which was nice for us. I don't get much

chance to play with Scofield, whom I love. He's such a great player. So every tune was from a different era—different feeling, different sound, different attitude. Each piece had its own life to it. And it's just amazing to think that it all came from one person. Overall, I think the whole event had a very powerful impact on Miles. Everybody was so happy to be there. It was like his birthday party. I really regret that a couple musicians who should've been there couldn't make it. Keith [Jarrett] should've been there. Tony [Williams] should've been there. Jack DeJohnette should've been there. They were very much a part of his groups over the years. For whatever reasons they weren't there, but a lot of musicians did show up. Just to see this whole amazing canvas of music, played briefly in condensed form—it was like repainting a picture. It was an amazing event and a very moving experience.

How did he seem to you at the time?
I could see that Miles was not in top form, health-wise. And I was a little worried about it. But for many years I had been worried about him. I remember 16 years ago I was in his house with Herbie and we both thought he was gonna die. This was in 1976. We had to help him into the hospital. I thought he was gonna die *then*! But he had always been very tough, very resilient. You could never imagine that Miles would die. It's like family. You never think that anyone in your family is going to die. But I think he must've had an idea at that Paris concert, because when he went in the hospital later he had double pneumonia and bronchitis and had one heart attack. Around that time I was speaking to Peter Shukat, who was an old friend of mine and had been handling Miles for the last few years. And I would ask Peter, "Does he want to live? Does he really want to?" And Peter would say, "I don't know." This was most worrying of all. Because you can get sick, but you need the will to get better. And nobody knew if he had it at that point.

That was also true of Jaco [Pastorius] in the end. So many people thought he was indestructible because he always bounced back from whatever he put himself through. But at some point, he gave up.
I agree with you. I saw Jaco quite some time before he died and I agree. I think he had given it up already, and that really, really hurt me, because he was a young man with such talent. I mean, how can you give up?

Some of his closest friends were really angry at him for that.
Yeah, I'm angry myself. I'm still angry about it. Yeah, it was sad. I met Jaco in 1974, before he joined Weather Report. He arrived [in New York] from Miami and found out where I was rehearsing. I had a great bass guitar player at the time in Ralphe Armstrong but Jaco came by and basically said, "I wanna play." He was really such a live wire, so full of vitality. So we jammed and he was amazing. He was looking for a gig and was broke. I loaned him money to get his car fixed and he paid me back 11 years later. I called Tony and said, "You should hear this bass player. This guy is amazing." But Jaco went back down to Florida and eventually hooked up with Joe and Wayne, and that was the start of a beautiful period. I actually got to know him better around '76–'77 when Shakti did a lot of touring with Weather Report in the U.S. and in Europe. Every night we would be checking each other out and it was really a wonderful combination because the two bands were so different. Jaco was playing so great then and Weather Report was such a great band. They really had a great impact on contemporary music. And to see Jaco really in his element was wonderful. So I knew him very well during his heyday. Then I saw him at Seventh Avenue South some years later and I was really shocked. He was drunk, acting crazy. He just seemed like a different person. You could see it in his eyes. But even so, I don't think we can ignore the great music that he made with Weather Report and on his own. These are great records, in my opinion. And Jaco played outstand-

ingly on them. But something happened. Something happened to his mind during that period so that instead of evolving he was devolving.

What was that notorious Trio of Doom gig in Cuba at the Havana Jam [1979] like?
It was such a shame! Tony and Jaco and I had rehearsed here in New York, and what a trio that was! What a pleasure it was to play with them! Tony and Jaco were just so much together. After one rehearsal, we actually went in to record with Joni Mitchell [for *Mingus,* Asylum, 1979]. We recorded one tune and then later they wiped Tony and me off the tracks, which I thought was a shame. But rehearsals were happening and we went down to Havana with high expectations. We each had a tune that we brought into the trio. We started off our set with my tune, "Dark Prince," which was an up-tempo C minor blues with altered changes. It was really a chance to stretch, but Jaco just threw the music down, walked back to his amp, turned it up to 11, and started playing A major really loud against it. I was looking at Tony like, "What is going on here?" It was nothing like the rehearsals. He did the same to Tony's tune. Then he went out and did his whole audience routine. It was a fiasco. The Bay of Gigs, I call it. And I was so mad at Jaco. He came off stage saying, "Yeah, man, that was the shit!" And I told him, "I have never been more ashamed in my life to be on stage with somebody. That was the worst shit I ever heard in my life. I don't wanna see your face for at least a week." I really was mad at him. Tony was mad at the time, but he wouldn't say anything. But he got mad later. We went into the studio later to try to do something, but there was a big fight between them…. Not really a big fight, Tony just flipped out and smashed his drums and walked out of the studio. And that really tore Jaco to strips.

So it was evident to me during this period that something was going on with Jaco that didn't really have too much to do with music. There was something happening in his mind. I don't know what it was. It was some kind of idea or image of himself of what he had to do or what he was supposed to do. And it was really crazy. It certainly had nothing to do with what we were playing. It was strictly show time. It was sad. But you can never take away from what he's done. He single-handedly revolutionized bass guitar—his sound, his chords, his harmonics. I mean, Jaco just blew the shit open. It's amazing what he did to bass guitar. Even today, Jaco stays unique. In the bass guitar firmament, he's unique. And nothing can take that away. Nothing! Whatever happened afterwards is just tragic, because we all loved Jaco. He was a loveable guy. He had his faults, too, but who doesn't? He was a lovely person. And everybody just wanted him to—to be alive and just play. That's what we're here for.

In your current trio you have such a strong hookup with [percussionist/drummer] Trilok Gurtu.
Well, Trilok is an Indian musician by training and a jazz musician by affection, so we have a lot in common. He can shift at a moment's notice from an Indian groove to an Elvin Jones kind of groove. So we're able to move together in a very easy way—very instant communication. At any point, we can dramatically change the musical derivative, and this means we have a big field to play in. We're not restricted to just one or two particular ways of communicating. And he has a great sense of humor, too, in the way he plays. I love humor. I take myself very seriously, but there's a point beyond which you take yourself so seriously you get heavy. And I don't want that to happen to the music.

Are you doing any other playing outside the trio?
Yes, I continue to play with a symphony orchestra. I do several concerts a year. I have a couple scheduled with a great American orchestra, the New World Symphony in Miami, which is an orchestra of musicians between the ages of 20 and 35. It's my second concerto and we'll probably record it sometime next year. I also have a group with Katia and Marielle Labeque [world-renown classical piano duo], which only exists in Europe called 20th Century Living. The music is all by 20th century composers, classical and jazz—Stravinsky, Bartók, Bernstein, arrangements of Thelonious Monk tunes with

everything written out. In Europe we're able to play with this group in great concert halls and have really mixed audiences, classical and jazz. It works very well. We tried to get some gigs over here but nobody's interested. The difference is, in Europe you have art subsidies, whereby the governments contribute money to make these programs happen. They see them as cultural events that need to be promoted simply because it's a good cultural event, that's all. You don't need another reason.

That's the failing of shortsighted American politicians. They don't see the connection between cultural events and social problems.
Exactly, and when I see symphony orchestras going bankrupt in America, this really frightens me.

The group that is supposed to be funding artistic expression in the States, the National Endowment for the Arts, is being raped by the Bush Administration and the whole fundamentalist right wing.
Well, money is petrol in the motor, isn't it? No money, no orchestras.

So we may never see you perform here in the States with 20th Century Living.
It's unlikely, yeah.

Other than that gig you played with Miles last summer, you probably don't have much use for electric guitar these days?
Not at all. Since I formed this trio back in 1988, I've been concentrating strictly on acoustic gut string guitar, which is the guitar I discovered when I was 11. So maybe I'm reverting back to my childhood. But there's definitely something there for me. I love the tone and it's a very percussive instrument, much more responsive in the upper register than a steel string guitar. No comparison. But I would like to play electric guitar again some day. As a matter of fact, I would like to record with Elvin and a Hammond organ player, and for that I would have to play an electric guitar. [John did eventually record *After the Rain* (Verve, 1995) with Elvin on drums and Joey DeFrancesco on organ.] Or with Tony. I love those guys. Tony is still today the great revolutionary on drums. And Elvin, who I never had the chance to play with, is so much a part of my growing up—listening to him and Trane. I really like this idea.

*Elvin did a record last year with Sonny Sharrock [Ask the Ages, *Axiom, 1991] that was a very powerful blowing album.*
Really! I haven't heard Sonny Sharrock in a long time. I remember playing with Sonny on one of Wayne's records, *Super Nova* [Blue Note, 1969]. I knew Sonny from back in 1968 when we played the Berlin Anti-Festival together.

Does your switch to acoustic guitar have anything to do with hearing loss from playing so loud with electric guitar?
No, although I do have a little dip around 4K, but just a small one. So I'm in pretty good shape. Actually, I have other problems with listening to loud music. When it's above a certain volume, I really miss the tenderness that's part of music, part of human life—the subtlety and feelings. And that all goes by the board for me when everything's cranked up. I'm not interested in doing that. I don't want to blast people, I want them to go into the music. I don't want to confront them with a wall of pressure. I am convinced, personally, if the music is open, if it has more space in it, then the listener's mind will go inside and his or her imagination will start to play inside the music. And that, for me, is really what's happening. At that point, the listener becomes lost in an individual sense and is found in a greater sense, just as we are when we play the music. And if we are able to do it, then the listener is going to be able to do it. And the music will be able to do its thing, which is, in fact,

heal. That's the great power of music. It heals the human spirit. So I am convinced now that people shouldn't be bombarded by music. Maybe I did before, but 20 years ago was another era.... The Vietnam War and the whole thing—Freedom Now, the black intellectual movement and how it was repressed, flower power, LSD, and all of that... Where we were going... It was a very different period, certainly for me. So I consider things differently today. And I see things actually differently. And for me, I would prefer to see more space and more subtleties in music, because the act of listening to music is very intimate, as it is to play. And if some kind of intimate action can take place inside the music, I think this is what's really happening.

Now that you're so immersed in more intimate acoustic music, how do you feel about being confronted by your own electric past? In the last couple of years, Columbia has reissued [A Tribute to] Jack Johnson *[1970] and* Johnny McLaughlin, Electric Guitarist *[1979], for instance.*
They're great, I love them. They're all part of me. And today there's still a Johnny McLaughlin Electric Guitarist inside me. I love that, too, but it's another way. And I don't rule out the possibility of playing the electric guitar again, especially if I get a chance to do something, as I say, with Elvin or do something with Tony again. But I don't know about the sound anymore. What you hear on *Que Alegria,* that's what my sound is all about now. That's my voice now. And I don't know if it's feasible to play an acoustic guitar with somebody bashing drums. That's tough. This guitar doesn't like it. At a certain volume, she freaks out. And the only way to get around that is to plug in the electric guitar. And I don't know what my voice is on that instrument anymore. It would require going back to the lab and finding out where my head is at as far as an electric sound is concerned. Maybe it'll come back quick, maybe it won't. I don't know.

That's a whole other woodshedding period.
You bet it is. And I may find the time, even if it's just a couple of days, to go in the studio and thrash around and flounder and find out what I don't like. Sometimes by the process of elimination you find out where you need to go. So we'll see what happens.

I recently saw a bootleg album of that jam you and Hendrix did together. It was selling for something like $40.
What a rip-off! There was not too much to that. It was just like a party in the studio. That was never intended to be released. That's terrible, but what are you gonna do? These people have no scruples. They have no honor. They're just looking to make a buck off a dead man's name. It's really a shame. This just disgusts me. They're just mercenaries with no morals, these people. But they're out there, so what can we do?

Keep playing.
That's it. That's all we can do.

DAVID MURRAY

SAXOPHONIST DAVID MURRAY enters a room with a gruff, swaggering demeanor, which is also an apt description of his tenor style. Few on the scene today play as forcefully and with as much abandon as the charter member of the World Saxophone Quartet, and no one has been so thoroughly documented as he has. My own CD shelves are teeming with a seemingly inexhaustible supply of David Murray releases on a plethora of labels. He is indeed the playingest man in the avant-garde.

My 1992 interview with the tenor titan took place in the Manhattan offices of Columbia Records, which was distributing his Japanese DIW releases in the States at the time. David seemed somewhat perturbed that this piece for *Down Beat* was not going to be a cover story. Always one to speak his mind, David barked, "Come on, man! When am I gonna get a cover, man? I been out here too long. I want a cover!" In fact, the cover subject of that January '93 issue of *Down Beat* was one Harry Connick, Jr. While I don't profess to understand the editorial wisdom that determines just who does and who doesn't get on a cover of any of these monthly music magazines, I did notice that David did indeed have a *Down Beat* cover all to himself in the June '95 issue.

OCTOBER 13, 1992

A prolific composer, a frequent collaborator, and relentless road warrior, reedman David Murray is more than eager to place his distinctive horn in as many contexts as possible. "I would like to be able to play with everyone who plays jazz—everyone who plays any kind of music," he says. "By the time I die, I would like to be able to play with any musician on the planet and know something about what they do as well as they know about what I do. I think that's the process that Duke Ellington went through in his lifetime. He learned a little bit from every culture and he reflected that in his suites about different cultures."

It has been 18 years now since Murray arrived on the New York scene. During that time he has been widely regarded by New York critics as one of the leaders of the avant-garde, having put in his tenure in the '70s loft scene and emerged as a force to be reckoned with in the '80s. His delicately balanced work with the World Saxophone Quartet and his recent work with the American Jazz Orchestra have helped to bring him to the attention of a wider international audience. While his ongoing collaborations with the likes of guitarist James "Blood" Ulmer; drummers Milford Graves, Andrew Cyrille, and Sunny Murray; and violinist Billy Bang have allowed him to keep one foot firmly planted in the cutting edge. Now, in the '90s, Murray stands as one of the most vital voices on tenor sax or bass clarinet, ready to attain the mantle of greatness. (Murray was unanimously selected as recipient of the 1991 Jazzpar Prize, a Danish jazz award with an international nominating committee, often referred to as The Nobel Prize of Jazz.)

Born in an Oakland ghetto 38 years ago, David Murray first picked up the tenor saxophone at the age of nine. After learning the rudiments of harmony from his mother (a pianist in the Pentecostal church) and learning the proper fingerings from his older brother (an aspiring clarinetist), Murray began sitting in with experimental bands in Berkeley and San Francisco. He later enrolled at Pomona College in Los Angeles and came under the wing of drummer, music critic, and (then) faculty member Stanley Crouch, who was one of the first to champion David when he arrived in New York in 1975. Other musicians on the Pomona campus at that time included Charles Tyler, Wilber and Butch Morris, Bobby Bradford, and Arthur Blythe.

Crouch and his star pupil David Murray ended up making the journey East together, renting a loft above an East Village jazz club, and producing their own concerts there. Some of those early sessions were documented on the five-volume *Wildflowers* series, co-produced by Alan Douglas and Michael Cuscuna in association with Sam Rivers, who ran the Studio Rivbea space where the concerts took place.

Throughout the '70s and '80s, Murray's explosive tenor style was marked by a relentless flow of energy, daring intervallic leaps, and frequent ascensions into the tenor's upper reaches to sustain a high squeal over his last few choruses. This style caused several critics to proclaim him the stylistic heir of Albert Ayler. But in recent years, some of the more romantic aspects of Murray's playing have come to the fore, inviting comparisons to the likes of Coleman Hawkins, Ben Webster, and Paul Gonsalves—all important influences on David.

These qualities can be heard on the most recent batch of David Murray releases (he is one of the few jazz artists who releases albums in batches). Due for release on DIW this fall are: *Picasso* by the David Murray Octet, featuring trumpeters Hugh Ragin and Rasul Siddik, trombonist Craig Harris, alto saxophonist and flutist James Spaulding, pianist Dave Burrell, bassist Wilber Morris, and drummer Tani Tabbal; an as-yet-untitled bass clarinet album by the David Murray Quartet featuring John Hicks on piano, Ray Drummond on bass, and Idris Muhammad on drums; and an as-yet-untitled tribute to saxophone legends by the David Murray Quartet featuring Dave Burrell on piano, Fred Hopkins on bass, and Ralph Peterson on drums [*Saxmen*, Red Baron, 1993].

But Murray is hesitant to acknowledge his ascending star on the jazz scene. As he says, "I'm not here to be a star show. I'm not here for that. I just wanna be known as one of the cats who can play." I spoke to David Murray following his duet performance with percussionist Khalil El' Zabar at the Time Cafe in Manhattan.

You seem to be constantly busy, always creating things in different contexts. By the time your records come out you're already two projects down the road.
That's true. I stay busy. I'm not making none of that Marsalis money, but I'm working. I gotta figure out a way to get to that level, man. Maybe I'll get me a new suit. [laughter] Or a real slick agent or manager or something. I don't know, man. I always feel like I'm in the doorway, but I can't really get in the door. I'm almost there, but not quite.

Your creative output is really staggering but one of the criticisms against you is that you actually record too much.
Well, I'm constantly making all of these records, hoping that one day some record company will say, "Wow, this guy has such an incredible output. Why don't we just sign him and make him slow down." I figure that if I demonstrate that I can do these things, then maybe somebody will pick me up. But too many artists just wait around to record. They get to be 50, then they get 60, then their life is over. At that age, they ain't got no life in them anymore. And they just live out their lives never doing what they really wanted to do. They get to be 80 and they look back on their careers and moan, "Oh, I really wanted to write this suite or this opera." My attitude is, "Do it now!" So I keep writing, keep documenting what I hear in my head. And in my dreams I'm hoping that somebody will come along and say, "Here's a million dollars. Stop doing all this shit. Slow down! Let's make one great record a year instead of five." I can't wait for that day. I would love that.

You have a very strong, very personal voice and you seem to be continually seeking new outlets for it. What are you interested in these days?
Well, suites seem to be the thing of the day, I guess. Most record companies want some kind of angle. So rather than going at the angle of mixing up musicians who would never, ever play with one another... To me, it's better to have an angle of having the music performed in a suite. It keeps the music from being trite, to me. So in the past couple of years I've been involved in performing and recording suites like Bobby Bradford's "Have You Seen Sideman?," which was dedicated to the late John Carter, and I also composed "The Baltic Suite," which I performed in Europe with the Baltic Ensemble. And of course, there was the "Picasso" suite. This kind of expression, to me, seems more honest than the gimmicky ways that producers threw musicians together in the '80s. I was getting tired and weary of producers wanting to throw me in with people who didn't have anything to do with jazz. I couldn't understand it and a lot of those dates were terrible. I did some of them just to make some money but my heart wasn't quite into it.

Are you referring to strictly electric projects?
Some type of fusion, I guess you'd call it. Yeah, I guess some of it was electric. It just never gelled to me. The only guy who I was really able to gel with who did that kind of stuff was Kip Hanrahan. I worked on his project *Conjure* [American Clave, 1988] and I did a tour on that with Billy Bang, Little Jimmy Scott, and Ishmael Reed. That was most satisfying. For something that's in that mode, that's probably about the best there is, I would think.

You weren't that happy playing with Blood and Jamaladeen in the Phalanx band?
Oh, I loved playing with Blood. But he has a concept. Some of the other things that we've done in

the studio never even came out. But playing with Blood is always exhilarating because Blood is the best at what he does. Jamaladeen is also the best at what he does. I have no problems there. The electric thing doesn't bother me as long as somebody's got a concept. I use electric guitar in the Shakill's Warrior band. So I have no problem with electric instruments.

I thought that Shakill's Warrior [Columbia, 1991] *was one of the best jazz albums of last year.*
Yeah, a lot of people said that to me. It was certainly great to hear Don Pullen playing Hammond B–3 organ again. He is sounding as good as ever on that instrument. He used to play it a lot in the early-1960s before he started concentrating on piano. So it was nice to hear him on organ again. Tani Tabbal also sounds great in that band. And my homeboy [guitarist] Stanley Franks, he's also sounding really good. I actually had a band together with him in high school, so it was sort of a homecoming to get back together with him for that record.

You also had the chance to do one of the last recordings with drummer Ed Blackwell when you did the "Have You Seen Sideman?" project together.
That's right. Blackwell, to me, is a genius. He is full of information and he was able to share that with anyone who would listen. People talk about African drum masters. He is a neo-African drum master for sure, as is Andrew Cyrille and Victor Lewis. I think, to me, those are the top drummers. And with Blackwell, especially, you hear Africa in his playing.

I know that near the end he was in constant pain, but by the time he hit the bandstand he would be transformed.
Yeah, I think the music kept him alive. I'm sure he broke the record of persevering for any kidney patient. I mean, he was on that kidney dialysis machine for 20 years, man. He called me one day and said he broke the record. He is a living testament that music is a healing force.

You also had a tight relationship with another great drummer who passed away, Steve McCall.
That's right. I miss him still in my music. I can't seem quite to get the replacement for him. I'll never get the replacement for Steve McCall, especially that left-handed way that he had. He was able to swing differently than anybody I know, even other left-handers. Steve was a brilliant man. He's like having a painter who plays drums. Steve was a thinker behind the traps set as he was off the bandstand. We've lost a lot of great drummers recently—Art Blakey, Blackwell, Phillip Wilson.

Phillip was in particularly bad shape near the end. [Wilson was viciously beaten to death in the East Village while trying to score some heroin.]
Yeah, it's a shame. And I hate to see a person in their latter years that frustrated. These kind of frustrations seem to be dictated by certain powers that be in the jazz world. Those are the kinds of things that I would like to see cease. Because there's so many good musicians out here, so many good jazz musicians in New York, that to focus on just a few, to me, is just obscene. It doesn't make any sense.

The media seems to only have room for one trumpet hero and one sax hero at a time.
That's a problem. And even if I thought in that vein if I may be one of the ones that is chosen, for me it's no good because I didn't come here to be a scapegoat of any kind. I'm in love with the art of jazz. And there's a lot of players, man, that are being overlooked. And it's really a shame. One of these days... If things don't get fixed correctly, I don't know what I'm gonna do. Maybe I need to be a producer or something—try to record these people myself. [Saxophonist] Carter Jefferson hasn't gotten his due. We could go on and on. Bobby Bradford hasn't gotten his due, Rasul Sadik hasn't gotten his due, Hugh Ragin hasn't gotten his due, Craig Harris hasn't gotten his due. I could make a

list, man. Look, there's a lot of people out here who can really play. And not just in that particular genre but in other genres, too. There's a lot of bop players that haven't got their due that are being pushed aside for the younger generation of kids that seem to pose at being bebop players.

Who are you thinking of in particular?
Oh, you got [trumpeter] Dizzy Reece, for one. He's a great player who is one of the pioneers. I mean, he played with Bird, man. Why isn't he being championed out here? Does he have to be 85 years old like Doc Cheatham to start getting a little play? You know, there's a lot of guys, man, and if I start naming them we'll be here all day. On every instrument there are great, great players being ignored. I just don't understand it. Jazz has never been the kind of business when you get old you get pushed aside. Most musicians play until they die. Clifford Jordan should've had a much bigger push than he got. There's a tenor saxophone player over in Europe named Andy Hamilton. He's like the Lester Young or Ben Webster of England. I did a recording with him called *Silvershine* [World Circuit, 1991]. Man, he's a great player and he's been overlooked, even by the English. So there's a lot of great players that are out there. All over the world.

It's commendable of you to bring some of these players to light in your big band.
Look, everybody in that band either has their own band or is trying to get some kind of record deal. And they're being turned back. People are saying, "Well, we already have the David Murray big band." Well look, the tides could be turned and I could be playing in their big band. And if they ask me, I certainly will because I respect the players.

You don't seem to be frustrated by this situation.
I try not to let it get to me. I can't really complain in terms of myself because I get the work. I don't have a real manager right now. I don't really have the team yet that I need to do all the jobs that I need to do. I probably turned down half the work that I could do because I just can't stay on top of the business end of it. I'm gone on the road or I just can't handle all the calls. There's only so much you can do.

I've seen you around town in some contexts that may or may not have been recorded. One was the duet you did with Milford Graves last year at the New Music Cafe.
Yeah, we recorded that for DIW. And we named the album *The Real Deal* [1991]. That was Milford's idea. That was really a great experience playing with him. He is a wonderful drummer, man. So much energy. He's one of those guys that has his own concept. As long as a person has something that he's developed that really depicts what they think about all the time, I will have no problem playing music with that person. When a person has a concept, you can hear the agony, you can hear the blissfulness, you can hear everything in his playing. You can see the whole world in somebody's playing if they have a concept. In Milford Graves, you can hear Africa, you can hear Brazil, you can hear everything. It's the same with Blood Ulmer, Craig Harris, Dave Burrell, and Billy Bang. These are people who really have a concept. And I have a concept. It took me a long time to really develop it. As far as a saxophone player, I probably developed my own sound when I was 27 or 28. And today I encourage my students around the world to keep trying to develop their own sound because that's their ticket to success. You have to have your own individual sound. A sound is like a signature, to quote Cecil Taylor.

Where were you at in terms of your development when you first came to New York back in 1975?
I was studying everybody, probably sounding like them. Like any younger player who wants to sound good, you have to study others. You're not just going to come upon it all by yourself, not

unless you're Charlie Parker or somebody. They threw away the mold when he died. So you've gotta study other people to be good. You can't be a great writer without acknowledging the great works. You just can't get around James Joyce, you can't get around Ralph Ellison, you can't get around Albert Murray, you can't get around Chaucer. You can't get around these people. You don't just come up with a concept all on your own, because they didn't either.

Why do you put yourself in all these different contexts while some musicians are content to remain in one bag?
Well, there is the artistic part of it. But the other part of it is, you have to be a little more flexible if you want to survive financially playing jazz. That's something I need to do very much, is to survive financially. And I have to have my feet in different camps in order to do that.

Do you hope that your sons follow in your footsteps and become musicians?
Well, I'm looking for Kahil to come on as a musician. He played on my *Big Band* album [Columbia, 1991]. He's at William Patterson College right now and soon he'll be starting out with his own band and DIW has sort of promised to record him. So his future is taken care of. And I'm assuming my other son, Mingus, will come on as a musician, too. He's mostly doing karate right now but he certainly has a lot of music inside of him. I'm just waiting maybe—another year or so—to stick an alto sax in his mouth. I think he's really going to be something else. I guess it's inevitable. There's a history of musicians in my family, going back many generations. So I just think the future holds a lot for jazz, as far as the Murray family is concerned.

Any thoughts on that Special Quartet session you did last year with McCoy Tyner and Elvin Jones?
Oh yeah, that's a great album. I really dug McCoy's playing. I was just so impressed with him. His explosiveness is just really inspiring. He's got a lot of music under his belt. He probably has more in reserve than most people have out front all the time. He's a great player, and Fred Hopkins sounds so good on that one. Fred is playing great bass these days. Ray Drummond's also sounding great these days. Wilber Morris is playing good bass these days. I've been lucky to be around great bass players. I've been fortunate to be around such a high level of musicians in my career.

Are there any other projects that you hope will take off for you?
I'm still trying to push the duo with me and Dave Burrell. We did this record *Daybreak* [Gazell, 1989]. And we have another one, *Live in Victoriaville, Canada* [Victor, 1991] that is really a great album. People have written articles about that one saying it's an indication of where music in the '90s is going. I thought so, too, but it's really nice to hear other people comment along those lines.

You have been an outspoken critic of Wynton Marsalis and his very conservative curator's approach to jazz. What are your feelings about his brother Branford and what he's doing with "The Tonight Show" band.
I think what Branford's doing with that band is great. People keep asking me, "Isn't that horrible that Branford is playing with 'The Tonight Show' band." And I say, "Hell, I wish they would've asked me! I would've done it." That's a great gig. And I'm sure everybody else would've done it. It takes a special kind of person to do a job like that. It's just another phase in music and shouldn't be criticized. It should just be noticed as another change in the taste buds of America. It's good to be visible. Nothing wrong with that.

On your travels have you had an opportunity to jam with the local people in places like Turkey and Israel?
Oh yeah. Like this thing with the "Baltic Suite"—that's a collaboration with musicians from

Northern Germany and parts of Scandinavia. And there's a lot to learn there. Recently the World Saxophone Quartet went to Australia and we collaborated with some aborigines, some dijeridoo players. When I go to Japan there's always musicians who wanna play with me—koto players, shakuhashi players. I had a long conversation once with John Takamitsu about him composing a fanfare for the WSQ. So I've had the opportunity to be around some great composers. Probably one of the best of my generation, I think, is Julius Hemphill. His thought process is really on a high level. When he was in the WSQ it was quite a different band and I learned a lot from him. And although he's not with the band anymore, he's still writing good music. Bakida Carroll's music that he dedicated to John Carter is beautiful. And, of course, Bobby Bradford's suite is gorgeous. There's a lot of people out here doing good writing and arranging these days. Anthony Davis and James Newton are doing some beautiful things. Craig Harris is coming on like Mozart. He's got a wealth of music inside him—and on paper. There's another guy who's got a lot of music inside him, Leroy Jenkins. So it's time for the record companies to wake up and start recording all this music that's just sitting around.

Any thoughts on your upcoming appearance with the American Jazz Orchestra?
Gary Giddins called me up for that and it was really nice that he did because I always wanted to play with an orchestra. It's nice to be able to play with them, because I'll probably never get the opportunity to play with this orchestra they have at Lincoln Center, with Wynton Marsalis and all his cousins and all their dogs and cats, family, and generations.

Do you record a lot of stuff on tour, just to document it?
Yeah, I always get a tape, if I don't have my DAT with me—just to see where my sound is going every day. That's important to me. Where it's going, where I'm coming from. That's where you learn to edit yourself. I don't wanna play the same solo every night. I don't wanna play the same solo on the second tune even. There's a lot of people out there that play the same stuff over and over. But I'm constantly kicking myself trying to make myself change and do something different, so I won't become bored with my own self. So right now, writing fills that void. The more I write, the more strange the music sounds and the more strange my playing gets. And then the next thing I know, the strange playing becomes part of my concept. But you have to go through that strangeness and unassuredness to get to something that's normal or kosher enough for people's palate.

When you first came out in the late-1970s, some people couldn't deal with your sound. Now you are becoming closer to the mainstream in a way.
Yeah, well, I've tried to make it part of the mainstream because there's no way you're gonna make it in this life if you're not a part of the mainstream. But every once in a while I do something to throw people off, like when I make a record with Milford Graves. People will say to Milford, "Well, how's David Murray gonna play with Milford Graves?" Well, anybody that knows my history would know. I've played with him a lot. Just because we haven't done it recently doesn't mean we can't play together. I can play with anybody. Hopefully I can. I'd like to play with the Philharmonic. I'd like to be a soloist with them one day, but that's probably impossible. But I would be all ears for any of that. I try not to put any boundaries on myself. When you say can't you usually mean won't. My mother and father always taught me there's nothing you can't do if you have God behind you and if you put your heart into it. Eleanor Roosevelt once said "The things that you cannot do are the things that you should do." And to me that meant a lot. Because things that are difficult are things that are gonna be most satisfying once you accomplish them.

And your mainstream acceptance is typified by your upcoming week at the Village Vanguard.
Oh, I've been playing at the Vanguard for years. I played at the Vanguard when it meant something

to play at the Vanguard. When Max Gordon was alive I think it meant a lot more to play at the Vanguard, because his tastes were very rigid in a certain way, but in a positive way. First of all, you had to be good to play at the Vanguard. And he didn't go for no nonsense. I just remember him coming up to me and saying, "Keep playing the ballads. Keep playing the ballads. That fast stuff, I don't like. Play some ballads." And I thought about it. He had a point. It's just like, he's part of the old guard, and he's gone now. I dug Max. And his wife now, she's a little more flexible in terms of the choice of music she brings in. But at the same time, when it was difficult to get into the Vanguard, I was already playing there. Not like today—darn near anybody plays at the Vanguard. It doesn't have to fit the mold of the old Max Gordon Vanguard, which in a way is good because time must move on. But at the same time, I feel like I've been there a little longer. I've had more experience playing that gig than a lot of players do. So if somebody now tells me they're playing at the Vanguard, it's not like 12 years ago when they'd tell me they're playing at the Vanguard. It's a little more flexible now than it used to be. He would bring people in to play who he respected, nothing more, nothing less. I also continue to play at Condon's and I might even go back into Sweet Basil. The Blue Note has already told me that my music is too... They associate me with a certain crowd, avant-garde musicians or something. But I don't know what that's about. I always thought that avant-garde was a painting style of a certain period. I never knew that it applied to music.

VISIONARIES

FRANK ZAPPA

ROBERT FRIPP

BRIAN ENO

LES PAUL

JOHN ZORN

BOBBY MCFERRIN

JOHN SINCLAIR

BILL LASWELL

MILFORD GRAVES

GLENN BRANCA

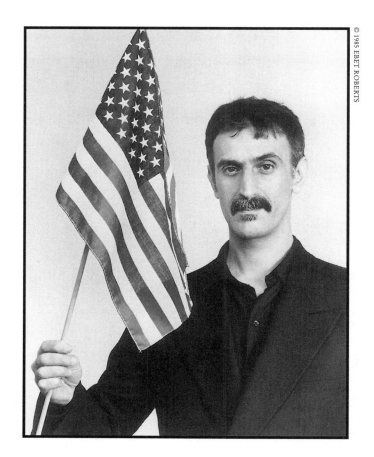

© 1985 EBET ROBERTS

FRANK ZAPPA

I INTERVIEWED FRANK ZAPPA on four different occasions. The first was memorable, if only for the fact that I showed up a bit late for the interview, very nervous and anxiety-ridden over a malfunctioning cassette tape. Zappa graciously lent me a cassette of music by Antonia Brico to tape over. I conducted this interview for *Good Times* magazine in conjunction with his latest release at the time, *You Are What You Is* (Rykodisc, 1981). It was a cover story for a December '81 issue. I would later interview Zappa for a February '83 *Down Beat* cover story and an August '84 issue of *Modern Recording* magazine.

A true renaissance man, Zappa integrated doo-wop, blues, modern jazz, and electric fusion into his rock music while maintaining a separate career as a contemporary classical composer under the influence of Anton Webern, Edgard Varèse, Igor Stravinsky, and Karlheinz Stockhausen. He wrote and recorded everything from silly pop tunes ("Valley Girl" and "Don't Eat the Yellow Snow") to grandiose orchestral suites (*The Perfect Stranger,* Barking Pumpkin, 1983), from '50s-styled R&B (*Cruising with Ruben & the Jets,* Rykodisc, 1968) to off-Broadway musicals (*Thing Fish,* Rykodisc, 1986), from biting satires (*Broadway the Hard Way,* Barking Pumpkin/Rhino, 1988, and *We're Only in It for the Money,* Rykodisc, 1968) to virtuosic displays of his instrumental prowess (*Shut Up 'n Play Yer Guitar,* Rykodisc, 1981) and MIDI technology (his Grammy-winning *Jazz from Hell,* Rykodisc,

1986). The scope of his discography, which totals over 60 records, would take months to fully absorb. Zappa had a huge impact on much of the progressive and experimental rock music of the past three decades. The likes of British art-rockers Henry Cow, New York noisemaker John Zorn, and funkmeister George Clinton owe a debt to Frank Zappa. In one of his last interviews, Zappa told *Pulse* magazine: "I never had any intention of writing rock music. I always wanted to compose more serious music and have it be performed in concert halls, but I knew no one would play it. So I figured that if anyone was ever going to hear anything I composed, I'd have to get a band together and play rock music. That's how I got started."

After a lengthy career as a prolific composer-conceptualist-guitarist-satirist, Frank Zappa died of prostate cancer on December 4, 1993, just a few weeks short of his 53rd birthday. A noted workaholic, he spent his final years working as though his life depended on it. Only a month before his death, he issued a new album of orchestral and chamber music entitled *The Yellow Shark* (Rykodisc, 1993) recorded live by the Ensemble Modern in Germany and Austria in September of '92.

NOVEMBER 17, 1981

Frank Vincent Zappa was born on December 21, 1940, in Baltimore, Maryland, the eldest of four children. His father, a Sicilian-born immigrant who worked for the military, moved the family to California in the early-1950s, eventually settling in Lancaster near the Mojave Desert. Zappa started playing drums when he was 12 and by his teenage years got seriously involved with R&B. At age 14 he discovered the music of his childhood hero, Edgard Varèse, and began emulating the contemporary classical composer in his own first orchestral works.

Zappa's first band was a racially-integrated combo called The Black-Outs. He started up his own recording studio in the early-1960s and recorded some obscure singles, including the Penguins' "Memories of El Monte," his first recorded performance on guitar.

In 1964, Zappa joined a Los Angeles area bar band called The Soul Giants. He grew tired of playing covers of top 40 hits and eventually persuaded a few of the other band members—vocalist Ray Collins, drummer Jimmy Carl Black, bassist Roy Estrada—to quit The Soul Giants and form the wildly experimental Mothers of Invention.

They quickly became the most talked about band on the Los Angeles underground scene and in 1966 they recorded their first album, *Freak Out!* (Verve, 1966), the first studio double-album of the modern rock era. They followed that up with other highly regarded albums like *Absolutely Free* (Rykodisc, 1967), *We're Only in It for the Money,* and Zappa's orchestral debut, *Lumpy Gravy* (Rykodisc, 1967). [An interesting footnote: The tune "Plastic People" from *Absolutely Free* became the anthem for a whole movement of dissidents in Czechoslovakia who centered around an illegal, underground band known as Plastic People of the Universe.]

In 1969, Zappa broke up the original Mothers of Invention and in 1971 began recording and touring with a new lineup called The Mothers. This band included former vocalists for The Turtles—Mark Volman and Howard Kaylan (also known as Flo and Eddie). Also in 1971, Zappa released his film *200 Motels,* a kind of mockumentary (pre-dating *Spinal Tap* by more than a decade) about the hardships of rock'n'roll road life.

In the mid-1970s, Zappa finally began to realize commercial success with albums like *Over-night Sensation* (DiscReet, 1973) and *Apostrophe (')* (DiscReet, 1974). In 1979, he broke into the top 30 with *Sheik Yerbouti* (Zappa, 1979), which included the pop satire hit, "Dancin' Fool." Earlier this year, Zappa formed his own Barking Pumpkin label to record and distribute his records. I spoke to The Grand Wazoo himself about the state of the record industry, the state of the union, and his latest release, *You Are What You Is.*

You've always been a social commentator of sorts. On your new album you're expressing strong views against drugs and ignorance in songs like "Dumb All Over" and "Charlie's Mouth." Who are you addressing these things to?

I'm addressing it to anybody who will listen to it, which right now isn't very many people because the only radio stations that are playing the album are in New York, Long Island, and Connecticut. It's totally dead every place else in the country. The album is not selling at all. It's one of the best albums that we've ever made and most people don't even know that it's out there.

What's the problem?

Today radio is not like it used to be. Most of the stations that matter are programmed by five people, who are not even located in the same town where the radio stations are broadcasting from. I'll give you a good example: When we played in Tucson, Arizona, the station that was co-sponsoring the concert asked me to come on the air and be a DJ like I did here [New York] on WPIX one time. I flew in right before the concert from Las Vegas, went to the station to do my DJ shot.... I go in there, shake hands with the regular DJ, and they announced that I'm on the air. I say, "Great, you got my album?" They say, "Yeah." Fine, I stick it on and play it. But as soon as I start playing my album the program director calls up and tells the guy not to let me do it. So I said on the air, "What is this? You invite me in to be a disc jockey and you won't let me play my own records? I'm not gonna stay here for this. Thanks, goodbye!" And I left. The station had just changed its format and had become an Abrams station, which meant that it was being programmed from remote control a million miles away. Somebody in another city was telling the people of Tucson, Arizona what they must hear. Prior to the time that they became an Abrams station, they had a record catalog of 2,000 LPs. After they became an Abrams station, they threw out 1,500 LPs—cut their library down to 500 albums, including none of mine. They went on to a total formula of what to play and what they wanted me to do on the air was play Pat Benetar, Foreigner, REO Speedwagon, and Journey and sit there and be a DJ announcing those records. And I wasn't gonna do it. There's no reason why I should have to front for somebody else's music when I think that what I'm doing is perfectly fine and that the audience would enjoy hearing it. So I told the audience the next day at the concert what had happened and they were upset about it. When I spoke to some of the kids there they said that prior to the time when the station became formatted it was a better station. People are grasping at straws in order to make more money during the present economic crunch. And when a programmer in another city says, "If you take my formula and use this formula, you will win in the ratings war," which means that you can charge more money for advertising, then a lot of people go for that.

Why is there no place for Frank Zappa in this formula?

There are many broadcasters who turn crimson at the mention of my name and just can't stand the idea of putting my stuff on the air. Because in the wisdom of the people who program stations, to them a song with an idea above drugs, sex, and rock'n'roll or a boy-girl situation is something that they don't want on the air. They are successfully removing all social content, moral content, and aesthetic content from what goes on the radio. You will hear the same ten songs for the rest of your life now. That's what it's down to. As long as an area refuses to take the responsibility of picking their own music... When they turn it over to an "expert" someplace else and the expert sends them a list and says, "Play this and you're gonna win in the ratings war..." As long as that's all that matters, that's all you're gonna get.

Why did you decide to market your collection of instrumentals [Shut Up 'n Play Yer Guitar] through mail-order only?

Because if I release it as a normal commercial release in the United States, it would be doomed. Radio stations wouldn't play it because they don't play instrumental music. And the other problem is that it would have been very difficult to advertise it. So I figured that by doing it the way I did, by letting people who already bought the other albums know about this one by putting information on the inner sleeve of the other ones—it's direct marketing to the people who would be the most likely consumers for it. And it's done better than any of the other albums I've had out recently. It's doing much better than *You Are What You Is*. Within two weeks of the first orders coming in, the album had paid for itself, which is more than you could say for any of the other albums that we've had out. And we've gotten letters back from people who say they really love it and want to have other episodes or editions. So I intend on putting out some more.

What does this album represent to you as an artist?
It's a collection of guitar solos that I think represents a lot of different styles that I can play—a lot of different guitar sounds and textures that would be interesting, not just to guitar players but to people who like good instrumental performance.

What was it that initially attracted you to guitar?
Well, let's face it, there's nothing that sounds like an electric guitar. Good 'ol distorted electric guitar is a universe of sound that transcends the actual noise that is coming out. I mean, you can take one fuzztone note from a guitar and look at it on a spectrum analyzer and calculate everything that's in it, but there's so much more in it than just the harmonic components. It says something that no other instrument says and that's what attracted me to it. It had emotional content that went beyond other instruments. I mean, nothing is more blasphemous than a properly played distorted guitar.

At what point did those blasphemous sounds catch your ear?
About the time I was 16 I started hearing some solos on records that really intrigued me. Johnny "Guitar" Watson was an extremely evil-sounding guitar player at that time. But the smuttiest one that I heard was Guitar Slim. Just pure smut. His solos on "Three Hours Past Midnight" and "The Story of My Life" were really what did it to me. The absolute manic way that he spewed out these notes in a phrase with little or no regard to the rest of the meter or what was going on but still being aware of where the beat was... He was just yelling it at you.

You have mentioned that you think about your own solos as going for that same vocal quality.
Yeah, I think that's the most direct way to communicate with somebody, using speech rhythms. That really makes a big difference. Because if you listen to a guy playing nice neat scale patterns and things like that, no matter how skillful he is in making his stuff land on the beat, you always hear it as Music—capital 'M' music—lines, chord changes, and stuff like that. But if you want to get beyond Music into emotional content, you have to break through that and just talk on your instrument—just make it talk. And there's a different rhythmic attitude in doing that.

You've done a number of film projects over the years. Anything in the works?
Not really. I'm always open for suggestions if somebody will want to put up the money. All the ones I've done so far I've financed myself, but I can't afford that anymore.

Do you find the same kinds of control in the film industry that you are now encountering in the record industry?
Oh yeah, it's all the same. If you think about it, it's frightening. But I would not focus this whole climate down to one man. I would never dump it on Reagan because I don't think he's smart enough. Reagan is just a guy, he's an actor. He gets his lines from elsewhere. Look at it this way— Reagan got elected by one of the smallest quantities of voters in history yet he stands in front of a

television camera today and talks about the mandate he got from the American people. Only 17% of the American voters went out and voted for him! It was a choice between Tweedle Dum and Tweedle Dee. That 17% was mostly Christian religious fanatics manipulated by those video organizations that motivate that stuff. He was elected by the Moral Majority and he owes his ass to them. The Constitution says there is supposed to be a separation of church and state, but we got a little paradox here where you've got a president in there who owes his success to the machinations of religious organizations who helped put him in there. And those people are not in the religion business, they're in the real estate business. They get their money from a lot of people who want to go to heaven and they take it and they put it in real estate. Or they buy television satellites and they have their own television studios. And as long as Americans are not interested in reading printed matter—they're illiterate, they come out of school and can't read or spell… Everybody wants it quick so they can get back to watching TV. These so-called churches get free TV time and all these tax breaks, and they're thriving. It's a whippin' business. Whenever times get tough everybody starts looking for an easy way out. So naturally, cults thrive, religions thrive, escapist material thrives, and that's what's happening right now. People are looking for a way out of the reality of what's going on, which is not very beautiful. In fact, it's disgusting.

Does this whole climate tend to make you more cynical?
No, it tends to make me more realistic about what's going on. I don't think that being cynical is necessarily a bad thing because if you're not cynical then you swallow the whole enchilada. You have to sit and evaluate what people tell you. You have to read between the lines, and there's a lot of lines to read between.

Does this all reflect a national shift toward the right?
It's a national shift toward nowhere. It's toward fake security. People withdraw into themselves. They keep their mouths shut, they're scared shitless. The reason why the Moral Majority has had success in stifling creativity in the United States is because if you take any small group of people and if they make enough noise, they can sound like a lot of people. The Moral Majority is neither moral nor the majority. There's not more of them than there is of us. They just make more noise. And when something good goes on the air, nobody ever calls up and says, "That's great!" So if a guy owns a radio station, what does he know? It's a business for him. They way he earns his living is by charging money for advertising time on the air. He doesn't care what he plays on his station. If the station ain't working as a rock station, he'll go country & western or whatever. He just wants to sell time. And if the only phone calls or responses he ever gets at the station are from people complaining and applying pressure, then he only gets one picture of what the community desires. If everybody in the United States who wanted to hear variety or any kind of expression on the air would call up the station and demand it, they would get it. But no, they keep their mouths shut. So the automatons, who are controlled by these little agitation groups, organize and apply their pressure by operating phone banks and sending thousands of telegrams to Congressman X. He thinks, "Hey, the world wants this." But it's not the world. It's a manipulative mailing campaign that influences that opinion. People engineer this stuff and it's made to look like more than it actually is. So until people realize that they still have some control over their lives, you can still make noise, you can still open your mouth and fight back… Don't expect to win in just 15 minutes but you don't just bend over. I never did want to bend over, I have no desire to bend over. When you're 40 years old and you bend over, it's harder to stand up again. And everybody should realize that. Don't bend over.

Is this a phenomenon that you've noticed taking hold within the past few years?

This year it's really taken a nose dive, since the Reagan Administration has gotten in. It's frightening. We're looking at the prelude to the New Dark Ages here. If you know anything about history, the Dark Ages we're going into now is gonna make the first one look like a company picnic.

What happens to those people who have creative ideas today? Where do they go?
Well, most of them aren't going anywhere because there's no place for them to go. There's no outlet for their creativity and there's also no way to support themselves while doing creative things. It's not easy, but that's the way it is. You gotta be brave and you gotta keep doing it.

Are you alarmed by the rising rates of illiteracy among young people today?
It disturbs me a lot. I think that the English language is a great creative tool. You can do stuff with the English language that everybody else should be jealous of. But nobody gives a fuck, you know? When you go to school, what are you there for? You go to party. You meet somebody of the opposite sex and go out and get pooched. Or you're gonna get just enough of an education to get a job when you get out. Who wants to be smart? There's no desire to be smart. It's not fun to be smart. You're not gonna get laid if you're smart. And if you don't get laid, you know, then what kind of a person are you? So the whole emphasis on building your brain power is gone. Nobody wants to build up their brains.

Hasn't that kind of attitude been prevalent through the '50s and '60s, too?
It started in the '50s. It started with the idea of coolness. We're the only society that has coolness as a way of life. It's just escalated from the '50s to a point where it's not cool anymore to be smart. These are troubled times and we are the people who are troubling them. We're our own worst enemy. You stop thinking, they're gonna stick the bag over your head. Next thing you know it's off to the slaughterhouse. You just have to think about what it is people are telling you or selling you. Think about what's really going on. There's so much make-believe crap out there and a lot of it looks like more fun than the real world. And if you go for that, then you're doomed.

Are there other artists today trying to voice the same message to people?
No, because in most instances to say anything pertinent on any topic is the kiss of death to your career. The people who are most successful in the rock'n'roll business are the people who never do interviews, who never say anything about anything, who have no content in their songs, who keep their mouths shut and only play the beat and sing about their boyfriend or girlfriend, drugs, sex, rock'n'roll. Those are the ones who get on the radio and make millions of dollars, and they never say nothing.

So why have you felt a conviction to jeopardize your career by being so outspoken?
If I stopped speaking out right now that doesn't mean that I would suddenly sell millions of units. They don't trust me anymore anyway so I might as well keep doing what I've been doing. And I'm not asking people to agree with what I'm saying. I'm just encouraging them to actively think. You have to stand up and say what you think. Whether you agree with me or not is not important. It's the idea that you get used to using your brain instead of just swallowing everything that everybody feeds you on television or radio and in newspapers. Think about it before you act on it. But thinking is just not fashionable anymore. Everybody just wants to be having a good time and usually what happens when you start thinking about stuff—it ain't fun anymore. But I think a lot and I manage to have a good time. You can balance it out.

Do you have a strong enough core following to support what you do?

Well, understand that if the core doesn't grow to keep pace with the costs of doing what I'm doing, then ultimately I will disappear. Remember, it's my money that makes these things. I mean, I don't stick the money up my nose and I don't buy yachts. It all goes right back into the music. If I get a sale of a concert ticket, part of that money goes back into buying equipment and the airplane tickets for the next tour and paying the salaries of the people in the band. And the cost of making the records keeps going up, too. So it's just like any other small business. The capital comes in to keep the business running so that people can consume it, and unless that consumer body grows in pace with the cost of running the business, then the business fails. That's the worst part of it. I'm not funded by grants. I can only do what I can afford to do.

Does it make you depressed at all?
Naw... I don't like it, but I'm not gonna get suicidal about it. It's better to face it than to kid yourself into saying, "Oh, if we just keep doing what we're doing, all of a sudden we're going to be as big as The Beatles." It ain't gonna happen. It's all make-believe.

The political climate seems so bad in the States right now. Have you ever considered moving elsewhere?
No, I'm an American boy. I like it here.

What are some of the misconceptions that people have about you?
People find it hard to believe that anybody can really do the spectrum of stuff that I do, because most of the people they deal with are too one-dimensional or narrow-focused on just a certain field. They stay in that field and that's all they do. But I don't operate that way. I'm interested in different kinds of music, film work, computer editing, politics, and sociology and I have pretty well-developed skills in all those areas. But I don't think it's possible for me to correct misconceptions about what I do. People prefer to believe what they think they already know, and to interfere with that is only going to confuse them.

You have no college degrees, you've never studied with anyone, and yet you have acquired all this knowledge. How did you do it?
I went to the library. It's free and it's there. And until they close down the public libraries in the United States, everybody has access to the same information. Just go and do it.

ROBERT FRIPP

HIS DEMEANOR IS EXACTING, his speech deliberate, though the content is somewhat elliptical. His thoughts are precisely organized, his elocution impeccable. He is coolly cerebral and wholly logical. The Mr. Spock of rock, Robert Fripp admits to being more comfortable with verbiage than with music. When asked a question, he pauses, reflects intently on the nature and nuance of your words, then, assured that he has formulated a proper answer, he launches into a flawless diatribe. His steely-blue eyes project an intensity that can be slightly unnerving to interviewers. His distaste for interviews is legendary and he adopts a let's-get-on-with-it-then attitude to help him through the whole tedious process. (I couldn't help but notice that the book he was reading as I greeted him one early Sunday morning at the Cupping Room in SoHo was titled *Systems of Organization*. How appropriate, I thought.)

My interview with the creative force behind King Crimson, the League of Gentlemen, the League of Crafty Guitarists, and that one-man show of looping technology he dubbed Frippertronics ("a small, mobile, intelligent self-sufficient unit") was fraught with technological disaster. Halfway into it, I realized (journalist's nightmare) that the tape recorder was indeed not turning. Should've checked the batteries. "Oh well, there it is," announced the fatalistic Fripp, proclaiming the interview over. I offered to dash across the street and buy fresh new batteries, but the deed had been done, the symbolism was clear. This interview was indeed ended. But we picked it up again the next day by phone. And, thankfully, Fripp was in a more congenial, cooperative mood.

I first interviewed Fripp in November of '81 for *Good Times* magazine, shortly after he had reformed King Crimson with Adrian Belew, Tony Levin, and Bill Bruford. The following interview was conducted for a story in the September '84 issue of *Guitar World*. In 1994, Fripp resurrected King Crimson once again—with Belew, Levin, Bruford, stick player Trey Gunn, and second drummer Pat Mastoletto—for an album, *Vroom,* and subsequent tour. They followed that up with *Thrak* (1995) and *THRaKaTTaK* (1996), both on Fripp's Discipline Mobile Fidelity label. In 1998 Fripp formed ProjeKct Two, a power trio off-shoot of King Crimson. They released *Space Groove* and followed up with an international tour. Fripp also simultaneously released *Gates of Paradise*, the latest of an ongoing series of Soundscape releases on Discipline Mobile Fidelity.

APRIL 7, 1984

Things might have turned out differently. Robert Fripp might very well be peddling real estate today in some quaint English country town had not some force—call it "The Good Fairy," as Fripp has—taken hold of him at an impressionable age, magically transforming him into a guitarist. Fripp confesses that he still doesn't fully understand the powers at work that changed his life at the tender age of 17 back in his hometown of Wimbourne. To this day, he still registers surprise in relating that tale.

Fripp's first band of note was the pop-oriented trio Giles, Giles and Fripp, circa 1967. They made two singles and one dismally-received album *The Cheerful Insanity of Giles, Giles and Fripp* (Deram, 1968). A year later Fripp formed King Crimson and recruited Greg Lake on bass and vocals, Mike Giles on drums, Ian McDonald on reeds and keyboards, and Pete Sinfield on lyrics, lights, and synthesizer. Their debut album, *In the Court of the Crimson King* (Atlantic, 1969) received universal acclaim, including a rave from The Who's Pete Townsend, who called it "an uncanny masterpiece."

Following a number of personnel changes, Fripp arrived at his strongest lineup in 1972 with Bill Bruford on drums, John Wetton on bass and vocals, David Cross on violin and mellotron, and Jamie Muir on percussion. This edition of King Crimson met its untimely death in the summer of 1974 following an extensive tour of the States and culminating in a free concert in New York City's Central Park (which later yielded King Crimson's second and last live album, *USA*, Editions EG, 1975). That triumphant concert in Central Park on July 1 would be their final gig together.

Prior to that tour, Fripp had made this statement to England's *Melody Maker* magazine: "This band is not very sensitive or interested in listening to everyone playing. So the improvisation in the band at the moment is extremely limited and more concerned with individuals showing off than in developing any kind of community improvisation."

Shortly after the Stateside tour, back in England, Fripp announced the final dissolution of the seminal group that had spawned a whole school of progressive art-rock during the '70s. As he told *Melody Maker*: "King Crimson used various classical ideas to take the vocabulary from one brand of music—a certain European harmonic tradition—and tried to find a way of blending it with the energy of rock. But all that became so much pastiche. The movement, as a vital force, actually ended in December of 1973. It's a movement which went tragically off course."

Citing the music industry's vampiric audience/performer relationship, Fripp retired to the academic environs of the International Academy for Continuous Education at Sherbourne-Hastings in Gloucester, England, where he lived a reclusive existence for the next year. Another two years passed before Fripp, who had become a disciple of the philosopher-mystic G.I.Gurdjieff, summoned up some inner resource to return to the marketplace. He reformed King Crimson at the end of 1981 with

Bruford on drums, Tony Levin on stick and bass, and Adrian Belew on guitar.

How did you come to take up guitar?
I'm not entirely sure why. I was tone deaf and had no sense of rhythm. But nevertheless, I wanted a guitar. There was no one player who inspired me to pick up the guitar. No, it didn't quite work like that. I wanted to play but I can't tell you the exact motivation. Now looking back on it, there was a certain rightness about it that I'm still discovering. And the intriguing thing for me is why someone so profoundly unmusical would end up becoming a professional musician. There has always been a significance in that for me.

When did you acquire your first instrument?
On December 24, 1957, my parents bought me a very cheap guitar. And almost immediately I realized that this was my life. But side-by-side with this, I knew that I was eventually going to take over my father's real estate firm. So there was this incompatibility, this contradiction in aims. I knew that the guitar was my life, but at the same time I knew that I was being primed to sell houses for a living. Then, when I was 17, I went to stay with my sister on holiday in Jersey and I took my guitar. I had lots of opportunities to practice there, which I found quite wonderful. It was there that I established a deeper relationship with the instrument. And upon returning home to England, I announced to my mother, "I am going to become a professional guitar player." My mother didn't try to dissuade me. She simply burst into tears. I took her reaction to heart and my decision was delayed until I was 20.

Who were your early guitar influences?
When I was 11 I loved American rock'n'roll. English rock'n'roll was pretty feeble, so I listened to people like Elvis and Chuck Berry. Bill Haley didn't convince me. And James Burton didn't speak to me in the same way he spoke to other guitarists in Bournemouth. I was more taken with Scotty Moore at the time. Instinctively, you knew who the real masters were.

What was your training ground?
I earned money for college playing weddings and bar mitzvahs at The Majestic Hotel in Bournemouth. Actually, I replaced Andy Summers, who went off to London to join Zoot Money's Big Roll Band. But that gig, as boring as it was, did provide me with an opportunity to hone my craft and experience the discipline of sight-reading. But there was so much exciting music in the air and I was just not a part of it on this gig. I remember driving over to the hotel one night and hearing *Sgt. Pepper's* on the radio. I didn't know who it was at first and it terrified me. At about the same time I was listening to [Jimi] Hendrix, [Eric] Clapton with John Mayall's Bluesbreakers, the Bartók string quartets, Stravinsky's *The Rite of Spring*, Dvořák's *New World Symphony*—they all spoke to me in the same way. It was all music, perhaps different dialects but it was all the same language to me. And at that point, it was a call which I could not resist. From that point to this very day, my interest is in how to take the energy and spirit of rock music and extend it to the music drawing on my background as part of the European tonal harmonic tradition. In other words, what would Hendrix sound like playing Bartók?

And that led to forming King Crimson?
More or less. We began rehearsing in the basement of a cafe in the Fulham Palace Road and our first gig was at the London Speakeasy on April 9, 1969. But a big breakthrough for us came when we played at a free Rolling Stones concert on July 5 [1969] at Hyde Park. There were half a million people there and we made quite an impression.

You recorded seven albums before folding King Crimson in '74 and going into a kind of self-imposed exile.
I left the industry thinking that it was not possible for me to do anything more in "this rancid business." I was gone for three years and I had no wish or intention to return to the world of the professional musician at all. In a sentence, I found it difficult to be a human being and a musician at the same time. When I had first turned professional at age 21, I thought, "This is the best liberal education I could ever receive." And I was right. But it ceased to be the appropriate education for me and I needed to go somewhere else for my education at that point. So I went to Gloucester.

And you've now returned with a new edition of King Crimson.
Yes, I upped the ante and reformed the band because I saw that there was useful work to do which required a powerful instrument. And that instrument was King Crimson. Any particular thought form that is charged with energy takes on a life of its own—an existence side-by-side with the people or person who triggered it. In that sense, King Crimson has a life of its own.

How is this edition of King Crimson different from past manifestations?
This is the first band that I've ever been a member of where I said, "I wish to define the parameters of the band." But that's not dictatorial in any sense. That's where one accepts the role of leader in order to enable the process to take place. It doesn't imply in any way that I'm special or more important or better than anyone else. And the fact that we share the money and credits equally certainly helps to make this idea real. But anyone in this band can lead. The role is there for anyone. It's like saying because I defined the area of the sports field, we can play any sport we want within that. If you're pouring wine from a bottle, you need a cup to hold it. But to go some way towards creating a cup doesn't govern what you're going to drink. So certainly I initiated this band. It just means that I put myself in a role in order to enable this process to take place.

Talk about your guitaristic role in the new band.
Well, I've already done the great-soloist thing to death. More importantly, I've taken a great interest in time and rhythm in general over the last several years. I find playing rhythm rather than lead much more rewarding. I enjoy stepping back into the group structure and blending into the communal dynamic.

You seem to rely heavily on the Roland GR–303 guitar synth in this band.
Yes, it's remarkably versatile. I'm using it on everything I do. It's really the first synthesizer which guitarists can use effectively. I feel that it's the single most important development in the electric guitar since the [Gibson] Les Paul.

What is the challenge now presented to you in keeping this band together?
The challenge is this: How can four individuals accept the personal discipline of being a community? It's very, very difficult. How do four established musicians subjugate personal egos and ambitions to work together? Phenomenally difficult.

You have adopted a uniquely non-Western attitude toward playing and toward music education, which I'm sure you apply in your current teachings at the American Society for Continuous Education. Can you explain what it is you try to impress upon students there?
I try to introduce them to the concept of establishing a relationship with the music. And to do that requires changing one's personal state, becoming an instrument for the music to play and going to the place where the music lives. In Eastern and most Asian cultures, the musician spends a lot of

time not learning to play the instrument but finding a relationship with himself so that if one changes state, one is in a position where music can occur. If you have an instrument beneath your hands, then you can play. The Western approach is to develop the functional mode in the form of organization so that one has endless chops, but one is not in a position to actually respond to the *impulse* of music. And it's not really possible to change a state unless you relax. So my classes involve yoga and other approaches to being a musician which are not specifically musical, but which in my judgment will help very considerably. Again, I'm not teaching music. I'm trying to help aspiring guitarists find a relationship with music for themselves by changing their personal states to put themselves in a place where the music occurs. And then if that becomes a discipline for them, the change of state can be made eventually almost at will. I mean, it's not quite that easy and it takes years. But it becomes easier over time.

You have mentioned techniques that you worked on to harness this quality.
Right. Well, you know what it's like when you've just done an amazingly good gig, when the music seemed to be playing itself. Most musicians have had that experience, where everybody in the band was "on" and they all felt it. They say, "Yeah, it was magic!" Well, I've always been fascinated by the questions of how you get to that point for yourself. That magic, that feeling comes by of its own. But how do you learn to harness it? That certain feeling happened to me in a big way quite often with the first King Crimson. Amazing things would happen—I mean, telepathy, qualities of energy, things that I had never experienced before with music. My own sense of it was that music reached over and played this group of four uptight young men who didn't really know what they were doing. And then Pete Sinfield, the lyricist of King Crimson, called it "The Good Fairy." He said, "We have a Good Fairy. We can't do anything wrong."

But then The Good Fairy went away. Obviously, we had done something wrong. So it was a question of how does one put oneself in a position where, as Pete would say, The Good Fairy can do you favors. And that questioning began a long and painful process. In retreat in 1974 outside the music industry I began to work seriously with the techniques of approaching it. And I'm still learning the techniques.

You've also talked about the four levels of working. What are they?
The first level is "Automatic," which is just playing your licks. The second is "Sensitive," where you're aware of what's going on—you're in contact with what you're feeling and what you're thinking and the sensation your body has while in the process of making music. You are, at that point, experiencing the life of your body from the inside of your body. You have a living relationship with your two hands from the inside, which you are placing on your instrument. The third level is "Conscious," where it's beginning to go beyond the picture. It's where you are aware of music as a living force quite apart from you as a musician, where you go beyond yourself. And the fourth level is "Creative," where one can say the music plays the musician—or more accurately, you can't tell whether the music is playing the musician or the musician is playing the music. And that one, in my own experience, I'm aware of when it's going on but I have no idea *how* it's going on. So the question is, how can we organize our energy to put ourselves in that place where music can play us? It's largely a matter of technique. Exercises for disciplining the mind.

How does this relate to the title of your recent King Crimson album, Discipline *[Warner Bros., 1981]?*
The musician is like a house, and the music is like a friend that's always out there knocking on the door, wanting nothing more than to come in. But you've got to get your house in order for music to come in. That's where discipline comes in.

BRIAN ENO

MY INTERVIEW WITH BRIAN ENO was somewhat like the movie *My Dinner with Andre.* He talked non-stop for two hours. I listened—enthralled. When it was finished, I was completely overwhelmed by the information he had generously and quite spontaneously dished out about things musical and extra-musical. I came away from that intellectual encounter with far more than any *Down Beat* article could handle. And so the cover story that appeared in the June '83 issue only scratched the surface of what Eno was putting down that afternoon.

Perhaps the most important tidbit of information that I came away with from that eye-opening interview with Eno was regarding the Nimslo 3-D camera. Eno was so impressed by this Britain-manufactured gadget that he invested in the company (which a few years later went belly-up). He flashed me just a few sample pictures—brilliant 3-D images of himself and some friends cavorting as artists tend to do. I was instantly sold on this otherworldly process. I went out the next day and bought one at Olden Cameras in the heart of the camera district near Herald Square. They had boxes of 'em stacked up, marked down from $350 to $50. Apparently, no one was interested in purchasing these novelty items, since you had to send away to get the film developed at a cost of about $1.50 per print. But the final amazing results more than justified the extra cost, I thought. In subsequent years, I have had endless hours of fun while amazing my friends with these incredible 3-D pictures. And I have none other than Brian Eno to thank for it.

Since the time of this interview, Eno has produced records by a number of artists, including Devo, Ultravox, David Bowie, Talking Heads, John Cale, Laurie Anderson, and U2. He continues to make evocative music for his Opal label.

MARCH 18, 1983

First, seven random facts about the enigmatic Eno:

1. He does not read music and for years has insisted that he is not a musician at all, preferring to think of himself as a systems manipulator.

2. He doesn't have a band, never tours, and his albums on the independently distributed Editions EG label sell in modest figures (positively anemic by major label standards).

3. His most recent album, *Ambient 4: On Land* (Editions EG, 1982) was inspired by such a diverse range of elements as Frederico Fellini's *Amarcord,* Teo Macero's sparse production on Miles Davis' "He Loved Him Madly" from *Get up with It* (Columbia, 1974), and the sound of croaking frogs on Lantern Marsh, a place only a few miles from where he was born 35 years ago in Woodbridge, England.

4. He is leery of grants and collaborations, after being bombarded by bogus requests from artists and musicians all over the world.

5. His current musical projects include soundtracks for a film about the opium trade in Burma, a documentary about the NASA Apollo moon missions, and an Australian film about a valley in the Himalayas that has more species of flowers per acre than any other place on the planet.

6. His current video project is an upcoming exhibit in Japan, sponsored by Sony, which involves 35 TV decks and monitors.

7. His full name is Brian Peter George St. John le Baptiste de la Salle Eno (really).

By the time Beatlemania swept England, carrying off a whole generation of impressionable adolescents in its tide, Brian Eno was safely tucked away in the cerebral solitude of the Ipswich Art School. It was there, at the age of 16, that he came under the spell of something far more intoxicating to him than John, Paul, George, and Ringo. At Ipswich, Eno discovered the tape recorder. It was perhaps the single most important find of his young life, launching an ongoing journey of sound experimentation that continues to this day.

Eno was encouraged to use the school sound taping facilities by the Ipswich faculty, a group of artistic revolutionaries bent on upsetting the preconceived notions about art that more conventional teachers espouse. They, too, played no small part in shaping Eno's view of the world. He thrived in this environment of "We're not going to tell you what is possible or isn't," as he continued to entertain all kinds of possibilities for both sound and visuals. At the Winchester School of Art, where he earned his degree in fine arts between 1966 and 1969, he became president of the student union and spent union funds on having prestigious avant-garde musicians such as Cornelius Cardew, Christian Wolff, John Tilbury, and Morton Feldman come to lecture.

Influenced by Cardew's "School-Time Composition," by John Cage's book *Silence,* and by the notions of other systems artists ("Their emphasis is on the procedure rather than the end product"), Eno was brought to Reading University by Andy Mackay to lecture the students there. Some years later, when Mackay and Bryan Ferry were forming the art-rock group Roxy Music, Eno was invited to join, playing Mackay's VCS3 synthesizer and mixing their sound.

It was the glitter and glam era in England. Marc Bolan and T. Rex were big. David Bowie was in his Ziggy Stardust phase. Elton John had just released *Honky Chateau* to critical acclaim and Roxy

Music was opening for groups like Alice Cooper and Gary Glitter. With his own flair for visuals, Eno jumped into the movement with enthusiasm, sporting pancake makeup, eye shadow, rouge, and lip gloss onstage. It was 1972 and Eno had become a full-fledged rock star.

But to balance these pop pretensions, he maintained a sort of Jekyll & Hyde outlet for his "serious stuff." As early as 1972 he began conducting sound experiments in his home studio with King Crimson guitarist Robert Fripp, resulting in two groundbreaking LPs—*No Pussyfooting* (Editions EG, 1973) and *Evening Star* (Editions EG, 1975). From the beginning, these collaborations explored a Zen-like flow of sound, combining Fripp's tonal clusters and unremitting sustains on guitar with Eno's seemingly infinite capacity for programming tape loops via synthesizer. This risk-taking approach was clearly at odds with Eno's standing as a pop star, and his management objected vigorously. Yet, the experiments continued.

With his celebrated split from Roxy Music in 1973, Eno began producing his own solo albums, beginning with *Here Come the Warm Jets* (Editions EG, 1973), followed by *Taking Tiger Mountain (By Strategy)* (Editions EG, 1974). These were both ambitious, clever, and dynamic pop projects, featuring Eno's vocals on all tracks. They are generally considered to be among the most adventurous and compelling statements '70s rock produced, though Eno now considers them a bit naive. His third solo album, *Another Green World* (Editions EG, 1975), marked a significant transition in his career. On this icy, evocative album (which featured few vocals), Eno The Pop Star and Eno The Artist were beginning to merge. He would make one more pop-oriented album, *Before and After Science* (Editions EG, 1977), before discarding his pop persona altogether. Some of his comments about the rock star syndrome have since been quite telling.

Over the years, Eno has been investigating sounds that encourage a dynamic relationship between people and their surroundings—music that responds to and enhances ambiance. Functioning as an alternative to the bland pop arrangements of Muzak, this ambient music is intended to induce calm and create a space in which to think. "The idea of making music that in some way related to a sense of place—landscape or environment—had occurred to me many times over the last 12 years," he writes in his notes to *On Land*. "My conscious exploration of this way of thinking about music probably began with *Another Green World* in 1975. Since then I have become interested in exaggerating and inventing rather than replicating spaces, and experimenting with various techniques of time distortion."

When not occupied with his own ambient music projects, Eno has found time to produce a number of albums—three by David Bowie, three by Talking Heads, a funk-rap tape collage collaboration with Head-man David Byrne called *My Life in the Bush of Ghosts* (Sire, 1981), an evocative project with trumpeter Jon Hassell, and albums by several new wave bands including Television, Devo, Ultravox.

You've made some anti-synthesizer statements over the years, yet you're often associated with them.
Yes. People are always trying to sell me complicated synthesizers or they write letters asking me what I think are the best synthesizers on the market—all this junk that people seem to think I know about. I haven't a bloody clue what the best synthesizer is to the others. I'm just not excited by them at all. I'm not thrilled by something that does exactly the same thing over and over. Why people are is beyond me. I mean, they're not excited by assembly lines. If that's the kind of thing you want, go to the Ford motor factory and watch the car shells come off the assembly line.

To me, synthesizers are a little bit like Formica. If you see it from a distance, it looks great—this big panel of blue or pink or whatever fits in well with your designer home. But when you get close to the surface of Formica and start looking at it, it's not interesting. Nothing's going on there. Contrast this with a natural material like wood, which looks good from a distance but also is still interesting at any level of microscopic inspection. It's atomic structure is even strangely interesting as opposed to Formica, which is regular and crystalline. Think of the forest, for instance. You look at it from the air and it's rich, complex, and diverse. You come in closer and look at one tree and it's still rich, complex, and diverse. You look at one leaf, it's rich and complicated. You look at one molecule, it's different from every other molecule. The thing permits you any level of scrutiny. And more and more, I want to make things that have that same quality—things that allow you to enter them as far as you could imagine going, yet don't suddenly reveal themselves to be composed of paper-thin synthetic materials.

So you aren't interested in the high technology hardware like the Fairlight or the Synclavier?
Not at the moment. I've been moving more in the direction of very low technology—found objects and other things that have some kind of interesting inherent sound to them—just anything lying around, really. I spend a lot of time around Canal Street [a long stretch of electronic shops and junk shops located in downtown Manhattan], hitting things and listening to what this little bolt might sound like or this metal pot or whatever. As for high technology, all of the work I've heard from those machines is so unbelievably awful to me. Boring things like yet another synthesizer version of Vivaldi's *Four Seasons*... Who needs it?

What synthesizer are you currently using?
One of my favorite instruments is the Yamaha CS–80, one of the first polyphonic synthesizers ever made. It's so simple—doesn't do anything like sequencing or hasn't got any digital apparatus. It was actually a development from the organ so it's very much like an electric organ with a sort of synthesizer panel, capable of really lovely sounds. It's perfect for me. I'd rather have six beautiful sounds from a synthesizer than a possible infinity of mediocre sounds.

You mentioned that you've gotten very suspicious of records lately. Can you elaborate?
I don't like the form very much, anymore. I've become more and more interested in music that has a location of some kind, like gospel music—you go somewhere and you become part of something in order to experience the music. You enter a whole different social and acoustic setting. There's a whole context that goes with the music. Just sitting in your living room and sticking on some record is a whole other thing.

I think one of the things we have to do now is realize that the products of recording studios are another form of art. That's not music. There's been a break between the traditional idea of music—which still continues in many forms—and what we do now on records. That's something different. It's just like... At the birth of photography in the middle of the 19th century, what people started off doing was to try to make cheap portraits. It was a way of replacing a portrait painter by getting similar results, but much more cheaply. And, in fact, to this end they used canvas-textured paper and they would tint the things and arrange everything to make it look as much like a portrait as they could. Similarly with film... The first films were just recordings of theater pieces. So film was really nothing more than the traveling version of a play. And the same thing happened when records were invented. They were invented to give everyone a chance to be at a Caruso performance, or something like that. Or to sell Caruso in a wider way than he had ever been sold before. Well, with each of those forms, a point was reached where it became realized that this medium had its own strengths and limitations, and therefore could become a different form through its own rules.

I think that's true of records as well. They've got nothing to do now with performances. It's now possible to make records that have music that was never performed or never could be performed and, in fact, doesn't exist outside of that record. And if that's the area you work in, then I think you really have to consider that as part of your working philosophy. So for quite a while now I've been thinking that if I make records, I want to think not in terms of evoking a memory of a performance, which never existed in fact, but to think in terms of making a piece of sound which is going to be heard in a type of location, usually someone's house. So I think, "This is going to be playing in a house, not on a stage, not on the radio."

So with your recent works, particularly the Ambient *series, you are more or less providing a sonic environment for listeners to project into.*
Yes, it's a different approach. It's an understanding that the record is only one part of the whole process, that actually what we're dealing with is the recording studio, this black thing in the middle called a record, and someone's hi-fi system. Of course, the assumptions you can make about how someone sits down and listens are a bit limited. In my case, I assume they're sitting very comfortably and not expecting to dance. The way most producers work is like this. They say, "Here's the listener sitting here, so we'll have a guitar here, bass there, drums over there, horns there, vocals over here..." And so on. They're seeing it in two-dimensional terms, like a cinema screen. But I've been trying to get rid of the screen altogether. Forget about having this nice logical arrangement of things. I've become more interested in transferring a visual sense to music. What I want to do is create a field of sound that the listener is plopped inside of and within which he isn't given any particular sense of values about things. It's much more like being in a real environment, where your choices are what determine the priority at a given time.

The first time I listened to Discreet Music *[Editions EG, 1975], I was at work. The day had ended. All the people had gone home and the place was completely empty. During the day the atmosphere was generally hectic, with phones ringing and people rushing about, arguing, typing, talking. But this night it was so quiet I could even hear the fluorescent lights humming. I was sitting comfortably in a reclining chair and I put on your record, not having any idea about what kind of music it was. It not only put me into a state of total relaxation, but it also sparked the most vivid memories of a special friend I hadn't seen in years—places we had been together, the smell of the air, the colors of the sunset.*
You know, a lot of people have said the same thing that you're saying now about *On Land* as well, which was definitely the impetus for that record, for me. When I was working in the studio, I always found that a piece would begin to come to life at the point where it would put me in that kind of mood, where I suddenly was in some way connected with another place or another time. And as the piece developed, I'd get a stronger and stronger sense of the geography of that place and the time of day, the temperature, whether it was a windy or wet place or whatever. I was developing the pieces almost entirely in terms of a set of feelings that one normally wouldn't consider to be musical, not in terms of "Is this a nice tune? Is this a catchy rhythm?" Instead, I was always trying to develop this sense of the *place* of the music. It was and still is very hard to articulate, because it's not part of the normal musical vocabulary.

I'm working on a piece now about an evening that I remember from a very long time ago in which nothing in particular happened, actually. For some reason this evening just stuck in my mind. I went for a walk—I was about 14—and where I lived, in Woodbridge, there's a dike that dams up the river. And there's a narrow path on top of it that goes for miles, just wide enough for one person to walk along. One night I went for a walk on it, and there was a low fog hanging over the marshes, just about at the level of this pathway, so the effect was exactly like walking on top of this cloud. But above, the air was absolutely clear. And it was one of those deep blue nights with lots of stars. So I started working on a piece of music, and something about it kept taking me back to that night. I don't think I had ever remembered it before. It was as though the piece suddenly reminded me of that place. And the problem all the time was I had to get those stars in there somewhere. I kept thinking, "How do you make in music the feeling of a lot of stars?" You know, there's no sense in just having some clichéd twinkling sounds or whatever.

Cue the star machine.

Right, so that was a problem. I worked on that for four or five days, experimenting with different things, and I had no idea where to start. There's no sort of tradition for making star sounds in music. Anyway, I came up with something that I like quite a lot. To me, it certainly gives that feeling of a huge space with lots of remote bodies that sort of cluster in apparently meaningful ways with one another. So that's the kind of thing that I think about mostly when I'm recording now. They don't seem to be musical considerations at all. They're more like descriptive thoughts. I think of it as figurative music in a certain way, where I'm actually trying to paint a picture of something. Well, people have said that for years. But I mean that in a fairly accurate way—an aural picture of some type.

Could you explain how you developed your so-called hologram theory of music?

I think two things started it. There was a book by Samuel Beckett that came out two years ago called *Company.* It's about a 90-page book with very big type, so in ordinary novel-size type it would probably be about 30 pages long, or less. And for me, it's a great book. It's almost the same few phrases being permutated, the same things being said over and over again in slightly different ways. Almost all the material that appears in the book is there within the first two pages. Once you've seen the first two pages, you've effectively read the entire book. But he keeps putting them together in different ways. And one of the things that struck me about the book was you could take half a sentence from it, and first of all know instantly that it was Beckett—just something about the way the words were strung together. Also, from that half-sentence you would have a foggy impression of the feeling of the whole book. And that, in turn, reminded me of two things.

When I was in school—I went to Catholic school—we were told that the host, the thing you get at Holy Communion, could be broken into any number of minute parts and that each part was still the complete body of Jesus Christ, even if it was only a tiny fragment. This always puzzled me. I thought about that a lot as a fine theological point. And then when I was about 18, I went to a lecture by Dennis Gabor, who invented the hologram. He said that one of the things that's interesting about the hologram is that if you shatter it and you take a fragment from the whole, you will still see the complete image from that piece, only it will be a much less distinct and fuzzier version. It's not like a photograph, you see, where if you tear off one corner, all you see is that corner. The whole of the image is encoded over the whole of the surface, so the tiniest part will still be the whole of that image. And I thought this was such a fantastically grand idea, and for the first time it gave me some understanding of the Catholic idea of the host—there was some scientific parallel to it.

So those two ideas stuck in my mind for a long time. And when I started looking at this series of Cézanne paintings, I got the same feeling. You could take a square inch of one of those Cézanne paintings and somehow there was the same intensity and feeling and style within that one piece as there was within the whole picture. It's as if you saw the whole painting in that one piece because every brush stroke was charged just like the whole painting was charged—similarly with the Beckett book.

So I thought, "This is really how I want to work from now on. I don't want to just fill in spaces anymore." You know, a lot of the hard-edged paintings from the mid-1960s had to do with geometry and clarity of shape and so on. And the thing that made it disappointing as a movement for me was the fact that a lot of what those guys were doing was purely mechanical, just filling in colors, almost like following a blueprint or a paint-by-numbers scheme. It seemed to me they were cheating themselves, because I think every stage of the procedure should be as vital as every other stage. There shouldn't be one stage where you just fill in, where it's too predetermined. At that point, it's just hack work. You can farm it out to assistants, which is what a lot of them did. In fact, I was an assistant to a painter for a while. I painted his pictures for him, and it was a similar-type thing, where he just had color areas sketched out that had to be filled in. It's done, but that's not what I want to do. I want to be alive through every stage of doing any project.

Besides the obvious influence of painters on your work, you've also mentioned such names as Philip Glass, Steve Reich, Terry Riley....
And Lamonte Young. He was sort of the conceptual father of that whole minimalist school, I suppose. At least in music. It's interesting, though, because that movement actually happened in painting before it did in music—this idea of a kind of continuum. Jackson Pollock and Barnett Newman are two good examples. But in music, Lamonte Young began experimenting with very long drones and continuous musical environments in the early-1960s. He had a piece called "Dream House," which was a series of generators that repeated single notes. These were very carefully built generators so they didn't wave at all. The notes were as constant as possible for—months. This contraption was actually running for months and months. It was an idea that I'm very sympathetic to now. It was a piece of music that you walked into and you stayed for a while and you left it again. That was what *Music for Airports* [Editions EG, 1978] was meant to be.

That idea of a continuum has been a running theme in your music since your first collaboration with Robert Fripp back in 1972 on No Pussyfooting. *Using the analogy of painting, how would you say your own brush stroke has changed from that early work to your most recent ambient album,* On Land?
Well, I think the palette is much broader now. There's a wider choice of colors, if you will. *No Pussyfooting* is very much an album of musical types of sound—discernable guitar, electric instruments, mutable harmonies, chord clusters, and so on. What's happened, then—with *On Land*—a lot of that has been broken down. There are far more types of sounds that aren't musical in a traditional sense. They're not sounds that you connect with any particular instrument or with any particular object. As an aside to this, whenever I release an album it has to be copyrighted, so someone has to try to score this stuff. I saw a bit of the score for *On Land,* and the poor guy obviously had a real problem with it. You can't express it in notation. It doesn't work. So it rather came out as a kind of painting—a red spot here and a sort of blue stripe going across here and a roughly green area. So the difference is that at the time of *Pussyfooting,* I actually thought I was making music. Now with this new stuff, I feel that the connection has more to do with the experience of paintings or films or even non-cultural artifacts, like palaces. I'm quite inarticulate about it because I don't quite know what it is. There isn't any tradition for it.

With *Pussyfooting,* it's almost like being in some sort of tunnel. You don't have many choices about your direction within that. You sort of move forward as the piece streams along, and you can go a bit to the side as you're going. But with this landscape stuff, you are disoriented within it. As you listen to it more and more, you attach yourself to certain little clusters that happen that you may recognize. You can then start making the choice about which journey you take through that music. The problem is always calling it music. I wish there were another word for it.

Do you feel that musicians are too preoccupied with technique and results?
I think it's more a case of... Whenever you get into a spot, you can make yourself feel better by doing something clever. It's almost a sort of symptom of nervousness. I've seen musicians stuck for an idea, and what they'll do between takes is just diddle around, playing the blues or whatever, just to reassure themselves that, "Hey, I'm not useless. Look, I can do this!" But I believe that to have that to fall back on is an illusion. It's better to say, "I'm useless," and start from that position. I think the way technique gets in the way is by fooling you into thinking that you are doing something when you actually are not.

As you strip down your process from album to album, has it become more difficult for you to work in the studio with other musicians?

I think it's getting harder for me to work with musicians who don't understand recording studios. Most musicians have their own idea about what the ingredients of a piece of music are. And one of the things that most of them think is that it's got to have a few tricky licks in it—something skillful. So they sit down and get all their ingredients together and sort of stick them all into a pot, thinking a piece of music will come out of it. It's like the recipe book without the procedure, where you just get the list of ingredients but you don't bother to read about how to put them together or how to prepare them. You just bung them all into the pot and hope that you'll get lemon soufflé out of it in the end. Sure, you can work with the same set of ingredients all the time, but if you are going to keep yourself interested in it, then the procedure is where you have to direct your attention. So I don't like this ingredient way of working. It's like the formula disco style where it has to have this or that and it has to have the girls doing a refrain. You hear so much of this junk coming out all the time.

The difficult thing about working with skillful musicians is that sometimes I just can't explain to them the potential of something. Sometimes I know when I hear something that there are a series of operations that I can perform on it that will make it fabulous. This involves studio manipulation. And those kinds of manipulations—since they are in themselves ways of generating complexity out of sound—seem to work best on sounds that are initially quite simple. If the sound is musically complex to begin with, it's already a restrictive form to work with. So the problem with musicians is always telling them to have confidence in a simple and beautiful thing, to know that there's a whole world that can be extracted from a simple sound. And if they're not familiar with studios, they come in and give you some complex mess to work with, and then you have to spend two or three hours erasing all of that just to be left with this simple, beautiful thing. But to tell a musician who is confident of his abilities and knows he can do lots of better things... Sometimes people feel a bit insulted. They think you don't trust their intelligence. I think you can do the simplest thing well or badly. It's not that because it's simple, any idiot can do it. There's sensitivity in the way you can strike just one note. Funk bass players know this very well.

How does that relate to your work with Talking Heads?

Well, I did this a lot with Talking Heads, extracting from simple things. For instance, I would take just the snare drum and use it to trigger one of my synthesizers, and then I'd put that on a complicated delay. This allowed me to make cross-rhythms by using only that snare, just taking something that was there and shifting it in time, really, and putting it back into the mix again. And you weren't muddying the picture with these cross-rhythms, because as long as that snare drum stayed in time, this other fabricated rhythm stayed in relative time. It couldn't shift. So a lot of the cross-rhythms you hear on Talking Heads records are actually from the original instruments but are being delayed or treated in various ways. Sometimes we would run the tape backwards and delay the sound backwards so you hear the echo before the beat—that kind of thing.

Did working with Edikanfo in Ghana have any effect on your ideas about working with Talking Heads?

Yes, but after the event. Watching those guys playing and seeing the relationship they had with rhythm was so totally disheartening for me. After seeing Edikanfo, I thought, "There just isn't a chance of ever even approaching this." They were good musicians, but not great musicians. But just seeing how they worked with rhythm made me want to give up right away. All the interactions between players and all the kind of funny things going on with the rhythm—there's a lot of humor in it. And then when I started listening to the stuff that we did with Talking Heads, it was just so wooden by comparison. I couldn't get very excited by it anymore. I could still get excited about it in other terms, but not in rhythmic terms anymore. It seemed to be really naive.

It's like the same way I feel about the African sense of melody. Take King Sunny Ade, whom everyone is making a real big thing about lately. He has a great band, I must say, but I find him melodically quite uninteresting. I find his slide player [actually pedal steel], whom everyone is impressed by, quite boring. I've heard nine-year-old slide players who play better than that. It's like, if I want to hear great slide guitar, there are 150 bluegrass players in Nashville who can really play that thing and play it with a kind of feeling for the instrument that the guy in Sunny Ade's band is never gonna have. Just like they play their drums with a feeling that I'm never gonna have, that I'm only beginning to understand. My friend Robert Wyatt once said, "You commit yourself to what you're left with." It's very true. After all the trial and error, you realize that you end up with one or two things you think you can do. So I'm not terribly thrilled by all the trans-cultural things going on at the moment. They seem to be well-informed but...

Like mixing wood grain and Formica.
Yeah, it's a bit like that. It seems that too often you get the worst of both worlds rather than the best.

© 1984 EBET ROBERTS

LES PAUL

THERE ARE STILL PEOPLE WHO THINK that Les Paul is a guitar. After all, his name has been on the headstock of one of the most popular guitars in the world since 1952, when the inventor-guitarist struck a deal with the Gibson company. But the mercurial man behind the icon is indeed a living, breathing musician with a rich, colorful history in the music business. At age 83, Les continues to play to a packed house every Monday night at the Iridium nightclub in New York City, cracking corny jokes and flaunting the same inimitable fretboard flash that has been his calling card for more than half a century.

I had the pleasure of working with Les in the studio in 1996 on one track from Pat Martino's Blue Note debut, *All Sides Now.* We had planned to do an up-tempo version of Duke Ellington's "Caravan," a tune that Les played every Monday night with his trio at Iridium. We sent the sheet music to Pat in Philadelphia along with a recording of the tune, just so he could brush up on the piece. The day of the recording at Sound on Sound Studios in Manhattan, Pat was quite prepared for "Caravan." But after plugging in their guitars, Les turns to Pat and says with a mischievous smile on his face, "You know this one?" And he launches into the slow romantic ballad "I'm Confessin' (That I Love You)." Pat, who as a young developing guitarist idolized Les, had never played the song before but had a vague memory of it. And before we knew what was happening, tape was rolling. They hit on some spontaneous magic in the studio that day.

The following phone interview with Les was for a tribute to his guitar making colleague Leo Fender, who died in 1993. It was published in Japan's *Guitar* magazine.

MAY 8, 1993

Lester William Polfus (aka Les Paul, aka "The Wizard of Waukesha") is generally regarded as the god-father of the electric solid body guitar and the inventor of multi-track recording. A Django Reinhardt influenced improviser, Paul's natural eclecticism extended beyond jazz to pop, country, and blues. Born June 9, 1916, in Waukesha, Wisconsin, Lester began playing guitar and harmonica while a teenager in Chicago under the pseudonym Rhubarb Red. In 1936 he formed his first trio with Jim Atkins (Chet's brother) and Ernie Newton. After touring as featured soloist with Fred Waring's Pennsylvanians from 1937 to 1941, he settled in California and formed his own trio in 1944 while also making guest appearances on records by Red Callendar, Bing Crosby, and alongside Nat King Cole at a few Jazz at the Philharmonic recordings (under the name Paul Leslie). In 1948 he began making popular recordings for Capitol Records with singer Mary Ford. They were married in 1949 and their popularity peaked in the early-1950s with multi-track recordings of hit tunes like "How High the Moon," "Lover," "Vaya Con Dios," and "The World Is Waiting for the Sunrise." They hosted their own television show, "Les Paul and Mary Ford at Home," for seven years in the '50s.

In 1948, Paul's right arm was severely crushed in an auto accident. "They were just about to amputate," he recalls, "when one of the doctors recognized me and said, 'You can't amputate that man's arm. That's Les Paul, the guitar player.' They were able to save the arm, but they set it in a permanent position so I could continue to play the guitar."

After Paul and Ford were divorced in 1964, he veered away from music to concentrate on inventing. Following a coronary bypass operation in 1979, Les took a five-year sabbatical from performing before he began his steady Monday night gig at Fat Tuesdays, a Manhattan nightclub. Even though he suffered a broken eardrum and contracted arthritis in his left hand (limiting him to the use of only his index and middle fingers), Paul is still in a league all his own. "I've had to make a new way of playing, but in some ways it's proved to be advantageous. It stretches your head out, makes you think more."

Les was named to the Grammy Hall of Fame in 1977 and to the Rock and Roll Hall of Fame in 1988. The Smithsonian Institution also dedicated a wing of their American Music Exhibit to Les Paul and his many inventions, which include phase shifting, overdubbing, reverb, delay, and sound-on-sound recording.

Can you reminisce about Leo Fender?
I sure knew him well.

How did you meet him?
I met him in my own backyard. I had a recording studio that I built there in 1942 in Hollywood. And within a few months, a lot of people started coming in. One day a fellow named Joaquin Murphy, a very fine steel guitar player, brought over a fellow named Leo Fender and another guy named Paul Bigsby [who would later have a patent on a vibrato bar named after him]. So between Bigsby and Fender, they were more or less camping in my backyard. I had just finished building a guitar at the time. They saw that. And they saw me playing the Log [his prototype solid body electric guitar which he started working on in 1939] and that was the one that intrigued them the most.

I had a vibrola contraption on it, which is the device that Bigsby later got into. So that initial meeting obviously made some kind of impression on the both of them.

Now Leo Fender, he saw that the solid body guitar had a lot of things going for it. So he starts building 'em and fooling around with 'em himself. He asked me, "What are you gonna do with yours?" And I said, "Well, if it's the last thing I do I'm gonna chuck this Log down Gibson's throat. But when I took it to Gibson around 1945 or 1946, they politely ushered me out the door. They called it a broomstick with a pickup on it. It was maybe the late-1940s that Leo came over to my house with his first Fender. All it said on there on the headstock was "Fender," and he gave it to me. I still have it here. It's not a Telecaster, it's not a Broadcaster, it's not a Stratocaster. But it's a prototype with no number on it or no nothing. It's Leo's first guitar and it's still in mint condition. The only time it was played was when I picked it up one time and played it and told him what I would change on it.

In the meantime, Leo says to me, "I'm gonna start a business. Are you interested?" But I wasn't interested in going in with Leo Fender. I was more interested in hitting up the world's largest guitar maker, Gibson. So Leo went into business for himself [forming the Fender Electric Instrument Company in 1948] and he launched his first Broadcaster around 1950. Well, after that came out I immediately got a call from Gibson. The president of the company issued an order. He said, "You know that character who came in here, that weirdo who had the broomstick with the pickups on it? Find that guy and sign 'em up." I had been hounding them for five years or more with my Log and they kept turning me down. And now suddenly they were desperate to find me. This is 1950–1951, when Mary and I are just starting to make some noise. So the Gibson people came to me and got me to sign with them to make the first Les Paul guitar. And it was all because of Leo Fender. So Leo did me a favor. I couldn't move Gibson with an atomic bomb. It took Leo Fender to wake Gibson up.

How did Leo's philosophy about building guitars differ from yours?
The most interesting thing about Leo Fender—which is to me very intriguing—he had a very definite, simple way of looking at things. His philosophy was, "Why should I decide what the player wants. Let the player decide what he wants." So he would conduct surveys among players to find out what they wanted in a guitar. I remember he called me up one time and said, "Can you find eight good players that have good ears and know what it's all about." So between two of us—I picked from the jazz world and Joaquin Murphy picked from the country & western world—we came up with ten guitar players and they were to be very critical about his instruments. So Leo Fender made his decision as to how to make the guitar and how to make the amplifier by surveying all these great guitar players. We literally did his homework for him and he came up with his first guitar.

Was there any resistance on Gibson's part to naming their first solid body electric guitar a Les Paul?
Not really. When they signed me up the president said, "By the way, there's something I forgot to mention. In the contract it does not state what we're going to call that guitar." We had the agreement with the royalties and everything else but the thing that we didn't have worked out was what to call it. The fact was, they didn't want to call it a Gibson because it might turn out to be only a flash in the pan. So I says, "Why don't you call it a Les Paul guitar?" And he says, "Would you put that in writing?" And I made the deal for the first Les Paul guitar to come out in 1952. Again, thanks to Leo. He was the man who made me. If it wasn't for him coming around and sitting in my backyard, none of this would've happened. He was a sweetheart of a guy, I respected him as a businessman and as a thorough-thinking guy. He wasn't a guitar player, he was a businessman. He thought simply and efficiently. He didn't make 400 guitars like Gibson did, he only made four. And the parts are interchangeable—bolt-on necks—as simple as you can get it. He avoided getting complicated. If it didn't have to be there, he didn't put it there. The whole thing was geared to mass production.

Sort of like Henry Ford.
Exactly. So I had a great, great respect for the man, and as a person I loved him very dearly. I probably mentioned his name more times to Gibson than anybody I know of. I could see Gibson making 40 different banjos, 40 different mandolins, and 2,000 guitars. And this man was very, very methodical, very simple about the way he approached his four instruments. And while I went my way with the guitar and he went another way with the guitar, it didn't make any difference. We had different opinions on building a guitar. Mine was not so much finding out what the ten top guitar players wanted, it was what I wanted. Where Leo wasn't inclined to make a decision like that so he let others make it for him. And he did it extremely well.

When you first met him in your backyard, was he already making guitars?
I don't know what he was doing, because it came about gradually. I can remember Mary hanging some clothes on the line in the backyard and Fender sitting there. I was recording W. C. Fields at the time, I think. Then he and I would get into all kinds of discussions about things. No, I don't think he was building a guitar at that time. He may have been screwing around with them but I don't think he was making the Fender guitar.

He was doing radio repair, wasn't he?
That's right. He was just on the fringe area. He became a guitar man later on.

When did you first amplify a guitar?
Well, when I was 12 I was working in Chicago entertaining customers at a local hamburger stand. And some of these people would complain that they couldn't hear me. So I got the idea to jab a record player needle into my acoustic guitar, slide a telephone mouthpiece under the strings and wire it up to my parents' radio, which doubled as an amplifier. That was around 1928. A few years later I was playing electric guitar at the 1932 Chicago World's Fair and the speakers were separate from the amplifier. Well, finally one day it dawned on me. I don't know whether it was an original idea or not but I thought, "For God's sakes why don't I just go over to Bell & Howell and go get one of their projectors." It's got a handle, it's got a case. You pick it up and there you are, you got a speaker in there and an amplifier all together. It's all ready to go. So I just plugged my guitar into the projector and I'm on my way. And that was my first real guitar amplifier. It had no name on it, it was just a plain goddamn amplifier. I took it around Chicago and the only ones who could understand what I was onto was a company called Lyon & Healey. They picked up on the electric guitar, the pickup and the amplifier and started to make 'em there. And from that, Gibson saw it and noted that this thing was making some noise. So they got into it as well. That had to be 1934–1935.

And was this around the time that you developed the Log?
That came later, around 1939. By the way, that Log was made on 14th Street in New York City before I ever went to California. I just took a four-by-four piece of lumber and put some wings on it, just for cosmetic purposes. It had two pickups and an Epiphone neck attached to it. The Epiphone people let me use their place on Sundays because no one was working. The watchman was there and he let me in and out. And that's how I built it. But when I built that Log, Epiphone thought I was nuts, too. A lot of people thought I was crazy but I had played around with this idea back in 1930 when I took a railroad track and compared it with a piece of wood. And the railroad track sustained much longer than the piece of wood. And I said, "Well, I can't see Gene Autry with a piece of railroad track on top of a horse." But seriously, I knew that it had to be a piece of wood and not metal because of the expansion/contraction factor of metal.

And you finally sold Gibson on the idea?
Yes, but not until 1951.

And you've had a long lasting relationship with Gibson ever since.
Well, not the entire time. My contract was up with Gibson in 1963 and they wanted me to re-sign, but Mary and I were in the throes of a divorce. So I said, "I'm not gonna re-sign with Gibson because it'll show up in our divorce settlement. So I won't sign with Gibson until the divorce thing is settled." In the meantime, Leo came to me and asked me to join Fender. But I told him, "I can't do anything until the divorce is final." I says, "I'll let you know." So I called Gibson and said, "I wanna talk to you first before I make any decision about going with Fender. I just feel uncomfortable about having Les Paul's name on a Fender guitar." And Maurice Berlin, the president of Chicago Musical Instruments, which owned Gibson, said to me, "Odd that you should call. I'm at the plant in Kalamazoo. We just sold off the building and all the electronics. We're phasing out the electric guitar." This was probably the biggest shock of my life, and so few people know today that the decision had actually been made by Gibson to stop making the electric guitar. So I tell him, "Can I fly back there and talk with you about it?" This was a Thursday. By Friday I was there. By Monday we were back in the business of making the guitar. I totally turned his head around.

How did you do it?
It took 18 hours of hard work and persuasion. He had a partner and I had a friend with me. Between the four of us we batted out an agreement to go back in and make this guitar, which Maurice Berlin did not have any faith in at all. He really thought that the guitar was just a passing fancy. Now, I don't know what Leo Fender was doing at the time. All I know is I was saving Gibson from going under. So in 1967 I signed my agreement to go back with Gibson. And I had one agreement with Gibson and that is that Maurice Berlin said, "I'm gonna turn this thing all over to you. It's up to you. If you feel you can make it fly, then I'll back you up 100 percent." And he did. And we took Gibson and probably climbed higher than any time in history for Gibson. It just went sky high. Leo had been our big competitor from the beginning, but by that time he had already sold his company to CBS [in 1965] and was sort of semi-retired. Of course, even when Leo sold out [for $13 million] and others took over, they followed suit. The die was cast. But when Leo had his thing going, he was great.

Did you stay in touch with him over the years?
Well, we began to lose touch after I moved back to the East Coast to do the Listerine shows ["Les Paul and Mary Ford at Home," a series of six-minute television shows sponsored by the Listerine company]. I would see 'em once a year whenever I could get West. But so much was happening in the East then. It was very, very potent. You had "The [Ed] Sullivan Show," Milton Berle, Perry Como, Jackie Gleason—all broadcasting out of New York. So there was so much power back here that this was *the* place to be. And consequently, you lost track of these people way out on the end of the earth on the West Coast, like Leo way out in Fullerton, California. It was 19 hours flying time at that time. It wasn't convenient. So I did lose track of a lot of friends. Leo went his way and I went my way. We'd meet occasionally at conventions. Like many friendships, you just kind of drift apart. Eventually he moved to Flagstaff, Arizona. I was in Mahwah, New Jersey. So you call once a month, then once a year. You don't feel like writing. It gets kind of weak.

But I ran into Leo about 12 years ago. We were in Atlanta playing down there for the NAMM show and M. H. Berlin, president of the board of CMI, which ran Gibson, is now in a wheelchair. We were down in the basement by the cafeteria and a guy walked by and I say, "Hey Leo! How ya doin'?" And Berlin says, "Who was that fellow you just said 'Hi' to?" I says, "You're kidding!

That's Leo Fender." He says, "Geez, can you introduce me to him?" Here they've been competitors since 1950 and here we are in 1980... They never met each other! And both, two of the nicest people that you'd ever want to meet in your life. Mr. Berlin used to stop me in the hallway and say, "Les, don't let anybody change your mind." The last time I saw him was at the Mayo Clinic. I took a run up to see him up there and he wasn't feeling too well and was about to retire. And he says, "I gotta tell you something...." And he told me the story about the broomstick with the pickups on it and "go find that guy." Then he said, "Les, in your wildest dreams, did you ever imagine that the Les Paul guitar would be this successful?" And I said, "Of course," and sincerely meant it. I always had faith in the idea of that Log.

Did you know much about G&L [the company that Leo Fender founded in 1980]?
No, people were feeding me information about what was going on. If there was any innovation or anything happening, whether it was in marketing, design, inventing, I was kept well informed. But I didn't follow Leo that closely. After he left Fender... I could see they were floundering around with their own problems. Each company had their things they had to go through. So nobody had all good times.

When was the last time you saw Leo?
I saw him in Anaheim at a NAMM show a few years back. We had a hotdog or something and we were yackin' around.

Sounds like you were good friends.
Oh, I had a very high regard for the man. Sorry to see that guy go.

JOHN ZORN

WHEN I FIRST MET DOWNTOWN renegade John Zorn in the early-1980s, he was playing duck calls in a bowl of water. It was part of the times. Kindred spirits like Zorn, Fred Frith, Elliott Sharp, David Moss, and a host of others were boldly exploring sound, reinvestigating their chosen instruments and pushing the envelope with all manner of unorthodox, extended techniques. And while some thought that Zorn was merely bullshitting with his duck calls and alto sax squeaks—a bespectacled charlatan who could neither play his instrument nor truly improvise—there was a mad genius at work behind the zany facade. Zorn began working on organized systems of improvisation as early as the mid-1970s and by the '80s had developed a number of sophisticated "game theories" that involved strict rules, role playing, prompters with flashcards. Zorn pursued this notion of pure improvisation within structure in such game pieces as "Archery," "Pool," "Lacrosse," "Hockey," and his monumental "Track & Field," which was performed with a group of a dozen musicians at the Public Theater. As his experiments began to be taken more seriously by the critical community, there followed more prestigious gigs at New Music America, the Brooklyn Academy of Music, and the Whitney Downtown, where he premiered his sprawling piece *Spillane* (Elektra/Nonesuch, 1987). In the mid-1980s, Zorn landed an important record deal with Elektra/Nonesuch and pursued his interest in radical jump-cut music with his band Naked City, which included guitarist Bill Frisell, drummer Joey Baron, and Fred Frith on bass. The band released six albums on Zorn's Avant label and one on Nonesuch. Zorn has also recorded tributes to bop pianist Sonny Clark and to Ornette Coleman, performed punk-thrash style by his band Spy vs. Spy.

Ironically, at the time of this interview (for a February '84 *Down Beat* profile and later in an expanded Q&A form for *Option*) Zorn had not yet traveled to Japan. Now he is something of a celebrity there, performing regularly as well as composing music for commercials on Japanese TV. He speaks fluent Japanese with barely a trace of an accent and spends a great deal of time there each year. More recently, Zorn has been interested in exploring his own ethnic roots, which led to developing the Radical Jewish Culture series for his own Tzadik label (which to date has a catalog of some 90-plus releases). One disc from his Great Jewish Music series is a compilation of Burt Bacharach music, in which several downtown colleagues twist, and otherwise reinterpret, familiar Bacharach tunes. His most recent band was Masada, a brilliant acoustic jazz quartet that combines Ornette-ish heads with klezmer scales. This past summer of 1998 Zorn engaged in a duet with drummer Milford Graves, reunited with Bill Laswell and drummer Mick Harris for a Painkiller tour and also opened his own Lower East Side nightclub, Tonic.

NOVEMBER 2, 1983

John Zorn has this problem. It seems that large segments of the world's population refuse to take him seriously. In England, Germany, and Holland, and at home in America he has suffered "unspeakable abuse" from critics and audiences. Perhaps the fact that a significant portion of Zorn's current repertoire involves playing various duck calls into buckets of water has something to do with this antagonism.

The general public may never understand John Zorn or appreciate his music. He may never have had a hit record or even a moderately successful one. And his playing may never inspire legions of aspiring musicians to take up the duck call as their main "horn." He knows this. But Zorn is no joke. What Zorn is, as a steadily growing community of improvising artists and avant-garde music supporters have come to realize, is a serious composer and ingenious musical architect. Through his experiments with systems and sound relationships, Zorn is paving bold new directions in improvising. The fact that he looks goofy and plays duck calls is merely a distraction, a ruse that most people can't get past.

Is there an assumption by some that you're not a legitimate musician?
Right, well, people look at me and I'm playing duck calls all laid out on a table.... And at this point in my development, a lot of the work that I'm doing is involving the duck calls and the sounds I'm getting from them in the water. And I don't play the saxophone as much as I used to in concert, maybe only 15 percent of the time. Everything else is with mouthpieces and pieces of the horns laid out on this table. And it's developed over eight years or something.

When did you first buy a duck call with the intention of playing it?
The first one ever was a Greenhead duck call that Mark Miller, the drummer, gave to me. And I used that on Eugene's recording, *The English Channel*, from 1979. And from then on it just grew and grew. It got to a point where I would go into a hunting store and they didn't even want me in the store any more. At first I tried the duck calls in the store with my mouthpieces to see if they fit. Then they wouldn't let me try them anymore so I'd just go in and buy their stock. Sometimes I play them on their own, sometimes I attach them to my horns. But then, the guys in the hunting stores, man, they didn't wanna know about me. So now I get them mail order. I call this nice woman on

the phone at the Olt Game Call Company in Pekin, Illinois. She knows who I am. She thinks I'm a big hunter. "Yeah, they're hunting a lot of birds up there in New York City." And I order all my calls by mail. It's great.

Do you think what you're doing is coming to a sharper focus?
Well, I have a thing in my head and I'm focusing in on that pretty clearly. And what that's involved in is a lot of changing sounds. That's the most important thing to me—abrupt changes, very cleanly executed. That's my main thing.

Hearing it on a record, it sounds like studio edits. But to see it live is kind of disorienting. The sound jumps from one planet to the next.
Well, that's my whole trip in a nutshell. If I had to say it in one file card it would be those really fast changes, one world to the next, never staying on one thing for a long period of time—always defining a certain thing and then moving onto something else very quickly. It's something in improvisation that never really happens that much. The style that really developed through players like Derek Bailey and Evan Parker, the people who really legitimized it in many ways, was a style that wasn't involved with changes so much but rather slow progressions, a slow evolving of the music from thing to thing. There would be very few points where there would be a sudden change, and I think that's a really good way of playing. Things have changed a lot. Improvisation has grown a lot.

Was there any one event that sparked your interest in this concept of abrupt changes?
Well, I've always liked cartoon music. That's definitely one of the major influences on me. When I was in college [Webster College in St. Louis] I was working on my thesis on the cartoon music of Carl W. Stallings, who wrote for Warner Bros. The guy is really a genius. When you just listen to the music abstracted from the visuals of the Warner Bros. cartoons, it's amazing. That's the prime period, the '40s, for Warner Bros. I think they really did an incredible jump in film techniques. So that music is really important to me—a lot of changes in that music.

What was the basis of your college thesis?
It was just talking about Stallings' work and how it related to Stravinsky and Webern's experiments in the early part of the century. Stravinsky's whole thing is blocks, working with blocks and reordering them, which was also very, very important for me. He would have a block of instruments working in a certain pattern and then... Boom! He would change to another. *The Rite of Spring* is a typical example of this. Throughout the whole piece that's basically all that's happening.... Boom... Boom... Change... Change... Change, one thing to another.

So there's certain elements of your music that can be traced back...
Through Stravinsky and Varèse and Harry Partch. Even Philip Glass was very important to me, because of the idea of getting a group together to play your own music. Partch did this as well. Partch had his disciples working with him and Glass had his own troupe and Reich had his own troupe. That really made an impression on me when I was in college. The best way to get a good performance is to have a troupe of players that know your music fairly well—not writing an abstract score, giving it to people who don't know you at all. They just look at the music. There's always something missing in that, there's always something lacking in the performance of a symphony orchestra playing another composer's work. Especially if it's a work that really is difficult to play or provokes problems for people in the orchestra. There's a wall between the two—grumbling about performing it or whatever. But if you have your group that is interested in what you're doing, then they'll produce much better performances.

So it was in college when you first began experimenting with abruptly changing sounds?
I think it was always in my head. My very early music when I was just a teenager studying composition—13, 14, 15—that music, too, had that abrupt quality. But I was really into more traditional forms at the time. I was really into C. P. E. Bach and J. S. Bach. I was really into counterpoint. The way I put things together when I look at my old scores... There are real threads running to what I'm doing today in terms of those changing blocks. So it goes back that far, it was always there.

Can you go back to the very beginning of your interest in music and your actual serious pursuit of music?
I was very interested in the organ when I was a little kid because I liked monsters and saw *The Phantom of the Opera* and the guy was playing the organ and I thought that was really cool. At that time I was living in Queens, between Fresh Meadows and Flushing. I started writing music. I didn't know what I was doing. I couldn't play the piano. I was playing flute when I was maybe 13. Then I started playing guitar.

Did that whole Beatles phenomenon interest you?
Well, it interested me to a certain extent. But I cut myself loose from popular music when I got into classical. The Beatles attracted me a lot when I studied guitar. Then The Doors came along and I had always been interested in the organ and Ray Manzarek was playing the organ so I got into The Doors a bit. I remember seeing them at Hunter College, one of their first New York performances. But then I got more and more into Bach's organ music—studying it, trial and error writing.

Did you have a teacher?
Leonardo Balada was my teacher at the school I went to in New York City, which is where I was born and grew up. That was the U.N. School, and he was the music teacher there. Balada was an Argentinian composer. When I was very small, Balada wrote some modern music for the bandoneon and presented it at the school. And it totally flipped me out. Things began to churn in my head then, alternate ways of writing music. It was always a pain for me to write music in the traditional way. I still do it today, but it's a very laborious process. It's like I don't hear music that way. I hear in relationships and forms and shapes. Traditional notation always seemed like the long way around, to me. That's another way I got into improvising. It's more direct. You're right there making decisions then instead of sweating over them again and again day by day.

How were you regarded in school by your classmates?
I was kind of a fringe character, kind of some weird guy that was floating around doing these different things no one ever really took seriously. But this one guy, Steven Hartke, was really nice to me. He was the main pupil of Balada at the time in high school. I kind of looked up to him. He was a year or two older than me. He was really into counterpoint and loved to write. He was much more traditional than I was. The stuff that he wrote sounded a lot more like what you would imagine classical music is supposed to sound like, but he was really encouraging to me.

What got you to first pick up the sax?
I think it was hearing Anthony Braxton's *For Alto Saxophone* [Delmark, 1968], that two-record set. I was at Webster College at the time and wanted to know what was going on in St. Louis. Oliver Lake was teaching at Webster College and the Black Arts Group was there. Luther Thomas, who was one of my friends in school, was studying the saxophone there. Marty Ehrlich was there, too, but I never met him in St. Louis. Anyway, I remember asking someone, "What's going on? What kind of new music is around?" And he said, "Well, there's these guys in Chicago [AACM] and

they're playing this pretty wild stuff. You should check it out." This was when I was first in college, around '71. So I went to this record store and asked the guy, "What have you got by the AACM?" He pointed me to a bin and it was just packed. And I looked through it and I saw the cover of *For Alto* and it looked kind of interesting. I remember asking this guy, "What is this record?" And he said, "Oh, you buying that record? We got about a thousand of 'em down in the basement. Nobody wants to buy them." And I said, "Wow, sounds interesting... I'll take it." So I bought it and it just totally freaked me out. It was the greatest. There was something about the energy.... It had energy, but it also had that kind of structural clarity that I was interested in. He also dedicated one piece to John Cage, and I was always interested in Cage's music.

You weren't interested in John Coltrane and Ornette Coleman at the time?
No, that came much later. Once I started picking up the saxophone really seriously, which was when I was in college, I decided to really learn the instrument the right way and do the full trip with it. And jazz seemed like the literature of the saxophone. I studied with James Meyer, who was the bass clarinet player and saxophone player with the symphony orchestra in St. Louis. He was an incredible teacher. I said, "Look , I don't have that much money. I can afford to take lessons for four months. I'll come once a week. Just teach me everything you can." I'd go there and we'd just talk. Once in a while I'd play a little bit, he'd make a suggestion. I'd just keep notes and we'd talk about everything—about reeds, tone production, harmonics.

Did you go through classical repertoire, too?
Yeah, with him. It's important to get a good teacher when you're studying an instrument or forget about it, it's just gonna fall apart. I think one of the reasons I really gave up the guitar was because my teacher was such a dipshit. All he wanted me to do was play the chromatic scale, four octaves up and down the fretboard—in six seconds, he wanted me to do it! So I'd spend all my time trying to get it in six and I remember I couldn't get it in less than nine or something, and he was always really disappointed in me. Finally I said, "Fuck this guy, man! Forget it!" So Meyer was a fantastic teacher, and he was a jazz player when he was younger so he would always talk lovingly about playing jazz—how great it was, how he would go to these late night chili houses in Harlem and jam. He went to Juilliard during the day, then he'd go Uptown and play jazz saxophone all night, then he'd come home totally exhausted and flop on the bed. So it was always kind of a nice, romantic image.

Did he drop any names on you?
He turned me on a little bit to some people but he had pretty much left the jazz world by the bebop era. So when it came to producing the sounds that I was interested in producing—things like Braxton, Roscoe Mitchell—he was pretty much at a loss. It was almost like I was showing him some of the weird things I had found. And he was always interested, which made him so hip. I'd show him chord fingerings I had figured out by accident and he'd kind of look at it and go, "Yeah." And it would make sense to him, physically, on the saxophone. And he'd give me some other fingerings to try which would work or wouldn't work, depending. So it was a give and take, which I think is important with teachers. So that was an important period, St. Louis. I was only there a year and a half but I met a lot of people and wrote a lot of music. And my music really went through a lot of changes.

When did you start experimenting with improvisational systems?
I think the first time I really did anything similar to what I'm doing now was in college, a piece I called "Klarina." It was for three players, each of whom played three instruments. It was written in such a way that no one combination of instruments occurs more than once. So it's like all possible

combinations of these three players playing three instruments. So you get these kind of abrupt changes as well, but you also get all the possible combinations of instruments involved, which is something that was very, very important for me in the middle period of my composing pieces like "Archery" and "Pool."

It sounds almost mathematical.
It is. It is involved in that kind of stuff but I'm not such a math wiz. I don't work things out in a mathematical way.

You could program on a computer all possible combinations.
Right, and then work out an ordering in which none would be repeated.... Yeah, I could. I've talked to George Lewis about getting a hold of a computer and he said he was gonna lend me one of his and then it never happened. I am interested in working with computers and I'm sure when I do get around to that and I do get systems worked out, it'll really be another big step for me. So this was the first piece that involved systems in which I didn't talk about sound at all. I'm no longer interested here in a specific sound, I'm interested only in the relationships involved.

You're defining the territory and you're letting them play around within that territory.
Right, exactly. Which I think is a very important step. It's the kind of thing that composers like Henri Pousseur and Pierre Boulez dabbled with a little bit in the late-1950s, working in an open form, having things be able to be shifted around. Or Earl Brown's open form works where he'd have maybe six elements, totally composed, but they could be shifted around so the conductor could say, "OK. Play element number two. Now play number six. Now play number one." And that kind of thing grew into Stockhausen's mid-period work, like "Plus Minus" and "Kurzwellen," which depicted relationships of sound itself. Not players, but sound itself. You'd start with a short-wave sound, then you'd have a plus on your score and play something higher than that or louder than that—or a minus, you'd play something quieter or lower in pitch. And you'd go from symbol to symbol, and that's what the score would be. It could start with any sound, you'd never know exactly what you'd find on the short-wave receiver, but from there you'd bring the sound through these sets of relationships and moving the sound from here to here. Stockhausen's piece is involved in sound itself and defining where the sound goes. What I've done is taken it beyond that point to something that exists even outside of time. There's no timeline anymore in my pieces, where you begin at Point A, then you go to B, C, and end at Z. It's a set of rules, kind of like game theories that are meant to spark relationships among improvising musicians, who then will fill in their own music.

But isn't there a point where one chunk of music ends and the next begins?
The downbeat that you're talking about is an open system that I call a pool system. Someone gives a downbeat and the music changes. But within that system there could be X amount of time from one downbeat to the next. It could last five minutes or only 10 seconds before another system is called into play.

And that system is utilized in "Track & Field" and "Pool" and "Archery."
Not in "Archery." The pool system developed with the piece "Pool," which I wrote in '78. That piece was completely based upon the downbeat system. There is a set of orderings which you interpolate into this system but the main system involved in improvising in the piece "Pool" is the one where a sharp change happens at a downbeat. And it can be given by any one of the players at any time.

Was developing that system a culmination of your attempt to get these sounds changing rapidly and abruptly like the cartoon music you so admired?
It was the easiest way to do it and I'm surprised I never thought of it before. It's the easiest way to bring about the kind of change that I want to happen in a very clean way.... Boom. And all I say is: "Change on the downbeat." I don't say X number of people drop out, X number of people come in. I don't say play from loud to soft. Or if something was very high in pitch, the next thing would be very low. I just say: "at this point there's gonna be a change. If you're playing, you can drop out. If you do stay in, you should change the music that you're playing." So in a large group of maybe 12 players, a downbeat is given—the downbeat could lead to just one person playing or it could bring the whole group in, it could be just two players, it could be anything. But a change has to happen. Any kind of change.

Who designates?
Anybody in the group can make a decision.

And the players have sets of flashcards to designate. How does that work?
In "Track & Field" I have four sets of systems, each set had five systems within it. So there's a total of 20 systems involved. Instead of having cards that go 1–20, I arranged the groups into four little systems. One was drone systems, one was improvising systems, one was a set of roles, and the other one was features. So if you wanted to call, say, feature two, which is a duo... Feature four would be a quartet, feature one would be a solo. If you wanted to call F2, you would hold up your F card and hold up your two fingers.

So that was an example of democracy in music where each person has equal say.
I hate to say "democracy," but I guess that's what it is. Everybody has an equal say. But it doesn't really amount to that. Theoretically, that's the case, but what actually ends up happening is, there are players who are more familiar with my music than other players in the group and then there's always different personalities involved. Some people are very content to sit and play whatever system is up, other people are very interested in making dynamic changes, calling a lot of systems and having the control over the group. Maybe they have a certain set of relationships in their head, they want to actualize them. This system gives them the opportunity to do that.

Veto power.
Yeah, veto power. So... Through the roles in "Track & Field" I was able to give people positions where all they had to do was make decisions in terms of the group. Like, there was a marshal, a general, a runner—and these people weren't involved in playing music, per se. They were just involved in sitting and arranging players, maybe switching people who were playing with people who weren't playing, or cutting people off or making group decisions by system.

Let's say that I'm in the group and I get an idea for four different sounds that I want to hear together.... How would I get them together and enact that idea?
Well, see, each piece that I write gives all the players the abilities to do all these possible combinations, but always in different ways. That's what makes one piece different from the next. In "Track & Field," all you would have to do is call a feature.... Feature 4 or F4. That would mean quartet would play by itself, either on the downbeat or on what I call a meld, which would mean a slow drifting away of the players who are playing an older system and other players coming in slowly with the new system—kind of like a segue.

How would I communicate the specific instruments that I would want to hear?
Eye contact is the easiest and most direct way to do it. Eventually it would be great.... I have in my head the possibility with high tech having everybody have a little microphone system with an earphone and they could talk to each other and say, "Hey, let's do a duo at this point," or "This system is up, why don't we call a different system." That kind of communication, which in the past has been so taboo in improvising—you're not supposed to talk, you're just supposed to get up and blow. I mean, that kind of thing, I think, really inspires a lot of new directions in improvising—communication by word or by eye contact or by cue. These are things I'm very, very interested in.

So the function of the prompter is to kind of confirm these things?
Or convey. The prompter would act like a mirror or telegraph device. So that if someone wanted to make a cue clear to everybody, instead of getting everybody's eye contact, you'd do it through the prompter. And the prompter has everybody's attention. The prompter was used in "Pool" and in "Archery." "Archery" was the first piece I wrote that needed a prompter and I wrote it without a prompter in mind. I tried to create a system that with the minimum possible number of instructions, I could generate the most highly complex music possible. But the system ended up being a little more complicated than I had hoped, so I needed a prompter. But compared to the pieces I'm writing now, "Archery" is like really, really simple. So when musicians play "Archery" now it's like sight-reading time. They just come in and they read it, no problem. Before, it was a mess.

Can you give me the progression of your pieces?
There's so many from there. I can give you the major pieces. The next piece that really related was called "Baseball." That was for three saxophone players—Phillip Johnston, who plays in the Microscopic Septet, myself, and Leora Barish, who has since given up playing the saxophone and is now involved in writing movie scripts in Hollywood. And then I moved to "Lacrosse" [1977], "Hockey" [1978], "Fencing" [1978], then "Pool" [1979], "Jai Alai" [1980], "Croquet" [1981], and "Track & Field" [1982]. All of these pieces I tried to concentrate on a different aspect of improvising, almost as if to give the players that would be performing it a certain problem to think about so that when they play the piece, they learn something about improvising or other possibilities of improvising. So when they would go and play a free improvised piece with other people or any time that they would play, it gave them something to think about. "Fencing," for instance, was about harmony, mostly—what you play against someone else. Think through several possibilities before you come in and play, then you make your decision to get the most unusual combination.

Do you have a stable core of musicians who perform these pieces?
Using musicians has been a very slow process of developing people who are interested in what I'm doing and who have an affinity for the language that I myself developed on the saxophone, which is pretty...original. But the first people I worked with were Eugene Chadbourne and Polly Bradfield. Then Bob Ostertag came along, Tom Cora, Toshinori Kondo, Wayne Horvitz, and it moved on and on from there. And I found that as people would call me or as I would see performers and become interested in what they were doing and ask them to be involved in some of my work, my work would also change. Some of the rock stuff that I'm involved with now is definitely because I became friends with people like Anton Fier and Arto Lindsay, who are really involved in rock music. That's their music. It's not my music at all, but I heard them play and was intrigued. I heard Arto's band DNA and it totally floored me. It was incredibly organized, an incredible band. So as I met musicians and became friends with them and appreciated their music, it affected my own music. Now my music has become more eclectic as far as that is concerned.... Many different elements are kind of adjoined. And my music has really... Rather than becoming very exclusive, where it's only these

few people that made these weird, funny sounds, now I feel like anybody, any instrumentalist could be involved in playing these relationship systems and have a good time doing it. And the resulting music would be what I had intended, what I had in my head. The shape would be the same, which is pretty amazing for me. I was really lonely eight years ago when it was just a few people I could play with. And we'd do concerts with three people in the audience and if the critic did come, the review would end up being incredibly antagonistic: "Total bullshit... Forget about it! There's nothing there."

Have you made any European connections for this?
No, I was never too good at making phone calls and hustling gigs. I'm perfectly content to sit in my house and compose my music and play downstairs at The Saint [the tiny one-room underground club that Zorn operated for a brief period in the basement of his building on 7th Street in the East Village]. If someone calls me on the phone and the money's good and it seems like it'd be fun, I'll go. But I'm not gonna call up and try to get a gig.

How do European audiences respond to your music?
Europe is a funny thing for me. A lot of people have said how great Europe is in terms of audience. The money is there, I will agree. They bring me over. Here... Forget it. It's impossible to get a guarantee except at a place like The Public Theater or The Kitchen, and they give you a gig once every two years. There are smaller places where you can get maybe $100 a night. Tin Pan Alley is a great place that gives guarantees. But Europe has a mystique.... When I first went there it was amazing that there were pictures of artists on their money instead of politicians. That's been around for so long it's just like part of their life—going to see music and paying money for the arts. It's new in this country. This country hasn't been around that long, so they're way ahead as far as that's concerned. But as far as ability to hear the music, they're no different than anybody else on the planet, I don't think. I have just as many, if not more, problems in Europe with the press and with the audiences than I do here in New York. All antagonism. All I get is a headache from them—a lot of close-minded views of what music is supposed to be. Especially England. England is a total drag! The first promoter who brought me over there, Anthony Wood... I did a solo concert and he wrote a review after I split apologizing for bringing me to England and what a mistake it was. And I get the usual anomalies like "aquatic antics." I'm so tired of reading reviews where all they talk about is how I sound like a herd of elephants. And the second time I went there on tour with Derek Bailey's Company—Steve Lacy and Evan Parker were both in the band—we did a dozen gigs through England. People used to come up on the stage and splash water on my face from my water bowl before walking out, just to let me know that I'm full of shit. And then the reviews would be: "Lacy tells us what improvisation is all about, here he is defining the form. And here is John Zorn, the court jester, showboating, trying to get attention, just a bunch of bullshit." Italy I've never played, but from what I've been told it's the kind of audience that yells and applauds when you play really high or really fast, and then when you start playing music that you're really interested in, they just talk the whole time. Germany was good. I played the Wuppertal Festival, though I felt a little bit out of place there. Most of the music in that part of Germany has been more like the free jazz, screaming kind of sax players—Peter Brotzman, who I love, and Peter Kovalt, who I love. They're great players and I like to play with them. But the audiences are used to a certain type of thing and when they get something different, they react just the way American audiences react—kind of ambivalently, and "What the hell is this?" and "He doesn't know how to play."

Have you played in Japan?
No, I'm ready to go to Japan. I'd love to go. Japan must be great.

Talk about your own vocabulary that you developed on the saxophone.

Well, I think the main reason I picked up the saxophone as a possible instrument is that it really was like a sound maker. There was something about the breath I was attracted to. The saxophone's a great instrument for me. It's perfect. But I think I looked upon it as a sound maker more than anything else. And that's still the way I look at it. I remember doing tonguing experiments when I was just beginning on the sax, trying to get as many different squeaks and sounds and chords that I could out of it. It was that kind of vocal quality that I was drawn to. And to me, it fits right in with the literature of the saxophone, with the sound makers that existed in the '60s in a jazz tradition. They were all going for vocal kind of sounds and the very human, crying sounds—people like Albert Ayler, Roscoe Mitchell, John Coltrane, Pharoah Sanders.... Pharoah's solo on "Naima" from [*Live*] *at the Vanguard Again* [Impulse!, 1966] is one of the masterpieces of jazz history, I think. An incredible sound-oriented solo. All of these things were so far ahead of their time and no one really appreciated them.

The search for sound has been around, I think, for a really long time. Evan Parker took it a far, far way. I remember a friend coming back from England and saying, "Wow, you gotta hear this guy Evan Parker. I didn't hear him play one note the whole time!" And it's not a matter of whether it's a note or not a note, it's the concept of working with sound or noise and trying to depart as far as you can. A major departure, a major step, is when you take all the parameters of music and change them—not just one. Not just harmony, where you just work out something different harmonically... It's when you attack rhythm and harmony and melody, something like what Ornette Coleman did. Ornette was a big step in jazz because either consciously or unconsciously he really attacked all those parameters. And that's something I'm interested in doing and consciously thinking through and getting to a new place, in terms of time, in terms of harmony, in terms of melody, the sound that I'm doing, the dynamics of it. And I'm just at the beginning of it. Even with all the flak I've been getting, it's just the tip of the iceberg.

BOBBY MCFERRIN

THERE WAS A CASUAL BUT MEMORABLE listening party that I attended in 1982. A bunch of us critics and writers were huddled around a sound system, anxiously waiting for Bruce Lundvall to unveil the first batch of releases from his new label Elektra/Musician. Lundvall had for some years previous been associated with Columbia Records and had brought several big names to that label in jazz, pop, and country. Now he was heading up this ambitious new enterprise under the auspices of Elektra. We sat on chairs and patiently sampled some of this new music as Lundvall waxed enthusiastic about each artist. There was a bop outing from trumpeter Red Rodney with his sax playing colleague Ira Sullivan. There was an avant-funk release from Bill Laswell's band Material. And there were a few other offerings that have left my memory. But one album definitely jumped out from the rest. It was the self-titled debut of singer Bobby McFerrin. Amazingly fluid with the uncanny ability to alternate quickly between falsetto and deep bass notes, McFerrin impressed us all. He had a soulful, knowing presence, and made some remarkably creative choices. He did a cool, if conventional, duet with Phoebe Snow on Smokey Robinson's "You've Really Got a Hold on Me" and a hip rendition of the Orleans top 10 pop hit, "Dance with Me." It was a fine enough showing but only skimming the surface of what McFerrin would get into in subsequent albums. It wasn't until he started doing concerts in 1983 featuring his unaccompanied vocals that McFerrin really found his own voice, which involved producing notes while breathing in as well as out and producing cross-rhythms by drumming with his hand on his chest. His following release on Elektra/Musician, aptly titled *The Voice* (1984), was a startling collection of everything from baroque to Beatles—a conceptual, incremental leap to a new plateau. And he's been elevating ever since.

I spoke to McFerrin by phone on the eve of a 1993 clinic/performance at the University of Colorado at Greeley, where I have been covering an annual college jazz festival since 1987. I wrote a piece based on this interview for the *Greeley Tribune.* Another piece on McFerrin's vocal clinic at Greeley later appeared in *Down Beat.*

FEBRUARY 3, 1993

Bobby McFerrin is to sound what Michael Jordan is to gravity—defiantly creative with intuitive skills that separate him from the rest of us mere mortals. And it is precisely because their instincts are so right that neither of these geniuses can really describe what it is that they do. Whether it's Michael driving to the hoop or Bobby glissing his way through " 'Round Midnight," both are comfortably in the zone, purely on automatic pilot, just doing what comes naturally.

Born in New York City on March 11, 1950, Bobby McFerrin grew up in Los Angeles and began studying music theory at age six. He played piano in a high school jazz quintet, then dropped out of college in 1970 to work as a keyboardist, arranger, and sometime backup singer for a variety of gigs ranging from lounge acts to the Ice Follies. In 1977, he landed a straight singing job at the Hilton Hotel in Salt Lake City. He lived for a short time in New Orleans before eventually working his way to his current home base in San Francisco. After attracting a lot of local attention for his vocal acrobatics, he got a call from jazz scatting patriarch Jon Hendricks, who asked Bobby to join his four-voice Family. Following that short apprenticeship, he was signed to a two-record deal by Elektra Records. His big breakthrough came with the release of *Simple Pleasures* (EMI Manhattan, 1988), which included the infectious pop tune that swept the nation, "Don't Worry Be Happy."

In 1990, he released the spiritually-tinged *Medicine Music* (EMI Manhattan), a meditation on music as a healing force which featured his acclaimed 10-member Voicestra. As he told *New Age* magazine: "When I became a singer I found that there were times, after a really good sing, when it was like 'running energy,' a really good, positive energy. I could actually feel a difference in the way my body felt, particularly the way my mind felt at ease and lighter. When you're singing, you're employing the breath in a rhythmic way. It can do a lot to reduce tension and slow your thought process down."

More recently, McFerrin has focused on classical music. An appearance at Tanglewood in honor of Leonard Bernstein's 70th birthday in 1988 led to a friendship with master cellist Yo-Yo Ma. Their mutual admiration and musical rapport resulted in the intriguing recording *Hush* (Sony Masterworks, 1992), a unique duet album of classical pieces like Rachmaninoff's "Vocalise," J. S. Bach's "Air on a G String," and Rimsky-Korsakov's "Flight of the Bumblebee" alongside five McFerrin original compositions. Says Bobby, "We simply had a ball because Yo-Yo brings such a wonderful childlike attitude to new adventures. Working with him on that album was absolutely fabulous, among the most enjoyable four days I've ever had musically."

Simultaneously with *Hush,* Blue Note released *Play,* an ebullient romp through jazz standards and originals with pianist Chick Corea. Both records, like McFerrin's solo performances, are filled with the spirit of creative adventure. "I've always been interested in free association," he says. "I've always been interested in how things happen. And how, if you're very aware and very open, you can grab hold of things and use them for ideas. It demands an acute awareness of your environment. To me, it's like having big ears, like antennae that reach out to the audience and take in what they have to offer."

Following his passion for classical music, McFerrin has also been involved in conducting symphony orchestras around the country. His present to himself on his 40th birthday three years ago was to conduct the San Francisco Symphony in one of his favorite pieces, Beethoven's "Seventh Symphony." He is currently studying the score for Mozart's "Symphony No. 41" and has also been commissioned to write an opera for the San Francisco Opera Company. Tentatively titled *Gethsemane,* with libretto by Ishmael Reed, it is scheduled for the 1995 summer season.

Proving once again that you can't keep a good renaissance man down.

I've been to several of these college jazz festivals, and I've noticed that although the students are generally very well equipped in terms of book knowledge, they're missing something. So when people like yourself come in to perform and give clinics, they really respond. What types of things might you be able to impart to an audience of aspiring musicians who are looking for some kind of inspiration?
Oh boy... Well, the first thing that came to my mind was the word abandon. That has a lot to do with it. I was just reading this book by Natalie Goldberg called *Wild Mind: [Living the Writer's Life,* Bantam, 1990]. It's simply about the difference between the person who says, "I'm going to exercise," and goes out to a bookstore and buys a book about exercising, and the person who just begins to exercise. A lot of people say, "I'm gonna write," so they go to school to learn how to write, but they never write. Or they get a lot of information from other people rather than placing the same kind of value on their own ability to take chances in writing. And it's not about whether it's good or not in the eyes of other people, it's just a matter of sitting down and putting your pen to paper and going for it—the process of doing, which is where you learn a lot of stuff. For me, even though I went to school and studied theory and harmony and everything, I could not tell you when I'm onstage theoretically what I am doing. And it's not until maybe I go back later and pull it apart that I might be able to tell you: "Well, that run there was based on B diminished chord, then I went down to G flat, then I took off and did a retrograded version of the first whatchamajiggy." Even though I might be able to go back and analyze it, when I'm doing it there's absolutely nothing going on in my mind but the next note, the next thing, and grabbing onto whatever is there. I don't know how much of that is missing in education, but I do think the idea of teaching improvisation—not so much theoretically or what goes into it, but really the fact that improvisation basically is simply the courage to move from one note to the next. That's all it is.

Keith Jarrett said that anytime some musicians say, "Let's play some bebop," they've already defeated the purpose. They're not making music at that point, they're just imitating.
Yeah, I can relate to that. People in college seem to be hung up on transcriptions, which is fine for analyzing how people got in and out of stuff harmonically. But they aren't really learning how to improvise, they aren't overcoming their fears. Can this be taught? I hope that when I'm on stage I can communicate that I am simply abandoning myself to the moment. Lots of people don't get it unless I talk about it, or they might read about it in an interview. And they realize that I'm actually just sort of playing with what comes up. I'm sure that at least half of the audience thinks that they're set pieces, that I've actually done them before. There are some pieces that I do in concert, but I always try to make them a little different in some way.

A great example of your purely spontaneous energy was when you had the audience pass you around the room at Carnegie Hall recently.
Yeah, I've only done that a couple of times. That was the last time actually.

That graphically illustrates what you're talking about—just giving it up to the spirit.
And this is what we must do as musicians, as artists.

Why is audience participation important to you as a performer?
I think it goes back to the question of how do I think I'm imparting this sense of abandonment. They get it easier if they participate in the process instead of just passive listening. They can pick up on it a little bit better if they are actively involved in the process of making something, creating something. They're also in a relationship with me. I think they get it better that way. It's about adventure and discovery with an audience. They bring their stuff and I bring my stuff and we all make some discoveries along the way. We share our musical stuff. And they get a sense when they leave, I hope, that they were actively involved in the creative process.

Sounds like a description of a Baptist church service.
Well, my grandfather was a Baptist minister, even though I never went to his church. Maybe it's sort of a genetic thing.

Just the idea of being actively involved and partaking in the event.
That's real key to me. I just got commissioned to write an opera for the San Francisco Opera Company. And even though opera is traditionally something you sit and watch, I'm trying to figure out if I can in one instance get the audience involved in the action in some kind of way, even if it means they have a line, something they have to say at some particular part in the opera. I think it'll make a big difference. Before the opera begins, maybe I or someone walks out on stage.... Maybe in each program there is a slip of paper that has something for them to do. And I come out and say, "OK, in the third scene in the second act, you have to do something." I have no idea what that event is, but I'm very interested in making this opera not such an elitist kind of event. I want to open it up to everyone. And I think that might even make the opera more interesting if it spills out into the hallways.

I understand that you've stopped touring with your vocal group, Voicestra.
We spent three years putting together a tour, but economically it was really difficult to pull off. Too many elements. Besides the ten singers there were road managers, sound people, stage crew.... It just got too expensive. But we still get together and sing. Right now we're working on a dance piece with the Oberland Dance Collective, so we'll be on stage with a dance troupe. So we're just doing some isolated kinds of things but no extensive touring. It's not economically feasible at this point.

You probably don't do too much planning for a solo performance.
No, I don't do any at all.

Do you warm up before a solo performance?
I never warm up. I just consider the stage to be an extension of real life. I'm singing backstage before the show. I walk on stage and I'm singing. I drive home and I'm singing along the way. I get something to eat, I relax, I take a bath, I'm singing the whole time. It's no big deal.

You just go out and start getting involved in the moment. That takes a certain amount of discipline, I imagine.
Well, and I'm still trying to figure out what that is. I think it's just a matter of, you sort of step into this stream of consciousness and you go. You try not to listen to your judges and you just grab whatever is there. It's so simple but so hard to describe.

That's a pretty bold move for students who are too obsessed with playing the right notes, which is why your presence at this college festival will be very important to them in breaking down those barriers.
Oh yeah, it's funny... I was just listening to this piece today by the Yellowjackets. And there's this

tune called "Memoirs." And Russ Ferrante is playing a wonderful solo and all of a sudden he plays a very simple chord, a basic triad. And my first thought was: "What a plain chord that is." And then I realized that in some ways it was the simplest, most beautiful chord that he played. Because all the other things were augmented this and that.... We get so used to augmented and diminished, adding all these color tones to our chords. Chords have become four, five, six notes—two-handed, two-fisted, just all over the place. All of a sudden, right in the middle of that comes this minor triad. And that was the chord that stuck out for me. Of all the things that he played, that was the one that sucked me into it. And it was because it was the simplest one. And I realized that in jazz I'm not used to hearing things that simple anymore. Because jazz has gotten, in some ways, so convoluted.... There's so much stuff in it.

Well, that was the beauty of Miles and Basie—just hitting the right note at the right moment.
That's right. Less is more.

There's so many lessons for these college kids to learn. Unfortunately, most of them can't be learned in the classroom.
Right.

And being where they are, in Colorado, Nebraska, Montana... They don't have an opportunity to pick up much by osmosis. There's no Village Vanguard out there so they're dealing with textbooks and transcriptions, then picking up whatever inspiration they can at these festivals. So your presence there is going to deeply affect a lot of people.
Well, you know, the Bible is my favorite book. And there's this passage in Corinthians that says something to the effect: "Knowledge puffs up—sort of makes you big-headed when you know a lot of stuff. But love builds up." And I think the experience of performing, just letting it go, is more like the love of doing it rather than thinking about it, which is the knowledge. I mean, anybody can go to school. My conducting instructor here in San Francisco just blows me away with what he knows about scores and stuff like that. And fortunately, he's also a very good conductor. He's able to apply that knowledge. But I'm also aware of people who know a lot but they can't apply, they can't get it from their head into their heart. That's the most important thing. Because the bottom line is, if I'm standing on the podium, what I know about the music is secondary in terms of history and the composer's emotional state and where it was written and how long he lived and theoretically what he was into. The bottom line is: Do I love what I'm doing? And if I do, the musicians in the orchestra feel it and they play better. That's it. Music is about spirit.

What are you going to do at your vocal jazz clinic at Greeley?
Just spend some time with the students, answer a lot of questions. We might try a couple of tunes and do some jamming together. Again, whatever works out. I just play it by ear.

What helpful hints do you have for singers who are struggling with improvisation?
I tell them to choose four notes, any four notes, and then just begin improvising with those four notes. Alter the tempo, experiment with the texture of the notes, tell a story, see where they may take you. But above all, make sure you have the three most important ingredients in music—swing, soul, and sincerity. That's really where it's at.

And the bottom line at these clinics is to try and instill this sense of abandon in them.
That's right—the courage to move from one note to the next without thinking about it. To me, if someone wants to know what my definition of improvisation is, that's what it is—the courage to move from one thing to the next. That's it in a nutshell.

JOHN SINCLAIR

IT WAS 3 A.M. IN NEW ORLEANS. I had just kicked off The Monk Hour on another edition of "The Milkman's Matinee," my late-night weekly radio show on WWOZ. My shift was from 2 A.M.. to 5 A.M.. "This is the Milkman, makin' my early morning deliveries here on the dark side of Friday," went my regular refrain. And from 3 to 4 every morning I put out a solid hour of Thelonious Monk music across the airwaves in the Crescent City. Pretty radical for a town obsessed with second line grooves, funk, and N'awlins R&B. Musicians just getting home from their gigs around town would invariably tune me in and dig the sounds. One night, a rather gruff-voiced caller offered some encouragement. "Hey Milkman! Keep up the good work!" It was John Sinclair, WWOZ's resident blues authority who hosted the "Blues and Roots" late-night show on Saturday. He also happened to be a huge Monk fan and scholar. I finally met him face to face a couple weeks later at his 52nd birthday celebration in his Treme neighborhood. We shared a joint outside Trombone Shorty's brass band club and from that moment became fast friends. It was only later that I learned of Sinclair's notorious and colorful past.

Sinclair is also the author of *Guitar Army,* the 1972 counterculture classic that chronicles his bust and subsequent imprisonment for two and a half years in the State Prison of Southern Michigan at Jackson for possessing two joints of marijuana. The case became something of a cause célèbre, prompting demonstrations from the likes of John Lennon and Yoko Ono and one protest single, "Free John Sinclair." An accomplished poet with an impressive body of work, Sinclair regularly performs around New Orleans with his band, The Blues Scholars. He has also hit the road with his band, appearing in New York, Boston, Chicago, Los Angeles, and other cities. Sinclair has released three records of his poetry—*Full Moon Night* (Total Energy Records, 1994) with The Blues Scholars, *If I Could Be with You* (Schoolkids Records, 1995) with The Society Jazz Orchestra under the direction of composer-conductor Ed Moss, and a solo spoken word disc, *Thelonious: A Book of Monk* (New Alliance, 1995). All three CDs showcase the poet's keen eye for detail and storytelling, his love of jazz, his undying romanticism, and his frenzied, over-the-top delivery, which is chilling to witness.

This interview with the transplanted Detroiter was originally conducted for the Japanese *Music* magazine. It was subsequently excerpted for the December '96 issue of *Fi* magazine in the States.

J U L Y   1 2 ,   1 9 9 5

Poet–musicologist–political activist John Sinclair (he prefers to think of himself as an agitator and rhythm-chaser) vividly recalls the day they dragged his controversial ass to the slammer for possession of two joints of marijuana. It was July 28, 1969, the day after astronaut Neil Armstrong's "one small step for man, one giant leap for mankind." An auspicious day for millions of TV-watching Americans who took in the first moonwalk in hushed awe—not so auspicious for the counterculture icon, who would spend the next two and a half years of a nine-to-ten year sentence in the State Prison of Southern Michigan at Jackson.

"The punishment seemed kind of medieval to me," recalls Sinclair, puffing on a joint in his spacious New Orleans home some 25 years later. "My wife was pregnant with Cecilia. My other daughter, Sunny, was two years old. I was just in the middle of everything—and not only in the middle of it, but at the head of a lot of things. But then, that was kind of the idea behind putting me away." As chairman of the White Panther Party, a radical group of acid-eating counterculture politicos whose ten-point program called for the overthrow of the United States government, Sinclair was seen as dangerous. So he was iced. Simple as that.

As a political activist in the Detroit/Ann Arbor area, Sinclair always kept one foot firmly planted in the music world. His involvement with the notorious proto-punk band MC5 yielded some of the most kinetic sounds of a turbulent decade. And after his incarceration, he managed such Detroit bands as The Up, Mitch Ryder & The Detroit Wheels, and The Rockets.

Today, Sinclair has re-emerged as a poet and performer, fronting a scruffy band, The Blues Scholars. He's old enough to be profiled in *Mature Times,* yet young enough in spirit to tour the country in a funky van doing one-nighters. Living in New Orleans since 1991, Sinclair has made his mark on the Crescent City scene. Besides his own performances, he hosts a weekly late-night "Blues and Roots" show on WWOZ, and he's a columnist for *Offbeat,* a local music monthly.

Apart from his activities as poet, DJ, and rock'n'roll rebel, the founder of the White Panther Party also takes great pride and a bit of mischievous glee in programming the taped music heard by throngs of tourists every day in the Riverwalk, New Orleans' answer to every other sprawling shopping mall you've ever been in. Located on the banks of the Mississippi, it contains the same string of Gap, L. L. Bean, Disney, Warner Bros., and what-have-you stores that one encounters in malls all across America. But unlike the somnambulant Muzak generally heard in such commercial shopping venues, you get a healthy dose of Sinclair faves like Smiley Lewis, Dr. John, Professor Longhair, James Booker, the Dirty Dozen Brass band, and Ernie K-Doe when you stroll through the Riverwalk. It's John's way of making a statement, making a difference by throwing a monkey wrench in the mix. Still subversive after all these years.

Tell me first of all about the Detroit music scene as you remember it as a kid?
I grew up in a little bitty country town called Davison, Michigan, 10 miles east of Flint. The only other prominent Davisonian is Michael Moore, the documentary filmmaker. So my urban frame of reference was Flint. My whole experience with the music was from whatever was on the radio. I was born in 1941 and when I was seven I got my first radio. That's when radio was still the primary entertainment medium. Then I got interested in pop music when I was about 10 or 11—"Your Hit Parade" and that kind of stuff. I used to listen to this guy Bill Lamb who was a disc jockey on WBBC in Flint. And he had the top 10 every Saturday morning. I tuned in every week to see what the top 10 tunes were gonna be. It was Frankie Laine and "Mule Traine," Guy Mitchell—"Shrimp Boats Are Comin'." All the things that were pop music in the late-1940s and early-1950s—"Wheel of Fortune" by Kay Starr, "How Much Is That Doggie in the Window" by Patti Page, "Sixteen Tons" by Ernie Ford... That kind of thing. And I actually thought that all those artists were there in the studio performing these tunes live. So I was excited about this top 10 thing and always wanted to go to the radio station to see this, because it was so huge in my mind. It was just what life was about. All the interesting shit came from the radio.

So finally one Saturday morning my Dad took me to see the top 10 with Bill Lamb. So we go down to the studio and it was just two guys sitting in there playing records. No audience, no performers. That was a big disillusionment of my young life. I can still feel the sinking feeling when you looked in and saw that this was what it was gonna be. Anyway, so somehow I found R&B on the radio. And in Flint, Michigan, there was this great disc jockey named Frantic Ernie Durham. He was on WBBC and I must've picked up on him just about the same time he came to town, around '52. The Frantic One. He was my idol. He was the thing that I looked up to and aspired to be in life. This was right at the beginning of when white kids started listening to black radio stations. And I was kind of in that number because this other stuff was just so boring and lame. You were getting a little bit older and wanted something more, and then you'd hear something like "One Mint Julep" by The Clovers or Ray Charles' "I Got a Woman." Just all those kind of really hip records. And I beamed in on that. I had no idea where this music came from, it was just pure aural information. So I was involved with that from that point on all the way through high school.

Were you aware of what was happening in Detroit at the time?
No, I was pretty oriented toward Flint. The basic form of entertainment for us was disc jockey dances. And when I was in high school I was a fiendish collector of 45s and I was also a fiendish dancer, and I also wanted to be a disc jockey. So I used to do little disc jockey hops after the football game on Friday night in the gym.

What would you play?
I was in the 10th or 11th grade—had to be around '57, '58. I'd just play all the hip records of the day, like I play now on Saturday night. They were just good records, to me.

No Pat Boone?
Oh, no, no, no, no, no! All records by Negroes. Maybe two percent of what I might play or want to collect might be...

Elvis?
Yeah, I liked the Sun Records and maybe the first three on RCA. Carl Perkins, too. About anything on Sun was cool, up to Johnny Cash—a little too country for me. And Buddy Holly & The Crickets I liked. I was a freak for Bill Haley when I was about 13. I had all his records. But other than that it was all Negroes. I used "Walkin' with Mr. Lee" by Lee Allen as my theme song and I'd

play stuff like "The Big Wheel" by Clifton Chenier on Argo. And I used to close with Paul Gayten doing "Drivin' Home."

Sounds like your show now.
Exactly. I'm playing the same records. To me, frankly, the best records I play are the ones that were made in the '50s. That's when they really made the great records, just magnificent records. To me, 1945 to 1960 was the golden age of music on earth for jazz, blues, R&B, gospel. Everything was hittin' like a ton of bricks, man. Besides that, you had guys around from the earliest periods. You had guys like Ellington and Louis Armstrong still in their prime. You just had everything. Coleman Hawkins and Roy Eldridge from that generation were still at the top of their game. Bird and Dizzy and Miles, Trane, Sonny Rollins. I don't know, I could preach on the cultural superiority of the '50s forever. Not America, per se. Not in terms of popular culture, just in terms of African-American culture. That was the highpoint of Western civilization. It's just been downhill from there. To me, that was the shit. And I just felt tremendously blessed to be able to have this in my life. And as a kid, as a teenager, it helped define my whole view of life. So it was a big influence. I mean, after you hear Billy Ward & His Dominoes, The Moonglows, and The Flamingos, any Caucasian ideas of beauty just completely disintegrate. You know what I'm saying? It just redefined everything for me.

How were you regarded by your schoolmates? As a renegade?
Well, there was a crossover thing happening. Our school was divided into farmers and people who went into town. So there were kids who were into being hip. Commercial wide scale mass TV was in its infancy and it wasn't really aimed at the young people like it was later. I was like 10 or 11 when we got our first TV set and it just didn't interest me very much. They would take shows that you listened to on the radio and put 'em on TV and they just seemed really stupid. "Superman," you know? You listened to it on the radio and you could fill in all the pictures in your mind. Of course, most people were squares, but I remember people that I went to school with.... We would all go to somebody's house for lunch hour and listen to Little Richard records and "Gee" by The Crows and records on Specialty and Chess. When "Maybelline" came out, all the people that I knew were just leveled by that record. Their minds would just be shredded when they heard "Maybelline" for the first time. We'd go to this place where we hung out and played "Maybelline" on the jukebox six times in a row. You got six for a quarter. Then you'd put another quarter in and play it six more times. You just didn't want to hear anything else, it was just so far out.

So I wasn't like a weird loner or anything like that. I was a pretty sociable guy. And there was a set of really hip white kids who were really attenuated to the Negro cultural imperatives, just in terms of the records and clothing and styles. And that was a small group but it was very hip. That was the group that I ran with and we were all fantastic dancers. We'd go to all these huge rhythm and blues revues at the IMA Auditorium. They were basically like black dances and there would be like 25 or 30 white kids, and that would be us. And we would be trying to dance with the colored girls. Or we'd bring our own girlfriends and show off. The pinnacle of life would be to clear the floor at the IMA Auditorium so that everyone else stopped and stood in a big circle while you did your little thing. I did that two or three times. That was the pinnacle of achievement, like winning the big football game or something.

But my teenage years... I just had so much fun when I think about it. Now I do research and I look at charts for the week of October 25, 1956, and you look at the ten records on there for that particular one week and like eight of them are all-time classics. And I wasn't into jazz at the time. I didn't know anything about anything except rhythm and blues. But in that area, every week a number of records would come out that were just the baddest records you ever heard. Every week! And next week there'd be five more. These were labels like Chess, Vee Jay, Specialty, Aladdin, Imperial.

When you saw something with the Atlantic label on it, you wanted to hear that motherfucker right now! It might not be your favorite record you ever heard, but if it was on Atlantic you knew it was going to be tough. Same thing with Chess or Checker.

And the radio was playing all this great music?
Yeah. You'd drive around in your car at night and you could pick up this great station out of Nashville, WLAC. They had the greatest rhythm and blues program imaginable. 50,000 watts pointed in all directions. The shows were sponsored by mail order record shops and I used to send away for the records. This great disc jockey named John Richford, who went by the name of Jumpin' John R, would pitch you on one of these from Ernie's Record Mart, 1719 Third Avenue in Nashville, Tennessee: "The Blue Star Blues Special—six records, 12 big sides for the low, low price of $2.79 plus packing, mailing, and COD. Send no money, just your name and address to me, Jumpin' John R, WLAC, Nashville, Tennessee." And the six records would be like "Lonely Avenue" by Ray Charles, "King Bee" by Muddy Waters, maybe "Congo Mambo" by Guitar Gable. There'd always be something on Excello, always something on Vee Jay, like "Baby It's You" by The Spaniels. Maybe a Jimmy Reed record. And there'd be something on Atlantic, something on Chess like The Moonglows or Willie Mabon. You could order either 78s or 45s. Man, I get emotional thinking about these.

But they'd service the rural areas of the South, that was their primary function. Because you get into Mississippi, once you get outside of Jackson you are hard pressed to find a record shop, at least until you get to Clarksdale. So there's all these people in Alabama, Tennessee, and Mississippi, that was their primary audience. But because they were 50,000 watts, people picked it up all over the fuckin' country. And John R had this thing. Every night he would number the records. So if you heard a record you liked, you didn't even have to remember the name of the record or the artist. You could just say, "Send me number 5 that was played today, July 12." And they would send it to you COD. I thought that was fantastic. And a lot of these people couldn't write anyway so they just had to put the 5 and the date, you know? And you could get the fuckin' record you heard. It was a great system.

What eventually brought you to Detroit?
I went to graduate school at Wayne State University. That's kind of when I came of age in my own mental outlook, which has served me so favorably for so many years. [uproarious laughter] Far more than I had any reason to anticipate. But by the time I got to Detroit in '64 I was a jazz fanatic. I had already gotten to know the jazz scene pretty well from driving over from Flint. You could drive to Detroit from Flint in those days on 50 cents worth of gas. I remember driving in to see Cannonball Adderley at Baker's Keyboard Lounge just after Yusef [Lateef] had joined him and they had just a ridiculously high cover charge—something like $3.50! And the place was so stiff that we just left. We caught one tune and drove back to Flint. So I didn't go to Baker's. The Minor Key was really the place. I saw Miles there with J. J. Johnson and Philly Joe Jones. The cover charge was also $3.50, but you didn't have to buy any drinks. You could sit there all night and hear three sets of music from 9 P.M. until 5 A.M. for $3.50. That's the place where I got up and walked into a pole after 45 minutes of Elvin Jones. It was a great place. I used to see Trane there a lot playing hour and a half sets, half of which would be just him and Elvin blowing the roof off. There was another place called The Drone Lounge. Jimmy Smith would play at a place called The Grand Bar. So I was a jazz fanatic and, increasingly, an avant-garde jazz fanatic.

You also started to write around this time?
Yes, by the fall of '64 I got a gig with *Down Beat* as their Detroit correspondent and also had my

first reviews published in *Jazz* magazine. And then I met Charles Moore, this trumpet player from Alabama, and I also met my first wife. All this was going on the first six months I was in Detroit. I had a weed connection through the black jazz places that I hung out at, and I got some of the campus business, which led to my first arrest.

You were the Mezz Mezzrow of Detroit?
Much lower scale than Mezz. Mezz was a hero of mine, for sure. Jack Kerouac, William Burroughs, Allen Ginsburg. All those characters were my heroes. Malcolm X. Elijah Muhammed. Fidel Castro. I liked him a lot. I didn't like anything else. I was really into an avant-garde kind of thing and got totally unplugged from popular culture from '61–'65. For those four years I never read the newspaper or watched TV or listened to the radio except for jazz programs. So like all the time that Kennedy was president, I missed the whole thing. You know, after they had the Bay of Pigs I just wasn't even interested anymore. My attitude was just, like, "Fuck these people!" I was into a kind of urban withdrawal during that period. So my perspective on Detroit was more from a jazz point of view. And the more I met people and talked, the more I learned about the glorious history of jazz in Detroit in the '40s and '50s when it was like the Second City of Bebop. In fact, when I came there it was just after that era had ended and it was pretty slim pickings. They didn't have hardly any work for jazz around town.

Was there an avant-garde scene?
No, there were two or three guys who were interested in doing things beyond the norm. But there wasn't even a bebop scene as far as work. It was pretty slim pickings, maybe three things on the weekend and that was it. And that's when we started this thing called The Artists Workshop. That was more an outlet for Charles Moore and the people he was associated with. A group of musicians from Upstate and around the area eventually coalesced into a group around Charles called The Detroit Contemporary Five. And that's when I started writing poetry and I used to perform with these guys. Charles Moore and I used to live together and all we did was listen to records, smoke joints, and fantasize different things that should be happening and then try and figure out how to do them. We'd read our *Down Beat* and beatnik publications from the West Coast and New York, read the *Village Voice* and sit around going, "Man, this shit looks great! How come we don't have no shit like this?" So we were trying to figure out how you could do this, without having any idea of anything, which was a very interesting process. We had these templates from San Francisco and New York. We'd hear about something people were doing somewhere and we'd say, "Yeah, we should have this in Detroit." And we'd make some raggedy approximation of what it was supposed to be like. But we had pretty clear-cut models that we wanted to emulate. And somehow out of all this we came up with this unique thing called The Detroit Artists Workshop.

You mentioned an arrest?
Yes, I went from The Detroit Artists Workshop into a six-month prison sentence at the Detroit House of Corrections in 1966, from February to August. And when I came out, everything was different, everything had changed. Everything was hippie, drug-oriented, rock'n'roll, light show, posters, long hair. All this had emerged in these six months that I was away. I hadn't seen much sign of that before I went in. And so I kind of responded to this because it was a fresh thing—people you didn't know trying to do something different. And so from a base of The Artists Workshop I tried to relate to this new movement, and that's how I got to know the MC5 and pretty much became 100 percent involved with that thing.

What was your role with the band?

When I was with the MC5 our entire focus was on equipment—on getting equipment and keeping it in repair. As their manager, my main job, besides getting them the gigs and getting the money, what little there was, was to then take that money to Joe Massamino's store and use that money to get more equipment. Always more, always bigger, always blowed out. So we were always in and out of the shop.

What had they been doing before they met you?
They had developed into a very interesting band that considered themselves avant-rock. The lead singer was a guy who had taken the name Rob Tyner to express his admiration for McCoy Tyner. His real name was Bob Deminor. Rob's best friend was Gary Grimshaw who developed into the poster artist of the group. They were pals at Lincoln Park High School and were like the school beatniks. And then Wayne Kramer and Fred Smith were like a year under them and they were best pals and they both played guitar. And so they kind of came together from this idea of... Rob Tyner was a rock'n'roll beatnik. He wanted to be in a band. It was the medium to which a kid could think of expressing himself. I guess when I came up five years earlier it was poetry and writing about music. But when I met 'em they were into long improv things and feedback as a musical tool and loudness as an aesthetic unit. They played opening night at the Grande Ballroom and I said, "Jesus, these kids are great!" It wasn't like a rock'n'roll band singing, "Baby I want to hold your hand." I was a little too old for that. What I was really listening to at this time was Cecil Taylor, Archie Shepp, Pharoah Sanders, Sun Ra, Coltrane, Albert Ayler, Ornette Coleman. Then I heard these guys and they were trying to relate to that same kind of energy tapping, trying to get to that thing that was bigger than them, you know? And I related to that right away. And then it seemed like this was something that was really going to be exciting. It wasn't top 40, it wasn't pop, it was something different. These people were gonna be different. So I kind of invested everything that I had into them for about ten years, and at the end of it I realized they weren't going to be that different.... I had been wrong. I was really convinced until around '74.

Did you also produce their records?
I produced their second single. I started out being a fan of the band and then Rob and I became very close friends. We used to take acid together and then stay up all night ranting and raving about the way the world should be. This was like the fall of '66 and going into '67. I would go to their gigs at teen clubs and I would always just be struck at how un-together their whole operation was. But I didn't know nothing. I was just a beatnik. I liked to hear 'em, once they got all their wires untangled and their little bitty equipment set up, which was always blown to shreds. They had this concept of being very loud long before they had the equipment with which to affect this vision. When I first heard them they were already using Vox Super Beatle amps, then they graduated to a Shure four-channel mixer. We were always trying to get more equipment to realize that big sound that they were after. They had a very clear mental concept of what they wanted that shit to sound like.

So I hung around with them for a year—go to the gigs, hang out. And then in August of '67, the guy who ran the Grande Ballroom decided to start bringing in national acts. Up until then it was all local bands. And the first act he brought in was The Grateful Dead. And these were guys who were basically beatnik dope fiends. And I thought, "Wow, this is interesting. They got a record out on Warner Bros. and they're touring the U.S. and they're just guys like us." And that was where I really decided, "Well, shit, I could do this with the MC5. It would do 'em a lot of good." Up until that point I hadn't thought about it because I thought people in the music business were guys with cigars and sleeve garters, you know? Or earnest fraternity assholes, like Bob Seger's manager. They weren't very appealing either. But The Dead's management was cool. So that's when I started acting like the MC5's manager. We never signed a contract or had any discussion or anything. One day it was like this and the next day it was like that.

And you had other activities going on simultaneously?

I was a kind of a cultural activist and writer and cultural organizer through The Artists Workshop. We used to do jazz and poetry at Wayne State University. So I had a little organizational ability. Plus, we had developed The Artists Workshop Cooperative Housing Project, which was a big name for the fact that we took over six buildings on this one block and ran them all so that everybody we knew could have a place to stay, where you didn't have to turn their shit down. My poem called "The Drum Thing" is about those days, when there were three drummers practicing every day in the house and a trumpet player upstairs. So I had these little organizational skills. Plus, we put out our own poetry pamphlet series. We were in the early stages of the mimeograph revolution. My wife at the time worked at Wayne State University and she had the key to the office. We would go in there at midnight, purloin boxes of paper, and run off poetry on the mimeograph machine until 6 A.M. So that was our publishing venture. And I was associated with this little underground newspaper called *The Fifth Estate,* which came out every two weeks. So these were the things I was doing when I started dealing with them. I just tried to apply the different organizational precepts that I learned trying to do things to this band.

When I first started seeing MC5, they'd get to the gig 45 minutes after they were supposed to start playing. And then they would take another 45 minutes to an hour trying to sort the wires out and get this shit set up. And then they'd play two James Brown tunes and "Black Ticom" for 45 minutes. This wasn't real popular. I mean, this would be at a teen club where the kids would come to dance. So the other thing I'd start doing was getting the equipment together, making sure they were on time, getting more gigs.... I knew everybody on the scene already so I knew who to fuck with about the gigs and everything. And then I think the most important thing was we just started working on developing their repertoire and presentation. And they were an exhilarating bunch of musicians because they were totally fucking focused on what they wanted to do musically on stage. And they had some pretty advanced concepts musically.

When we started hanging out I had them listening to more various forms of energy music like Archie Shepp and Coltrane. And also more blues. 'Cause around '65 I had started listening to blues again and I was kind of struck by how the energy content corresponded between a Muddy Waters and a John Coltrane, which wasn't a real popular view at the time. 'Cause if anything, the music in the '60s was even more pigeonholed than it is today. There was jazz, and then avant-garde jazz over here and it wasn't even connected to jazz. That's the way they thought about it. They called it anti-jazz. "That shit isn't music, it's just noise. It doesn't have any principals. How can you tell if they are any good or not?" When I started writing about jazz I soon became embroiled in all the polemical disputes that were arising at that time. I was kind of lined up with Leroy Jones and A. B. Spellman, Frank Kofsky. It's hard to remember.... I did so many things in such a short period of time.

So MC5 was just one of many things that you were involved in at the time.

At first. The '60s, man... Every day was like six months is today. There was so much going on. And at the same time it was small enough that you could hook up. As part of what we did at The Artists Workshop, we put out a poetry magazine starting in '65 called *Work* and later that year we started an avant-garde magazine called *Change*—both mimeographed. A 150 page mimeographed magazine. *Change*... As in "Change! Motherfucker!" It was in the imperative. And I wrote a column for *The Fifth Estate* that focused on poetry and jazz and avant-garde. I was quite a polemicist. And I was also a polemicist for the legalization for marijuana. From the fall of '67 to the fall of '68, The Artists Workshop kind of faded out. We went from the mimeograph to the tabloid revolution. We tried to do our own nightclub. It failed. We didn't have any money. We were scuffling, always trying to do a lot of wild stuff with no money but with a lot of people, because we had quite a few people that we used to take acid together all the time. That's my standard disclaimer about this period—we were all on acid. And that's one reason why we were able to do so many things, we had so much energy and it was focused. There'd be a group of 20 or 30 people of whom maybe 10 took acid together once a week, for several months. And we kind of developed a group mind. We'd have these wild fantasies and... Others would understand them. It wasn't like you were just a nut, these other people would see the same thing. [laughter]

Your progress was interrupted by another jail sentence?
Yes... End of July of '69 to December 13, 1971. They sent me to prison for possession of two joints of marijuana the day after the guy [Neil Armstrong] walked on the moon.

Was the band still together when you got out?
Briefly. They broke up shortly after I got out. They had gone through different things of which I have no firsthand knowledge. Between '67 and September of '68 the MC5 kind of created themselves as this monstrous high-energy performance ensemble. They developed their own music, their own compositions. They developed a stage show. They created outfits, bought more and more equipment. They became tighter and tighter until the fall of '68, which is when we got the record contract with Elektra. And by that time they were an awesome thing to encounter in live performance. They were just fucking awesome! I heard them every night, and every night they blew me away. I've never seen anything like it. And to hear it on records, sometimes you can get an idea of the musical excitement. But their concept was beyond just playing tunes. Their model was James Brown. *Live at the Apollo* [King, 1963] was our bible. That and Coltrane's *Live at Birdland* [Impulse!, 1961]. We had one of those early four-track in-car players and we used to play these tapes at full volume on the way to the gig, smoking 15 joints along the way. So that when you arrived at the place to play, your state of mind was informed by this fuckin' ride and you were ready to just... Roar!
    Oh, they were fun days! When you'd go see the MC5 you didn't know what was going to happen, but you knew that your mind would be blown. The whole trip was just so exciting. I've been in the music business for a long time since then.... I've managed different bands and done promotions and productions, but none of it was like the MC5. That was like being on a religious mission. [laughter] And as the manager I felt my job was to lay down the boards in every way so they could just get up there and do their show and I could enjoy it. The exciting thing was they gained more and more followers. Legions of followers. It was all very localized and very fresh and exciting. Once we got a record contract and started traveling around, all that receded. It lost that real exciting part.

What happened with the record?
Elektra had called them in and were going to censor them. So we're on the West Coast at our own expense and we didn't have any records.

Why?
Because it had the tune "Kick out the Jams, Motherfucker." We had a single version as well, "Kick out the Jams, Brothers and Sisters" that we did for radio. The idea was: You hear that on the radio, you get the album, and you hear the real thing. Also, there were incendiary liner notes that also used the word "motherfucker" once or twice. And it also encapsulated our slogan: Rock'n'roll, Dope, and Fucking in the Streets, the motto of the White Panther Party. So they pulled our record off the market. What an experience. I'm blown away just thinking about it. We got so popular and we hated the authorities so much and they hated us so much. And that was a constant subtext that often rose over the text and became an overtext. Sometimes the shit would get so thick that the

police would come in and pull the plug. And then you wouldn't have anything but a bunch of pissed off kids who were ready to tear the police apart, egged on by us, of course. [laughter] Oh, we hated the fuckin' police, man.

So many of these things in rap music today—apart from its utter lack of musical interest for me and emotive power... The context rings so familiar. The Luther Campbell thing a few years back, when they were giving him all that trouble, reminded me of when "Kick out the Jams" came out. They were arresting clerks in stores for selling the record. Certain chains refused to carry our record. I was with another underground newspaper at the time called *The Ann Arbor Argus* and we made Elektra buy a full-page ad to kick back some money to the paper. And so we laid out the ad and it said, "Fuck Hudsons," the main record store chain in Detroit, which refused to carry our record. Some say that was the contract-breaker. Our contract with Elektra only lasted six months. See, we presaged so many things that have become clichés in the music business. We kind of had the initial Sex Pistols experience in the sense that we sold this thing to Elektra, they fired us, and then we sold it for more to Atlantic Records. The cover was submitted to Elektra, which they bought from Gary Grimshaw. We mutually agreed with Elektra to end the contract. They insisted that we take out "Kick out the Jams, Motherfucker." We wanted this as our artistic expression. So they pulled it off the market. I had to go to New York and argue about it. And we decided, "Let's just withdraw."

Danny Fields had been at Elektra and he was our champion. He left at the same time. He provided an entrée to Atlantic. So we went and made a deal with Jerry Wexler, one of my childhood idols. And we got a $50,000 advance, full control, half the publishing—a much better deal. But then we made this terrible mistake of hiring Jon Landau to produce it. It kind of led to the band rejecting its former direction and going in the direction that rock critics said they should. And they completely changed their whole approach. That was after I was gone.

And at that point you stepped out.
They stepped me out. I went to prison. I had my trial on a Friday afternoon, I was planning to go to the gig that night. Instead, the jury went out and came back with a guilty verdict and they remanded my bail and put me in right there. And of course, I didn't have any idea how long it would last. And then they brought federal charges against me—conspiracy to blow up the CIA office in Ann Arbor, which I really wasn't involved in but I was proud to have been charged. [laughter] I wish I had. I was proud to know the guys who did it. I was proud of them. But I wasn't really the military arm of the White Panther Party. I was more of the legal arm. Oh man, it's really a helluva fuckin' story. The problem is, the more years you get away from it and try and tell the story, the more implausible the whole thing seems because the whole context is missing.

Sounds like a kind of social disobedience that certainly doesn't exist today.
People were on acid—not at any given moment, but that was what was the prevailing attitude. That was the context of reality for quite a few months—people dropping acid, talking about all kinds of wild shit about "People should get together.... Why should we have these wars.... Why should we put up with this shit.... Let's not.... Let's fuck with these people.... Let's make it hard for 'em to keep this shit up." Seems like every 30 years people get a chance to act up. Maybe it'll happen again soon.... Not so much for me. I had my fun. These kids today, wandering around aimlessly with these expensive tattoo jobs. You just wish they had something more interesting to occupy their time—like fuckin' with the government. It's good for everybody! [laughter]

And the MC5 was part of it.
The MC5 existed as part of two scenes that overlapped. One was rock'n'roll bands and one was hippie

acid heads. And that was when the shit got interesting, when it started to overlap. There was a real interesting dynamic that took place between '66 and '69, where these kids who had been in rock'n'roll bands started to get high and take acid and adapt to the hippie lifestyle and worldview.... And the music got more interesting. There was a spirit of competition and camaraderie between the bands. They'd always be trying to blow each other away. MC5... When I worked with 'em our whole idea was to just blow everybody away. If we had a special gig where we'd be opening for Big Brother & The Holding Company, we'd spend the whole week—like a football team working on plays—trying to figure out a set that you could do that would destroy the audience to the point where when Janis Joplin came on with Big Brother & The Holding Company it was "ho hum." Cream... We tried to blow them away. You just try to get in there and just fucking blow people away. We wanted the audiences to just sit there with the tops of their heads flat back. That was our goal. That was what we lived for. That's why I loved these guys, man. They were so focused. They did not give a fuck about anything else. They had this aesthetic with the sound, how to make it different. It wasn't just a tone. They wanted to just invade people and get inside them with the sound. Oh, man... That was kicks! So that's how we got our reputation, getting on these bills with Cream and other bands. That's where that term kick out the jams came from—from taunting these English bands from the wings.

Did you have some success with that first Elektra album before it was pulled?
The first album was number thirty with a bullet—sold about 90,000 out of the shoot. Then they just killed it. It was such a fragile thing to keep this whole juggernaut going, and everybody at the proper mental and emotional pitch. A serious setback like that created the stage for more bad things to happen. I dunno... I guess we thought we'd take over the world or something. We were on acid, you know? We were out there. We'd do shows with Sun Ra. We played a lot of benefits because I thought it was important to play as much as possible. I thought that what they had was so dynamite, they were stupid not to have people hear it. So we played all the time.

And the Alantic album that followed was a detour?
Oh, I thought the second album [*Back in the U.S.A.*, Atlantic, 1970] was really a craven betrayal of all the things they had once stood for. When they made their second Atlantic album, *High Time* [Atlantic, 1971], this guy Jon Landau... He then went on to take Bruce Springsteen from his former management and make him into a huge star. Now he's a multi-millionaire. Bruce Springsteen is the opposite of MC5. I went to see him on his first tour and I thought it was a Broadway show about rock'n'roll—the precise cues, slick lights, songs about people and cars and working men. The MC5 was more about carrying a bomb up to the front door of the White House and knocking on the door and handing it to 'em. [uproarious laughter]

What are some of your more recent activities?
I formed Big Chief productions and am putting out some of the MC5 board tapes and rehearsals tapes from 1971. I've been clinging to those things for 25 years hoping that one day I'd get some of them out. So far we've put out two albums, *Power Trip* [Schoolkids, 1995] and *American Ruse* [Schoolkids, 1995]. I've also done some recent performances and recordings with [former MC5 guitarist] Wayne Kramer.

What are your future plans?
I plan to stay in New Orleans and continue to have fun.

BILL LASWELL

THE FIRST TIME I SAW BILL LASWELL play bass, he had woven a screwdriver between the strings of his instrument. He was whacking that bass, getting a percussive steel drum effect out of the thing. It was weird. I had never seen anyone do that to a bass before. And what Fred Frith was doing to his guitar was even more bizarre. It was the winter of 1980, my introduction to the Downtown improvisers scene in New York. Laswell was one of many Downtown "celebrities" performing that night at the Roulette performance space as part of Derek Bailey's Company, a loosely organized ensemble headed up by the British avant-garde guitarist. It was my first encounter with the enigmatic bassist. I would see him again in various settings including Curlew, Material, and the Golden Palominos—a kind of Downtown supergroup featuring such illustrious renegades as Frith, John Zorn, Anton Fier, David Moss, Arto Lindsay, and Jamaaladeen Tacuma.

Laswell got into the producing end of things with his band Material and scored his first commercial triumph with Herbie Hancock's album *Future Shock* (Columbia, 1983), which included the hit single "Rock-It." After that, the offers started pouring in—Mick Jagger's *She's the Boss* (Atlantic, 1984), Laurie Anderson's *Mister Heartbreak* (Warner Bros., 1984), as well as projects for Public Image, Motorhead, Iggy Pop, Sly & Robbie, Peter Gabriel, Ryuichi Sakamoto, Yoko Ono, and The

Ramones. In 1990, Laswell formed his Axiom label with an eye toward world music and provocative projects by kindred spirits like Jonas Hellborg (*The Word,* Axiom, 1991), Sonny Sharrock (*Ask the Ages,* Axiom, 1991), Ronald Shannon Jackson (*Red Warrior,* Axiom, 1990), Ginger Baker (*Middle Passage,* Axiom, 1990), Carlinhos Brown with Olodum (*Bahia Black,* Axiom, 1992), and Henry Threadgill (*Too Much Sugar for a Dime,* Axiom, 1993). Laswell's prolific output as a producer (more than 200 albums to date) has been documented on other labels like CMP (world music), Subharmonic (ambient/trance/dub), Black Arc (funk), and SubMeta (ambient). In 1996, he formed Third Rail, a swamp funk band featuring guitarist James "Blood" Ulmer, drummer Jerome Bailey, and organist Bernie Worrell. He also continues to play rare gigs with Painkiller, a ferocious power trio with drummer Mick Harris and alto saxophonist John Zorn. Laswell's most recent remix project is *Panthalassa* (Columbia, 1998), a reconstruction and mix translation of Miles Davis' *In a Silent Way, On the Corner,* and *Get up with It,* for Sony Columbia.

The following is a composite of interviews conducted for *Bass Player* and *MIX* magazines.

JANUARY 7, 1985, AND APRIL 18, 1991

The floor-to-ceiling shelves of Bill Laswell's studio in Greenpoint, a residential neighborhood in Brooklyn, are lined with master tapes bearing some celebrated names—Iggy Pop, Ryuichi Sakamoto, Miles Davis, Jimi Hendrix, Ginger Baker, Public Image, Deadline, Material, Afrika Bambaata, Gil Scott Heron, Yellowman, Last Poets, Herbie Hancock, Golden Palominos, Samalnuri, Foday Musa Suso, Bernie Worrell, L. Shankar, Sonny Sharrock, Motorhead, Jonas Hellborg, Sly & Robbie, Massacre, Last Exit, Jungle Brothers, Masabumi Kikuchi, White Zombie, Maceo Parker, and Bootsy Collins.

Over in one corner of the studio is an array of old Fender basses, a pink Gibson Thunderbird bass, a white pearl Gibson SG guitar that once belonged to Allan Holdsworth. "He gave it to Cliff Cultreri and Cliff sent it to Nicky [Skopelitis]. It sounds incredible," explains Laswell. One is set up so it resonates like a coral sitar. "This old Steinberger is one I had 12 years ago," he offers in this guided tour. "This other early-1960s Fender P-bass is one Robbie Shakespeare uses a lot. Five-string Fender fretless... Originally it was a four-string fretless that I used to use a lot when I was in Massacre, and one night it got stolen out of a truck. It was gone for about a year and I saw it hanging in the Music Inn on 4th Street and I bought it back for twice the amount. 1982 Alembic, four-string Wal fretless. It has a nice sound. That's on a lot of records."

A soft-spoken, enigmatic man, Bill Laswell remains a renegade figure on the music scene. As a producer, he has gained much power in the industry. He is also a potent force as a bassist through his work with Last Exit, the improvising rock ensemble featuring guitarist Sonny Sharrock, drummer Ronald Shannon Jackson, and saxophonist Peter Brotzman.

Born in Salem, Illinois, in 1955, Bill Laswell grew up in the Detroit area playing funk and R&B in various Midwestern bar bands. As he recalls, "Most of my early experience in music was playing black music. I started playing when I was 13 and did sessions around Detroit a few years later for the Invictus label. I also toured around a lot playing five nights a week."

Laswell arrived in New York in 1977 and established himself as a sought-after bassist on the Downtown improvisers scene, which also included the likes of John Zorn, Fred Frith, and Eugene Chadbourne. He began playing avant-garde rock with James Chance and in 1978 he formed the Zu Band, which later became Material. In July of 1979, they recorded their first EP for Red Records. Around the same time, Laswell formed a power trio with guitarist Fred Frith and drummer Fred Maher called Massacre. Laswell later joined Curlew. In May of 1980, avant-garde guitarist Sonny Sharrock joined Material. In early 1981, Laswell formed another band called Deadline with guitarist

Robert Quine and drummer Phillip Wilson. Later that year, Material recorded its major label debut, *Memory Serves* (Elektra/Musician, 1981). The group followed that up with *One Down* (Elektra/Musician, 1982) and then Laswell released his solo debut album, *Baselines* (Elektra/Musician, 1983). More recently he has also forged strong alliances with funkmeisters George Clinton and space bassist Bootsy Collins and the whole P-Funk gang.

Material continues to exist in name only, operating as a kind of production company for various Laswell projects. Bill's current vehicle of playing remains Last Exit, the raucous free improv thrash-jazz band he formed with saxophonist Peter Brotzman, drummer Ronald Shannon Jackson, and guitarist Sonny Sharrock, though he continues to perform on occasion in Japan with local improvising musicians there.

I met with Laswell on several occasions for this interview—at his studio, at Platinum Island in Manhattan where he does his mixing, over beers in a dark corner of his favorite low-profile bar in the Village. He admitted up front, "I don't do interviews so well. I'm not familiar with the form.... I just talk." And so he did, about anything and everything from recording techniques to the CIA. And, of course, there was plenty he had to say about the state of the bass world and his place in it.

What is your attitude toward the bass?
Whatever I do with the bass, what I value about it, is the way the sound and the feel relate to an environment and the creation of lines. No one really plays great lines anymore. There are very few bass players who I could actually listen to. I hear a lot of people with incredible technique doing exercises on the instrument. But as far as really playing great lines on a bass, playing with a great sound, incorporating it into the music, knowing how to make music really work... I see that very little. This area, where people are getting around more on the instrument, is not at all interesting to me. These are not artists. I as a bass player am more influenced by Gurdjieff or Alister Crowley than I am by some jerks who play fusion music. And the whole idea of these magazines glorifying these people is just a total waste. There's so very little of it that I can listen to. And I'm not talking about one person in particular. I'm talking about 99.9% of all that shit. Jonas Hellborg is an exception. And Bootsy is a great bassist. He has a limited style, but it's real. The stuff that he actually plays... He's playing himself. It's coming out of him. It's coming from a great experience and a real devotion to a certain style. It's real. But these people who are doing all these acrobatics on the bass, tapping and whatever, they don't play to what I value, which is again good lines and creative ideas of how to juxtapose rhythms with drummers. I think a lot of great rhythm sections have to do with direction and communication, not just someone who can play time. The feel is what's important, not the time.

So you must admire James Jamerson.
Everybody likes Jamerson. He played with a natural feel. He had a sound. He had a style. That's what he did. He had a natural gift for that. I admired Jamerson when I was a teenager. I heard a lot of great bass players growing up in Detroit.

What do you think of Percy Jones?
He has a lot of tricks. Bass playing isn't one of them. But he's good at tricks, if you like tricks. He'd probably sound great with a real bass player underneath. Maybe I should do that with him some day.

I understand you had some encounters with Jaco Pastorius?
Never under the circumstances where he was making any sense. I always liked Jaco. I felt like if I would've known him, I could've helped him out. I never actually knew him. I recorded him once.

By the time I actually got to him, he was sideways. That was Deadline, Phillip Wilson's project (recorded for Celluloid Records in 1984). We were recording and Phillip ran over to the old Lone Star to get Paul Butterfield, who was playing there. And Jaco tagged along. And it wasn't happening. We let him play for about three minutes at the end of one song ("Makossa Rock"). He was in and out. Both him and Butterfield were pretty much out of it then.... It's that Charlie Parker syndrome. When he died, these Japanese people came to my house asking about Jaco and I had to tell them: "I don't really know him." He wasn't my friend. But if he was and I saw him fucking up like that... If I knew anybody who was fucking up that bad and was actually a friend, I could do something about that. I could give him some money or help him out or get somebody to talk to him or listen to him. Somebody could've helped him out. But people love for somebody to die so they can have something to talk about. A lot of people right now are just waiting for certain people to die so they can have a big rap on the whole thing: "Yeah, he was my friend." But they can't say that shit when he was alive.

But I didn't know Jaco. I saw him play live in his early days when he first came out. He had a voice.... It wasn't even bass, it was a voice. I never thought about it being a bass. He just seemed to develop this unique voice. And it was really his. That stuff he did with Joni Mitchell was great. But then he got out there and lost it. The first time I ever met him was in an elevator at RPM Studios in1981. He had a black eye. He said, "Some fucker cold-cocked me last night." Then he pulls out these pictures of his daughter and starts crying. We were recording Oliver Lake and he walked into the studio when Oliver was playing with the headphones on and everything, just walked in and started talking to him in the middle of a take. He was totally out of it by then.

But what he did... His contribution was great. What came after him was all these idiots trying to sound like him, which is a major part of why bass players today are so fucking lame. They don't really play bass. And he wasn't either. He was not playing a bass, it was some other shit. But there's all these know-nothing never-bees trying to sound like Jaco, and it's so lame and obvious. They should have more respect for the guy than to just run with his shit. Nobody plays like him. There's just no way. They can forget about it, but I hear all the time these guys trying to cop that—no personality, no nothing. I don't think anyone's gonna play that particular instrument like that again. It would've been interesting to hear Jaco playing in a more rock situation. Like more open with drummers playing more simpler, heavier, more dedicated rhythms. Like Ginger [Baker]. Or anything that was real raw. It's too bad that didn't happen. I'm sure he would've been wide open to it.

I know that when Jaco heard I had a bunch of Hendrix tapes from Alan Douglas he was going around asking about that. He wanted to hear them. He was real curious about that, as far as over-dubbing on them. That would've been interesting.

The other night I was talking to Bob Quine [Lou Reed, Voidoid guitarist] and he paid you a real high compliment. He said you were the best bass player he ever played with, not because of notes or anything but because you listen and react so well.
Well, Quine's criticisms are probably in the right place. He never could stand people just dicking around on their instruments. He's got his own way of doing things. Zorn still works with him a lot. I saw Quine a couple of months ago on this session Zorn was doing for a Nike commercial. The director was Jean-Luc Goddard and Quine was playing. He sounded OK. To be honest, I'm not a fan of Quine, but I'd rather hear Quine in a second than some of this other shit that people are passing off as guitar playing. In a second. I'd rather hear him tune up than listen to that shit. It's not guitar playing, it's more like typing. It's not about anything. If you had to transpose that into painting or any other kind of art form, can you imagine how pitiful that shit would be to look at? There's just a lot of bad music being made available more and more.

What do you think of this neo-conservative trend in jazz?
That's just a bunch of guys wearing suits playing somebody else's music. You gotta look elsewhere. That's the key. Don't pay attention, because paying attention is like paying somebody. That's all it is, really. You're building these people up by paying attention to them. I don't endorse that shit, not even for a second. But they're not gonna disappear, so I have to look elsewhere. But there are people who come out of the genre that was referred to as jazz that I think are still natural, instinctive players and play with a really great gift and good spirit and do it naturally. And that's also the essence of world music. You just have to not think of it as being ethnic. That's really the essence of world music—just being a natural player and improviser of an instrument. Whether you're from northern Minneapolis or Marrakesh. And you'll find that real instinctive players and open, thinking people will communicate musically without any trouble—if they're just free of all the things that sort of get put on you in the whole education system of how music is supposed to work or how Western music is supposed to be a certain thing.

Have you been approached to produce any straightahead jazz projects?
No. I would see that as a huge waste of time for me. There's no reason to be there unless you really like the music. And most straightahead jazz I can't even listen to. So I don't see how I could even be there.

Has your interest in Middle Eastern, Asian, and Indian music affected your approach to the bass?
It has, probably in a gradual, indirect way. I can't really pinpoint it. You get sonically influenced, I suppose. Lately I've been working on a kind of North African music called gnawan music. There's an instrument they play in gnawan music called a sentir, which has a very low register. Sounds a lot like a bass. It's a three stringed instrument and has a really nice sound. And to hear that instrument actually played by the people who play it in those places is really an experience. I suppose that has influenced me to some degree.

What is the thrust of Axiom Records?
It's really just a continuation of what my work has been the whole time. Just now it has another name and it happens to be this particular year. But it's always really been the same thing. We just put out a compilation of all the stuff. There's a quartet record of Sonny Sharrock with Pharoah Sanders, Elvin Jones, and Charnett Moffett, which is really nice. And there's a record we did in France of a Turkish saz player called Talip Ozkan [*The Dark Fire,* Axiom, 1992]. There's also a new Material record [*The Third Power,* Axiom, 1991], which is really a bunch of things taped together. It's with Sly & Robbie, Herbie Hancock, Bernie Worrell, the Jungle Brothers, Shabba Ranks, Garry Shider, Michael Hampton, Bootsy, Fred Wesley and Maceo [Parker], Henry Threadgill... It's kind of a juxtaposition of styles sort of passing in and out of itself. It's a real collaboration featuring different characters at different times, sort of confusing the issue. All of that is part of this label. And there's five more records coming out, but it's not good to talk about them because things change. The one that's definite is a Brazilian record with Olodum [the Brazilian drummers who played in Paul Simon's last album, *The Rhythm of the Saints,* Warner Bros., 1990]. Wayne Shorter plays soprano sax on that and it also features Carlinhos Brown, a young Brazilian singer, percussionist, and guitar player who's just starting out.

You've greatly expanded beyond the Downtown community you were associated with ten years ago.
Well, there never really was, for me, a Downtown community in New York. What happens is, people call that—whatever that is I was involved in and people still are—they call that Downtown music. And all that means is that people don't have enough money to get a better place to live. And

when people start to make money they get out of there, so what they're doing is no longer considered Downtown. I associate Downtown with the sort of people who aren't making money. And I don't really have any affinity with not making money or being Downtown. So I'm not in that stuff at all. I did a few records associated with that scene because I was getting started and that's where I lived because I had no money.

Like Massacre, the power trio you had with Fred Frith and Fred Maher.
Massacre was a great thing at the time [late-1970s]. That's the only outlet I had and I actually learned a lot from Frith at the time. So that was a valuable situation for me. But you have to go on, you have to try to keep going and take the next step. What I've tried to do since then is not just to move out of the Village, but to branch out more internationally, to go everywhere and experience as much as possible in different places around the world. And not as a tourist but as someone who's traveling there for a purpose and who is actually making real contact with people that are doing things there musically. I'm documenting that and registering it in a way so that it's made available in maybe a more professional atmosphere, so things get presented maybe a little more efficiently than the idea of field recordings.

What were some of your first steps in this direction?
About eight years ago I began making inroads in Japan. Things developed and there was work. I ended up making something like 30 trips to Japan. And then from there I went more into Southeast Asia to Thailand and Korea. I also got interested in Okinawan pop music, which has some great guitar stuff. The *Neo Geo* [Epic, 1988] project I did with Ryuichi Sakamoto was sort of the beginning of that phase.

What's the latest on Last Exit?
Not happening, not right now. Right now is more, for me, a time of responsibility for organizing things. And Last Exit is the opposite of responsibility. It has more to do with playing out of tune because you're out of tune, or just playing loud because there's volume. It has to do with abandoning a lot of things.... There's a lot of clashes of different kinds, a lot of energy being thrown around. And sometimes it's powerful. Other times it's noise. But now is not the time to promote Last Exit or glorify any of the exploits of Last Exit. That was then and this is another time. I couldn't even do that right now. But again, it'll come around. There will be a time when that happens again, probably in another environment. But that was strictly based on fun. It's really based on relationships—knowing certain people, liking them, and just seeing what kind of collisions would occur.

Have you seen any bands that have impressed you lately?
I don't go to concerts. I can't concentrate for more than a few minutes on any one particular style of music. That's why lately I'm starting to like what John Zorn is doing with his band Naked City, because he jumps really quickly from one thing to the next. The information gets changed a lot quicker and all the events are squashed down to real precise statements—getting shorter and shorter and shorter. And I think that's actually really clever and it's probably one of the more interesting things that's going on as far as... I guess you could call it composition or structure. And that sort of comes from his discovery of hardcore, which has been a really positive thing for him. We have a group called Painkiller, which is a trio with me, Zorn, and Mick Harris, the drummer from Napalm Death. That was done at the studio. It's on the Earache label, which is Napalm Death's label.

Sounds like a '90s version of Massacre.
Yeah, it sort of is, but it was all improvised. It was done very quickly, but there's a real feeling of

improvising structure, which is good. I think that's what's missing a lot of times from bands.

What are you excited about these days?
Everything. Absolutely everything. There's a scene happening in Paris where there's a lot of young kids growing up in mixed neighborhoods—people from Africa, Martinique, the Middle East all living together in these neighborhoods in Paris. And they're all kind of hearing all this music. All these different cultures are clashing. So what it's producing is these kind of mutation of kids who have all this music in them. Like the way we would grow up with country & western, jazz, and blues, they're growing up with rock music, hip-hop, Morroccan music. And there's a group that's come out of this scene called FFF. The singer is from Toga, the drummer's from Martinique, the rest are French. It's like a mixture of their different cultures—jazz, reggae, Caribbean stuff, and yet they're totally devoted to James Brown and P-Funk. It's basically like a funk band with all these world music influences. So we got T-Bone from Trouble Funk and Mudbone from P-Funk, Ayib Deng and all these guys. I guess in the end it'll be some kind of new take on funk.

So you're helping them realize their musical ideas?
Just getting them on tape, actually. Not really trying to educate them. It's natural. What they're doing, they can't even discuss it intellectually. It's just natural growth. It's like the way somebody plays an instrument naturally. What they've assembled in their influences is natural. It's not like "I need to get this book on West African drumming. Then I'm gonna go to the Asian Society and check out this shit. Then I'm gonna go and read about Harry Partch." You know... This shit is natural. We predicted 10 years ago that it would be happening. And now it's in the earliest beginnings of it. I think it will develop more and more, become more and more clear.

How did you find them?
They contacted me. I did a record with these kids from San Francisco called The Limbomaniacs, and they liked that stuff. Plus, they knew I was also associated with Bootsy and Maceo and everybody. And there was also the fact that I've worked previously in Paris on a lot of African stuff. I created a real kind of controversy over there because I did all this shit with machines and people were saying, "Oh, he's killing African music." These books say I'm the one who came over and tried to destroy African music [particularly after his notorious production job on a Fela Kuti album in which he edited out the bandleader's sax solos and replaced them with Bernie Worrell keyboard solos]. But if young people in Africa had access to machines, computers, drum machines... Forget it. It'd be so space age. But we got a lot of flak for that, and it was fun. And actually, it was the Africans who wanted to do that anyway.

Is there anything that you're especially proud of that you've done as a bass player?
What I am sort of happy about is that a lot of times it sounds like a lot of different people, so it doesn't end up sounding like I'm just rescheduling the same events. I'm glad about that. And there's a lot of use of a lot of different instruments, which implies a different approach to making the sound. It's got a lot more to do with playing than it does the instrument and amplification. There's incredible amounts of technique that just go into touching strings and playing. With bass, very few people are doing that. There are guys who are beating the bass up and getting a bunch of notes out of it, but what I'm talking about is a lot more subtle.

Do you change up, sometimes play with fingers, sometimes with picks?
All the time, yeah. I stopped playing with my thumb maybe 15 years ago because I felt that was a style that was being mishandled, exploited without being understood or felt. When Larry Graham

played like that, it sounded good. He got a great sound. And Bootsy has his own style, which is not like Larry Graham's at all. It's very much Bootsy's style. There was a guy who played with Santana called Doug Rauch who had a real original style of playing with his thumb. And outside of those three people I don't think there's anyone else I would bother listening to that played with their thumb. As far as playing with a pick, I'm not really an authority on that, but that's another style, just another technique that works for different kinds of music—especially if you're going for some kind of conviction and intensity, regardless of the information. Playing with a pick has more to do with trying to maintain something really stable and intense.

How do you look back on your Baselines *record [his provocative 1983 solo album on Elektra]?*
I haven't heard it in a long time. I would probably think it was done a long time ago. I don't regret anything. I don't regret any choice, any decision, any line played, anything that's out of tune.... It's all part of the story. That was a point in time and everything should evolve. It was a very different album from my next record [world music–influenced *Hear No Evil*, Virgin/Venture, 1988], and I have plans to do another one which will be very different from that. I'll continue doing those things.

Are there examples of bad music in these exotic locales you travel to?
There's a lot of terrible pop music everywhere. It's unbelievable, but it's so funny because it's all misinterpreted versions of American pop. I've heard music in Thailand that sounded like... The number one record in Thailand when I was there had a verse that went: "I hate America...." And it sounded like Black Uhuru, but twisted. Real cheesy and not quite working. Basically, somebody got ahold of some reggae records. There's horrible pop music all over that's selling. That's not to say pop music is a bad thing, but that's usually the area where people blatantly try to make money— "Make that again for me and I'll buy it." But again, not to say that it's all bullshit. There's a lot of really valuable stuff.

To what extent has American pop culture infected the world?
It's everywhere. It's pretty much devastated the Japanese. They're just trying to be different people. Like, "Today I'll be Bootsy, next year I'll be David Byrne." That's really a helluva way to look at what you're going to do with music. A lot of Japanese people are caught up in that. It's a direct influence of how Western pop culture is just devastating people. A lot of their music is completely contrived and derivative of something that's directly copied up. I had beginnings of working with some of the bigger pop artists—if I can use that word. Their idea for making music was to take a couple of records... Take the rhythm track from this one, a vocal idea from this one, and that would be their idea of writing music.

Feed the elements into a computer.
Yeah, basically. Just copy it and change the lyrics to whatever they want to say. But there are really great musicians in Japan. In the hardcore scene there's some really impressive bands and young people who are from the streets, which really has nothing to do with what's selling or what you hear about. You'd have to be there to see most of them. Some of that's starting to leak out. And John Zorn is helping a lot to make that kind of activity known internationally. So without him and other people making it known, you wouldn't know about it in America.

Americans are attracted to familiarity.
But that can be manipulated a lot of different ways. You can get people to do pretty much anything. America's the real center of telling somebody to do something and they run and do it without questions.

As long as it's done with authority and backed up with a little money, you can get people to do absolutely anything. I mean, if you can get people to buy the shit that they're buying now I'm convinced you can get them to buy anything—*anything*. It's just a matter of presentation and how you manipulate the situation and how you're gonna make the whole thing work in terms of money. When people see money they change their whole perspective about anything and everything. Especially here in America.

So how do you think FFF is going to get over in America?
No idea. I never think about that—never.

Do you feel the musical climate has changed at all since the Reagan years, that people at record companies are opening up now to more challenging music?
I don't think people at record companies would know challenging music if it was right in their face. I've been hearing challenging music since I started listening. I've heard it in the streets, in the Middle East, in Africa, in India, in Asia. I've seen combinations of influences of young kids who will go from listening to hardcore hip-hop to like skateboard thrash and hardcore music. That's a fusion that's inevitable and it's totally inspiring. And at the same time there's people that actually play with a natural gift, who have a natural voice and a vision. There's still actually people, living musicians, who have a vision, but there's very few. Ornette Coleman is one. But I think as far as times changing and Reagan era and record companies... That's all bullshit. The shit's been here the whole time. If people decide to write about it, that's their business. If somebody likes it or dislikes it... It's always been great, it's always been challenging, it's always been here. It doesn't even need a chance. It just needs to *be*. And the chance is the people who want to get with what's really happening. They want to take a risk and look around, find what's great, write what's totally invisible to them— they can do that. But to do that you have to give up something. You have to take a chance with yourself, find out who you really are, and is it really worth it to risk what you've built or what you have or what you're known for. The shit is wide open and it's incredible. It's always been incredible. It's just a matter of whether you know it or not. It's right here, but to most people it's invisible. It's got nothing to do with business or the times or anything.

Did you happen to see the James Brown pay-per-view concert recently?
It was beyond pathetic. But it was a setup. There's no way that that happened naturally. It was like the selling of James Brown. To me, it looked like it was meant to make him not appeal to young people, to have nothing to do with being any type of a symbol of black power in this country. It looked like a total setup. The horn section, those guys couldn't even begin to play—guys who looked like accountants playing trumpet and alto sax, totally out of time, out of tune, not on the same planet. And Rick James at the end doing a bass solo? This guy can't even hold a fucking bass. And Bootsy's over there trying to downplay the fact that he's got the same instrument. He came on at the end with Catfish and that was probably the only time where it actually resembled anything that had anything to do with the real music. They needed Maceo desperately. Seemed like it might've been set up by the CIA. There's definitely a lot to that.

Too bad you weren't the musical director.
Well, then it wouldn't have been on TV. That's why they were able to set him up like that, because it was TV. I think this country has been pissed off at James Brown for a long time. They got him in jail, then they get him out and set him up for Vegas. Like an Elvis thing. He's still great, he can sing, he can do his stuff—but it was clearly a setup.

Are there any new players around that you'd like to bring to our attention?
Yeah, this guy Buckethead is good. He's from Nebraska and wears a Colonel Sanders bucket over his head and a plastic mask. He's been hanging around all these kids in Limbomaniacs, which is how I met him. He has a style.... He plays fast and the way he's playing you'd think he was coming out of a Holdsworth thing but it's not those choice of notes, it's another conversation totally, it's a different language. And it's really deep. Watch out for Buckethead! Raised by chickens. Any second now, everybody's gonna start talking about him. Guitar has been so fucked up by these guys trying to do fast, whatever that shit is—typing guitar solos. It's unbelievable. But Buckethead is something else.

Did you ever get into that as a kid, trying to sound just like somebody?
No, I never got into it then, I'd never get into it now. To me, bass is some serious shit. It has to do with moving time and personality—it's like a religion, it's like a good western. And it's not like any of this other shit, it's beyond music. It's about character and how you get in and out of shit.

You didn't obsess on a particular player as young musicians tend to do?
No, all I wanted was for a good drummer to say, "He's bad. I wanna play with him."

MILFORD GRAVES

TO WITNESS MILFORD GRAVES in performance is like encountering a shaman in the forest. His endurance on the drum kit is positively superhuman, though balanced by awesome technique and a fertile imagination that allows him to consistently create that "sound of surprise." I've seen Graves nearly levitate off his drum stool in duet performance with tenor titan David Murray (documented on their 1991 DIW album, *The Real Deal*). On other occasions, with Reggie Workman or solo, he would incorporate dance and tai chi movements around his kit for a performance that was both highly provocative and entertaining while also being indelibly tied to Africa. The criminally under-recorded Graves has recently been documented on John Zorn's Tzadik label. The typically provocative and astonishing *Grand Unification* (Tzadik, 1998) is his first solo drums recording in 15 years.

The following interview was done for a story on half a dozen drummers associated with the so-called avant-garde. It was entitled "Masters of the Free Universe" and appeared in the December '92 issue of *Modern Drummer*. I took the subway out to the end of the F line in Jamaica, Queens, for a personal audience with this living master.

JUNE 11, 1992

In one corner of Milford Graves' basement sits a multi-colored, hand-painted drum kit. Dangling down from above are two thick link chains with leather wrist bracelets attached at the ends. A pair of heavy-duty coils connects the chains to the ceiling. At first glance, it appears to be some kind of strange S&M love slave contraption. It turns out to be an ingenious exercise machine for drummers, as Milford demonstrates.

He sits down at the kit, sliding his wrists through the bracelets. He picks up the sticks and begins to play, unleashing a whirlwind of energy. As his arms move down to strike a drum, the springs offer resistance, pulling his arms back. Going through the motions of drumming, he resembles a manic marionette attached to the puppeteer's strings. But the effect is similar to what baseball players get from swinging a weighted bat in the on-deck circle.

After a few minutes of this aerobic drumming, Milford's forearms are bulging like Popeye's. I suddenly understand why the 51-year-old drummer is in such incredible shape. But physical exercise is only a part of how Graves gets his amazing energy and stamina. A highly disciplined, deeply spiritual individual, he is also a strict vegetarian, a knowledgeable herbologist, and an acupuncturist as well as a trained martial artist. He grows vegetables and herbs in his Queens backyard, his basement is stocked with jars of ginseng and other exotic roots. On one wall is a poster of the human body with all the pressure points clearly marked and over in another corner is a human skeleton for further study. It's clear from just glancing around this basement that Milford is into more than just drumming. And when you watch him perform, you get an understanding of just how deep the act of drumming can be.

Graves' uncompromising performances are ritual invocations of the spirit that involve dancing, singing, primal screaming, and flailing on the kit with superhuman abandon. Much too severe for some, entrancing for others. And, amazingly, he exhibits as much energy today as he did back in 1966 with his historic duets with pianist Don Pullen. As he told Valerie Wilmer: "Most people will play for the average person's senses. I try to go above the average person's senses."

Milford's innovative approach to the drums involves astonishing speed and multi-directional rhythms that create a dense undercurrent of pure energy. Only the most forceful soloists can survive on top of this kind of tidal wave, which explains Milford's rapport with tenor titans like the late Albert Ayler, Charles Gayle, and David Murray.

Born in Jamaica, Queens, on August 20, 1941, Graves started out playing bongos and timbales in a neighborhood group. He played strictly Afro-Cuban hand percussion through his teens, working and jamming with Latin jazz bands in the neighborhood. At one fateful jam session in Boston in 1963, he sat in on the traps set with alto saxophonist Giuseppi Logan and instantly lit up the room. Though he still considered himself a hand percussionist, his occasional forays on traps started to attract attention from other players.

He bought his first traps set later that year from pianist Hal Galper and began learning the rudiments while also incorporating aspects of Latin, Haitian, and Cuban drumming onto the kit. He picked up other jazz rhythms by ear.

In 1964, he joined the New York Art Quartet with trombonist Roswell Rudd, saxophonist John Tchicai, and bassist Lewis Worrell. Later that year, they participated in the October Revolution in Jazz, a series of performances at the Cellar Cafe in New York intended to introduce "the new thing" to a wider audience. In the following year, Graves appeared on several recordings for the renegade ESP label, including sessions with the NYAQ, with pianist Lowell Davidson and bassist Gary Peacock, with pianist Paul Bley, and with Giuseppi Logan's group. Perhaps the most provocative of these sessions were his duets with fellow drummer Sunny Morgan.

In 1966, Graves and Don Pullen appeared in concert at Yale University. The performances, documented and released as two separate records on their own SRP (Self-Reliance Project) label, stand as an important landmark in free drumming. Three years later, Graves and Andrew Cyrille teamed up for the astonishing *Dialogue of the Drums* (Institute Percussive, 1974), a manifesto for the melodic approach to the kit, released on their own IPS label. Graves joined Albert Ayler's group in 1967. That summer they performed together at John Coltrane's funeral. A month later, they began recording the first part of Ayler's *Love Cry* (Impulse!, 1967). Graves is heard in constant motion throughout that provocative album. Two years later, Ayler was found floating in the East River. The cause of his death remains a mystery.

Since 1973, Graves has been teaching at Bennington College in Vermont. One course, entitled "The Influence of Music," touches on the healing aspects of music. He continues to play around New York at performance spaces like the Alternative Museum, the New Music Cafe, and the WeBo gallery. He says his goal as a drummer is to inspire other young drummers to get deeper into their instrument.

It strikes me that too many young drummers today are obsessed with technique.
Amen.

They don't really have an approach to the instrument, they don't have a philosophy of what they're doing. They're mostly concerned with keeping time and imitating a drum machine.
That's sad, but true.

I think they need to be reminded that there's a deeper meaning behind playing the drums, that there's a difference between making music and learning technique. And you personify that attitude.
Well, one thing that I find is... I was listening to Pharoah Sanders on WKCR and the interviewer was trying to pull out certain things from him. Pharoah didn't really talk on an academic level about what he's doing, other than that he's self-taught. He talked about his experience of just really getting involved with this music—going out to California, hitchhiking, no money, hanging on the scene, and just being around a lot of musicians who really had a similar kind of situation in not having schooling in a sense of entering a building where you try to pick out this and pick out that. I really wanted to almost pick up the phone and call Pharoah and say, "Be careful that you don't put down what you were doing as not being schooled." Because he *did* go to school, and it's a large school. The school of life.

A lot of the older musicians dealt with music because music was feeding one or the other sense apparatuses of the body. To be able to survive on the planet, people eat food, they feel things, they smell things, they see things. And there are people who need to hear things as well to survive. If you think about gospel or blues, that is definitely true. When there was no such thing as civil rights in this country and black people didn't have the opportunity to go to the conservatory, you played music because there was really a *need*. It wasn't like something hip to do: "Well, I wanna do this here because that's what everybody is doing." Playing music or singing was something you had to do to be able to survive on the planet. So every sound that you dealt with, every rhythm that you played with, it had to really stimulate you in a way to make you say, "Yeah, well, I wanna live, you know?" And not dealing with constantly being depressed all the time.

A lot of young guys today... They don't have this thing. They have certain opportunities today. You can go to school and study music. But people forget about what it is to go deep into yourself to find the music, to really go after that thing and really work hard. People today get things a little easier. I remember times when if you didn't pass your exams with high grades, you couldn't get into places like Queens College or Brooklyn College. Now you can go into a school where they let you in because people think they're doing you a favor to calm down your anger. So people take it for granted, and they don't have that thing where they really go inside and say, "This is what I wanna do. I gotta work." It's like cheating people from really understanding what the truth is.

So I think it's terrible that a lot of the younger folks who wanna play drums... They don't have this opportunity to really feel a deeper, deeper connection with themselves, to ask themselves, "Does this really turn me on inside spiritually? Or does it just satisfy a social need." They have lost that connection deep inside. Consequently, drumming today is about seeing what kind of strokes I can do, how fast my hands are, how loud I can play, instead of saying, "Well, is my inner soul, my spirit, being satisfied?"

There are no instructional videos on satisfying the inner soul.
Exactly. I mean, with all the high technology today I just think that... What I try to tell a lot of the younger musicians is that this may be just a temporary thing as we're moving into the next century. But if there ain't some major changes made, then we might as well forget about it. I think it's intelligent to understand what's happening as opposed to that superficial, mechanical, materialistic level. So I say young musicians today ought to familiarize themselves with what it is to go back and really touch that inner thing. Because there will be a time when there's no machines or nothing outside of yourself that's gonna help you play music. It's gonna have to come from deep within.

Maybe people today are just too concerned about paying rent to consider such an adventurous, alternative route.
Yeah, well, the money thing is a drag. My advice is always to tell people that you have to think like a lot of ancient cultures, and that is in a more holistic way. I'd say, do things other than drumming. There must be something you can do other than drumming. That if you never could drum, there must be something that really satisfies your soul. So I'm saying, do that so that you never get to the point where you *have* to make money off your drumming or your music. Because then you gonna start making some compromises that may not be the best for you. That's one of the reasons I think that things have moved on all levels in all professions to a level where it's almost like anti-human, to a certain degree. People are becoming specialists in just one area instead of becoming a complete type of person. So when one thing is not working... OK, then you do something else. And I say this a lot because I'm constantly meeting people who say they are making money but they ain't happy with what they're doing. They say, "Well, what else am I gonna do?" And that hurts in a way, when you hear something like that. Or else they get past a certain point and give up. They say, "Well, I can't go back now 'cause I'm older, you know?" But that's what I try to avoid. So I can do music and drumming. Whereas, I know that I'm not being confined to make that compromise to be able to stimulate or appease somebody who wants to manufacture some kind of machine. And that means limitations.

You had some significant collaborations with Albert Ayler, notably the 1967 Impulse album, Love Cry. *What can you tell us about him?*
Albert was two kinds of musicians. He was a musician who played for the record company and also to an audience that may not understand what he'd do if he went to the deeper stuff. Certain things he did that were not major concerts.... We'd play up in Harlem or he'd come to my house and we'd do stuff. And that Albert Ayler was a different Albert Ayler. That's the thing I tell horn players: "It's a shame you didn't hear Albert Ayler another kind of way and not just those little tricky, corny melodies he used to always go out and play."

So he was very conscious of commercialism?
Definitely, he was always trying to find those tricky melodies. And a lot of our playing that I felt people should hear... Unfortunately during that time in the '60s there weren't things like they have

today, video cameras and really fine smaller recording equipment. So a lot of that stuff you can only talk about. All the records we did were OK. But the real heavy-duty stuff we never recorded.

What were your earliest playing situations like?
I actually came up playing in the lots around here. I'd play in the lot with a tin can. Everybody knew me. They couldn't see me, but they could hear me. It was more wooded around here then and I'd always be playing tin cans and everybody knew it was me. I don't know what it was but I had this thing where I always wanted to be the drummer in the community, stimulating people. I was living in the top floor of the building I was in. My window was wide open and everybody knew at a certain time they could come around and sit on the park benches and check me out. A friend of mine came to this country from Cuba when he was 11. His father was a Cuban religious drummer and he turned me onto a lot of that stuff. So we formed a percussion group playing with bongos, timbales, and congas, playing traditional and non-traditional things. We would play for the assembly programs in junior high school, jam during the intermissions at school dances. And by the time I had graduated from high school, everybody was saying I played real good timbales and congas. I had been playing timbales and congas since I was 12 or 13. And at 19 I formed this Latin jazz group with this piano player around here. Then I got the word that there was another piano player coming down from Boston who was better than the guy I had. It turned out to be Chick Corea. So Chick came by the next time we rehearsed. He started playing this Latin stuff and I said, "That's it, man. This guy is in the band." So I formed a whole new band with Chick on piano, Lyle Atkinson on bass, and Pete Yellin on alto sax. All of us was between 18 and 20. That's when we really started doing gigs around here. Everybody was saying, "Them young guys can really play!" The conga player's name was Bill Fitch. He went with Cal Tjader in '62, through Willie Bobo's recommendation. That was a blow, man. We could really do some stuff together with me on timbales and Bill on congas.

How did you make the transition to playing jazz on the kit?
In the summer of '63 I went up to Boston to play some Latin jazz gigs with [percussionist] Don Alias. And at one point they said, "Let's play some jazz." So I took my timbales and played it like it was a snare drum. And I was playing my cymbal like a ride cymbal. And the guys was telling me, "Man, you play good jazz!" And I said, "Yeah, but I wanna play some Latin and African, man." Anyway, I met the piano player Hal Galper there in Boston. He called me up later and said he needed some money because he was a little broke and he offered to sell me his drum set for $100. He brought the drum set over and I gave him the $100, then about two weeks later he wanted the drum set back. I said, "No thanks, man. I got it now." I had it in this little place I was staying at in Boston and took it along to jam sessions. One day I heard this alto player at a jam.... I remember nobody wanted to play with him because they said he was too weird. His name was Guiseppi Logan. He was up there playing all alone so I came up out of my seat, went up on the traps set, and I started playing with him. Everybody started looking at me like I was strange. "What the hell is he doing?" So later Guiseppi came over to my place with this really good trumpet player named Fred Ballard. And we got up there and jammed and jammed. Don Alias heard me and said, "Man, I like the way you play them trap drums." People would come up to me and say, "Man, you're so different!" But I wasn't even thinking about it. Then [drummer and teacher] Alan Dawson saw me, introduced himself, and encouraged me. So with all this encouragement, I said, "Hmmm, maybe I ought to think about doing this more seriously." At the same time, the Latin gigs was not happening too much. During that time, late-1950s, early-1960s, it was extremely difficult for a non-Latino cat to get a job playing timbales or bongos. Extremely difficult, man, unless you had your own thing. So I said to myself, "Well, it looks like you ain't gonna get too many calls." Meanwhile, all these guys were

telling me how hip I was sounding on the traps set, so I thought, "Man, I'm gonna do it."

Where did you learn about the rudiments of jazz drumming?
My uncle taught me the basics about how to play with brushes and what the concept of a snare drum was, how to use my right hand. But the feeling was there in the way he taught me. It wasn't about looking at a blackboard or counting it out or notating. When you put music to paper, you mechanicalize it—just take it so outside of yourself so that you can grab the sucker like a frame that's so nicely put together with screws and hooks and lock it in so that you can't even move it. It's so damn stiff, man! Whereas, in the old days, if somebody showed you a rhythm, they would sing it out to you. And the way they talked, they would bounce, the tonality—each tone, each word—it was so full of life, man! It moved you when somebody explained it to you that way. It was a human connection. In those times, if you didn't get it, you played it and the guy would say, "That's not right." You'd say, "What's wrong?" And they'd say, "You not doing it right. Listen to me." And you'd say, "What is it, man?" And you be there for days, playing it over and over and over. And all of a sudden you do it right and the guy would say, "That's it, that's it!" You could tell by the guy's tone of voice, the expression on his face, his body movement, that you struck something in him that was hitting the real essence of what life is all about. Movement, man! And, see, that's what people miss today.

Yeah, they're into an instant, paint-by-numbers aesthetic.
That's right, man. And there's nothing inside, nothing for the soul with that. This instrument we play has always been looked at—in this country—as a non-musical instrument. We were never considered as really musicians, just timekeepers. But to me, drummers are not timekeepers, we're life givers—because the drum is a very powerful instrument.

You must be disturbed by the current obsession with drum machines?
It's unbelievable, man. This is what people don't understand about time and spacing: Nothing in the universe is metronomic in the sense that it's an exact. Everything changes according to what the situation is. So all this stuff about the avant-garde and new music not being in touch with time is ridiculous. The way we do things is the way nature does things. The true musicians are in touch with that big vibration, the big drum of the universe. To me, the drums is about vibration and energy. Each one of us has his or her own internal vibration. It's related to the heart beat, the sound of blood flowing in your veins. And once you get in touch with that vibration, you will find that there is no such thing as playing out of time. The only way you play out of time is by playing things that will be detrimental and hurting to your own soul. You don't calculate time by saying one-two-three-four or by putting on a clock and practicing all day to a tick-tock metronome. Those are just machines, man. It's got nothing to do with the essence of life. We've gotten so machine-like that we've really forgotten how to get out there and get deep into ourselves.

And the tempered scale is really a man-made system that takes us out of this deep inward focus.
Exactly. The piano is an industrial compromise. It doesn't represent the true way a string vibrates. Once you hit an open string it vibrates into all its component parts. The tempered scale doesn't reflect that. The tempered scale is only a part of that. It leaves out all of the vital things that make the connection that will cause a sympathetic vibration in our soul. That's what's taken out of the piano. The tempered scale was developed when the world started getting industrialized. It's a compromise because to make a piano they used mathematical calculations to make a scale. They couldn't make a mathematical system with too many different Es, too many different Ds within an octave. So they had to make everything—from one octave to the next—the exact same double of that pitch. So

they had to deal with a certain kind of mathematical system that would give them only one E in that octave and not two different types of Es. So it became very neat, but at the same time they did something that was totally against the way we vibrate, the way we sympathetically respond when we hear drum skins vibrating or a string or a reed or whatever else. So when you're constantly bombarded by the tempered scale, programmed by that, and somebody else comes in and plays in a real natural way, the way our inner selves are, people automatically say, "That's not happening." And that's terrible, because unfortunately, there's a large majority of people who feel like that.

So there are no wrong rhythms and no wrong notes.
I talk about this all the time up at the college. Something hit me years ago about the concept of right note/wrong note. I would hear some people say that this person hit the wrong note even though this person was playing totally what they felt. And I said, "Wait a minute. That was a beautiful note he hit. You have trained yourself to listen to only 12 tones. You're telling me that all the rest of sound contained in there has no value, is no good?" Well for me, it's just like a person eating brown rice and white rice. If you eat white rice all the time, then brown rice will taste terrible to you. If you eat white rice, because they put additives in, your taste buds have been reduced to only handling a limited amount of frequency from that white rice. When you taste brown rice, you're tasting those frequencies plus other substances in that brown rice, so what it's doing is it's causing your taste buds to react in a much more energetical way. You got more nutrients stimulating you and your system is not used to that. So you're rebelling. But don't say the brown rice is no good. You gotta say, "Well, my body has to get more of an understanding and get regulated to this particular type of thing." And it's the same thing with the tempered scale. People say, "Oh, that sound was 'out,' this is 'in.'" I say, "No way." It's only out if you think it's out. If you hit what you think is a wrong note or wrong rhythm... If you think something is supposed to be there, you gotta make it right and let it come back in with feeling.

None of that is happening in this culture. Too many musicians are too concerned about commercial viability.
Exactly. And I think there's gonna have to be a big change. I'm confident of that. I think something is happening now but there has to be another creative period that's going to come. People said that this music was going around in the '60s because there was so much of a revolutionary vibe in the air. The Vietnam War was going on. It was just like "Challenge! Change!" in the air. And I reflect back.... I remember if you was a black musician playing this music constantly, people would say it was hate music or revolutionary music and so on. And at the same time that people were saying that, there were some great responses we were getting from people. It really looked like something was getting ready to break through in a big way with this music. All of a sudden... Boom! Musicians started saying, "Well, you know, man, I gotta start playing some music that people can relate to." And so on. And that's one of the sad parts. Maybe we wouldn't have drum machines today if musicians would've said, "That's it, man, we gonna really fight to keep this in." Not realizing that a lot of times you gonna have to do it yourself. You can't depend on the establishment in that sense, which is really committed to doing commercial stuff.

Do you think that musicians playing this liberating music in the '60s were perceived as a threat by the government?
Well, that was told to me by many people, that the FBI was watching the musicians. A lot of the bands were playing at political rallies, where people were protesting the war and so forth. So they had to have said, "Wait a minute, what is this?" I heard all kind of talk like that, sure—a conspiracy and a plot to stop so-called avant-garde, new music in this country. This music poses a threat, you

see, because it allows people to act in a way that they will really get true wisdom. And then they will be able to perceive things that are really no good for them. But [noted jazz writer] Nat Hentoff said something very interesting at the time. He made a prediction that people who were playing this so-called avant-garde music would end up teaching on the campuses. And that totally came true. Most all of us went that way. I'm still there, up at Bennington. We all headed that way. Instead of getting record dates and the big festivals and so on, people get a chance to hear us on campuses. That's the sad thing about it, man, because when you do these things you get a great response from the people. All over the world, people are just like, "Wow!" when they see the energy of it. And I wish I could reach more people with it.

Do you have any general advice for young drummers?
I would tell them, whatever you wanna do, experience both sides. Before you put this down, check it out. Play in tempo, play out of tempo. Try both of them. Do it with sincerity and not as a put-down, just to see how it feels. And I think you will find it will feel good for you. What really inspires me is to play before drummers, not as an ego thing of like "Look what I can do." It's more like, "Man, if I can pass something along to help you out, to be a teacher or one of the elders... If I can inspire you, take this and go on with it, man." That's what we're supposed to do as musicians anyway—turn each other on, man. We inspire the hell out of each other. I recall one time in 1965 I was playing in the Village, might've been on Bleecker Street. I was playing with Giuseppi Logan and John Coltrane came in with Elvin Jones. I was a little nervous, man. Next minute I know, Elvin was sitting right down in front of my drums and he was grooving with me, man. And he took me to another level. Roy Haynes did it once, too. I was with Albert Ayler at Slugs and he ran up to the stage, man. Philly Joe [Jones] did it once, too. Max [Roach], too. It was like one drummer to another saying, "That's it! That's right!" Those guys was feeding me, taking me to another level. And I like to do the same thing when I see a young drummer doing something different. "Take it out there!" Because we the brotherhood. We the drum brotherhood.

Even if I never make no money, don't win no drum poll, don't get in magazines, I'll always continue to reach out and inspire people that way. To me, the high point of a performance is not so much the hand claps and the smiles, it's when a young drummer comes over and looks at you and you can see the amazement on their face, like: "Who is you? Where you been? I never heard of you?" It feels good to know that I stimulated them, from one drummer to another drummer. My payoff comes when they tell me, "Thank you, man... I didn't think you could approach drums like that." So that's what I want to do. I wanna take that instrument and inspire every drummer to dig deeper inside and go farther than they ever thought they could. And if I can do that, I'll feel as though I will have accomplished something.

GLENN BRANCA

THE FOLLOWING INTERVIEW with Downtown composer-conceptualist Glenn Branca was my first assignment for *Guitar World* magazine. It appeared in the January '83 issue. There is absolutely no way that such a story would ever appear in *Guitar World* today, particularly not at such a length. The magazine now seems strictly devoted to charting bands and the latest paint-by-numbers guitar shredder. No way that they would ever cover someone like Branca, let alone give the guy five whole pages of coverage (in the same issue, by the way, with a story on Ornette Coleman guitarist Bern Nix). But those were more enlightened times—probably not as profitable, but certainly more adventurous editorially. And for that we can thank the open-minded, forward-thinking genius and risk-taking tendencies of the great Noe "The G" Goldwasser, former editor-in-chief of *Guitar World*. Noe was not afraid to cover jazz, country, blues, and experimental music. After all, the name of the magazine was *Guitar WORLD*, wasn't it? Since Noe's unceremonious departure from the magazine, the post-G *Guitar World* began focusing its attention on two things: heavy metal and Eddie Van Halen. Today it is strictly a fanzine for teenagers into the latest pop trends.

And to think that I used to interview players like Jimmy Raney, Danny Gatton, Tiny Grimes, Eugene Chadbourne, Robert Quine, and Glenn Branca for this same magazine. Seems like a few lifetimes ago. Thanks, Noe!

SEPTEMBER 10, 1982

Tucked away in the New York Union Motor Truck Terminal near the Hudson River on Manhattan's Lower West Side, somewhere up on the third floor of that massive Port Authority warehouse building, weird and wonderful things are going on at night. There, in the privacy of his small studio space cluttered with the remains of what used to be conventional guitars, Glenn Branca is busy concocting aural schemes to assault your senses.

Like Thomas Alva Edison at his Menlo Park laboratory, absorbed in a tireless search for just the right filament for his light bulb, or more appropriately, like Dr. Frankenstein devising some unholy aberration of man, Branca is totally wrapped up in his un-ending experiments with the guitar, exploring the limitless potentials of the little metal string and its inherent properties of resonance.

Upon the release of his first EP, *Lesson No. 1* in July of 1980 and his follow-up last year *The Ascension* (99 Records, 1981), Branca was hailed by the New York press as something of a genius. On those recordings, he was basically concocting orchestral guitar pieces of symphonic scale using an array of elaborately-tuned guitars. The dense textures that he created with six or at times as many as ten interlocking guitar patterns were lauded by critics as revolutionary. John Rockwell of the *New York Times* called Branca, "The most prominent composer working in the increasingly active field of rock/avant-garde experimentation," while Gregory Sandow of the *Village Voice* said, "Branca is now frighteningly good, one of the best composers alive; the exuberance, intelligence and newness of his music make everything else around sound stale and tame."

But in spite of those impressive accolades, Branca now considers his innovative work with guitar symphonies in *The Ascension* as hopelessly outdated. "*The Ascension* might as well be from the 19th century as far as what I'm into now with my music," says the 33-year-old composer. "I mean, I like the record, but most of that stuff was written over two years ago and I've gone through a lot of changes in the last two years. Musically, I've been progressing so quickly that it's almost ridiculous. The ideas are really snowballing and I can't keep up with them. Right now I'm about six months behind, which is to say that my musical ideas are about six months ahead of what I've actually written. *The Ascension* is all just regular guitar. What I'm involved with now is a whole other world," he explains with all the zeal of the chemist who accidentally happens onto the discovery of DNA.

Branca is continually evolving beyond the basics of guitar. By breaking the instrument down to its most elemental level, he is now discovering certain properties and principles that intrigue him enough to continue experimenting within the realm of sound. Looking over his current arsenal of "staircase guitars," which are patterned after steel guitars and are played with mallets, and his latest experiments with what he calls his "harmonic guitar," an incredible discovery he stumbled onto that affects organ-like resonations of the strings and opens up a whole new world of harmonic possibilities, it's hard to imagine that at one time Glenn Branca actually did play a conventional six-string guitar in the accepted manner. But, of course, that's all in his past now. Branca is thoroughly immersed in more exploratory pursuits today, which may inevitably lead him entirely away from the instrument as we now know it.

As he says, "When I really started breaking down the guitar and examining it's properties, I began to realize that I wasn't working with the guitar so much as with a metal string which is stretched over a microphone. If you look at if from that point of view, the potential for what you do with it increases considerably.

"Then when I saw the difference between an untempered metal wire and a tempered metal guitar string, it was incredibly interesting to me because the harmonic series of the wire is so totally different from the guitar string. It didn't have a real fundamental tone, but instead the harmonics are much more random, like a bell or a piece of metal. So I believe that the potential of the metal string is absolutely incredible, yet the potential that is realized in music today is incredibly small, at most about ten percent. This idea of keys and specific notes and scales... I won't say it's ridiculous, but the reason behind it is really to make life a little easier for the musician, to make the instruments kind of reasonable. The reason for this tempered tuning was that on the piano you could play in all of the keys without going out of tune, but that tuning doesn't adhere to the natural tuning of the string. It was invented by man, it has nothing to do with the reality of sound."

It's clear that as Branca gets deeper and deeper into his experiments with resonance and sound, he is actually delving into physics more so than music, although he believes the two are inextricably linked. In fact, at this point, Branca neither considers himself as a guitarist or a musician at all. "I'm not necessarily interested in developing my technical prowess on the instrument," he says. "Actually, I haven't played a regular guitar for about five or six months now. And I'm not interested in simply playing games with the interaction of notes and rhythms. At the time of *The Ascension*, I was writing music but I don't really think of myself as writing music anymore. I don't like to think of myself as an inventor necessarily and I'm not really interested in being an instrument builder either, but it seems necessary at this point and it seems like it may be continually necessary. I'm not really trying to improve the instrument or anything like that or make a better new instrument. I'm trying to make an instrument that gets what I want to hear."

What Branca is hearing these days is difficult to put into words, although he does seem to be drawn to this idea of resonance and harmonics involving non-tempered instruments. It's as if he's evolved beyond the standard notions of what music is and has developed his own new language of sound. He speaks about the relationship between matter and music and is intrigued by the psychic implications: "This is something I've been experiencing with my music for the past couple of years. I'm definitely getting into some deep water with my music now, but I'm trying to stay down to earth as much as possible. I'm starting to study physics, because there is a clear connection between the harmonic series and a lot of mathematical and scientific thought, yet the harmonic series has been almost totally ignored in music within the last five hundred years. This is why lately I've been looking at a lot of early music and I've discovered that it's clear that some of these ideas were used back then and for some reason have been lost. It has something to do with the Catholic Church and the tempered scale and the evils of certain kinds of music. I'm intrigued by it."

In addressing his current state of mind with regard to his experimentations in resonance and harmonics, Branca says, "I'm a thinker and that's what I want to be. It's very possible that I may come to the point where I'm doing exactly the same thing but it's not music at all, having nothing to do with sound. I think that's very possible. It seems to be heading in that direction at this point. I'm sure I'll be making sounds for a couple more years, but it may come out somewhere else. Someone like John Cage has sort of reached that point. His work is more about philosophy, I think, than it is about music."

At the time of this interview, Branca was beginning preparations for the debut of his next symphonic work, entitled "Symphony No. 3," to be premiered at the Brooklyn Academy of Music as part of its "Next Wave" series.

Can you describe what happens at one of your concert events and how people react to the whole thing?
I'll have to admit that someone seeing my music for the first time probably won't get into it. It's definitely an acquired taste because everyone is so used to hearing music in a very specific way. It's almost impossible to get used to hearing this music, which has absolutely nothing to do with conventional structure at all. Musicians and composers have gotten more into complexity of structure, and so have the audiences. In the same way that we used to watch a solo performer and be amazed at the technical feats that he could perform on the instrument, people are now listening to music and

being amazed by the production and by the technical complexity of the compositional elements. And that's something that I'm just not interested in. Another thing that is difficult about my music is that on the outside, superficially, it can sound very irritating and grating and unpleasant. But once you are listening to it and kind of immerse yourself in it, it starts sounding very rich. And my music takes a long time to develop. There's a necessity for that. The room has to be warmed up, literally. The room gets glowing. It's almost like feedback, continually building up. Dance music affects you viscerally to get your feet moving. This music I think sparks the imagination and gives a kind of field or playground where the imagination can play in. I think you can kind of dream into this music. I know of many people who have seen my concerts who have had experiences which are incredibly powerful. There's always that room there. I'm not telling them: "This is the way it has to be. This is the way you have to perceive it." People can perceive it on any level that they want. Some people like to see the sexual aspect of it, some people want to see the philosophical aspect of it, or the political aspect, or you name it. And it's all there.

In spite of all the experimentation you are involved in now, there was a time when you were actually playing a conventional guitar in a conventional way.
Well, let's see... When I was a sophomore in college I played in a band. We played cover tunes—any tune that came out between 1965 and 1967. But that was about the one time that I was in a real conventional band situation.

But didn't your interest in guitar go back beyond college?
Oh yeah. I started playing the guitar when I was 15. I've been totally in love with the instrument ever since, although I never really considered myself to be a musician. That's the one thing that's a little strange about all this. I'm not really a musician. I did study for about three months when I was 15, but then I didn't touch the guitar again for a year. I've never been interested in anything that had anything to do with school so I couldn't deal with lessons. Then later I picked up a chord book and learned how to play a few chords. From there I just basically improvised and it was through the improvising that I came up with a few new ideas. I couldn't stand to practice, so whenever I touched the guitar I would just play it, just experiment.

What struck you about the guitar? What made you pick up that instrument as opposed to a saxophone or piano?
At this point I don't even remember. I just wanted to play it. I think it was getting fairly popular at the time and actually when I first started playing it I didn't get into it at all. It was funny. You have to realize that for years I wasn't studying to be a musician or wasn't even necessarily interested in being a musician. I was an actor when I was real young and I wanted to be involved in the theater. I studied theater in college and after I got out of school I started writing plays. But all the while I also had a guitar.

When did you begin inventing our own instruments?
When I finally put together my own theater group. Of course, my plays weren't the kind of plays with characters and plots, they were more like collage-type performance events. So I would use a lot of music within the context of the pieces. Most of it didn't even require that the person who was playing it be a musician because I was interested in working with the structure of sound and with non-tempered instruments like gongs, cymbals, bells—basically anything I could get my hands on at the pawn shop or find in the street. During this period I made a few of my own instruments. One was an absolutely amazing instrument which turns out to have a lot to do with what I'm experimenting with now, although I didn't realize it at the time. I found a bolt—it was about six feet long

by three-quarters of an inch in diameter—and I wanted to use it somehow as an instrument. I was using garbage cans lids at the time as little sounding boards for different percussion instruments so I got the idea to place this bolt on top of the garbage can lid to amplify it. Then I put a microphone underneath that and with a very thin metal rod I would rub the bolt from the top to the bottom along the threads. I got some really beautiful spirally effects—these very high tones which were actually the harmonics of the bolt, which I didn't even realize at the time. I made some tapes of this and when I played it back at very slow speeds the sound was absolutely incredible. The pitch was lower so the harmonics became much more prominent, and I could hear whole orchestras from this. I knew there was something there, but I didn't know what it was. So I created a few musical pieces using this bolt as part of the music for my theater group in Boston, around 1973–1974.

Were you at all influenced by ethnic music at the time?
If I was influenced by anything at that point it was probably the "Ramayana Monkey Chant" from Bali. I think it was on the first gamelan album released by Nonesuch. You can still get it. It's all part of a festival—a whole lot of people standing around for hours and hours just chanting. Very rhythmic, very percussive, very abrasive. It's a vicious kind of piece. So I was listening to that but was probably more influenced by people like [Olivier] Messiaen and [Krzysztof] Penderecki, and I suppose to some extent I was trying to emulate their music at the time.

With this interest in more exotic music, did rock music lose its appeal for you?
Oh no. I was always interested in rock. I was completely addicted to it. Occasionally, I would think about starting a band, getting together with people and playing, but it never really happened. The theater thing was much more of the work I was really making, but I was also interested in any kind of music that was experimental. But I never really saw the relationship between rock music and experimental work. Even when I listened to Brian Eno I could hear one side that was rock, maybe with a bit of a twist, and one other side where he did his experimental stuff. He never seemed to be able to find this formula of joining the two. So I started getting ideas of my own along those lines. But when I'd go to a rock club and visualize the type of band I would want to put together, I also visualized the entire audience walking out and the club never booking me again. I mean, at the time it was totally impossible to do what I was thinking. But then when I came to New York it was like a whole new world. There's actually an audience for this kind of stuff in New York. And it just so happened that when I got the bug to start this band the time was right for this kind of off-the-wall thinking. So I started this band in New York called Theoretical Girls. If I had started that band in 1975 or 1976, it wouldn't have gone anywhere. But the time was right. The whole punk thing had kind of died down but people were still really hot. They wanted something to happen.

Did Hendrix interest you at all during this phase?
He was very much involved in electronics and what I'm doing has nothing to do with electronics at all, it has to do with amplification. It doesn't have anything to do with the actual electronic distortion of a signal. That was mainly what he revolutionized, that use of electronic distortion, which I think is interesting but not for me. Recently though I've been able to see some old films of Hendrix and you can see from how he was playing that the man was obviously into a lot more than the people promoting him wanted his audience to know about. I saw one incredibly vicious concert he did where he almost looked like he was having an epileptic fit on stage with the guitar, and this is something I can relate to because I was interested in this kind of guitar playing when I had Theoretical Girls and I never realized that anyone else had ever played the guitar like this—a completely spontaneous, intuitive, emotional approach to the instrument. At the time I was working with the guitar in this way I felt as though I could actually project my psyche through the instrument.

What events led up to your departure from conventional guitar playing?
As I became more interested in working with these fields of sound, I started working with more than two or three guitars. Outside of the band I had an opportunity to put together a number of guitars for a special Easter festival at Max's Kansas City in 1979. I wrote this piece called "Instrumental for Six Guitars" and really didn't know what would happen with all those guitars together, but I knew it was something I wanted to look into. In the first rehearsal of the piece it was the most amazing thing I ever heard—period. None of us could believe what we were hearing. So at this point it was absolutely set as to what I was going to do. I mean, there was absolutely no doubt that I was going to work with this. When you hear something that is so clearly—I mean, I was crying! I just could not believe it, especially the last section dealing with very dense textures. It was like nothing I had ever heard. And this was also the first time I had used a different tuning, something I call the "Octave Tuning." I broke the guitar down to three octave notes—the two low strings were tuned to a low E, the two middle strings were tuned to an E an octave higher, and the next two strings were tuned to an E an octave higher than that. At this point I was still using exactly the same stringing as a conventional guitar. One reason for that was that I only had one guitar and I didn't think the other musicians would've wanted to restring their guitars, so I had to come up with a° tuning that worked.

So where did you go from the three E octave tuning?
My next step was the unison tuning, in which I broke the guitars down to tenor, baritone, alto, and soprano—like saxophones. Each guitar was tuned to one note and one octave of that note—exactly the same tone on all six strings. In this situation I was able to control what happened within each octave more specifically. You can play single notes with this tuning but I'm not interested in chords. It was at this point that I discovered the very common technique in classical music of doubling—17 violins playing exactly the same pattern, the same note.... There's an effect that happens there. So what I was really doing was trying to create the most resonant quality I possibly could. I soon found myself becoming more interested in the sound of the open string, but I didn't have the variety of notes with the open strings. So my next step was to make a tuning where I could get my unison effect but also have as many notes as possible that could be played open. What evolved from this was a kind of chromatic scale tuning.

Around this time I wrote a piece called "Indeterminate Activity of Resultant Masses," and in this piece I used ten soprano guitars. I was very interested in close harmonies so I wanted to kind of squash everything down and get as many notes together as possible just to see what would happen. So I broke it down to each one of the ten guitars tuned open in the unison tuning to a different note.

You don't really feature any solos in your music.
No, I'm not interested in featured instruments. After my "Symphony No. 2," some guy came up to me and said, "I thought that was really great. I'm a guitar player and I could really put down some hot licks over that stuff." I couldn't believe it! How could this guy have sat through an hour of this intense music and then tell me he's gonna have *his* guitar wailing over ten guitars in the background. There are a lot of solo players who are absolutely brilliant, but my music is clearly meant to stand on its own without a solo player. I suppose I shouldn't put that idea down. A lot of people have said to me, "It would be wonderful if you had some kind of melody going over that." But my idea is that the melody is inside it. It's there! You just have to listen for it. My music really requires more from an audience than music usually does.

INDEX

INDEX